DECIPHERING THE GENOME OF CONSTITUTIONALISM

Constitutional identity has become one of the most important and hotly contested concepts in contemporary constitutional theory and practice. It has been repeatedly invoked in debates concerning EU integration, constitutional reform and revolution, and the spread of ethno-nationalist populism, democratic backsliding, and constitutional retrogression. Yet the concept's precise foundations, meaning, scope, and dynamics of continuity and change remain somewhat unclear and under-explored. This contemporary and definitive volume aims to address this stark gap. Featuring some of the world's leading scholars of comparative constitutionalism, constitutional theory, and constitutional politics, this book provides a comprehensive, first-of-its-kind theoretical, comparative, normative, and empirical account of the concept of constitutional identity. It will be of great interest to scholars, students, jurists, and constitutional drafters alike.

Ran Hirschl is the David R. Cameron Distinguished Professor in Law and Politics at the University of Toronto and a Fellow of the Royal Society of Canada.

Yaniv Roznai is an Associate Professor at the Harry Radzyner Law School and Co-Director of the Rubinstein Center for Constitutional Challenges, Reichman University (Interdisciplinary Center Herzliya).

COMPARATIVE CONSTITUTIONAL LAW AND POLICY

Series Editors

Tom Ginsburg University of Chicago
Zachary Elkins University of Texas at Austin
Ran Hirschl University of Toronto

Comparative constitutional law is an intellectually vibrant field that encompasses an increasingly broad array of approaches and methodologies. This series collects analytically innovative and empirically grounded work from scholars of comparative constitutionalism across academic disciplines. Books in the series include theoretically informed studies of single constitutional jurisdictions, comparative studies of constitutional law and institutions, and edited collections of original essays that respond to challenging theoretical and empirical questions in the field.

Books in the Series

Deciphering the Genome of Constitutionalism: The Foundations and Future of Constitutional Identity Ran Hirschl and Yaniv Roznai

Courts that Matter: Activists, Judges, and the Politics of Rights Enforcement Sandra Botero

The Story of Constitutions: Discovering the We in Us Wim Voermans

Democracy Under God: Constitutions, Islam and Human Rights in the Muslim World Dawood Ahmed and Muhammad Zubair Abbasi

Buddhism and Comparative Constitutional Law Edited by Tom Ginsburg and Ben Schonthal

Amending America's Unwritten Constitution Edited by Richard Albert, Ryan C. Williams, and Yaniv Roznai

Constitutionalism and a Right to Effective Government? Edited by Vicki C. Jackson and Yasmin Dawood

The Fall of the Arab Spring: Democracy's Challenges and Efforts to Reconstitute the Middle East Tofigh Maboudi

Filtering Populist Claims to Fight Populism: The Italian Case in a Comparative Perspective Giuseppe Martinico

Constitutionalism in Context David S. Law

The New Fourth Branch: Institutions for Protecting Constitutional Democracy Mark Tushnet

The Veil of Participation: Citizens and Political Parties in Constitution-Making Processes Alexander Hudson

Towering Judges: A Comparative Study of Constitutional Judges Edited by Rehan Abeyratne and Iddo Porat

The Constitution of Arbitration Victor Ferreres Comella

Redrafting Constitutions in Democratic Orders: Theoretical and Comparative Perspectives Edited by Gabriel L. Negretto

From Parchment to Practice: Implementing New Constitutions Edited by Tom Ginsburg and Aziz Z. Huq

The Failure of Popular Constitution Making in Turkey: Regressing Towards Constitutional Autocracy Edited by Felix Petersen and Zeynep Yanaşmayan

A Qualified Hope: The Indian Supreme Court and Progressive Social Change Edited by Gerald N. Rosenberg, Sudhir Krishnaswamy, and Shishir Bail

Reconstructing Rights: Courts, Parties, and Equality Rights in India, South Africa, and the United States Stephan Stohler

Constitutions in Times of Financial Crisis Edited by Tom Ginsburg, Mark D. Rosen, and Georg Vanberg

Hybrid Constitutionalism: The Politics of Constitutional Review in the Chinese Special Administrative Regions Eric C. Ip

Constitution-Making and Transnational Legal Order Edited by Tom Ginsburg, Terence C. Halliday, and Gregory Shaffer

The Invisible Constitution in Comparative Perspective Edited by Rosalind Dixon and Adrienne Stone

The Politico-Legal Dynamics of Judicial Review: A Comparative Analysis Theunis Roux

Constitutional Courts in Asia: A Comparative Perspective Edited by Albert H. Y. Chen and Andrew Harding

Judicial Review in Norway: A Bicentennial Debate Anine Kierulf

Constituent Assemblies Edited by Jon Elster, Roberto Gargarella, Vatsal Naresh, and Bjorn Erik Rasch

The DNA of Constitutional Justice in Latin America: Politics, Governance, and Judicial Design Daniel M. Brinks and Abby Blass

The Adventures of the Constituent Power: Beyond Revolutions? Andrew Arato

Canada in the World: Comparative Perspectives on the Canadian Constitution Edited by Richard Albert and David R. Cameron

Constitutions, Religion and Politics in Asia: Indonesia, Malaysia and Sri Lanka Dian A. H. Shah

Courts and Democracies in Asia Po Jen Yap

Proportionality: New Frontiers, New Challenges Edited by Vicki C. Jackson and Mark Tushnet

Constituents before Assembly: Participation, Deliberation, and Representation in the Crafting of New Constitutions Todd A. Eisenstadt, A. Carl LeVan, and Tofigh Maboudi

Assessing Constitutional Performance Edited by Tom Ginsburg and Aziz Huq

Buddhism, Politics and the Limits of Law: The Pyrrhic Constitutionalism of Sri Lanka Benjamin Schonthal

Engaging with Social Rights: Procedure, Participation and Democracy in South Africa's Second Wave Brian Ray

Constitutional Courts as Mediators: Armed Conflict, Civil-Military Relations, and the Rule of Law in Latin America Julio Ríos-Figueroa

Perils of Judicial Self-Government in Transitional Societies David Kosař

Making We the People: Democratic Constitutional Founding in Postwar Japan and South Korea Chaihark Hahm and Sung Ho Kim

Radical Deprivation on Trial: The Impact of Judicial Activism on Socioeconomic Rights in the Global South César Rodríguez-Garavito and Diana Rodríguez-Franco

Unstable Constitutionalism: Law and Politics in South Asia Edited by Mark Tushnet and Madhav Khosla

Magna Carta and Its Modern Legacy Edited by Robert Hazell and James Melton

Constitutions and Religious Freedom Frank B. Cross

International Courts and the Performance of International Agreements: A General Theory with Evidence from the European Union Clifford J. Carrubba and Matthew J. Gabel

Reputation and Judicial Tactics: A Theory of National and International Courts Shai Dothan

Social Difference and Constitutionalism in Pan-Asia Edited by Susan H. Williams

Constitutionalism in Asia in the Early Twenty-First Century Edited by Albert H. Y. Chen

Constitutions in Authoritarian Regimes Edited by Tom Ginsburg and Alberto Simpser
Presidential Legislation in India: The Law and Practice of Ordinances Shubhankar Dam
Social and Political Foundations of Constitutions Edited by Denis J. Galligan and Mila Versteeg
Consequential Courts: Judicial Roles in Global Perspective Edited by Diana Kapiszewski, Gordon Silverstein, and Robert A. Kagan
Comparative Constitutional Design Edited by Tom Ginsburg

Deciphering the Genome of Constitutionalism

THE FOUNDATIONS AND FUTURE OF CONSTITUTIONAL IDENTITY

Edited by

RAN HIRSCHL

University of Toronto

YANIV ROZNAI

Reichman University

CAMBRIDGE
UNIVERSITY PRESS

Shaftesbury Road, Cambridge CB2 8EA, United Kingdom

One Liberty Plaza, 20th Floor, New York, NY 10006, USA

477 Williamstown Road, Port Melbourne, VIC 3207, Australia

314–321, 3rd Floor, Plot 3, Splendor Forum, Jasola District Centre, New Delhi – 110025, India

103 Penang Road, #05-06/07, Visioncrest Commercial, Singapore 238467

Cambridge University Press is part of Cambridge University Press & Assessment, a department of the University of Cambridge.

We share the University's mission to contribute to society through the pursuit of education, learning and research at the highest international levels of excellence.

www.cambridge.org
Information on this title: www.cambridge.org/9781009473248

DOI: 10.1017/9781009473194

© Cambridge University Press & Assessment 2024

This publication is in copyright. Subject to statutory exception and to the provisions of relevant collective licensing agreements, no reproduction of any part may take place without the written permission of Cambridge University Press & Assessment.

First published 2024

A catalogue record for this publication is available from the British Library

Library of Congress Cataloging-in-Publication Data
NAMES: Hirschl, Ran, editor. | Roznai, Yaniv, editor.
TITLE: Deciphering the genome of constitutionalism : the foundations and future of constitutional identity / edited by Ran Hirschl, Yaniv Roznai.
DESCRIPTION: Cambridge , United Kingdom ; New York, NY : Cambridge University Press, 2024. | Series: Comparative constitutional law and policy | Includes bibliographical references and index.
IDENTIFIERS: LCCN 2023050345 | ISBN 9781009473248 (hardback) | ISBN 9781009473194 (ebook)
SUBJECTS: LCSH: Constitutional law. | Constitutions.
CLASSIFICATION: LCC K3165 .D425 2024 | DDC 342/.001–dc23/eng/20231031
LC record available at https://lccn.loc.gov/2023050345

ISBN 978-1-009-47324-8 Hardback

Cambridge University Press & Assessment has no responsibility for the persistence or accuracy of URLs for external or third-party internet websites referred to in this publication and does not guarantee that any content on such websites is, or will remain, accurate or appropriate.

Contents

List of Figures	page xi
List of Contributors	xiii
Preface, by Gary J. Jacobsohn	xvii
Acknowledgments	xxi

Introduction: The Quandaries and Parables of Constitutional Identity   1
Ran Hirschl and Yaniv Roznai

PART I FOUNDATIONS, THEORY, AND CONCEPTS

1   Rousseau's Sovereignty and the Concept of Constitutional Identity   23
Howard Schweber

2   Constitutional Identity: Cracking the Genetic Code of the Constitution   34
Monika Polzin

3   Constitutional Identity as Discourse: Mis-identity and Dis-identity   44
Jaclyn L. Neo

4   Constitutional Identity and Constitutional Revolution   56
Stephen Gardbaum

5   The Death of Constituent Power   63
Victor Ferreres Comella

6   Constitutional Identity as a Source of Ontological Security   76
Joanne Wallis

7   The Crisis in, and of, Constitutional Identity   89
Upendra Baxi

PART II COMPARATIVE PERSPECTIVES

8   Confucian Constitutional Identity 101
    Ngoc Son Bui

9   '(A-)Religious & Democratic' Militant Dual Constitutional
    Identities and the Turn to Illiberalism: The Case of France 113
    Eugénie Mérieau

10 Constitutional Identity in Bangladesh: Complexity
    and Contestations 125
    Ridwanul Hoque

11 Clashing Identities? Traditional Authority and Constitutionalism
    in Africa 138
    Heinz Klug

12 Imposed Revolution? "August Revolution," "Imposed
    Constitution," and the Identity of the Constitution of Japan 150
    Keigo Komamura

13 India: A Constitution in Search of an Identity 163
    Gautam Bhatia

PART III AMERICAN CONSTITUTIONALISM
AND CONSTITUTIONAL IDENTITY

14 "This Is (Not) Who We Are": Reflections on 1619
    and the Search for a Singular Constitutional Identity 179
    Sanford Levinson

15 Constitutional Aspirationalism Revisited 193
    Justin Buckley Dyer

16 The Constitution at War with Itself: Race, Citizenship,
    and the Forging of American Constitutional Identity 204
    George Thomas

17 Constitutional Identity, Constitutional Politics, and Constitutional
    Revolutions 216
    Mark A. Graber

18 American Constitutional Exceptionalism, Constitutional
    Identity, and Democracy 229
    Miguel Schor

PART IV EMERGING TRENDS

19 Constitution Making and Disharmonic Identity 245
   Aslı Bâli and Hanna Lerner

20 Constitutional Identity and Unamendability 259
   Oran Doyle

21 Illiberal Constitutionalism and the Abuse of Constitutional
   Identity 272
   Gábor Halmai and Julian Scholtes

22 Deconstructing Constitutional Identity in Light
   of the Turn to Populism 286
   Michel Rosenfeld

23 Unconstitutional Constitutional Identities in The European Union 300
   Pietro Faraguna

24 What Counts as Constitutional Identity? 312
   Mila Versteeg

25 Contrariness and Contradiction in Constitutional Law 330
   Zachary Elkins and Tom Ginsburg

26 Conclusion: The Past, Present, and Future
   of Constitutional Identity 345
   Christina Bambrick and Connor M. Ewing

Index 357

Figures

24.1 Represented by the constitution (United States)   *page* 319
24.2 Represented by the constitution (China)   320
24.3 Represented by the constitution (Japan)   320
24.4 Represented by the constitution (Korea)   321
24.5 Represented by the constitution (Taiwan)   321
24.6 Who feels represented? (United States)   323
24.7 Who feels represented? (China)   323
24.8 Who feels represented? (Japan)   324
24.9 Who feels represented? (Korea)   324
24.10 Who feels represented? (Taiwan)   325
25.1 The Aristotelian square of opposition   334

Contributors

Aslı Bâli is Professor of Law at Yale Law School.

Christina Bambrick is the Filip Family Assistant Professor of Political Science at the University of Notre Dame.

Upendra Baxi is Emeritus Professor of Law at the University of Warwick and former Vice Chancellor of the Universities of South Gujarat and Delhi.

Gautam Bhatia is Postdoctoral Research Fellow at the SCRIPTS Centre for Excellence at Humboldt University.

Ngoc Son Bui is Professor of Asian Laws in the Faculty of Law at the University of Oxford and a Fellow of St Hugh's College, Oxford.

Victor Ferreres Comella is Professor of Constitutional Law at the Pompeu Fabra University.

Oran Doyle is Professor of Law at Trinity College Dublin and Research Professor at the Academia Sinica, Taiwan.

Justin Buckley Dyer is Executive Director of the Civitas Institute, Professor of Government, and Jack G. Taylor Regents Professor at the University of Texas at Austin.

Zachary Elkins is Professor of Government at the University of Texas at Austin.

Connor M. Ewing is Assistant Professor in the Department of Political Science and Fellow of Trinity College at the University of Toronto.

Pietro Faraguna is Associate Professor of Constitutional Law at the University of Trieste.

Stephen Gardbaum is the Stephen Yeazell Endowed Chair in Law at UCLA School of Law.

Tom Ginsburg is the Leo Spitz Distinguished Service Professor of International Law at the University of Chicago School of Law.

Mark A. Graber is a University System of Maryland Regents Professor at the University of Maryland Francis King Carey School of Law.

Gábor Halmai is a part-time professor at the Robert Schuman Centre at the European University Institute and Director of the project "TRust, Independence, Impartiality and Accountability of Legal Professionals under the EU Charter – Part 2" (TRIIAL 2).

Ran Hirschl is the David R. Cameron Distinguished Professor in Law and Politics at the University of Toronto.

Ridwanul Hoque is formerly Professor of Law at the University of Dhaka and currently a university professorial Fellow at Charles Darwin University.

Gary J. Jacobsohn is the H. Malcolm Macdonald Professor of Constitutional and Comparative Law in the Department of Government and Professor of Law at the University of Texas at Austin.

Heinz Klug is the John and Rylla Bosshard Professor of Law at the University of Wisconsin Law School.

Keigo Komamura is Professor of Law and Vice President of Keio University.

Hanna Lerner is Professor and Head of the School of Political Science, Government and International Affairs at Tel Aviv University.

Sanford Levinson is the W. St. John Garwood and W. St. John Garwood Jr. Centennial Chair in Law and Professor of Government at the University of Texas at Austin.

Eugénie Mérieau is Associate Professor of Public Law at the University of Paris 1 Panthéon-Sorbonne and a member of the Sorbonne Institute of Philosophical and Legal Research (CNRS).

Jaclyn L. Neo is Associate Professor of Law and Director of the Centre for Asian Legal Studies at the National University of Singapore.

Monika Polzin is Professor of Public Law and Public International Law at the Institute for European and International Law at Vienna University of Economics and Business.

Michel Rosenfeld is University Professor of Law and Comparative Democracy, the Justice Sydney L. Robins Professor of Human Rights, and Director of the Program on Global and Comparative Constitutional Theory at the Benjamin N. Cardozo School of Law of Yeshiva University.

Yaniv Roznai is Associate Professor and Vice Dean at the Harry Radzyner Law School and Co-Director at the Rubinstein Center for Constitutional Challenges at Reichman University.

Julian Scholtes is a Lecturer in Public Law at the University of Glasgow.

Miguel Schor is Professor of Law and Associate Director of the Constitutional Law Center at Drake University.

Howard Schweber is Professor of Political Science and Legal Studies at the University of Wisconsin–Madison.

George Thomas is Burnet C. Wohlford Professor of American Political Institutions at Claremont McKenna College.

Mila Versteeg is the Henry L. and Grace Doherty Charitable Foundation Professor of Law at the University of Virginia.

Joanne Wallis is Professor of International Security in the Department of Politics and International Relations at the University of Adelaide.

Preface

Gary J. Jacobsohn

It has become a staple of much contemporary discourse that ample space be provided for airing both the misgivings and the endorsements that have accumulated around the vexed subject of *identity politics*. For some, the invocation of that term makes possible a necessary discussion of the injustices that have too often burdened marginalized groups, while for others it is an impediment to achieving progress in fulfillment of a societal common good. So far as I know, constitutional identity, this volume's focus of interest, has not had a direct association with the politics of identity, which perhaps partly explains the congenial ambience that until recently has marked its relatively brief conceptual history. That may be changing.

My first engagement with the *genome* question had nothing to do with the controversies that now commonly attend discussions of the specific variant of identity that relates to constitutional orders. It was initially a decidedly academic exercise in an intellectual progression that followed several efforts to understand the role of antecedent principles in constituting a polity. What became plainly evident in the three cases that I had examined in some detail – the United States, Israel, and India – was that the presence of great variability in constitutional design and development did not cause me to question my increasing appreciation for the ubiquity of the process by which constitutional identity evolves.

To be sure, the very supposition that an evolutionary process is critical for thinking about the identity concept may be questioned. It presumes a dynamic aspect that is not obvious when viewed through the lens of centuries-old classical theories of personal identity, in which, as the eighteenth-century Scottish philosopher Thomas Reid argued, "an uninterrupted continuance of existence" is the essence of what *constitutes* an individual as a person. Moving from the individual to the community of individuals who collectively inhabit a polity, we might expect to find something similar, so that once constituted a state must, in James Madison's famous account, rely on continuity to achieve its "requisite stability." To the extent that a constitutional order's identity is in flux, sadly we will accordingly find it "deprived of that veneration which time bestows on every thing."

But, as the United States illustrates in a way that is in some respects more discernible in Israel and India, a stable identity is at odds with the disharmonic reality that is endemic to the constitutional condition. For Americans who have often heard their exceptionalism described with reference to the people-constituting function of their founding text, it is chastening to be reminded of the alternative visions that were contained within the folds of that document. If creating a people was a hallmark of the Constitution, the tensions and incongruities with which it was encumbered ensured that this project would be ongoing and protracted. Add to this that it is no part of exceptionalism in the United States or elsewhere that a constitutional order also encompasses disharmonic interactions between the aspirations inscribed in its governing charter and the social order within which it functions, and the mutability of constitutional identity can no longer rightly be called into question.

Or so we might conclude if the scope of our vision extended no further than the rarefied confines of scholarly inquiry. Concepts, however, do not necessarily retain the properties of their rationally derived meaning when removed to the less detached setting of political contestation. Consider, for example, how the idea of democracy has fared in the grasp of political actors determined to obscure their autocratic aspirations through the assuasive and tendentious invocation of a popular-sounding system of rule. With identity, too, it should come as no surprise that there will be those who stand to benefit from a strategically deployed exercise of concept manipulation. Thus, in the three cases that provided me with the resources to begin theorizing about the instability of constitutional identity, the historical record is replete with examples of opportunistic denial of what an objective assessment of the concept divulges. Instead, a static conceptual understanding, according to which identity is selectively discovered in text or history and then largely regarded as unalterable, has often emerged at moments when the effects of constitutional disharmony have fashioned an outcome that is viewed as unacceptable to endangered holders of power.

Such a moment has arrived in a profoundly significant way in the wake of recent developments in Europe and elsewhere. Thus, invocation of constitutional identity as an integral cog in the scheme by which the concerning phenomenon of democratic backsliding has progressed is increasingly evident in the radical politicization of the concept. What had previously been prized for its heuristic properties is now appreciated as well by some for its instrumental value in preserving a particular regime type whose essential features manifest unmistakable authoritarian proclivities. Accompanying the resistance to this development are the governmental incumbents' indignant allegations of illicit intrusion into the prerogatives of sovereign autonomy. Yet notable too is the reaction within the academic community to the nefarious purposes to which constitutional identity has been deployed. While some scholars have pushed back against the transformation of a conceptual tool into an implement of power maintenance, others have called for its terminological abandonment, or at least for an acceptance of a seriously restricted scope for the idea's application.

How, then, can we make sense of this abusive appropriation of the concept of constitutional identity by political actors intent on facilitating the demise of liberal constitutionalism? Perhaps by attempting to understand what they are doing in light of that other terminological adaptation, which is how we arrive at the door of identity politics. To be sure, the controversy surrounding this term underscores its elusiveness as an analytical marker; still, its ubiquitous usage is generally meant to convey important information about the historical injustices visited upon marginalized groups, and the consequent necessity for political action on behalf of those whose exclusion and subjugation have left them believing there are no options other than to pursue an identity-based effort to achieve rightful recognition in the social order. When viewed through this prism, identity politics is essentially inclusionary, as the goal of its promoters is integration – though not necessarily assimilation – into the broader societal mainstream.

Constitutional identity's current quandary is the direct result of its having been implicated in the recent rethinking of identity politics to support an exclusionary *raison d'être* at odds with the political dynamic that inspired its early proponents. While this development is not confined to one geographic locale – in the United States, for example, it plays out in the rise of a Christian nationalism whose champions desire nothing more than a reconstruction of constitutional identity to conform to a presumed distant past – its most advanced progression is evident in Europe, and most unequivocally in the Hungarian case. As is clear in many of its populist-inspired undertakings, and especially notable in its response to the European Union's migratory policies, that country's government (abetted by a compliant supreme court) has embraced, for explicitly exclusivist purposes, an historically rooted inviolable concept of constitutional identity. Indeed, an imagined "historic constitution" now functions as the principal protective shield against what is tendentiously portrayed as a threat to the survival of the nation's ethno-cultural identity. If the familiar version of identity politics is fueled by a felt need to counter a majority culture's domineering denial of minority group self-determination, the legal narrative that we find increasingly associated with the phenomenon of democratic decline is best understood in opposition to it, namely as a grievance-generated constitutionally framed instantiation of majoritarian identity politics.

My hope is that this disturbing conceptual misappropriation will be short-lived, or at least that its insidious influence will diminish over time. To break the linkage between constitutional identity and identity politics will require more than any volume of essays can by itself achieve. Scholars, however, who analyze and reflect on the nuances of constitutionalism can through their efforts contribute to the necessary work of those in the political and judicial arenas whose resistance to the weaponization of constitutional identity should be encouraged. As will be gleaned from many of the pages in what follows, that effort is best situated in an appreciation for the dynamic dissonance in constitutional identity rightly understood. Purging the idea of its disharmonic aspect enables its ill-intended guardians to attain their desired outcomes with unwarranted ease. The danger thus arises and becomes concerning when the failure to acknowledge ambiguity and incongruity in the genome of constitutionalism is allowed to go unchecked. If there is a salutary takeaway from this book, it lies in the greater awareness of what can be done to mitigate this possibility.

Acknowledgments

The idea to curate a volume of original essays centering on the key concept of constitutional identity, and on Gary J. Jacobsohn's essential contributions to its formulation, was born in the pre-COVID era. Like many other dimensions of scholarly life, it was put on hold due to the pandemic. We enthusiastically picked it up again in late 2021. All the chapters included in this volume have benefited considerably from discussion and detailed feedback during a three-day authors' workshop in November 2021. We thank Antonia Baraggia, Amnon Cavari, Joey Cozza, Federico Fabbrini, Meital Pinto, Adam Shinar, Manal Totry-Jubran, and Han Zhai for chairing and commenting on the various papers. We thank the many contributors to this volume for their dedication, responsiveness, and of course for their rich, thought-provoking takes on constitutional identity. We are likewise grateful to Marianne Nield at CUP, as well as to the three anonymous reviewers for their exceptionally helpful suggestions on a draft of this project.

As anyone who puts together a volume of this scope and caliber knows, having excellent research, editorial, and logistical assistance is essential. We thank Julius Ott, Jen Rubio, and Nicholas Slawnych for their superb research and editorial assistance at different stages of this project. Special thanks go to Adi Zaharia for her invaluable editorial and coordination assistance over the last couple of years. This volume would not have come to fruition without her commitment, good judgment, and tireless work.

We dedicate this volume to Gary J. Jacobsohn, a great thinker, mentor, and friend. Winner of the American Political Science Association Law and Courts Section's 2019 Lifetime Achievement Award, his many writings over the years contributed considerably to the rise of comparative constitutional studies as one of the most vibrant areas of inquiry and practice in contemporary public law. Our understanding of constitutional identity – arguably one of the most important concepts in contemporary constitutional thought, constitutional law, and constitutional politics – would not be nearly as sophisticated without Jacobsohn's decades-long groundbreaking scholarship in comparative constitutional theory.

Introduction

The Quandaries and Parables of Constitutional Identity

Ran Hirschl and Yaniv Roznai

Constitutional identity has become a crucial concept in contemporary constitutional theory, constitutional jurisprudence, and constitutional politics. Courts, jurists, scholars, and politicians alike have often invoked (and occasionally misused) this term. Fierce debates on the status of member-state constitutional identity vis-à-vis that of the emerging pan-European constitutional order – debates given added vigor by the rise of ethno-nationalist populism and a corresponding form of illiberal constitutionalism in Central and Eastern Europe – have triggered a host of landmark rulings in recent years by the German Federal Constitutional Court, the Constitutional Court of Hungary, Poland's Constitutional Tribunal, Italy's Constitutional Court, Ireland's Supreme Court, the Court of Justice of the EU (CJEU), and the European Court of Human Rights (ECtHR). These decisions follow an earlier spate of milestone rulings on such matters as the place of the crucifix in Italy's national and constitutional identity (*Lautsi v. Italy*) and the relationship between *laïcité* and France's naturalization and citizenship laws (*S.A.S. v. France*).

Meanwhile, in other parts of the world, the scope and nature of constitutional identity features centrally in debates about the place of Hinduism in India's political and constitutional order; the extent to which Japan's post World War II constitution reflects that country's own history, tradition, and aspirations; the place of Shari'a law and official state ideology of *Pancasila* in the Indonesian constitutional order; and the tension embedded in Israel's self-definition as a "Jewish and democratic state." In other countries, moreover, from Turkey (*Türkiye*) to the Czech Republic (*Czechia*), and from Bangladesh to Brazil to Taiwan, apex courts have developed an "unconstitutional constitutional amendments" doctrine, which enables the judiciary to invalidate constitutional amendments deemed incompatible with a polity's core self-defining constitutional ideals (Roznai 2017).

It comes as no surprise then, to witness a rapidly growing scholarly interest in the concept of constitutional identity (Toniatti 2013, 62), arising in multiple conversations: the literature on populism; democratic backsliding and constitutional retrogression; challenges surrounding definitions of constitutional transformation and revolution; the place of religion and religion-infused morality in public life; struggles over gender equality, sexual preference, immigration or education policies; and debates concerning national constitutional traditions, "global constitutionalism," and the legitimacy of judicial reference to foreign constitutional jurisprudence. *Google Books Ngram Viewer* (which covers a large corpus of books in English since the 1950s) shows a rise in recent years in searches for constitutional identity, illustrating the continuously expanding interest in the concept since 2005 (Google Books Ngram Viewer n.d.).

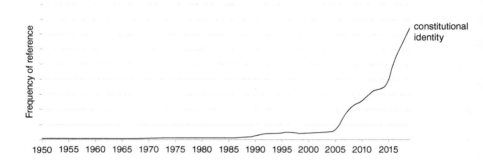

1 THE BASIC QUESTIONS AND CHALLENGES

In his now-classic *Constitutional Identity*, Gary Jacobsohn argues that constitutional identity "emerges dialogically and represents a mix of political aspirations and commitments that are expressive of a nation's past, as well as the determination of those within the society who seek in some ways to transcend the past" (Jacobsohn 2010a, 7). The identity of the constitution is a mixture of universal values with particular attributes that reflect the nation's particularistic history, customs, values; it is an intermingling of established features and aspirations (Jacobsohn 2006, 2010a). Importantly, constitutional identity is never static, but rather emerges from the interplay of inevitably disharmonic elements embedded in any given polity's constitutional tradition (Jacobsohn 2010b, 47). In this sense, and as is visible in many of this book's chapters, constitutional identity is conceived as "a fluid concept" in which "constitutional assertions of self-definition are part of an ongoing process entailing adaptation and adjustment as circumstances dictate" (Jacobsohn 2010a, 13). The dynamic nature of constitutional identity arises from such disharmonies and internal tensions, not to mention the external tensions between the constitution and the existing reality. For this reason, as Jacobsohn argues, we must understand constitutional identity as being changeable, continuously developing over time.

Despite its increased importance, however, the concept itself remains elusive. As Michel Rosenfeld puts it, constitutional identity "is an essentially contested concept as there is no agreement over what it means or refers to" (Rosenfeld 2012, 757).

Identity seems to refer to certain defining features of something or someone, a certain subject (Martí 2013, 21). But what exactly is that something, someone, or subject? Is it the constitutional document? The everyday, so-called "small-c" constitution that includes practices, customs, and interpretations? The identity of the constitution makers? Or perhaps it is the identity of those who are to be subjected to the constitution? These challenging questions remain largely unsettled in the scholarship on constitutional identity (Rosenfeld 2009, 18–19).

Where in the constitutional sphere is a given polity's constitutional identity to be found? While most authors agree that a given country's constitutional identity has some sort of connection to its constitutional documents, there is considerable disagreement about the exact nature of this relationship, especially with regard to the causal directionality between constitutional documents and constitutional identity. Michel Troper (2010), for example, identifies the relationship between the two as essentially unilateral, with the "hard core" of a given polity's constitutional document(s) determining that polity's constitutional identity (Rosenfeld 2012, 759). According to this view, identifying a country's constitutional identity is simply a matter of extracting a constitution's indispensable principles, without which it would lose its essential character and cease to represent the polity it was meant to serve (Rosenfeld 2012, 759). Because Troper then views constitutional identity as supervening on constitutional documents, he conceives of a limited role for constitutional identity, whereby the concept essentially serves as an interpretative guide toward faithful constitutional adjudication.

A diametrically opposed view is taken by George Fletcher (1993), who envisions an inherently dichotomous relationship between constitutional documents and constitutional identity qua the unwritten legal context in which constitutional documents are written and interpreted. This conception of constitutional identity inheres in supra-constitutional values; in contrast to Troper's recommendation for judges to look to the constitutional text to determine the essence of constitutional identity – and, by extension, the constitutionality of a particular amendment – Fletcher argues that the acceptable way to resolve questions of constitutional consistency is "to turn 'inward' and reflect upon the legal culture in which the dispute is embedded" (Fletcher 1993, 737).

Prominent authors such as Michel Rosenfeld and Gary Jacobsohn occupy a middle ground between these two positions, with both authors locating constitutional identity in the continuous reinterpretation of constitutional documents by the judiciary over time. For both authors, constitutional identity "neither exists as a discrete object of invention nor as a heavily encrusted essence embedded in a society's culture" (Jacobsohn 2006, 363). Rather, a polity's constitutional identity is to some extent, but not exclusively, characterized by its textual constitution, although it can also consist in what Jacobsohn describes as the polity's "prescriptive constitution": "long-standing commitments and sanctioned practices that may be at odds with the language of the document currently in force" (Jacobsohn 2010a, 345).

Importantly, constitutional identity develops out of the political conflict and resolution characteristic of constitutional change for Jacobsohn (2006, 363), or in strikingly similar terms for Rosenfeld, "constitutional identity emerges from the confrontation of the very paradox [between identity and difference across constitutional reform] on which its corresponding constitution rests" (2009, 10). Both these views further characterize constitutional identity as inherently mutable up to a limit, or, as having "bounded fluidity" in the sense that it circumscribes both limits and possibilities for constitutional reform (Jacobsohn 2010a, 349), the legitimacy of which always depends upon a sufficient connection with previous interpretations and manifestations of constitutional identity. The main driving force here is constitutional discord or disharmony, which in Jacobsohn's view is critical to the development of constitutional identity (2010, 4). Such disharmony may reflect a variety of inconsistencies, including simultaneous constitutional commitments to incompatible legal or political ends, conflicts between dual or multiple constitutional hierarchies or, more generally, discrepancies between a given polity's formal constitutional commitments and its real-life "political constitution."

Rosenfeld's account deemphasizes the role of disharmony while accentuating the discursive process of negation, metaphor, and metonymy in the formation of constitutional identity (Rosenfeld 2012, 759). France's constitutional identity, for example, with its roots in the destruction of the *ancien régime*, was initially characterized by a bare rejection of the French feudal system, and only later evolved into the positive self-image required to maintain the fiction of a constituted imagined community through the subsequent developments of *égalité*-based metaphor and metonymy, giving shape to a new constitutional identity rooted in legal commitments (Rosenfeld 2012, 759). In contrast to Jacobsohn, who characterizes the purpose of constitutional identity as resolving disharmony within a constitutional document or between that document and broader social values, Rosenfeld's view suggests that constitutional identity has the broader goal of mediating "conflicts and tensions between identity and difference ... that shape the dealings between self and other within the relevant polity committed to constitutional rule" (Rosenfeld 2012, 761).

The puzzle surrounding the concept of constitutional identity becomes more complex when one considers the fuzzy distinction between national identity and constitutional identity (Wischmeyer 2015, 415). The conventional view is that, more often than not, the people or the political community precede their constitution; constitutions are created when "we the people" or their representatives come together and decide on how to shield their core ideals, values, and political system and institutions from passing whims and the vicissitudes of everyday politics. Other accounts point to the dynamics whereby constitutions at the same time help constitute the people and create a sense of community and of a common founding narrative. In a magisterial recent book, Wim Voermans (2023) shows how both processes take place simultaneously. Human evolution, human nature, and the history of thought have all played their part in shaping modern constitutions. Constitutions, in turn, have shaped our societies, creating imagined communities of trust and recognition that allow us to successfully cooperate with one another.

In direct accounts of national and constitutional identity, these terms may overlap but are not fully synonymous, even though they are often used interchangeably (Cloots 2015, 118; Drinóczi 2020; Martin 2012, 29). In many jurisdictions, the basic principles and system of values are determined by or directly reflected in the constitution itself. The United States is a paradigmatic example of a country in which national and constitutional identity are strongly connected: "our self-definition as a nation is bound up with the Constitution," in Justice Kennedy's words (Toobon 2005).[1] Indeed, the United States Constitution plays a vital role in defining its national identity (Bassok 2015, 289). But just north of the US border, in Canada, the linkage between national identity and constitutional identity was relatively loose until 1982, when core values such as multiculturalism and the rights of Indigenous populations were written into the Constitution. So, the question remains: Is a given polity's identity shaped by its constitution, or vice versa? And how significant are disharmonies and mismatches between national and constitutional identity, let alone disharmonies within a given constitutional order or text, in explaining constitutional transformation or revolution? What are the circumstances that justify such change in the name of harmonizing national and constitutional identity?

Importantly, Rosenfeld distinguishes constitutional identity from national identity, although the exact relationship between these two kinds of identities remains somewhat elusive. In Rosenfeld's view, constitutional and national identity "differ though they may overlap and though they may comprise the same exact membership or closely intertwined ones," and "constitutional identity is constructed in part against national identity and in part consistent with it" (Rosenfeld 2012, 758). His characterization of national identity as enabling the creation of "imaginary communities" (Rosenfeld 2012, 758), however, along with his distinction between Spain's multi-ethnic *constitutional* identity and the United States' multi-ethnic *national* identity (Rosenfeld 2012, 161), suggests that rather than an ethnic notion, national identity should be understood as consisting in a polity's general social inclinations, whereas constitutional identity consists in a polity's codified legal commitments, a stricter threshold.

The common ground between Jacobsohn's and Rosenfeld's perspectives is then the view that constitutional identity enables a constitution to respond to societal pressures while ensuring continuity between past and present. At minimum, both Jacobsohn and Rosenfeld seem committed to the idea that constitutional identity has descriptive value in that it supplies a framework that gives coherence to

---

[1] Justice Kennedy made this remark in an interview concerning his support for the practice of referring to (if not relying on) foreign law in the course of adjudicating constitutional cases. Kennedy differs from Justice Scalia in seeing no necessary conflict between borrowing and constitutional identity.

constitutional change. By referring to the core values and principles embodied in a constitutional document, one benefit of constitutional identity is that it allows courts and other lawmakers to understand constitutional provisions in light of the ideals originally animating the enactment of a given constitutional document, and this sense of constitutional identity gives a useful label for the kind of interpretation implicit in constitutional adjudication. Furthermore, for both Jacobsohn and Rosenfeld, constitutional identity has normative value in that it provides a standard for the legitimacy of constitutional change. Constitutional identity not only serves as a means for the judiciary to overcome "hard cases" of constitutional adjudication but also furnishes the criterion by which we can evaluate constitutional change as successfully preserving the authority of the constitution.

Constitutions are situated between the past and the future, looking at once forward and backward (Scheppele 2008, 1377). For this reason, the temporal element is crucial for shaping and understanding constitutional identity: It is rooted in the past but also encompasses commitments and aspirations for the future (Millet 2013). Indeed, the distinction between national and constitutional identity seems to be the sharpest where the express purpose of a new constitution is to separate the future from the past in ways that will have transformative effects on society. This in turn raises another set of important questions this volume aims to address: Can a polity's constitution be different – perhaps even expressly disconnected from – that polity's "true" or "authentic" constitutional identity? Does constitutional identity have a meta-political dimension to it that is not subject to constant construction, deconstruction, and reconstruction, or is it ultimately as politically contingent as any other national and collective meta-narrative? And how does constitutional revolution reflect a foundational disconnection or reconnection with the polity's constitutional identity? (Jacobsohn and Roznai 2020).

To add another layer of complication, the rise of transnational constitutional or quasi-constitutional orders – the emerging pan-European constitution is a prime example here – creates a new frontier of contestation: national versus transnational constitutional identity. While the idea of protecting national identity amid the European integration process is not new, it was only in the early 1990s that the first formulation of the identity clause was included in the European treaties.[2] Moreover, beginning with the 2009 Treaty of Lisbon, European treaties have included judicially enforceable identity clauses, affording a much greater range of protection to the national identities of EU member states. Art. 4(2) of the Treaty on European Union ("TEU"), for example, reads as follows: "The Union shall respect the equality of Member States before the Treaties as well as their national identities, inherent in their fundamental structures, political and constitutional, inclusive of regional and local self-government." Following the adoption of the Lisbon Treaty,

---

[2] The Treaty of Maastricht, provides in Art. F(1) that: "The Union shall respect the national identities of its Member States, whose system of government are founded on the principles of democracy."

Article 4(2) TEU made its way into the jurisprudence of the Court of Justice of the European Union (Besselink 2010; Faraguna 2016).

Across Europe, multiple crises in recent years have complicated or raised new challenges associated with national identities. Examples abound. Recall the financial crisis of 2008 and its challenge to pan-European solidarity. There is also the continuing so-called "refugee crisis" (and questions of incoming immigration more generally), portrayed by nationalist leaders and parties as a threat to both their respective countries' identity in addition to Europe's identity. Another example is the transformative rights jurisprudence of the European Court of Human Rights, which frequently touches upon matters of national and constitutional identity. Finally, contestations surrounding Belgian or Dutch national identity, as well as the Britishness debate related to Brexit, all contribute to this same tension surrounding identity. Meanwhile, in an increasing number of landmark rulings, the ECtHR has scrutinized pillars of Irish, French, and Italian national and constitutional identity (e.g., famously in *Lautsi v. Italy* and *S.A.S. v. France*). Other rulings in Europe's high courts frequently address matters such as reproductive freedoms, citizenship and naturalization, entitlement for benefits, and recognition of same-sex marriage and parenthood; matters perceived as elements of national and constitutional identity in some countries.

More generally, it may well be argued that identity of any sort, certainly political or constitutional identity, must be relational in nature as it ultimately relies on real or perceived "Others" to clearly demarcate itself as unique or distinct from other identities. What is more, any political and constitutional identity must rely, at least to some extent, on a sense of "folk," peoplehood, or other collective meta-narrative of belonging and the common good. In that respect, liberal constitutional identities may feature an inherent weakness in their tendency toward inclusivity, especially in comparison to communitarian and nationalist approaches which underscore the role of "folk" elements in political and constitutional identity.

Constitutional identity may then become exclusionary rather than unifying. This trend assumes very specific contours in some Central and Eastern European member states, where constitutional identity has been increasingly used (or abused, as some argue) by both judicial and political actors to mark a stark differentiation of the domestic constitutional traditions, fostering strong defiant and separatist sentiments (Fabbrini and Sajó 2019; Halmai 2018; Kovács 2017; Scholtes 2021). In some instances, these sentiments add fuel to new trends of "constitutional capture" and the undermining of judicial independence which challenge pan-European norms of liberal constitutionalism and the rule of law. Against such a background of new contrasts and challenges, the European "constitutional path" of identity seems to be subject to a new process of transformation.

Much has been written in recent years about populist threats to democracy, constitutionalism, and the rule of law, as well as what has been termed democratic backsliding, constitutional retrogression, and the rise of illiberal constitutionalism.

The nationalist and exclusionary reformulation of constitutional identity in Viktor Orbán's Hungary is featured centrally in these accounts. In 2018, to pick but one example from Hungary's recent shift toward an ethno-nationalist constitutional order, Orbán's majority government enacted the Seventh Amendment of the Basic Law of Hungary. The Amendment introduced a number of clauses codifying the role of Hungary's constitutional identity as a limit to the nation's legislative capacity, with Article 3 providing that all government bodies "shall protect the constitutional self-identity of Hungary," and Article 2 prohibiting Hungary from fulfilling its treaty obligations as a European Union Member State in any way which violates "Hungary's inalienable right of disposal related to its territorial integrity, population, form of government and governmental organization" (Kelemen and Pech 2019, 68). As Dimitry Kochenov and Petra Bard have argued, the "constitutional self-identity of Hungary" is a concept "so vague that it can be considered an attempt at granting a carte blanche type of derogation to the executive and the legislative from Hungary's obligation under EU law" (12), and Orbán has subsequently invoked these sections to skirt Hungary's obligations under EU refugee settlement quotas in order to, as Orbán explains, protect Hungary's constitutional self-identity from an influx of "Muslim invaders" (qtd. in Kelemen and Pech 2019, 68).

Orbán's use (or misuse) of constitutional identity has been widely criticized as undermining fundamental EU legal principles such as the rule of law and judicial independence. However, some observers have argued that Orbán's application of constitutional identity reflects an inherent weakness of the very concept of constitutional identity rather than an abuse of an otherwise valuable concept. For these critics, it is no accident that constitutional identity plays such a key instrumental role in the enactment of discriminatory constitutional amendments in Hungary and other European jurisdictions, as some intrinsic feature of the concept enables populist and authoritarian governments to interpret constitutional identity in whatever manner required by their own political purposes. Although such critics offer slightly different accounts of the relationship between constitutional identity and its routine application toward illiberal ends, most identify the concept's inherent vagueness as making it susceptible to perversion (Faraguna 2017; Körtvélyesi and Majtényi 2017; Sajó and Uitz 2017).

Federico Fabbrini and András Sajó (2019) advance what is perhaps the most rigorous account of constitutional identity's susceptibility to illiberal constitutional development. They focus, in a nutshell, on the conceptual vagueness inherent to the notion of constitutional identity. First, "constitutional identity" is indeterminate in the sense that the concept has no identifiable formal definition (Fabbrini and Sajó 2019, 467). As the two argue, simply defining "constitutional identity" as the hard core of a constitution provides little guidance with respect to the kind of legal commitments which will actually form a given country's constitutional identity. As the concept is indeterminate, they argue, a given country's constitutional identity could possibly include *any* given commitment, including illiberal ones, that plausibly emanates from or reflects an aspect of that country's constitutional history. The concept's arbitrary content, therefore, allows illiberal reformers to enact exclusionary, xenophobic, and otherwise illiberal amendments (464). Picking up on a point of equivocation identified by J.L. Martí (2013, 17), the two further argue that the notion "constitutional identity" can refer to both the identity of a given constitution (as a legal concept) and the identity of the people constituting a given polity, with the latter interpretation potentially accommodating ethnic and religious elements. While Fabbrini and Sajó grant that constitutional identity can be defined wholly in terms of a country's legal commitments and consequently that the concept does not inherently involve any ethnic or religious dimensions in principle, they argue that even a purely legal concept of constitutional identity can thereby incorporate components of national identity which promote nationalist ends.

In his recent engagements with some of these criticisms, Jacobsohn (2023a, 2023b) suggests that the Orbán-influenced Hungarian Constitutional Court's interpretation of constitutional identity reflects a misuse of the concept as it overlooks the inherent mutability of constitutional identity. By locating Hungary's constitutional identity in the nation's historical constitution which is "acknowledged" rather than "created" by Hungary's fundamental law, Jacobsohn argues that the Court employs a static conception of constitutional identity that is confined to Hungary's Christian past and immune to future change. It is this non-dynamic application, and not the fluidity of the concept, which enables the Court's abuse of the concept for illiberal ends, and privileging a historical period in the construction of Hungarian constitutional identity is then what empowers constitutional adjudicators in that country "to establish fixed constitutional meanings that advance their political projects, whether noble or ignoble" (Jacoboshn 2023a, 51). Since constitutional identity only insulates itself against future reinterpretation when it is articulated in a manner which neglects the disharmony endemic to the concept, it only becomes a tool for exclusivist ends when lawmakers ignore the contradiction which is central to the concept. An appreciation by legislators and courts alike of the disharmony, conflict, and incongruity intrinsic to constitutional identity, Jacobsohn argues, will mitigate the deleterious consequences that have been associated with the concept by its critics.[3]

To be sure, this view's inherently dynamic and mutable conception of constitutional identity still admits to some possibility for populist application, provided that the concept is employed in such a way which retains a modicum of disharmony.

---

[3] Jacobsohn (2023a) approvingly cites earlier landmark rulings of other national high courts in Central and Eastern Europe on the Treaty of Lisbon as an application of constitutional identity which accommodates this mutability. The Czech Court's understanding of their relationship with the EU as a "dialogue of equal partners," as well as their conclusion that "state sovereignty is not an aim in and of itself, in isolation, but is a means to fulfilling ... fundamental [constitutional] values" (Jacobsohn 2023a, 55), correctly recognizes the flexibility of constitutional identity and seems to preclude, according to this view, an application of the concept which privileges past societal values at the expense of alternative constitutional projects.

We might imagine a country that perpetually makes some progress toward liberal constitutionalism before backsliding into illiberal constitutional arrangements soon after, all the while grappling with some tension in its self-identity, as an example of the "correct" use of the concept without any normative payoff. In recognizing this possibility, Jacobsohn notes that "fluidity is bi-directional, and so movement along the continuum [of constitutionalism] is subject to pressure and influence that may emanate from sources with opposing objectives as far as liberal democratic aspirations are concerned" (2023a, 26).

Tensions surrounding the scope, nature, utility, and proper application of constitutional identity characterize constitutional jurisprudence and politics in other, non-Western settings. The constitutional order in many African and Latin American countries is marred with conflicts and disharmonies concerning Indigenous cultures, colonial legacies, and the diverse, "plurinational" essence of the polity. As the recent failed attempts to adopt a new constitution for Chile illustrate, public perception of over-representation of one competing identity among others (in this instance of Indigenous people's rights and status) may generate backlash and rejection. Constitutional disharmonies readily present themselves in what have been termed *ethnic democracies* (e.g., Smooha 2002), which subscribe to general principles of democratic governance yet are committed to prioritizing the status and well-being of a certain ethnic or religious group within the polity. The inherently conflictual mode of constitutionalism identified by Ran Hirschl (2010) as *constitutional theocracy* provides another prime example. Here, a single religion enjoys primary constitutional status as the official state religion, often with strong political backing and autonomous jurisdiction over certain legal and public policy areas, while minority rights and principles of freedom of religion are constitutionally enshrined and adhered to various degrees. To complicate matters even further, there are disagreements, at times fierce, among followers of the state religion regarding the degree of strictness or leniency that should be applied to the translation and enforcement of religious precepts in public life.

In virtually all these settings, constitutional identity reflects elements of cultural, ethnic, or religious heritage within a given polity, frequently combined with an aspirational facet. The simultaneous formal (constitutional) or informal (political) prioritization of such particularistic facets, alongside the commitment to core universalist values, can and does provoke frequent clashes over constitutional identity. Countries as diverse as India, Israel, Malaysia, Indonesia, Pakistan, Egypt, Sri Lanka, and Thailand (to name but a few) have experienced varying levels of turbulence in their constitutional spheres because of such clashes. More often than not, these clashes pit progressive, reform-seeking social movements and non-governmental organizations against religious establishments, conservative leaders, and traditionalist groups, featuring diametrically opposed views on issues such as personal status and family law, gender equality, and LGBTQ rights, alongside issues related to denominational education, blasphemy, heresy, and conversion.

As noted above, courts in these and other polities have developed an "unconstitutional constitutional amendments" doctrine that permits judicial invalidation of constitutional amendments that are deemed discordant or otherwise in conflict with core constitutional ideals that define the polity as such (Roznai 2017). In adjudicating such "existential" identity matters, which address the very definition of the polity, courts and judges have knowingly embraced the Dworkinian idealist vision of Herculean judges tasked with preserving the "enduring values" (Dworkin's term) of their respective polities. This in turn raises another question. Are courts the right forum to decide contested matters of constitutional identity, and by extension fraught questions of history and memory, restorative justice, and of collective metanarratives, which define and divide entire nations?

In addition to these key substantive challenges, the fluid and inherently mutable nature of constitutional identity raises a host of methodological questions of operationalization and measurement. How are we to operationalize, measure, or otherwise quantify such a fluid and abstract concept? And how are we to empirically address the distinction – essential to understanding constitutional identity – between what has been termed "large-C" constitutionalism (referring to the formal dimension of a given polity's constitutional order) and "small-c" constitutionalism (referring to the less formal, "real-life" practice and acceptance of constitutional norms and constitutional law)? What is more, as we discussed at some length earlier in this introduction, constitutional identity is understood by many to be a dynamic and all-encompassing concept. So, we may pose yet another question, alluded to previously: what is not included in it, or how are we to refute claims for its significance? In other words, does the concept lose its analytical precision and explanatory power by being overly abstract, too inclusive, ever-evolving, and thus potentially non-falsifiable and irrefutable?

To address these questions, and to offer what may well be the most comprehensive scholarly account to date on the question of constitutional identity, its various meanings, constitutional and political significance, and its potential future(s), this unique volume brings together leading scholars of comparative constitutionalism, constitutional theory, and political theory. The contributors to this volume hail from diverse backgrounds and experiences, offering an impressive range of national and regional expertise with which to tackle these questions.

2 STRUCTURE AND CONTENTS OF THE BOOK

Fittingly, the volume opens with a preface by Gary Jacobsohn, who emphasizes the concept's development and manipulation from a constantly changing concept that reflects constitutional disharmony to a static and selective discovery of identity for political aims and identity politics. Jacobsohn, who has been the source of inspiration for this book, raises the danger of failing "to acknowledge ambiguity and incongruity in the genome of constitutionalism" – precisely those elements this book aims to explore.

The volume consists of four main parts: Foundations, Theory and Concepts; Comparative Perspectives; American Constitutionalism and Constitutional Identity; and Emerging Trends.

Part I: Foundations, Theory, and Concepts, begins with Howard Schweber's chapter *Rousseau's Sovereignty and the Concept of Constitutional Identity*. Schweber analyzes the concept of constitutional identity in relation to Jean-Jacques Rousseau's theory of constituent power. Drawing on Rousseau's idea of a founding legislator who is able to impose constitutionalism before the existence of a popular sovereignty, Schweber differentiates and explores the relationship between sovereignty, political authority, and constituent power, which represent three dimensions of constitutional identity. He goes on to suggest that the points of agreement and difference between Rousseau's model and the current theory of constitutional identity, as reflected in the writings of Gary Jacobsohn, reveal both the possibilities and the limitations of the latter view.

In the following chapter, *Constitutional Identity – Cracking the Genetic Code of the Constitution*, Monika Polzin applies the concept of constitutional identity to analyze German constitutional conflict on legally binding electoral gender quotas. The German system is a critical and curious case study for constitutional identity not only because of Germany's unprecedented constitutional transformation, indeed constitutional rebirth, following World War II but also as it conflicts the fluid or dynamic nature of constitutional identity with the German Basic Law's eternity clause, which aims to shield certain core values from future change.

The German eternity clause, like its Indian "sibling" – the basic structure doctrine – provides special protection to certain basic foundational constitutional principles and values, often based on their rightness, in the name of "the people." But as Jaclyn L. Neo shows in her chapter *Constitutional Identity as Discourse: Mis-identity and Dis-identity*, even these foundational values are contested when considering "the people" from a realist perspective rather than a mythical one. It is indeed contestation that is at the focus of Neo's chapter in which she demonstrates how constitutional disharmonies give rise to constitutional identity contestations through an examination of the narratives employed by constitutional actors. She recognizes "constitutional mis-identity" and "constitutional dis-identity" as two modes of argumentation that challenge existing claims about constitutional identity in this way.

The tension between stability and change is also at the core of Stephen Gardbaum's chapter *Constitutional Identity and Constitutional Revolution*. Exploring the relationship between these two concepts, Gardbaum posits that certain constitutional revolutions, especially of what he terms the "new beginnings" type, are best defined according to their ability to substitute an existing constitutional identity with a new, modified one.

Whereas Gardbaum focuses on the result of revolutionary changes, Victor Ferreres Comella focuses on the motivation behind revolutionary constitutional changes. In his chapter *The Death of Constituent Power*, he calls for the rejection and ultimate abandonment of "the idea that there exists a sovereign people, endowed with the unlimited power to enact a constitution whenever and however it wishes." In a liberal democracy, he claims, constituent power must be regarded as a limited power.

The relationship between continuity and change is also central in Joanne Wallis' chapter *Constitutional Identity as a Source of Ontological Security*. Here, Wallis applies the conceptualization of constitutional identity in constitutional theory to international relations, using the concept as an analytical tool to define a given nation-state's self-identity by narrating a sense of biographical continuity. As Wallis argues, this understanding of self-identity is valuable for the notion of "ontological security" for that state and its people. Finally, drawing on the case study of Timor-Leste, Wallis then demonstrates how the concept of constitutional identity can successfully "travel" to the lexicon of international relations.

Closing the first theoretical and conceptual part of the book is Upendra Baxi's chapter *The Crisis in, and of, Constitutional Identity*. Here, Baxi examines three core conceptual queries surrounding constitutional identity: What is the relationship between national and constitutional identity; can constitutional identity be "abused"; and what are the theoretical implications of the plurality of constitutional identities in multicultural and pluractional societies? Taken together, these tensions highlight the dialectic, disharmonic, and perhaps even crisis-ridden nature of constitutional identity.

Part II of the book provides comparative perspectives on constitutional identity, exploring the various conceptual and theoretical challenges presented in Part I, through the lenses of various case studies.

The opening chapter here is *Confucian Constitutional Identity*, by Ngoc Son Bui. He considers the role of Confucian values in the formation of constitutional identity in three Confucian-influenced countries in Asia: China, South Korea, and Singapore. In his comparative analysis, Son demonstrates how Confucian commitments and Confucian heritage are embodied in these countries' formal constitutions and in their dynamic nature, and how the disharmony embedded in constitutional identity provokes judicial, social, and political change of Confucian-infused constitutional identity.

In the following chapter, *"(A-)Religious & Democratic" Militant Dual Constitutional Identities and the Turn to Illiberalism: The Case of France*, Eugénie Mérieau draws on the case of France to elucidate the tension between democratic and religious components of dual constitutional identities. Mérieau argues that constitutional identity needs to be understood in light of what she terms "the regulation of constitutional alterity," and in particular, through the various tools of militant democracy: banning political parties, constitutional unamendability, and the state of emergency, guarded also by the judiciary.

In the French case, constitutional identity ties a secular identity to democratic principles and is protected by militant democracy in order to guard constitutional faith. It is exclusionary in many ways. Constitutional identity is also contested in

Bangladesh, as Ridwanul Hoque argues in his chapter *Constitutional Identity in Bangladesh: Complexity and Contestations*, because of the Muslim majority citizenry's alleged ignorance toward religions. Similarly, the identity of Bengali nationalism is also exclusionary, and Hoque shows that the founding of Bangladesh has merged the country's national and constitutional identities. The resulting identity, he claims, is based on nationalism, secularism, democracy, and socialism, principles that have evolved with time while still remaining contested in several key respects.

Taking the idea of disharmony and contestation a step forward, in his chapter *Clashing Identities? Traditional Authority and Constitutionalism in Africa*, Heinz Klug asks whether the existence of forms of governance that clearly challenge the founding values of a constitution (e.g., traditional, pre-statist communities and identities) are merely disharmonic with the constitutional order or whether they pose a direct threat to its very existence. Drawing on constitutions and constitutionalism in Africa, Klug demonstrates how traditional norms and authorities have continued to assert their influence and to enjoy different levels of legitimacy across the continent. Constitutional identity in Africa thus reflects an ongoing relationship between forms of traditional authority (colonial or incorporated into post-colonial constitutions) on one hand, and nationalist and African-socialist ideologies articulated by post-colonial elites on the other.

Disharmony, the various chapters in this book reveal, is an integral part of constitutional identity. This is also the story of the Japanese Constitution, as highlighted by Keigo Komamura in his chapter *Imposed Revolution? "August Revolution," "Imposed Constitution," and the Identity of the Constitution of Japan*. Komamura illustrates how the Japanese constitutional revolution of 1946 produced contrasting internal and external disharmonious factors. Internally, the new constitution substantively deviated from the old regime while maintaining procedural continuity; externally, it was an imposed constitution within an international legal framework, triggered by Japan's defeat in World War II. The tension between the denial of the Emperor's sovereignty on the one hand, and the symbolic importance of the Emperor system on the other hand, remains an integral part of Japan's constitutional identity.

Closing the second part of the book is Gautam Bhatia's chapter *India: A Constitution in Search of an Identity*. Constitutional identity in India may be regarded as static, due to the unamendability as expressed in the Indian basic structure doctrine. Yet, in this chapter, Bhatia suggests that even when analyzed according to Indian Supreme Court's jurisprudence on the basic structure doctrine, Indian constitutional identity is best understood as dynamic and contested. He further argues that, as the Indian constitutional experience indicates, accounts of constitutional identity should be expanded to encompass struggles over the allocation and distribution of powers among states and among branches of government.

Part III of the book focuses on American constitutionalism and constitutional identity, and its implications for theory of constitutional identity more broadly. It opens with Sanford Levinson's chapter *"This Is (Not) Who We Are": Reflections on*

1619 and the Search for a Singular Constitutional Identity. Here, Levinson focuses on the useful yet fiery search for an American constitutional identity by politicians and others. To that end, he discusses the case study of the "1619 project" – a series of published essays in the *New York Times Magazine*, in which it was argued that since 1619, slavery has effectively become part of America's constitutional DNA. This debate concerning "who we are" and a given polity's "true" constitutional identity, Levinson explains, is as necessary as it is potentially painful, volatile, and perhaps even dangerous.

Corresponding with Levinson's piece, slavery is also a central element in Justin Dyer's chapter *Constitutional Aspirationalism Revisited.* Revisiting the notion of constitutional aspirationalism, Dyer considers the twists and turns (as reflected in the thinking of Lincoln, Douglass, and Martin Luther King) and, ultimately, the disharmonies embedded in American constitutional identity, given its constitutional aspiration for the principle of equal liberty to all. He makes a point of acknowledging the central contributions of Black Americans to the formulation and realization of America's core national ideals and aspirations.

The centrality of constitutional disharmony to forging American constitutional identity recurs also in George Thomas' chapter *The Constitution at War with Itself: Race, Citizenship, and the Forging of American Constitutional Identity*, only this time by looking at the place of Black citizenship prior to the Civil War. Thomas demonstrates how the exclusion of Blacks from the social compact was a construction of constitutional identity, while also highlighting the existence of alternative understandings from the time of America's founding. However, although there are authoritative arguments that the Constitution could be seen as anti-slavery, Thomas argues that those who were anti-slavery still did not give much thought to the question of Black citizenship – an issue that was forced into the polity by events like the second Missouri Crisis of 1821 – thereby bringing into the debate competing understandings of the Constitution. Such competing understandings of citizenship have been a central feature of the American disharmonic Constitution.

Still more on the struggle for racial equality in America, in his chapter *Constitutional Identity, Constitutional Politics, and Constitutional Revolutions,* Mark A. Graber highlights the critical importance of constitutional politics in understanding the ever-dynamic nature of constitutional identity. Constitutional identity in the United States and abroad, he argues, is constituted, transformed, and even revolutionized through real and concrete struggles over different constitutional ideals, commitments, aspirations, and outcomes. Graber draws on various episodes in American nineteenth- and twentieth-century constitutional development pertaining to the framing and treatment of racial equality to illustrate his claim that constitutional politics matter considerably in shaping and reshaping a given polity's constitutional identity.

This part concludes with *American Constitutional Exceptionalism, Constitutional Identity, and Democracy* by Miguel Schor. He argues that scholars need to pay greater attention to structure and the role that constitutional design plays in halting or enabling democratic erosion rather than to the traditional focus on courts, rights, and values. When put in a comparative perspective, he claims, the core structure of America's constitutional order tends to obstruct majorities from governing, all while it does not adequately limit the freedom to erode institutions, unlike Germany's militant democracy, for instance. The troubling times of democratic erosion and demagogues' leadership, Schor claims, further accentuates this comparatively exceptional weakness. This conclusion in turn connects Schor's essay to the new trends identified in Part IV of the book, and especially those related to pressures on constitutional identity at times of populism, democratic backsliding, and constitutional retrogression.

Part IV of the book, and the concluding section of it, deals with emerging trends in the practice and study of constitutional identity. Opening this part is Asli Bâli and Hanna Lerner's *Constitution Making and Disharmonic Identity*. Drawing on the tumultuous constitutional experience of Turkey, India, and Israel, the authors examine the relationship between political and constitutional revolutions, and between political rapture and transformations of constitutional identity. Revolutionary changes of constitutional identity, Bâli and Lerner argue, may occur over an extended period of time, but they often result from short-term events such as founding a new political order or adopting new constitutional arrangements. Such events, however, often do not radically transform the constitutional identity of the polity but rather preserve many of its basic features, oftentimes strategically as a means to allow acceptance of the said change, launching an incremental process of transformation over time.

Oran Doyle's chapter *Constitutional Identity and Unamendability* concerns a question that, as indicated earlier in this introduction, is of major significance in contemporary constitutional politics: the notion of unconstitutional constitutional amendment, or, in other words, the constraints imposed on constitutional amendment powers by a given country's constitutional identity. Doyle explores this key issue by focusing on Ireland and, in particular, on two seminal court cases involving questions of unamendability. The analysis allows Doyle to elaborate on the distinction between generic constitutional identity, which conforms to moral values of constitutionalism, and particular constitutional identity, which refers to a country's distinctive constitutional features, traditions, and ideals. This distinction, Doyle argues, is crucial for constitutional unamendability as the former type (generic constitutional identity) may constrain constitutional amendments under specific circumstances, whereas the latter (particularly constitutional identity) should not be regarded as a substantive constraint on amendments but rather an argumentative frame for debate about the legitimacy of amendments.

The following chapter also concerns an issue of crucial significance in contemporary constitutional law and politics: the use and abuse of constitutional identity. In their contribution, *Illiberal Constitutionalism and the Abuse of Constitutional*

Identity, Gábor Halmai and Julian Scholtes focus on a recent trend within the European constitutional arena, in which the concept of constitutional identity is being drawn upon by ethno-nationalist populist regimes in Europe to justify deviation from EU law, as well as to prioritize particular national constitutional (and more often than not, illiberal) values and ideals over universal or European (and more often than not, liberal) ones. Drawing on recent developments in constitutional jurisprudence and constitutional politics in Hungary, Poland and elsewhere in Europe, the authors aim to define when and how the concept of constitutional identity is abused, in a search for a theoretical account of which forms of constitutionalism are compatible with legitimate, as opposed to manipulative or abusive, constitutional identity claims.

Delving deeper into this trend of abusing constitutional identity and its roots, Michel Rosenfeld's chapter *Deconstructing Constitutional Identity in Light of the Turn to Populism*, focuses on the challenge populism poses to the concept of constitutional identity. If the objective of constructing constitutional identity is to integrate the polity as a whole, contemporary populism, with its emphasis on anti-pluralism and rejection of the Other, shifts the construct of constitutional identity in the opposite direction, toward disaggregation and exclusion. Reaching similar conclusions as Halmai and Scholtes, Rosenfeld argues that populism demands exclusionary constructs relating to constitutional identity, which directly conflicts with the normative prerequisites of modern constitutionalism, or at least its canonical liberal stream.

Addressing the same phenomenon of the use and abuse of constitutional identity in justifying departures from fundamental values of constitutionalism, albeit from a different angle, Pietro Faraguna concentrates on EU jurisprudence to trace the abusive and selective borrowing tactics by domestic courts in his chapter *Unconstitutional Constitutional Identities in The European Union*. Importantly, he argues that constitutional identities should be respected only as long as they are compatible with the fundamental principles of constitutionalism.

As the various chapters in this volume demonstrate, constitutional identity is a complex, multi-faceted and rather elusive concept. In her chapter *What Counts as Constitutional Identity?* Mila Versteeg elucidates how large-N empirical studies that aim to operationalize the concept and make it "measurable" may provide a more rigorous account of the meaning of constitutional identity. Specifically, Versteeg identifies express statements of identity in constitutional texts (notably in preambles and amendment provisions), and the study of core values assigned to the constitution by the people governed by it as two promising scholarly avenues. Drawing on original data from nationally representative surveys conducted in five countries, Versteeg then illustrates the utility of the second, less intuitive, proposed avenue. As the data analysis shows, members of socially, culturally, and economically privileged groups tend to feel better represented by their given country's constitution. In other words, constitutions disproportionately reflect elite interests.

The theory of constitutional identity identifies tensions within constitutional systems (e.g., conflicting norms or ideals within the same constitutional text) and between the constitutional text and societal norms within which it operates (e.g., freedom of and from religion in a highly religious society, or gender equality in a largely conservative gender-segregated society). In their chapter *Contrariness and Contradiction in Constitutional Law*, Zachary Elkins and Tom Ginsburg explore empirically the nature and scope of the first type of these tensions: tensions within constitutional systems. To that end, they develop and apply a taxonomy of disharmonies that frequently appear within national constitutions, thereby "testing" canonical insights regarding disharmony vis-à-vis a much larger number of observations and data points. Taken together, the chapters by Versteeg and by Elkins and Ginsburg contemplate the possibility of deploying the potential of large-N empirical studies to measure empirically certain dimensions of constitutional identity and constitutional disharmony.

Part IV, and in fact the entire volume, concludes with Christina Bambrick and Connor M. Ewing's chapter *Conclusion: The Past, Present, and Future of Constitutional Identity*. In it, Bambrick and Ewing outline the important contributions that extant literature on constitutional identity and the essays featured in this collection make to the study of constitutional and political development. They highlight the fluidity and indeterminacy embedded in constitutional identity as both a potent tool for better understanding constitutional and political development, as well as a potential weapon for undermining or transforming a polity's established constitutional order. The chapter then turns to elucidate a range of future research avenues that scholars may fruitfully pursue, armed with the conceptual tools that existing work on constitutional identity and the ideas put forth by the various contributions to this volume both forged and inspired. Importantly, the authors highlight the call for further conceptual refinement of constitutional disharmony, which, as manifested in many of this volume's chapters, is indeed a vitally important component of any future inquiry related to constitutional identity. It is our hope that, taken as a whole, the essays included in this volume provide the grounds for such, and many other, studies, aimed at further refining and sharpening our understanding of the "genetic code" of constitutionalism.

REFERENCES

Bassok, Or. 2015. "Interpretative Theories as Roadmaps to Constitutional Identity: The Case of the United States." *Global Constitutionalism* 4: 289–327.

Besselink, Leonard FM. 2010. "National and Constitutional Identity Before and After Lisbon." *Utrecht Law Review* 6(3): 36–49.

Cloots, Elke. 2015. *National Identity in EU Law*. Oxford: Oxford University Press.

Drinóczi, Tímea. 2020. "Constitutional Identity in Europe: The Identity of the Constitution. A Regional Approach." *German Law Journal* 21: 105–130.

Fabbrini, Federico and András Sajó. 2019. "The Dangers of Constitutional Identity." *European Law Journal* 25: 457–473.

Faraguna, Pietro. 2016. "Taking Constitutional Identities Away from the Courts." *Brooklyn Journal of International Law* 41: 491–578.
Faraguna, Pietro. 2017. "Constitutional Identity in the EU-A Shield of a Sword?" *German Law Journal* 18(7): 1617–1640.
Fletcher, George P. 1993. "Constitutional Identity." *Cardozo Law Review* 14(3–4): 737–746.
Google Books Ngram Viewer. N.d. "Constitutional Identity." https://books.google.com/ngrams/graph?content=constitutional+identity&year_start=1950&year_end=2019&corpus=26&smoothing=3&direct_url=t1%3B%2Cconstitutional%20 identity%3B%2Cco
Halmai, Gábor. 2018. "Abuse of Constitutional Identity. The Hungarian Constitutional Court on Interpretation of Article E) (2) of the Fundamental Law." *Review of Central and East European Law* 43: 23–42.
Hirschl, Ran. 2010. *Constitutional Theocracy*. Cambridge, MA: Harvard University Press.
Jacobsohn, Gary Jeffrey. 2006. "Constitutional Identity." *Review of Politics* 68 (3): 361–397.
Jacobsohn, Gary Jeffrey. 2010a. *Constitutional Identity*. Cambridge: Harvard University Press.
Jacobsohn, Gary Jeffrey. 2010b. "The Disharmonic Constitution." In *The Limits of Constitutional Democracy*, edited by Jeffrey K. Tulis and Stephen Macedo, 47–65. Princeton: Princeton University Press.
Jacobsohn, Gary Jeffrey. 2023a. "The Exploitation of Constitutional Identity." In *The Jurisprudence of Particularism*, edited by Krista Kovács, 33–55. London: Bloomsbury Publishing.
Jacobsohn, Gary Jeffrey. 2023b. "How to Think about the Reach of Constitutional Identity." *Comparative Constitutional Studies* 1 (1): 6–28.
Jacobsohn, Gary Jeffrey, and Yaniv Roznai. 2020. *Constitutional Revolution*. New Haven: Yale University Press.
Kelemen, R. Daniel, and Laurent Pech. 2019. "The Uses and Abuses of Constitutional Pluralism Undermining the Rule of Law in the Name of Constitutional Identity in Hungary and Poland." *The Cambridge Yearbook of European Legal Studies* 21: 59–74.
Körtvélyesi, Zsolt, and Balázs Majtényi. 2017. "Game of Values: The Threat of Exclusive Constitutional Identity, the EU and Hungary." *German Law Journal* 18(7): 1721–1744.
Kovács, Kriszta. 2017. "The Rise of an Ethnocultural Constitutional Identity in the Jurisprudence of the East Central European Courts." *German Law Journal* 18 (7): 1703–1720.
Martí, José Luis. 2013. "Two Different Ideas of Constitutional Identity: Identity of the Constitution v. Identity of the People." In *National Constitutional Identity and European Integration*, edited by Alejandro Saiz Arnaiz and Carina Alcoberro Llivinia, 17–36. Cambridge: Intersentia.
Martin, Sébastien. 2012. "L'identité de l'État Dans l'Union Européenne: Entre 'identité Nationale' et 'identité Constitutionnelle.'" *Revue française de droit constitutionnel* 91: 13–44.
Millet, Francois Xavier. 2013. *L'Union Européenne et l'identité constitutionnelle des Etats membres*. Paris: Lgdj.
Rosenfeld, Michel. 2009. *The Identity of the Constitutional Subject: Selfhood, Citizenship, Culture and Community*. London: Routledge.
Rosenfeld, Michel. 2012. "Constitutional Identity." In *The Oxford Handbook of Comparative Constitutional Law*, edited by Michel Rosenfeld and András Sajó, 756–775. Oxford: Oxford University Press.
Roznai, Yaniv. 2017. *Unconstitutional Constitutional Amendments – The Limits of Amendment Power*. Oxford: Oxford University Press.
Sajó, András, and Renáta Uitz. 2017. *The Constitution of Freedom*. Oxford: Oxford University Press.

Scheppele, Kim Lane. 2008. "A Constitution between Past and Future." *William and Mary Law Review* 49(4): 1377–1407.
Scholtes, Julian. 2021. "Abusing Constitutional Identity." *German Law Journal* 22: 534–556.
Smooha, Sammy. 2002. "The Model of Ethnic Democracy: Israel as a Jewish and Democratic State." *Nations and Nationalism* 8(4): 475–503.
Toniatti, Roberto. 2013. "Sovereignty Lost, Constitutional Identity Regained." In *National Constitutional Identity and European Integration*, edited by Alejandro Saiz Arnaiz and Carina Alcoberro Llivinia. Cambridge: Intersentia.
Toobon, Jeffrey. 2005. "How Anthony Kennedy's Passion for Foreign Law Could Change the Supreme Court." *The New Yorker*, September 12, 2005. www.newyorker.com/magazine/2005/09/12/swing-shift
Troper, Michel. 2010. "Behind the Constitution? The Principle of Constitutional Identity in France." In *Constitutional Topography: Values and Constitutions*, edited by András Sajó and Renata Uitz. The Hague: Eleven International Publishing.
Voermans, Wim. 2023. *The Story of Constitutions: Discovering the We in Us*. Cambridge: Cambridge University Press.
Wischmeyer, Thomas. 2015. "Nationale Identität Und Verfassungsidentität. Schutzgehalte, Instrumente, Perspektiven." *Archiv des öffentlichen Rechts* 140(3): 415–460.

PART I

Foundations, Theory, and Concepts

1

Rousseau's Sovereignty and the Concept of Constitutional Identity

Howard Schweber

Throughout Gary Jacobsohn's writings a core concept has been his idea of "constitutional identity," most explicitly in *Constitutional Identity* and *Constitutional Revolutions* (Jacobsohn 2010; Jacobsohn and Roznai 2020). As Jacobsohn observes, the reference to constitutional identity necessarily points to the working of constituent power; the same power to create a constitution is the power required to replace, amend, or reconceive its underpinnings. The assignment of constituent power to "the people" means both that the people create a constitution with the capacity for an identity – or multiple claims to identity existing in disharmonic competition – and that the people have the authority to change a constitution's identity without thereby affecting their own.

These seemingly simple observations raise a whole series of questions: Are there real and "sham" exercises of constituent power?[1] Democratic theorists talk about assertable claims of representation and constituency; should we think of "constitutional identity" and "constituent power" as the names of other assertable political claims rather than descriptions of political phenomena and thus turn our attention to the relative strength of different versions of that assertion? (Saward 2006).[2] Are there normative standards for good or genuine expressions of constituent power – as we may speak of constitutional orders that produce evil results – or would the normative evaluation of a claim of constituent power reduce to a judgment of superiority among "peoples"? (Jacobsohn 2010).[3]

In this chapter, I propose to get at some of these questions by considering constitutional identity in relation to a particular theory of constituent power, that of

---

[1] The idea of a "sham constitution" goes back to Giovanni Sartori's classic description as one that is "disregarded" in practice (Sartori 1962). David Law and Mila Versteeg have extended the concept by compiling empirical measures of the degree to which constitutions are shams by this measure (Law and Versteeg 2013).
[2] On the idea of claims of constituency – assertions of the characteristics required to be the objects of political representation – see Schweber (2016).
[3] Mark Graber and Jack Balkin, among others, have explored the possibilities of "constitutional evil" (Balkin 1998; Graber 2008). On the various versions of constituent power that appear in American political development, see Frank (2010).

Jean-Jacques Rousseau. Rousseau is recognized as one of the three major modern or early modern theorists of constituent power along with Sieyès and Schmitt, but of the three Rousseau's stands out for his attempts to deal with what Bonnie Honig calls "the paradoxes of democracy": the problem of legitimating a founding moment, the relationship between constituent power and time, and the question of the identity of a people in relation to its constitutional commitments.[4]

Rousseau's model of constituent power is nicely captured in his description of three moments of the people in action following the creation of the state.

> This public person, so formed by the union of all other persons, formerly took the name of city, and now takes that of Republic or body politic, it is called by its members State when passive, Sovereign when active, and Power when compared with others like itself. Those who are associated in it take collectively the name of people, and severally are called *citizens* as sharing in the sovereign authority, and subjects, as being under the laws of the State.

The same three moments appear in three dimensions of citizens' self-aware actions. "[T]hey collectively take the name people; individually they are called citizens, insofar as participants in the sovereign authority, and subjects insofar as they are subjected to the laws of the state" (Rousseau 2002). The active sovereign is the people engaged in constitution making, "the action of the entire body acting upon itself – that is, the relationship of the whole to the whole, or of the sovereign to the State." The distinctions among the State, the Sovereign, and Power capture three moments (or dimensions) of constituent power. An exploration of the points of consistency and difference between this model and Jacobsohn's theory of constitutional identity demonstrates both the power and possibly some problems for the latter.

1.1 ROUSSEAU'S THEORY: SOVEREIGNTY, REPRESENTATION, AND THE PARADOXES OF FOUNDING

Rousseau asserted the classical republican position that the constitution (in the Aristotelian sense of the term) shapes the people.

> National institutions are what form the genius, character, tastes, and morals of a people, what make it itself and not another, what inspire in it that ardent love of the

---

[4] This chapter is not intended to be a contribution to Rousseau scholarship. Nevertheless, I am constrained to operate from a position within that scholarship. In particular, I am adopting two assumptions in my discussion: first, that Rousseau was intellectually consistent such that his writings on the constitutional systems of Poland, Corsica, and Geneva were expressions of his larger political theory rather than departures from his ideas expressed elsewhere, a view I share with David Rosenfeld (Rosenfeld 1987; Putterman 2001); second, I assume Rousseau to have been sincere in his prescriptions for political states rather than engaging in an exercise of disingenuous favor-seeking or presenting an "esoteric" argument. Here I follow Berlin (2002) and Williams (2007).

fatherland founded on habits impossible to uproot, what make it die of boredom among other peoples in the bosom of delights of which it is deprived in its own. (Rousseau 2014, 174)

Maintenance of such national identities required homogeneity and separateness, as in the case of Moses and the Israelites. "In order to keep his people from dissolving among foreign peoples, he gave it morals and practices incompatible with those of other nations; he overburdened it with distinctive rites, ceremonies" (Rousseau 2014, 172). In turn, that meant that republics had to be small to succeed. "Almost all small states, republics and monarchies alike, prosper because they are small.... All great peoples crushed by their own mass groan" (Rousseau 2014, 183). In order to achieve the virtues of a republic in a larger, modern state the only solution was confederation, but confederation in a form that maintained a shared and singular sense of national peoplehood capable of sustaining an assertion of constitutive power. "In the present state of things, I see only a single means of giving it that stability it lacks; that is to infuse, so to speak, the soul of the confederates into the whole nation" (Rousseau 2014, 174).

Rousseau's description raises the paradox of founding: By what democratic processes can the *demos* itself be constituted? Rousseau's answer, of course, is his particular model of the social contract. "The people, being subject to the laws, ought to be their author: the conditions of the society ought to be regulated solely by those who come together to form it" (Rousseau 2002, 193). What about nonsigners? "They are foreigners among citizens. When the state is instituted, residence constitutes consent; to dwell within its territory is to consent" (Rousseau 2002, 250). The theme is echoed in his description of the liberator General Paoli's address to the people of Corsica: "Corsicans, be silent. I am going to speak in the name of all. Let those who do not agree leave, and let those who do agree raise their hands" (O'Brien 2002, 302).

An implication is that "the people" of a given state are not coextensional with "all persons residing in the state." And indeed, Rousseau frequently refers to the idea of citizens as an elite and empowered class. "The real meaning of this word [citizen] has been wholly lost in modern times; most people mistake a town for a city, and a townsman for a citizen. They do not know that houses make a town, but citizens a city" (Rousseau 2002, 75). As a theoretical matter, these are distinctions that emerge subsequent to the social contract; it is the sovereign – the people exercising constituent power – that has the authority to "set up several classes of citizens and even lay down the qualifications for membership of these classes" (Rousseau 2002, chap. 6).

Rousseau famously declared that the sovereign cannot be represented, but Rousseau's sovereign is the people exercising its power in assembly wherein each participant expresses their view of the general will.

> When a law is proposed in the assembly of the people, what is asked of them is not exactly whether they approve the proposition or reject it, but whether it conforms or not to the general will, which is their own; each one in casting his vote expresses

his opinion thereupon; and from the counting of the votes is obtained the declaration of the general will. (Rousseau 2002, 230)

It is estimated that Geneva's General Council numbered fewer than 1,600 in a "town" of 20,000 (Rosenfeld 1987, 100). This was the legislature that exercised constituted authority, an elite and representative body charged with making laws as opposed to constituting *loi*. Yet in Rousseau's telling the General Counsel also spoke for the general will. "In a State such as yours [Geneva], where the sovereignty is in the hands of the People, the Legislator always exists.... It is assembled and speaks authentically only in the General Council" (Rousseau 2001, 236). In its operations, the General Council appealed to this role in the two questions with which it opened each session. The first is, "Does it please the Sovereign to preserve the present form of government?" The second is, "Does it please the people to leave its administration in the hands of those who are actually in charge of it?" The formulation "does it please the people" indicates that the actions of the General Council only became actual exercises of constituent power once they were ratified by the people. "The laws, although received, only have a lasting authority so long as the people, being free to revoke them, nevertheless does not do so" (Rousseau 2002, 324), leading Colon-Rios to describe the initial creation of a constitutional order as "provisional" (Colon-Rios 2020).

Yet this seems to raise problems for Rousseau's theory. How is the General Council not a representative of the sovereign, something Rousseau says is impossible? One answer turns on the meaning of the term "represent." The General Council cannot act for or stand for the people, but it can assert a claim to *speak* by expressing the general will. Hence the significance of subsequent ratification. The expression of constituent power, in other words, would be episodic. In between such moments – apparently marked by the calling together of a constituent assembly containing all the citizens – the state would operate through a government that represented the popular will by the authorization of the general will. In these periods of the operation of the General Council and the other councils of Geneva's government, is its constituent power present or does it lie dormant?

Rousseau confronted an even more difficult second paradox. How is "the spirit of the Constitution" to be "infused" among the Polish people before the creation and adoption of that same constitution? A people would learn to be virtuous citizens, he said, through the experience of living in a republic – that is, under an appropriate constitution. "[T]he voice of duty replaces physical impulse and right replaces appetite." Yet until they became virtuous a people would lack the will to act collectively to create such a constitution: "the effect would have to become the cause" (Rousseau 2002, 272).

Rousseau's famous solution was the founding Legislator, a figure capable of using religious authority to compel a people to live virtuously, *as if* they were collectively possessed of virtue. But, as we have already seen, Rousseau also identifies "the Legislator" with the general will, articulated through the actions of the General Council. Prior to the time when the people have been made virtuous by the experience of their constitution, do they possess constituent power? Or is the *legitimate* authority of the people to create or alter a constitution something that arises by virtue of the constitution's effects over time?

The easy reading of Rousseau is that constitution making is an episodic exercise of constituent power/sovereignty, after or in between which moments liberty consists in self-government through representative institutions. But this reading becomes problematic because the question of exclusion in representation – a principle that follows analytically if not practically from the imagined moment of foundation – makes authorship of constitutional identity the authority of a closed and elite group who then rule over others as well as each other. This is consistent with some modern descriptions of constitution making in practice (Hirschl 2007; Ginsburg 2014), but by freezing the identity of the people it makes constituent power little more than the name attached to an outcome, essentially definitional and hence tautological. As Rosenfeld puts it, "The contract is unanimous only in an axiomatic way, as a logical deduction from the meaning of the terms themselves: it is unanimous among the contracting parties, which, of course, it would have to be, if not they would not be contracting parties" (Rosenfeld 1987, 93).

1.2 CONSTITUTIONAL IDENTITY, CONSTITUTIVE POWER, AND THE QUESTION OF LEGITIMACY

Jacobsohn wrestles with some of the same potential problems that troubled Rousseau. The idea of constitutional identity immediately points to a consideration of constituent power as the authority of the people to engage in constitution making in the first place. But while Rousseau conceives of constitution making as episodic and formal, Jacobsohn sees constitutional identity as something that emerges over time. "[A] constitution acquires an identity through experience … this identity exists neither as a discrete object of invention nor as a heavily encrusted essence embedded in a society's culture, requiring only to be discovered" (Jacobsohn 2010, 7). The process of acquisition of identity is not only dialogical; it is "transactional" (Jacobsohn 2010, 326). The term "acquisition" is particularly interesting here; in Jacobsohn's view the creation of a constitutional identity is not simultaneous with the creation of the constitution. But just as constituent power is required to legitimate the creation of a constitution, it is equally an essential element of legitimate actions creating or altering a constitution's identity. What, then, is the role of the people – Rousseau's sovereign – in imbuing a constitution with an identity or altering that identity through constitutional revolution?

> The creation of constitutional identity, by this telling, is not only not the action of the whole of the people, even the identification of who among the people exercises this constituent power is *itself* not decided as Rousseau's sovereign. Instead it is the outcome of messy political conflicts occurring within an environment of contested and conflicting constitutional disharmonies. (Jacobsohn 2010, 4)

All of which raises the question of whether a constitution has an identity at all prior to the initiation of that dialogue. That is, like Rousseau's people learning virtue, does a people living under a constitution learn to invent its identity not present at the founding?

Of course a constitution may also be founded or changed another way, through a violent moment of disruption; is there a constitutional identity in that moment? If so, that identity cannot derive from the exercise of constituent power because constituent power cannot be authorized until after there is a constitutional expression of its recognition, creating a problem of infinite regress. "The people who participate in the referendum ... were already constituted. Rules regarding who would be eligible to vote and participated in such an expression of the people's will were already established: thus the famous paradox of constitutional democracy – 'the constitution constitutes the people who in turn constitute the constitution'" (Jacobsohn and Roznai 2020, 248). Consider Srinivassan's description of the first example of a constituent assembly. Srinivassan identified the source of the concept in seventeenth-century English Levellers' 1648 call for authorized representatives acting on behalf of "the well-affected of every county" to meet with representatives "chosen by the Army" to create a new local political order (Srinivassan 1940). This makes the claim of constituent power nothing more than the assertion of "brute historicity" (Schweber 2021); it was the case that in this place at this time a sufficient number of people accepted the process of selection as legitimate as to make the conclusions reached by the assembly enforceable over objectors, essentially Rousseau's solution of treating nonparticipants as "foreigners." Can this satisfy any meaningful definition of constituent power in a way that provides a legitimating theory for the exercise of political authority?

As Jacobsohn notes, several solutions to this potential problem have been proposed. One solution is to simply abandon the idea of constituent power altogether. Treat the creation of constitutions as a purely positivistic act, and thereafter the assertion of authority in terms of competing legal and political forces seeking control. Another is to treat constitutive power as a purely narrative device, a purely symbolic expression of a claim of representation. "By telling ourselves a fictional story about 'the people,' we satisfy a 'sort of psycho-legal need'.... According to this conception, the people's constituent power should not be regarded as an 'actual aggregate entity in the real world,' but rather as 'a concept that helps explain the normative basis for a constitution's claim to authority'" (Jacobsohn and Roznai 2020, 252; Tushnet 1983). And yet a third solution is to propose that constituent power is a kind of political dark matter, visible only retrospectively in its effects. Interestingly, the approach that favors purely retrospective assertions of constitutive power is consistent with theories that claim that power is always potentially present, as in Albert Venn Dicey's theory of parliamentary supremacy limited only by the ever-present possibility of resistance from the populace (Venn Dicey 1885).[5] Nonetheless, that

---

[5] For a review of the theory of parliamentary supremacy in British constitutional practice, see Goldsworthy (1999).

approach cannot gain explanatory purchase on the idea of constitutive power as an element of founding, only as an element of the operation of the fully formed Rousseauian triumvirate of people/state/government.

Jacobsohn rightly rejects the solution of abandoning constituent power as a legitimating concept. But he recognizes the paradox of trying to find an expression of constituent power before such power has been constituted in an institutionalized form.

> [T]he exercise of constituent power, even if regarded as extralegal, necessitates a certain representational form; that is, the will that we attribute to "the people" ought to be revealed through some kind of representation. Therefore, to be exercised, constituent power must in some way act as an already-constituted power…. [T]he initiation or emergence of constituent power can be spontaneous and direct … but the execution and formulation of the decisions of the constituent power require certain procedures and organization. (Jacobsohn and Roznai 2020, 259–68)

Colon-Rios makes the same point with specific reference to the idea of constituent assemblies as occurring somehow outside of law. "Both extraordinary and periodic assemblies could only be convened in accordance with the law: only a public meeting that complies with the forms established by the entire citizenry in their constitutional framework could be taken as authorised to pronounce the people's voice" (Colon-Rios 2020, 104). Andrew Arato describes "post-sovereign" constitution making in which procedural legality defines the exercise of constituent power (Jacobsohn and Roznai 2020, 234); Jacobsohn's and Colon-Rios' arguments point to the possibility that procedural legality is a necessary element *of* an exercise of sovereignty as anything more than a Schmittian exercise of will.

Thus we are returned to the problem of legitimacy. For an assertion of constituent power to be considered legitimate, it must be considered true; that is, even as a purely positivistic description of the nature of the governing narrative, one must recognize that the internal norm is the assertion that "the people" have truly acted. The possible tests for such validity seem quite different depending on whether one is talking about a moment of violent rupture occurring outside an existing constitutional system or a revolutionary change in meaning occurring within the operation of existing institutions.

Jacobsohn seems to try to elide that possible difference by making the distinction between real and sham assertions of constituent power turn on procedures.

> [F]or constituent power to approximately manifest the popular will, its exercise should incorporate actual, well-deliberated, and thoughtful free choice by society's members. It should be inclusive, participatory, time consuming, and deliberative…. Important to this enterprise is the maintenance of freedoms: speech, fair elections, assembly, and association, the absence of which spells the death for the legal concept that is constituent power. (Jacobsohn and Roznai 2020, 2357)

For example, Jacobsohn points to Ireland's experiment with deliberative jury of randomly selected ninety-nine citizens as part of the process of constitution making along with referenda and representative democratic politics; taken together these elements present a "legal approximation of constituent power" (Jacobsohn and Roznai 2020, 255). Subject to these limitations, constituent power may be exercised in either a moment of founding or a moment of revision. "Constituent power does not collapse into constituted power. The former can be exercised outside the constitutional order or through constituted organs" (Jacobsohn and Roznai 2020, 250–51).

But the two paradoxes – the problem of infinite regress and the problem of majoritarianism – remain troubling, particularly insofar as they seem to pose different problems for exercises of constituent power outside or through the existing constitutional order. Is "a legal approximation" of constituent power sufficient to resolve the tension between a legitimating norm of constituent power and democratic norms of ongoing deliberation, contestation, and pluralism?

1.3 REVISITING THE ROUSSEAUIAN MODEL OF CONSTITUTIONAL IDENTITY

Return to Rousseau's resolution of the paradox of virtue by the invocation of a Legislator able to impose constitutionalism before there exists a popular sovereignty capable of creating it. For Rousseau, the idea was that, over time, people become virtuous, then citizens, then imbued with spirit of the constitution. This is a classically republican ideal in which the constitutional order of the polity shapes, not reflects, society and psychology. In Jacobsohn's terms, at least until such time as public virtue is universally realized, such a constitution is "militant" rather than "acquiescent" (Jacobsohn 2010, chap. 5), operating as a "sail" that "serve[s] as a foundation for the construction of a social order embodying the transformative hopes of its revolutionary promise" (Jacobsohn 2010, 215).

One potentially superior alternative is to reconsider Jacobsohn's distinction between a dialogic emergence of constitutional identity and a violent, disruptive moment of constitutional establishment. Considered fully, Jacobsohn's argument presents a powerfully persuasive case that *only* constitutional change occurring within an existing constitutional system *can* express constituent power, because only in that situation is there the possibility of a developed constitutional identity. That is, constituent power is subsumed into constitutionality not as a matter of distribution of decision-making power but as an expression of identity. One cannot have constituent power without a people, nor a people without an identity in a system based on an ideal of constitutionalism that required a fully formed *constitutional* identity.

This is very close to Habermas' solution – later developed further by both Jacques Derrida and Bonnie Honig – of the infinite regress problem. It is, indeed, impossible to legitimize a moment of founding rupture based on appeals to any subsequently emergent norms and values. Instead, according to these arguments, one treats the founding moment as the establishment of a set of discursive resources that are drawn upon in the ongoing, dialogic, contested process of creating a constitutional identity (Honig 1991).

Jacobsohn acknowledges that a constitutional identity may be unknowable at the moment of founding. "Can we then know with certainty what is and is not irrevocable...? I would suggest that an affirmative response ought to be received skeptically. The reason for such uncertainty ... lies in the dynamic quality of identity and the dialogical process by which it is formed and develops" (Jacobsohn 2010, 332). An "unfinished symphony..." (Jacobsohn 2010, 333)

> ...a constitution is a large piece of a nation's constitutional identity, but it is not conterminous with it. In most cases it lays down key markers of that identity that are then adapted to changing political and social realities in ways that modify, clarify, or reinforce it through the dialogical engagement of various public and private sources of influence and power. (Jacobsohn 2010, 334)

But is this enough? Are these discursive resources not necessarily poisoned at the well by the brute historical fact of majority? If the mere assertion of the claim to constituent power is enough to bind future generations, then the answer is "yes" and the project is self-defeating: The only authoritative constituent power is one which lacks all the essential characteristics of constituent power that has any capacity for legitimation. The US founders were concerned with economic rights and interests, so they created a constitutionalist reservoir of meaning oriented around a conception of rights as a species of property. It required a violent disruption (such as the American Civil War) and new founding text (the Reconstruction amendments) to create a new reservoir of meaning on which we now draw in formulating our assertions of constitutional identity. An assertion of identity requires stability across time. "Imagining a polity in which the live hand of the present was the animating and sole directive source for its constitutive choices is to imagine a polity without a constitutional identity" (Jacobsohn 2010, 324). But, at the same time, the sail model implies an aspirationist and transformative understanding of constitutional identity, which raises the question in the US case: Should we conceive of those aspirations as already present at the beginning – as in Lincoln's invocations of the Declaration of Independence – or as the product of the dialogic process of creating constitutional identity?

Presumably any good answer will take the form of "both", but moments of disruption – including Rousseau's imagined signing of a social contract – cannot be conceived as exercises of constituent power. At most they are moments in which a bunch of potentially interesting ideas are recorded. Those ideas are not in any way determinative; in the dialogic process of contesting and creating a constitutional identity one or another of them may prove useful, but the choice of whether and how to use those ideas is the true exercise of constituent power that results in the emergence of a constitutional identity.

Two final thoughts emerge from this discussion. First, the demands of democratic citizenship are quite high. There would appear to be an affirmative obligation to engage in dialogue about constitutional identity and thus to participate in its creation and development. There is the expectation here of citizens being changed by the experience of that dialogue and of the dialogue itself changing its contours over time. This is the perfectionist element of the story – constitutional identity working itself pure would be the ideal Dworkinian case – that is the parallel to Rousseau's unsatisfying reliance on the inculcation of virtue through the experience of citizenship.

The second closing observation is that while each individual assertion of constitutional identity must be assessed in terms of its specific elements, history, and conditions, the model in which constitutive power inheres *only* in the operation of a constitutional system appears as a universal analytical necessity. As Jacobsohn says, "What this suggests is that the dynamics of constitutional identity are less the result of any specific set of background cultural or historical factors than the expression of a developmental process endemic to the phenomenon of constitutionalism" (Jacobsohn 2010, 348).

REFERENCES

Balkin, Jack. 1998. "The Meaning of Constitutional Tragedy." In *Constitutional Stupidities/Constitutional Tragedies*, edited by William N. Eskridge and Sanford Levinson, 121–28. New York: New York University Press.

Berlin, Isaiah. 2002. *Freedom and Its Betrayal: Six Enemies on Human Liberty*, edited by Henry Hardy. Princeton: Princeton University Press.

Colon-Rios, Juan. 2020. *Constituent Power and the Law*. Oxford: Oxford University Press.

Frank, Jason. 2010. *Constituent Moments: Enacting the People in Postrevolutionary America*. Durham, NC: Duke University Press.

Ginsburg, Tom ed. 2014. *Comparative Constitutional Design*. Cambridge: Cambridge University Press.

Goldsworthy, Jeffrey. 1999. *The Sovereignty of Parliament: History and Philosophy*. Oxford: Oxford University Press.

Graber, Mark. 2008. *Dred Scott and the Problem of Constitutional Evil*. Cambridge: Cambridge University Press.

Hirschl, Ran. 2007. *Toward Juristocracy: The Origin and Consequences of the Rise of New Constitutionalism*. Cambridge, MA: Harvard University Press.

Honig, Bonnie. 1991. "Declarations of Independence: Arendt and Derrida on the Problem of Founding a Republic." *American Political Science Review* 85 (1): 97–113.

Jacobsohn, Gary Jeffrey. 2010. *Constitutional Identity*. Cambridge, MA: Harvard University Press.

Jacobsohn, Gary Jeffrey, and Yaniv Roznai. 2020. *Constitutional Revolutions*. New Haven: Yale University Press.

Law, David S., and Mila Versteeg. 2013. "Sham Constitutions." *California Law Review* 101: 863–952.

O'Brien, Connor Cruise. 2002. "Rousseau, Robespierre, Burke, Jefferson, and the French Revolution." In *Social Contract*, edited by Susan Dunn, 310–24. New Haven: Yale University Press.

Putterman, Ethan. 2001. "Realism and Reform in Rousseau's Constitutional Projects for Poland and Corsica." *Political Studies* 49 (3): 481–94.

Rosenfeld, David. 1987. "Rousseau's Unanimous Contract and the Doctrine of Popular Sovereignty." *History of Political Thought* 8 (1): 83–110.
Rousseau, Jean-Jacques. 2001. *Letter to Beaumont, Letters Written from the Mountain, and Related Writings*, edited by C. Kelly and E. Grace. Hanover, UK: University Press of New England.
Rousseau, Jean-Jacques. 2002. *Social Contract*, edited by Susan Dunn. New Haven: Yale University Press.
Rousseau, Jean-Jacques. 2014. "On the Government of Poland." In *Rousseau: The Plan for Perpetual Peace, on the Government of Poland, and Other Political Writings*, edited by Christopher Kelly, 169–240. Hanover: Dartmouth College Press.
Sartori, Giovanni. 1962. "Constitutionalism: A Preliminary Discussion." *The American Political Science Review* 56 (4): 853–64.
Saward, Michael. 2006. "The Representative Claim." *Contemporary Political Theory* 5 (3): 297–318.
Schweber, Howard. 2016. "The Limits of Political Representation." *American Political Science Review* 110 (2): 382–96.
Schweber, Howard. 2021. "Constitutional Revolutions: The People, the Text, and the Hermeneutic of Legitimation." *Maryland Law Review* 81 (1): 226–42.
Srinivassan, N. 1940. "The Theory of the Constituent Assembly." *Indian Journal of Political Science* 1 (4): 376–92.
Tushnet, Mark. 1983. "Constitution-Making: An Introduction." *Texas Law Review* 91 (7): 1983–2013.
Venn Dicey, Albert. 1885. *An Introduction to the Study of the Law of Constitution*. New York: Macmillan and Co.
Williams, David Lay. 2007. *Rousseau's Platonic Enlightenment*. University Park: Penn State University Press.

2

Constitutional Identity

Cracking the Genetic Code of the Constitution

Monika Polzin

INTRODUCTION

When I was first introduced to Gary Jacobsohn's book on constitutional identity in 2010, I discovered a new and fascinating understanding of constitutional theory's most glamorous notion. His book inspired me to write my German post-doctoral (*Habilitation*) thesis on the German idea of constitutional identity. Since then, it has remained a constant source of inspiration and continues to teach me to reflect more deeply on constitutions and their identities. This leads me to the present chapter, which analyses (through the lens of Jacobsohn's concept of constitutional identity) the German constitutional debate on whether to introduce legally binding electoral gender quotas.

The chapter begins with a brief description of the importance of Jacobsohn's work to constitutional theory in general (see Section 2.1). It then analyses the German constitutional conflict on binding electoral gender quotas and illustrates the pertinence of his theory (see Section 2.2) and concludes with the finding that, in terms of constitutional theory, Jacobsohn has indeed cracked the genetic code of a constitution (see Section 2.3).

2.1 SIGNIFICANCE FOR CONSTITUTIONAL THEORY AND THE UNDERSTANDING OF IDENTITY

The significance of Jacobsohn's concept of constitutional identity is that it relies on the ideas of dynamism, fluidity, disharmony and imperfection to describe a constitution's functioning and to visualize the nexus between the struggles within a society, constitutional courts, and constitutional interpretation.

First, fluidity is crucial, as constitutional identity is understood as a dynamic state. The key statement is: '*In the end, constitutional identity will be fashioned – and refashioned – through the struggle over constitutional identity*' (Jacobsohn 2010, 135). This insight is very important to an understanding of constitutions and their functioning. Constitutional identity is in fact neither a treasure to be discovered nor an idea to be invented. It is a developmental concept or, as Jacobsohn puts it, *'a constitution acquires an identity through experience'* and *'this identity exists neither as a discrete object of invention nor as a heavily encrusted essence embedded in a society's culture, requiring only to be discovered'* (Jacobsohn 2010, 7).

The second important aspect is the reliance on *'disharmony'*. Constitutional identity is driven by disharmony either in *'the text of the constitution or in the society itself – in particular historical changes or political contestations'* (Jacobsohn 2010, 4, 13, 135, and 351–355). The disharmony component *'inherent in the constitutional condition'* (Jacobsohn 2010, 149) underlines differences in society. Furthermore, it aptly describes the beauty of heterogeneity and a democratic constitutional society's ultimate need to live in disharmony.

Thirdly, Jacobsohn emphasizes that what all constitutions have in common is *'their state of imperfection'* (Jacobsohn 2010, 202), which manifests itself in different forms, but always exists as a gap between the actual and the ideal constitution (Jacobsohn 2010, 202). Examples referred to are contradictions (a) at the core of constitutional arrangements (which is the case in Israel), (b) between constitutional ideals and reality (as in India), and (c) between the normative setting in the constitution and fundamental societal differences as regards the changing status of institutions (which is the case in Ireland).

2.2 GERMAN CONSTITUTIONAL IDENTITY AND ELECTORAL GENDER QUOTAS

The current German constitutional debate regarding the question of whether to introduce rigid electoral gender quotas currently centres around conflicting definitions of equality and democracy on the part of conservative and progressive voices, respectively. It therefore illustrates that the dynamics of constitutional identity are the expression of a natural developmental process that is intrinsic to constitutional orders (Jacobsohn 2010, 348) and that the key characteristics of constitutional identity are disharmony and fluidity. Moreover, it also points to imperfections in the German Constitution. The identifying feature of this constitutional tussle is that it is also a dispute concerning the content of the eternity clause and therefore implicates the identity of the constitution itself. The gender quota example also illustrates how Jacobsohn's theory on constitutional identity overlaps with the German legal concept of constitutional identity as the German Constitutional Court has conceived it. This court established the German doctrine of constitutional identity (for further English readings on the German concept see Thym 2012 and Calliess 2020) in its landmark Lisbon Judgment (BVerfG 2009). The doctrine is based on the eternity clause, Art. 79 (3) German Constitution (*Grundgesetz – GG*). According to the Court, Art. 79 (3) constitutes an impermeable boundary in the sense of protecting the identity of the constitution – constitutional amendments affecting the division of the German Federation into states (*Länder*), their participation in principle in the legislative process, and the principles laid down in Articles 1 and 20 are not permitted.

2.2.1 The Political Movement in Favour of Electoral Gender Quotas

In Germany, the introduction of a rigid (50 per cent) electoral gender quota is currently being discussed. A prominent political movement comprised of the German left-wing political parties (the SPD, the German Social Democrats, the Green Party and the former SED-party (Die Linke)), citizens, academics (e.g. Laskowski 2014) and NGOs[1] argue that only electoral gender quotas can ensure gender parity and thus implement true democracy. Ulrike Liedtke, the President of the Brandenburg Parliament provided a specific example of this approach when she argued that *'(i)f one half of the population are women, democracy requires that women be equally represented in parliament. This means: without gender equality democracy remains unfinished'* (Redaktion des Landtages Brandenburg 2020). This argument is based on a new understanding of democracy in German constitutional thought. Proponents of this notion argue on an abstract level that the German Constitution's democracy requirement is aspirational in nature and that it should finally be fulfilled by recognizing that the legislature must be composed equally of men and women. Different notions of representation underlie the idea of rigid gender quotas. They share the view that true representation, or rather democracy, exists only when the legislature is equally composed of men and women (e.g. Röhner 2019). In other words, true representation requires true gender parity. Rodríguez Ruíz and Rubio-Marín even use the term 'parity democracy' (Rubio-Marín and Ruíz 2008, 311) in this context and argue that parity is a 'democratic must' (Rubio-Marín and Ruíz 2008, 314). The assumption behind this reasoning is basically that only women can appropriately represent women in the legislature. A legislature dominated by men is simply not in a position to represent female ideas and perspectives (Phillips 2006). Another idea (Mansbridge 1999) is to implement the concept of 'descriptive representation' (Pitkin 1972, 60–91; Pitkin 2004, 335).[2] Descriptive representation requires that the legislature mirror the demographics of the society of which it is a part. A similar approach was previously articulated in 1776, during the American Revolution (Pitkin 1972, 60–61). John Adams argued that the legislature *'should be an exact portrait, in miniature, of the people in large, as it should think, feel, reason and act like them'* (Adams 1776).[3]

---

[1] See in particular the activities of the 'Deutscher Juristinnenbund e.V.' (German Female Lawyer's Association) www.djb.de/; 'Deutscher Frauenrat' (The German Woman Council) www.frauenrat.de/ or the 'Verein Parité in den Parlamenten' (Association for Parity in Parliaments) www.parite.eu/verein/.
[2] Pitkin herself rejected this concept of representation as the only truth of representation and did not discuss its linkage with democracy.
[3] For further details on the inconsistency of the assertation of John Adams, see Pitkin (1972, notes to Chapter 4, n. 2).

A further argument is that constitutional provisions promoting equal rights (*Gleichberechtigung*) for men and women, such as Art. 3 (2) of the German Constitution, must be understood as incorporating a right to be placed on an equal legal footing (*Gleichstellung*), thus also guaranteeing that men and women are equally (i.e. in accordance with their population share) represented. Therefore, the legislature is obliged, or at least has the right to, introduce gender quotas to ensure that men and women are equally represented in that institution (Laskowski 2014; Klafki 2020).

2.2.2 A Partial Victory: The First Parity Laws

The movement scored a partial and temporary victory in 2019 when two German federal states (Brandenburg[4] and Thuringia[5]) adopted the first parity laws in Germany. The key provisions of these laws were that electoral lists at state level would have to be made up equally of male and female candidates. The parties were obliged to nominate a man and a woman alternately, but were free to elect either gender for the sole leading role.[6] If first place were given to a woman, second place would be reserved for a man and vice versa. If parties did not nominate their candidates equally, the electoral body responsible could reject the electoral list in its entirety or in part,[7] and the parties would be entirely or partially banned from running. Individuals identifying as neither male nor female could decide whether to run in the male or female position on an electoral list.[8]

2.2.3 The Setback: The Decisions of State Constitutional Courts in 2020

However, in 2020 the State Constitutional Courts in Weimar (Thür.VerfGH 2020, 2/20) and Potsdam (VerfGBbg 2020a,b, 55/19 and 9/19) found that these laws violated the relevant state constitutions and were therefore void. The key findings were that the electoral gender quotas violated constitutional electoral principles (free and equal elections) and the freedom of political parties. Gender quotas

---

[4] Zweites Gesetz zur Änderung des Thüringer Landeswahlgesetzes – Einführung der paritätischen Quotierung (Second Act to amend the State Voting Act of Brandenburg – Parity Act) February 12, 2019, GVBl I, vol. 30, no 1.
[5] Siebtes Gesetz zur Änderung des Thüringer Landeswahlgesetzes – Einführung der paritätischen Quotierung (Seventh Act to amend the State Voting Act of Thuringia – Introduction of the Parity Quota System) July 30, 2019, GVBl 2019, no 9 at 322.
[6] Sec. 29 para. 5 s 1 Thüringer Landeswahlgesetzes in der Fassung des Paritätsgesetzes (State Voting Act of Thuringia in the version of the Parity Act); sec. 25 para. 3 Brandenburgisches Landeswahlgesetz in der Fassung des Parité-Gesetzes (State Voting Act of Brandenburg in the version of the Parity Act).
[7] See, for example, sec. 30 para. 1 s. 4 and 5 of the State Voting Act of Thuringia in the version of the Parity Act.
[8] See, for example, sec. 29 para. 5 s. 2 and 3 State Voting Act of Thuringia in the version of the Parity Act; sec. 25 para. 3 s. 5 State Voting Act of Brandenburg in the version of the Parity Act.

interfered with the principle of free elections, as citizens were obliged to vote using party lists equally populated with male and female candidates (Thür.VerfGH 2020, 2/20, 28). Moreover, the nomination process was no longer free since female candidates could not run or be elected for a male place and vice versa (Thür.VerfGH 2020, 2/20, 31; VerfGBbg 2020a, 9/19, para. 115). The freedom of political parties was restricted because the parties could only have lists with equal numbers of men and women (Thür.VerfGH 2020, 2/20, 31; VerfGBbg 2020a, 9/19, para. 115). The relevant courts found that this interference with constitutional rights could not be justified. The reasoning for this was that the democratic principle could not serve as a basis for electoral quotas. The Thuringian Constitutional Court expressly declared that the idea that the legislature must mirror the demographics of a society is not part of German constitutional law (Thür.VerfGH 2020, 2/20, 34–35). The Constitutional Court in Brandenburg emphasized that no part of the population could argue, based on the principle of democracy, that it had to be represented in the legislature in accordance with its share of that population (VerfGBbg 2020b, 55/19, para. 186; VerfGBbg 2020a, 9/19, para. 134). These two State Constitutional Courts therefore defended the traditional and liberal understanding of democracy and followed a widespread view in German constitutional literature in finding that gender quotas were unconstitutional (Ungern-Sternberg 2019, 528–529; Morlok and Hobusch 2019, 14–15).

2.2.4 *The Movement Battles on*

However, the electoral gender quota movement still advocates for the introduction of rigid quotas, either by way of reinterpreting the relevant constitutional provisions or, as a last resort, by constitutional amendment (Süssmuth et al. 2020; Hohmann-Dennhardt 2020). In addition, the debate has moved from a state to a federal level.

2.2.5 *The Constitutional Conflict and the Meaning of Democracy and Equality*

Consequently, there is currently a conflict in Germany regarding how to define democracy and equality. Does equality simply mean equal rights (*Gleichberechtigung*) or also the right to be placed on an equal legal footing (*Gleichstellung*)? What does democracy mean? Does it signify descriptive representation and guided elections to assure a particular representation of gender or other groups in the legislature, or does it mean the formal representation of the people as such in the legislature is guaranteed by free elections?

The German Constitutional Court has not yet decided the matter. In a recent admissibility decision (BVerfG 2020), the Court outlined the constitutional issues surrounding electoral gender quotas without deciding on them. However, the Court made it clear that introducing these quotas would change the current democratic model in the German Constitution. It would replace the current principle of total representation (*Gesamtrepräsentation*) with a group or gender-related democratic model (BVerfG 2020, para. 83). The current democratic model in the German Constitution is based on the principle of total representation – each Member of Parliament is a free representative of the whole people (BVerfG 2020, para. 66). This is also codified in Art. 38 (1) sentence 2 German Constitution, which states that Members of Parliament '*shall be representatives of the whole people, not bound by orders or instructions and responsible only to their conscience*'. As each Member represents the whole people and is not bound by instructions or orders, the German Parliament ultimately represents the people even though it is not a smaller replica of the voter demographic (BVerfG 2020, para. 66). The legitimation of the German Federal Parliament depends on free elections and not on the gender of its Members (BVerfG 2020, para. 72).

Germany is not the first European Country to entertain these thoughts.[9] For example, Belgium[10] France,[11] Greece,[12] Poland[13] and Slovenia[14] have also introduced measures to increase the number of women in the legislature.[15] However, the legislation is generally less strict than the ideas put forward by the German Parity movement. Even though certain other European countries also reject electoral lists that do not meet the applicable gender quotas, they have quotas below 50 per cent and do not require a strict rotation of female and male candidates on electoral lists.[16]

---

[9] According to the International Institute for Democracy and Electoral Assistance (International IDEA)'s 'Gender Quotas Database' www.idea.int/data-tools/data/gender-quotas/database (April 21, 2023) 12 Member States of the European Union (Belgium, Croatia, France, Greece, Ireland, Italy, Luxembourg, Malta, Poland, Portugal, Slovenia, and Spain) have electoral gender quotas. However, these states do not have identical quotas and there are a variety of rules for different elections.

[10] Belgian Electoral Code, art. 117.1
https://legislationline.org/sites/default/files/documents/81/Belgium_ELECTORAL%20CODE%20 as%20of%202014_en.pdf (March 15, 2023).

[11] French Constitution, art. 1 para. 2, www.legifrance.gouv.fr/loda/article_lc/LEGIARTI000001924099 7?init=true&page=1&query=constitution&searchField=ALL&tab_selection=all (March 16, 2023); Loi n° 88-227 du 11 mars 1988 relative à la transparence financière de la vie politique (elections of the National Assembly), art. 9 para. 1, www.legifrance.gouv.fr/loda/id/JORFTEXT000000321646/ (March 16, 2022).

[12] Greek Constitution, art. 116 para. 2 www.hellenicparliament.gr/UserFiles/f3c70a23-7696-49db-9148-f24dce6a27c8/001-156%20aggliko.pdf (March 15, 2023); Presidential Decree 26/2012 modified by the Supreme Court, art. 34, www.hellenicparliament.gr/UserFiles/f3c70a23-7696-49db-9148-f24d ce6a27c8/PD%2026-2012.pdf (March 15, 2023).

[13] Amendments to the Polish Election Code adopted in January 2011, art. 211 para. 3, https://legislationline .org/sites/default/files/documents/40/POL_Election%20Code.pdf (March 15, 2022).

[14] Slovenian National Assembly Elections Act 2006, art. 43 para. 6 para.7, https://legislationline .org/sites/default/files/documents/44/Slovenia_law_elections_national_assembly_2006_en.pdf (March 15, 2023).

[15] For an overview of national legislation relating to gender quotas, see the gender quota database of the 'The International Institute for Democracy and Electoral Assistance' www.idea.int/data-tools/data/ gender-quotas.

[16] Only Belgium demands a different gender for every third name. A strict 1:1 rotation does not exist (Belgian Electoral Code, art. 117.1 para. 1).

Examples are Poland (35 per cent female quota),[17] Belgium[18] (at least one-third women or men) and Slovenia[19] (35 per cent). France[20] sanctions breaches only by way of the loss of state subsidies. Currently (2023) only the Spanish government is planning to introduce the same rigid electoral quotas (Reuters 2023) as discussed by the German approach. However, the European Parliament suggested in May 2022 similar quotas for the European elections (Polzin 2022). A role model for these rigid quotas can be found in the Bolivian legislation,[21] in which fixed gender quotas determine that the ratio between men and women on the lists of candidates for any election should be equal to, or in favour of, women; and Art. 107 of the Bolivian electoral law sanctions any failure to meet the quota by rejecting the list of candidates.

2.2.6 Content of the Eternity Clause

The unique feature of the ongoing debate is that there is also a conflict regarding the content of the German Constitution's eternity clause and therefore, by extension, a dispute concerning the identity of the Constitution itself. The German eternity clause in Article 79 (3) German Constitution protects the basic content of the democratic principle from constitutional amendment. Some academics, including me, argue that there is an absolute prohibition in Germany against introducing a rigid electoral gender quota (Burgmeister and Greve 2019; Polzin 2019; Pernice-Warnke 2020; Volk 2022). This means that rigid electoral gender quotas can neither be introduced by law nor by way of constitutional amendment because this would violate the constitutional identity of the German Constitution protected by Art 79 (3). The thinking is that binding electoral gender quotas will replace the principle of the sovereignty of the people with group- or gender-related sovereignty. The idea that the legislature represents one people is abolished in favour of the idea that there are several groups, in this case, men and women, who must be equally represented in the legislature. This approach is similar to the former constitution of estates that existed in nineteenth-century Europe (Di Fabio 2018). In addition, one needs to consider the potential radical effects of gender parity laws driven by the notion that the legislature must mirror societal demographics appropriately (Burgmeister and Greve 2019; Polzin 2019; Pernice-Warnke 2020). This is a particularly dangerous notion as it is not limited to men and women. When it is thoroughly thought through, there may be further groups requiring representation in the legislature. The German people could potentially be divided into groups based on religious beliefs, age, salary, and race, for example. Drawing a boundary here would seem to be difficult. Moreover, if this idea were extensively applied, free elections would become a peril.

---

[17] Amendments to the Polish Election Code adopted in January 2011, art. 215 para. 5.
[18] Belgian Electoral Code, art. 119. para. 5.
[19] Slovanian National Assembly Elections Act 2006, art. 56.
[20] Loi n° 88-227 du 11 mars 1988 relative à la transparence financière de la vie politique, art. 9 para. 1.
[21] Bolivian Electoral Law 201, art. 11 and art. 54 para. 2 https://bolivia.infoleyes.com/norma/1888/ley-del-regimen-electoral-026 (March 18, 2023).

Free elections could result in a legislature that does not mirror society and therefore leads to an 'incorrect result'. The ultimate measure to ensure that the legislature mirrors society would be for its composition to be determined by a computer.

The current debate will probably be tentatively decided by the German Constitutional Court at some point. We will then see how the German Constitutional Court positions itself. Will it protect the democratic principle as understood by the framers of the German Constitution or will it side with the supporters of the new constitutional identity who argue for a radical new understanding and redefining of democracy? We will also see whether the German eternity clause fulfils its stated purpose of protecting the basic principle of democracy in the face of (powerful) social movements seeking to redefine its content.

2.2.7 Fragility and Fluidity

As highlighted in Gary Jacobsohn's book, the current debate demonstrates the fragility of the boundaries for developing constitutions. A struggle pertaining to identity can also affect eternity clauses and make the risk visible that, through the emergence of radical new constitutional identities, a constitution can even change its very soul.

The ongoing German constitutional conflict shows clearly how true and pertinent is Jacobsohn's work on constitutional identity. The key characteristics of constitutional identity are disharmony and fluidity. We can see here how the emergence of new disharmony in society itself can lead to a battle over constitutional identity.

This conflict clearly demonstrates the fluidity of constitutional identity. It is always changing. New movements or ideas can even attempt to influence or transform a constitution's soul. Jacobsohn's assertion that history has shown that nothing is immutable is made visible. The same is true for his argument that it is crucial to know the acceptable limits of constitutional change.

Finally, the current debate also proves the correctness of Jacobsohn's assertion that every constitution is imperfect. This is also true for the German Constitution and its eternity clause. The negative aspect of an eternity clause, which was already discussed during the preparatory work, is that it cannot prevent state coups and revolutions. In this regard, the perspective of one of the founding fathers of the German Constitution, Rudolf Katz, is particularly pertinent. Katz argued that such a clause is 'ridiculous' (Deutscher Bundestag and Bundesarchiv 2002b, subvol. II, 707 and 717. Translation by the author) and stated that

> …(s)uch a provision would only make sense when imagining a scenario where one day Stalin takes over power in Germany and starts overriding certain laws. In that case, one would have to imagine that one day Mr Molotov runs to Stalin pale with terror and tells him: That's not possible because Article so-and-so of the Bonner Constitution says this and that – so that means we cannot act that way. – Well, that is completely unimaginable. (Deutscher Bundestag and Bundesarchiv 2002a, subvol. I, 503 and 532–533)

2.3 FINAL REMARKS

This leads me to my final remarks. For me, Gary Jacobsohn's work on constitutional identity is so central because it provides us with an abstract description of how a constitution functions. One could go so far as to say that he has cracked the genetic code of a constitution. His book makes clear that every constitution is both fragile and resistant. The spirit of constitutions is aptly captured in the final sentence of his book: '*In this sense, constitutions are a lot like music: their disharmonies are intrinsic to their nature, conditioned by local circumstance and tradition, and necessary for the realization of the enterprise.*'

REFERENCES

Adams, John. 1776. 'II. Letter to John Penn 27 March 1776'. *Founders Online, National Archives* https://founders.archives.gov/documents/Adams/06-04-02-0026-0003.

Burgmeister, Jörg and Holger Greve. 2019. 'Parité-Gesetz und Demokratieprinzip: Verfassungsauftrag oder Identitätsverstoß?' *Zeitschrift Für Gesetzgebung* 34 (2): 154–173.

BVerfG, Judgement of 30 June 2009, 2 BvE 2/08 – Lisbon Judgement.

BVerfG, Order of 15 December 2020, 2 BvC 46/19 – Unsuccessful Electoral Complaint.

Calliess, Christian. 2020. 'Constitutional Identity in Germany: One for Three or Three in One'. In *Constitutional Identity in Europa of Multilevel Constitutionalism*, edited by Christian Calliess and Gerhard von der Schyff. Cambridge: Cambridge University Press, 153–181.

Deutscher Bundestag and Bundesarchiv (eds.). 2002a. *Der Parlamentarische Rat 1948–1949, Akten und Protokolle, Vol. 13, Ausschuss für Organisation des Bundes/Ausschuss für Verfassungsgerichtshof und Rechtspflege*. subvol. I. Oldenbourg: Wissenschaftsverlag.

Deutscher Bundestag and Bundesarchiv (eds.). 2002b. *Der Parlamentarische Rat 1948–1949, Akten und Protokolle, Vol. 13, Ausschuss für Organisation des Bundes/Ausschuss für Verfassungsgerichtshof und Rechtspflege*. subvol. II. Oldenbourg: Wissenschaftsverlag.

Di Fabio, Udo. 2018. 'Staatsrechtler hält Gesetz für mehr Frauen im Parlament für verfassungswidrig'. *Der Spiegel*, December 28. www.spiegel.de/politik/deutsch/udo-di-fabio-gegen-frauenquoten-vorschlag-von-katarina-barley-a-1207777.html

Hohmann-Dennhardt, Christine. 2020. 'Der Kampf geht weiter'. *Verfassungsblog*, July 17. https://verfassungsblog.de/der-kampf-geht-weiter/.

Jacobsohn, Gary Jeffrey. 2010. *Constitutional Identity*. Cambridge: Harvard University Press.

Klafki, Anika. 2020. 'Parität – Der deutsche Diskurs im globalen Kontext'. *Die Öffentliche Verwaltung* 73 (19): 856–866.

Laskowski, Silke. 2014. 'Pro Parité: Ohne gleichberechtigte Parlamente keine gleichberechtigten Gesetze und keine gleichberechtigte Gesellschaft! Eine juristische Streitschrift für ein modernes Wahlrecht'. *Zeitschrift des deutschen Jurisstinnenbundes* 17 (3): 93–142.

Mansbridge, Jane. 1999. 'Should Blacks Represent Blacks and Women Represent Women? A Contingent "Yes"'. *The Journal of Politics* 61 (3): 628–657.

Morlok, Martin and Alexander Hobush. 2019. 'Ade parité? – Zur Verfassungswidrigkeit verpflichtender Quotenregelungen bei Landeslisten'. *Die Öffentliche Verwaltung* 72 (1): 14–20.

Pernice-Warnke, Silvia. 2020. 'Parlamente als Spiegel der Bevölkerung'. *Deutsches Verwaltungsblatt* 135 (2): 81–90.

Phillips, Anne. 2006. 'Dealing with Difference: A Politics of Ideas or a Politics of Presence?' in *Contemporary Political Philosophy: An Anthology.* 2nd ed. Robert Goodin and Philip Pettit (eds.) Oxford: Blackwell, 171–182.

Pitkin, Hannah F. 1972. *The Concept of Representation.* Berkeley: University of California Press.

Pitkin, Hannah F. 2004. 'Representation and Democracy: Uneasy Alliance'. *Scandinavian Political Studies* 27 (3): 335–342.

Polzin, Monika. 2019. 'Parité-Gesetz in Brandenburg – Kein Sieg für die Demokratie'. *Verfassungsblog,* February 8. https://verfassungsblog.de/parite-gesetz-in-brandenburg-kein-sieg-fuer-die-demokratie.

Polzin, Monika. 2022. 'Transnational Lists, Diversity and Quota Regulation'. *EU Law Live,* December 3. https://eulawlive.com/app/uploads/weekend_edition_123.pdf.

Redaktion des Landtages Brandenburg. 2020. 'Landtagspräsidentin verteidigt Paritätsgesetz vor Verfassungsgericht – Landtag Brandenburg'. August 20. www.landtag.brandenburg.de/de/aktuelles/neuigkeiten/aktuelle_meldungen/landtagspraesidentin_verteidigt_paritaetsgesetz_vor_verfassungsgericht/12452.

Reuters. 2023 'Spain Announces Law Promoting Gender Parity in Politics and Business'. March 3. www.reuters.com/world/europe/spain-announces-law-promoting-gender-parity-politics-business-2023-03-04/.

Röhner, Cara. 2019. *Ungleichheit und Verfassung.* Weilerswist: Velbrück Wissenschaft.

Rubio-Marín, Ruth and Blanca Rodríguez Ruiz. 2008. 'The Gender of Representation: On Democracy, Equality and Parity'. *International Journal Comparative Law* 6 (2): 287–316.

Süssmuth, Rita, Jelena von Achenbach, Frauke Brosius-Gersdorf, Christine Hohmann-Dennhardt, Renate Jaeger, Silke Laskowski, and Friederike Wapler. 2020. 'Es Gibt Keinen Besitzstandsschutz Im Wahlrecht'. *Verfassungsblog,* October 21. https://verfassungsblog.de/es-gibt-keinen-besitzstandsschutz-im-wahlrecht/.

Thür.VerfGH. 2020. Judgment. July 15. 2/20.

Thym, Daniel. 2012. 'Attack or Retreat? Evolving Themes and Strategies of the Judicial Dialogue between the German Constitutional Court and the European Court of Justice'. In *Constitutional Conversations in Europe,* edited by Monica Claes, Maartje de Visser, Patricia Popelier and Catherine Van de Heyning. Cambridge, UK: Intersentia, 235–250.

Ungern-Sternberg, von Antje. 2019. 'Parité-Gesetzgebung auf dem Prüfstand des Verfassungsrechts'. *Juristenzeitung* 74 (11): 525–534.

VerfGBbg. 2020a. Judgment. October 23. 9/19.

VerfGBbg. 2020b. Judgment. October 23. 55/19.

Volk, Laura. 2022. *Paritätisches Wahlrecht.* Tübingen: Mohr Siebeck.

3

Constitutional Identity as Discourse

Mis-identity and Dis-identity

Jaclyn L. Neo

INTRODUCTION

Many see constitutional identity as the conceptual category through which to critique constitutional changes – as affirming, realizing, or deviating from a particular constitutional identity. 'Constitutional identity' has been linked to doctrines on the unamendability of the constitution. For instance, in their articulation of the basic structure doctrine in India, the Supreme Court invoked the idea that the constitution has an 'identity' that has to be maintained against constitutional amendments (*Kesavanada Bharati v State of Kerala* 1973). Embedded within this discourse is an assumption that constitutional identity is something fixed and identifiable, against which constitutional reality and changes can be measured and evaluated. The claim is that constitutions cannot be amended in a way that destroys or deviates from their fundamental constitutional identity.

Gary Jacobsohn's work upends this understanding of constitutional identity, arguing instead for a more contingent, contested, and contestable idea of constitutional identity (Jacobsohn 2006, 2010). According to him, constitutional identity is not a 'discrete object of invention nor as a heavily encrusted essence embedded in a society's culture, requiring only to be discovered' (Jacobsohn 2006, 363). Instead, it is acquired through 'experience', emerging 'dialogically' as a 'a mix of political aspirations and commitments ... expressive of a nation's past, as well as the determination of those within the society who seek, in some ways, to transcend that past' (Jacobsohn 2006, 363). This constitutional identity 'is changeable but resistant to its own destruction, and it may manifest itself differently in different settings' (Jacobsohn 2006, 363). According to this line of thought, constitutional identity is the confluence of different constitutional values and aspirations at any point in time, which can nonetheless be changed. In particular, Jacobsohn points to disharmonies in the constitution that provide the foundation for this fluid enterprise (Jacobsohn 2010).

The term 'dialogical' does not fully capture the complexity of this process which is more a multi-dimensional conversation involving multiple actors, rather than a dialogue, strictly speaking. Nevertheless, the critical insight stands, as it reflects that identifying constitutional identity is not a matter of discovery, but a matter of contestation. This rightly reflects the big C constitution as less deterministic, and small c constitution as far more dynamic. The 'big C' constitution is central; it is the anchor upon which the multi-dialogical enterprise concerning constitutional identity hinges. There is a 'bounded fluidity', even while 'constitutional disharmony is critical to the development of constitutional identity' (Jacobsohn 2010, 4), 'meaning within which dissonance and contradiction play out in the development of constitutional identity' (Jacobsohn 2010, 4).

This point is critical – to see constitutional identity as characterized by contestations, rather than consensus. Where there is consensus, it is a mere modus vivendi, subject again to change. This is highly unsatisfactory for those of us who like to think of the constitutionalist project as a triumph of enlightenment reason over petty tribalism, as a vindication of the individual from the excesses of abusive regimes, and as an effective constraint over absolute power. Indeed, the impulses of constitutional drafters and judges to eternalize certain basic foundational principles and values within the constitution are often, though not always, premised upon a belief in the rightness of those principles and values. And they do so in the name of 'The People'. But who is 'The People'? This is a question that can give rise to no permanently satisfactory answer and this can be a good thing as a historical idea of 'The People' may exclude minorities and other marginalized groups. Even the United States, whose constitutional mythology relies heavily on the constitution's 'We, the People' has had to grapple with the idea that historically, 'the People' excluded women and African-Americans, among others.

Once we abandon the mythical, imagined creature called 'We, the People', we find a society that is far less cohesive, and most times, far less agreed or agreeable about certain fundamental ideas. Within this realistic view of society, constitutional disharmonies and contestations make more sense. My intention in this chapter is to drill down on how these constitutional disharmonies and contestations can be understood as competing claims about constitutional identity. I look at the modalities of disharmonies and the narratives that constitutional actors employ in relation to 'constitutional identity' and I identify two modes of argumentation that challenge extant claims about constitutional identity: 'constitutional mis-identity' and 'constitutional dis-identity'.

The prefix 'mis-' is commonly used to falsify the root word whereas the prefix 'dis-' serves to negate the root word. In this regard, mis-identification or dis-identification are two distinct ways of challenging an existing consensus, the status quo. Furthermore, the prefixes bring attention to the differentiated processes of change. A claim of 'mis-identity' is a claim for reversion to past values assumed to be more 'authentic'; 'mis-identity' suggests that current claims about constitutional identity are *mis*taken and that changing the constitution, whether through interpretation or amendment, would realize its more authentic self. This 'mis-identification' appeal for a return to authenticity can be extremely powerful among those who disagree with the contemporary direction of the country. This nostalgic view of the constitution can be a serious point of mobilization for certain constituencies, as evidenced in countries where politicians have successfully campaigned to 'restore' a glorious constitutional identity for the people. Oftentimes, this nostalgic version of constitutional mis-identity serves to elevate the status of a dominant majority over the rest.

In contrast, 'dis-identification' challenges dominant views about constitutional identity by suggesting that those views no longer reflect what the actual society values. It is an argument to imbue the constitution with new values claimed to be more 'progressive' and reflective of current society: the displacement of constitutional identity to establish a refreshed constitutional identity through new interpretations and/or new provisions. This progressive claim of constitutional identity can be a powerful source of mobilization for those seeking to transform the existing status quo.

Both 'mis-identification' and 'dis-identification' claims build on constitutional disharmony and force a reconsideration of the status quo. However, they constitute different modes of disharmony and give rise to different conversations about disharmony and identity. For this reason, they should be treated distinctively and analyzed differently. At times, they may produce reinforcing claims, while at other times, under different conditions, they produce competing claims, pulling away from an existing 'consensus' on constitutional identity. We see this, for instance, where a particular constitutional identity is subject to both conservative and progressive pressures for change on the two extremes. Having a disharmony idea of constitutional identity and a framework that allows us to identify different modalities of contestations accommodates a more pluralist view of the constitution, where the constitution serves as a cauldron of pluralist constitutional values and legal meaning, rather than a fixed monolithic text.

The rest of the chapter will expound upon these two modalities of contestations within a disharmonic constitution to show that the idea of disharmony is even more dynamic than we might sometimes assume. To illustrate the dynamism of this contestation over constitutional identity and the utility of my proposed framework in highlighting these nuances, I use two permutations of contestations around religion in two constitutional settings – Malaysia and the United States. Both these countries, despite having different constitutional provisions on state and religion – Malaysia has a confessional constitution while the United States has a non-establishment constitution – have religious societies and have experienced significant religious mobilization over the public role of religion. There are nuanced modalities of disharmony in the context of contestation over religiously motivated claims about the constitution, and the framework of dis-identity and mis-identity would allow us to better appreciate the different forms of contestations over constitutional identity.

3.1 CONSTITUTIONAL IDENTITY AND THE DISHARMONIC CONSTITUTION

Questions have been asked as to what contribution 'constitutional identity' provides to our understanding and discourse of constitutionalism. Is it a descriptive idea, a normative idea, or an explanatory idea? I take constitutional identity as a *site* of contestation, in which a dynamic constitutional discourse revolves around disharmonies arising from the constitution. It is a site of ideas, speech, and action concerning what matters the most to us about our constitutional state. The disharmonic nature of the constitution is the condition that allows for this contestation, as we acknowledge and proceed on the basis that constitutions include 'alternative visions or aspirations that may embody different strands within a common historical tradition' (Jacobsohn 2010) and entail 'a confrontational relationship between the constitution and the social order within which it operates' (Jacobsohn 2010). It entails seeing the constitution as necessarily pluralist. The dialogic engagements occur in the actions and decisions of judicial, legislative, and executive authorities, and in the meaning that other interpreters, both public and private, give to the constitution (Kommers 2012). It should be emphasized that this contestation involves not only official institutions but also civil society and citizen discourse.

The constitutional identity of the disharmonic constitution could be inevitably far more contingent and subject to change. Even if, as has been argued, there 'is a presumption in favour of settled practice' this 'still leaves open the possibility that what is settled is also mutable' (Jacobsohn 2010, 100). The dynamics of change can involve several possibilities. Accepting constitutional identity as a site of contestation means that constitutional identities are never fixed. Instead, they evolve out of the tensions or incongruities within the framework of a single documentary text or between the text and external realities. This means that 'constitutional identity-formation is a matter of conflict within consensus' (Kommers 2012). But what exactly is constitutional disharmony? Broadly, disharmony can arise in three forms. The first is *internal disharmony* due to seeming contradictions within the text itself. The second is *external disharmony*, which arises due to a seeming contradiction between the text of a constitution and the context. For instance, there might be divergence between the text of the constitution and a socio-political consensus about a matter. The third is *silent disharmony*, which arises because the constitution fails to address a matter that political actors and society deem to be of fundamental importance. Within these different forms of disharmony, claims of constitutional mis-identity and constitutional dis-identity can emerge as sometimes reinforcing and other times competing claims.

3.2 CONSTITUTIONAL MIS-IDENTITY AND CONSTITUTIONAL DIS-IDENTITY

3.2.1 *Constitutional Mis-identity and Dis-identity as Reinforcing Claims*

Mis-identification and dis-identification form reinforcing challenges when the 'new' constitutional identity both sets of proponents seek to construct overlap. Allow me to illustrate using the example of Malaysia where a major site of contestation has been its secular/religious identity. Article 3(1) of Malaysia's Federal Constitution states that 'Islam is the religion of the Federation; but other religions may be practised in peace and harmony in any part of the Federation'. This may suggest a religious constitutionalist state, where Islam is the established religion in a substantive sense. However, the drafting history of this clause reveals a different reality. The Federal Constitution of Malaysia was the result of a 'grand bargain' among political elites and the product of protracted negotiations between the British colonial representatives on the one hand, and the local elites on the other. The local elites comprised three race-based political parties, each of which sought to champion its own community's ethnic interests. On the surface, at least, these political elites shared the common aim of independence from the British colonials and the creation of a pluralistic independent state. Non-Muslim elites supported the inclusion of Article 3(1) on the assurance of their Muslim counterparts that the provision would not affect the civil rights of non-Muslims and that 'Malaya would be a secular state' (Fernando 2002, 162–163). The political consensus (then) was that the 'constitutional identity' of Malaysia would be secular. Article 3(1)'s reference to Islam was meant to permit religious symbolism, but not to institute theocratic rule in Malaysia. This secular consensus remained in place throughout the first generation of Malaysia's independence. Islam was understood to be limited to representing the symbolic power of the state and laws personal only to Muslims. The Supreme Court of Malaysia (then its highest court) affirmed in 1988 the 'secular' constitutional identity of Malaysia. According to the court, 'the law in this country is still what it is today, secular law, where morality not accepted by the law is not enjoying the status of the law' (Che Omar Bin Che Soh v PP 1988). As for Article 3(1), the Supreme Court held that it only refers to the use of Islamic 'rituals and ceremonies' in public and official events (Che Omar Bin Che Soh v PP 1988, 561-F). Malaysia's constitutional identity was conceptualized as secular. The external disharmony was resolved by harmonizing the terms of the constitution with the known political consensus concerning the identity of the constitutional state.

However, with demographic and political changes, and the passage of time, this first generational secular consensus became fractured, creating pressure for a greater role for Islam in Malaysian public law, a challenge that we can characterize as an attempt to displace the secular identity. This constitutional contestation was grounded partly in interpretations of Article 3(1) but was not driven by the courts. Instead, it was the social transformation of Malaysian society that drove political changes. Mutalib (1993, 1–16) points to the influence of a worldwide revivalism of Islam which started in the 1970s whereby Islam provided the ideological resources for political mobilization fuelling nationalist and reformist movements. Muslim reformers impressed upon the masses that the preservation of Islamic identity could only be achieved through independence of the country and an appreciation of the past grandeur of the Muslim people and civilization (Mutalib

1993, 6–7). These global changes provided the background for growing social pressure for recognition of public Islam, which was capitalized upon by Malaysia's main Malay–Muslim political parties that were competing for the Malay–Muslim votes by trying to out-Islamicize one another. Their narratives portrayed the secular as a dis-identification of Malaysia's constitutional identity, taking into account the new social context and necessitating its displacement with a 'new' more religious constitutional identity.

The dis-identification challenge to the constitutional identity of Malaysia as secular is reinforced, in this instance, with the mis-identification challenge strongly anchored within a post-colonial narrative. As Rosenfeld points out, a common dialectic that presents itself in the post-colonial constitution is 'an ongoing struggle between absorption and rejection of the former colonizer's most salient relevant identities' (Rosenfeld 2012, 766). The post-colonial constitution's identity is therefore forged through 'identification with, and differentiation from, the colonizer's constitutional identity' (Rosenfeld 2012, 766). While this process takes place within the colonizer's constitutional framework, the framework is nonetheless subject to change according to the post-colonial state's institutional and identity-based needs (Rosenfeld 2012, 766).

Critics thus argue that the secular constitutional identity is a mis-recognition of Malaysia's true identity, which is Islamic. Narratives are constructed to present the precolonial past as a glorious Islamic society administering Muslim law under Muslim sultans. The aspiration is to restore the 'supremacy of Islamic law' (Ahmad Ibrahim 1988, 14) where Islam was primary and core to Malaysia's constitutional identity. This entails a 'restoration' of Islam as the (supposedly) proper *grundnorm* of Malaysia, a move that would reclaim the autochthonous nature of the Malaysian legal system and thereby its 'authentic' constitutional identity generally (Abdul Aziz Bari 2008).

The confluence of the mis-identity argument and dis-identity argument provided a powerful challenge to the (then) extant constitutional identity of Malaysia as secular. While not immediately producing a change in views, such challenges to the very core of constitutional meaning deprive defenders of the status quo 'a priceless advantage – their claims to self-evidence' (Ackerman 2006, 1433). The mis-identity and dis-identity claims successfully reinforced one another, resulting in an expanded and public role for Islam in Malaysia. Malaysia has since acquired a far more 'Islamic' constitutional identity than its initial secular consensus.

3.2.2 Constitutional Mis-identity and Dis-identity as Competing Challenges

Another constitutional dynamic emerges from a contest between competing claims of mis-identity and dis-identity, thereby pulling the constitutional identity in opposite directions. To illustrate, at a point in time, there may be a consensus about a particular aspect of the constitution that one can identify as part of its constitutional identity C_1. However, C_1 could subsequently be challenged by those who think that C_1 does not go far enough in advancing a particular value within society, and propose instead a move towards C_2. These C_2 'progressives' put forward a claim of dis-identification, challenging an existing 'consensus' on constitutional identity by suggesting that it does not reflect actual social values, and arguing that there is a need to reinterpret the constitution 'progressively' to reflect those new values.

In contrast, and perhaps sometimes even in retaliation, those who oppose C_2 could mount a claim that proponents of C_2 are gravely misguided. C_2 opponents may not just seek to preserve the status quo C_1 but go further by suggesting that C_1 was mistaken anyway and that there is a need to revert to the constitution's 'true' (original) identity. This would entail the revival of ideas to reconstitute a supposedly prior constitutional identity C_0. This claim of mis-identity links the identity of the constitution with claims of 'authenticity' and 'consistency' to its original intent.

Such contrasting claims of dis-identity and mis-identity complexify the disharmonic constitution and the manner in which it produces change. They show that the language of 'dialectics' or 'dialogue' may not always fully capture what happens in the process of such contestation. 'Disharmony' may not merely be the result of challenges to a contested constitutional identity, but may also arise from competing challenges to the status quo where actors do not merely seek to defend it but also advocate changes that would draw the constitution further away from their opponents.

This dynamic arises in the context of contestations about the disestablishment clause vis-à-vis the position of religion and religious values in the United States, for instance. For some time, the cornerstone of jurisprudence on the First Amendment's non-establishment clause was separationism. The 1947 Supreme Court judgment in *Everson v. Board of Education* was a turning point for the contestation over the religious/secular constitutional identity of the United States (Everson v. Board of Education 1947). In that case, the Supreme Court extended the establishment clause of the First Amendment beyond the federal government to state and local governments and affirmed that '[t]he First Amendment has erected a wall between church and state', which 'must be kept high and impregnable' without the 'slightest breach' (Everson v. Board of Education 1947, 18). Gunn observes however that *Everson* provoked an academic argument that was to later spill over to the 'culture wars' of the 1980s (Gunn 2012, 16). As he notes, '[d]uring the following sixty years, a lively and often polemical debate ensued that ultimately was joined by scores of scholars arguing back and forth about the appropriateness of the wall metaphor' (Gunn 2012, 16). Proponents of strong disestablishment argue that any state/public support for religion would display a constitutional dis-identity, especially as Americans have simultaneously become more religiously diverse and less religious. Prior state prioritization of Christianity fails to respond to this new social-political reality and needs to be displaced in favour of a 'new' separationist secular constitutional identity. This became the motivation for challenges to public religion over several decades, including against the practice of conducting prayers and devotional Bible readings in public schools;[1] against the display of the Ten Commandments in courthouses;[2] against the teaching of creation science in public schools as an alternative to evolution;[3] and against cities and towns from erecting crèches that appear to endorse Christianity.[4]

Opponents of this strong form of disestablishment see it as a mis-identity of the American Constitution, which is supposed to protect religion, and not exclude religion from the public sphere entirely. McConnell suggests, for instance, that the Supreme Court's jurisprudence under the First Amendment – premised upon 'abstractions', such as 'advancement of religion', 'entanglement', 'coercion', 'endorsement', 'neutrality', and above all the 'wall of separation between church and state', are removed from actual historical experiences motivating disestablishment and accordingly, are 'oversimplifications' at best and 'misleading' in some respects (McConnell 2003, 2205). According to McConnell, the historical records suggest that 'one of the principal arguments against establishment was that it was harmful to religion, and many sought disestablishment in order to strengthen and revitalize Christianity' (McConnell 2003, 2205). Similarly, Witte notes that '[s]eparationism needs to be retained, particularly for its ancient insight of protecting religious bodies from the state and for its more recent insight of protecting the consciences of religious believers from violations by government or religious bodies', but that there should not be an overzealous interpretation of the principle lest it 'runs afoul of other constitutive principles of the First Amendment – particularly the principles of liberty of conscience and religious equality' (Witte 2006, 44). Witte argues that '[t]he Court must be at least as zealous in protecting religious conscience from secular coercion as protecting secular conscience from religious coercion' (Witte 2006, 44). Such arguments see the extant constitutional identity of non-establishment as not anti-religious, but as protection of religious liberty whereby some public religion is not *ipso facto* objectionable.

---

[1] See, for example, *Engel v. Vitale*, 370 U.S. 421 (1962) (invalidating school-sponsored prayer in public schools); *Abington School District v. Schempp*, 374 U.S. 203 (1963) (invalidating the reading of verses, without comment, from the Bible and the Lord's Prayer in public school settings); *Lee v. Weisman*, 505 U.S. 577 (1992) (prohibiting prayer at school-sponsored activities in public schools); *Santa Fe Independent School District v. Doe*, 530 U.S. 290 (2000) (invalidating a school policy of beginning football games with a prayer led by a nominated student body representative, etc.).

[2] See, for example, *McCreary County v. American Civil Liberties Union*, 545 U.S. 844 (2005) where the Supreme Court held 5-4 that Ten Commandment displays in two Kentucky county courthouses violated the establishment clause of the First Amendment. Notably, the Supreme Court held, also 5-4 and on the same day in *Van Orden v. Perry*, 545 U.S. 677 (2005) that a monument depicting the Ten Commandments in an Austin, Texas public park did not violate the establishment clause.

[3] See, for example, *Edwards v. Aguillard*, 482 U.S. 578 (1987) (striking down a Louisiana law mandating instruction in creation science whenever evolution was taught in public schools).

[4] See, for example, *County of Allegheny v. American Civil Liberties Union*, 492 U.S. 573 (1989) (a split Supreme Court upheld a display containing a menorah, a Christmas tree, and other decorations outside, a block from the courthouse as not violating the establishment clause, but conversely that a creche display inside a county courthouse violated the establishment clause).

The mis-identity challenge has been taken to further extremes by political constituents who believe that Supreme Court has abandoned the country's true constitutional identity as a Christian nation. People in this camp not only decried the term 'separation of church and state' as a 'historical error', but also accused the Supreme Court of being involved in a 'deliberate attempt to impose un-American values on the Constitution' (Gunn 2012, 16). They find evidence in history and the political context – from the history of Americans as religious refugees to early state constitutions establishing state religions, to Christian faith being taken as an informal but highly salient factor for high political office to invocations of 'God' in political speech and even in its currency. These ideas are encapsulated in what has been termed the 'Religious Right'/'Christian Right' (see generally, McVicar 2016), or 'Christian nationalism' (e.g., Whitehead and Perry 2022). Further, Gorski and Perry observe a strand of white Christian nationalism premised upon the myth that the country was founded as a Christian nation by white Christians, divinely favoured, and that its laws and institutions are based on Protestant Christianity (Gorski and Perry 2022, 4–5).

Noll et al. note the following thinking among political constituents with strong claims of constitutional mis-identity:

> For those who hold to the 'Christian America' view, the situation may be summarized as follows: America was founded as a 'Christian nation.' But the nation turned from its Christian foundation and in recent decades has been taken over by secular humanism. The goal today is to become a Christian nation once again – by *restoring* America to its 'biblical base,' to the 'biblical principles of our founding fathers,' to a 'Christian consensus,' etc. ... Stated in this way then, the only alternative seems to be an all-out battle between the forces advocating a return to 'Christian America' and the ruling forces of 'secular humanism' – so that America can become a Christian nation once again. (Noll et al. 1981, 129, emphasis added)

This ideological movement based on the idea of America as a 'Christian nation' coincides with religious diversification in America. Straughn and Feld note that Christian nationalism is 'a discursive practice that seeks to align the boundaries of authentic national belonging with adherence to the dominant religious faith' (Straughn and Feld 2010, 281). At its peak in 2005, about 71 per cent of Americans regarded the United States as a 'Christian nation', according to Pew research data (Pew Research Center 2006). The proportion has since declined but a 2022 report shows that almost half of respondents still think that the Bible should have a great deal of influence (23%) or some influence (24%) on the laws of the United States (Pew Research Center 2022) and 45 per cent of Americans surveyed say that the United States should be a 'Christian nation' (Smith et al. 2022; see also Gorski and Perry 2022).

Opponents of strong disestablishment in the United States have also started to employ strategic litigation to 'restore' the place of religion in the constitutional order, that is, to correct the country's constitutional mis-identity. Recent judicial developments show that these cases have chipped away at the constitutional identity of separationism. In *Kennedy v Bremerton School District*, the US Supreme Court ruled that a public school district in the state of Washington violated the constitutional rights of a Christian part-time high school assistant football coach when it suspended him for leading prayers with players on the field after games (*Kennedy v Bremerton School District* 2021). Justice Gorsuch, delivering the opinion of the court, held that the district's 'reprisal' against the assistant coach 'rested on a mistaken view that it had a duty to ferret out and suppress religious observances even as it allows comparable secular speech'. According to the court majority, '[t]he Constitution neither mandates nor tolerates that kind of discrimination' and that a 'historically sound understanding of the Establishment Clause' does not make it necessary for government to be hostile to religion in this way.

In *Carson v Makin*, the US Supreme Court ruled that the exclusion of private schools that promote religion from a Maine state tuition assistance programme amounted to unconstitutional religious discrimination (*Carson v Makin* 2021). In a 6-3 ruling, the majority opinion held that the Maine program 'operates to identify and exclude otherwise eligible schools on the basis of their religious exercise'. The programme provided public funds for tuition at private high schools of a family's choice in sparsely populated areas of the state that lacked public secondary schools, but required eligible schools to be 'nonsectarian'. This excluded schools promoting a particular religion and presenting material 'through the lens of that faith'.

Proponents of strong disestablishment decry these recent rulings by the Supreme Court (see also *Ramirez v Collier* 2022; Shurtleff v. City of Boston 2002) as 'eroding American legal traditions intended to prevent government officials from promoting any particular faith' (Hurley and Chung 2022). The contestation about America's constitutional mis-identity or dis-identity vis-à-vis religion/disestablishment is set to continue.

CONCLUSION: CONSTITUTIONAL IDENTITY AND CONSTITUTIONAL CHANGE

As sites of contestation, constitutional identity is bound by the constitution, but, often, little else. This bounded fluidity is highly unsatisfactory for some. Jacobsohn identifies two types of changes that he considers problematic. The first are changes that could subvert the essentials of constitutional government which he contends has 'at the core' the 'rule of law and the administration of impartial justice' (Jacobsohn 2010, 70). The second are changes that 'could substantially transform or negate a fundamental political commitment of the constitutional order that had been central to the nation's self-understanding' (Jacobsohn 2010, 70). But if we accept disharmony and the possibility of dynamic change, there is little to constrain or prevent against the erosion of liberal constitutionalist values. But one should imagine the alternative, which is whether one may similarly object if the existing constitutional settlement is antiliberal, tribalistic, and/or authoritarian. Would not the possibility of contestation and change be a better alternative? When a constitution is changed to introduce or reinstate liberal values, do we similarly oppose these changes? Imagine for instance that the Islamic/Christian/Jewish nature of the state is declared to be the basic feature of the constitution, unalterable, unchangeable, unamendable, indestructible – what recourse could there be for secularists? Would it not be better to have the possibility of contestation and change within a recognizably disharmonic constitution? At the end of the day, value-normativism requires a certain commitment to democratic process-normativism – in which case liberal constitutionalism becomes a worthy struggle rather than a self-evident truth that all who seek will discover.

REFERENCES

Abdul Aziz Bari. 2008. 'The Indigenous Roots of the Malaysian Constitution – The Provisions and the Implications'. *Current Law Journal* 6: xxxiii.
Ackerman, Bruce. 2006. 'Interpreting the Women's Movement'. *California Law Review* 94: 1421–1437.
Ahmad, Ibrahim. 1988. *Ke Arah Islamisasi Undang-Undang di Malaysia*. Kuala Lumpur: Yayasan Dakwah Islamiah Malaysia.
Carson v Makin, 597 U.S. (2021).
Che Omar Bin Che Soh v PP [1988] 2 MLJ 55 (Malaysia).
Everson v. Board of Education, 330 U.S. 1 (1947).
Fernando, Joseph M. 2002. *The Making of the Malayan Constitution*. Kuala Lumpur: MBRAS.
Gorski, Philip S. and Samuel L. Perry. 2022. *The Flag and the Cross: White Christian Nationalism and the Threat to American Democracy*. New York: Oxford University Press.
Gunn, Jeremy T. 2012. 'The Separation of Church and State versus Religion in the Public Square: The Contested History of the Establishment Clause'. In *No Establishment of Religion: America's Original Contribution to Religious Liberty*, edited by Jeremy T. Gunn, and John Witte. New York: Oxford University Press.
Hurley, Lawrence and Andrew Chung. 2022. 'U.S. Supreme Court takes aim at separation of church and state'. *Reuters*, June 29, 2022. www.reuters.com/legal/government/us-supreme-court-takes-aim-separation-church-state-2022-06-28/.
Jacobsohn, Gary Jeffrey. 2006. 'Constitutional Identity'. *The Review of Politics* 68: 361–397.
Jacobsohn, Gary Jeffrey. 2010. *Constitutional Identity*. Cambridge: Harvard University Press.
Kennedy v Bremerton School District, 597 U.S. (2021).
Kesavananda Bharati v State of Kerala, 4 S.C.C 225; A.I.R 1973 SC 1461 (India) (1973).
Kommers, Donald P. 2012. 'Review: Constitutions and National Identity'. *The Review of Politics* 74 (1): 127–133.
McConnell, Michael W. 2003. 'Establishment and Disestablishment at the Founding, Part I: Establishment of Religion'. *William & Mary Law Review* 44: 2105–2208.
McVicar, Michael J. 2016. 'The Religious Right in America'. Oxford Research Encyclopedia of Religion, 3 March 2016; accessed 28 May 2023. https://oxfordre.com/religion/view/10.1093/acrefore/9780199340378.001.0001/acrefore-9780199340378-e-97.
Mutalib, Hussin. 1993. *Islam in Malaysia: From Revivalism to Islamic State?* Singapore: Singapore University Press.

Noll, Mark A., Nathan O. Hatch, and George M. Marsden. 1981. *The Search for Christian America*. Westchester: Crossway Books.
Pew Research Center. 2006. 'Many Americans Uneasy with Mix of Religion and Politics'. 24 August 2006. www.pewresearch.org/religion/2006/08/24/many-americans-uneasy-with-mix-of-religion-and-politics/#1
Pew Research Center. 2022. 'Religion in Public Life'. 27 October 2022. www.pewresearch.org/religion/2022/10/27/religion-in-public-life/.
Ramirez v Collier, 595 U.S. (2022).
Rosenfeld, Michel. 2012. 'Constitutional Identity'. In *The Oxford Handbook of Comparative Constitutional Law*, edited by Michael Rosenfeld and Sajó András. Oxford: Oxford University Press.
Shurtleff v. City of Boston, 596 U.S. (2002).
Smith Gregory A., Michael Rotolo and Patricia Tevington. 2022. '45% of Americans Say U.S. Should Be a "Christian Nation"'. 27 October 2022. www.pewresearch.org/religion/2022/10/27/45-of-americans-say-u-s-should-be-a-christian-nation/
Straughn, Jeremy Brooke and Scott L. Feld. 2010. 'America as a "Christian Nation"? Understanding Religious Boundaries of National Identity in the United States'. *Sociology of Religion* 71 (3): 280–306.
Whitehead, Andrew L., and Samuel L. Perry. 2022. *Taking America Back for God: Christian Nationalism in the United States*. New York: Oxford University Press.
Witte, John Jr. 2006. 'Facts and Fictions about the History of Separation of Church and State'. *Journal of Church & State* 48: 15–45.

4

Constitutional Identity and Constitutional Revolution

Stephen Gardbaum

In his seminal volume *Constitutional Identity* (Jacobsohn 2010), Gary Jacobsohn succeeded, along with Michel Rosenfeld's contemporaneous monograph (Rosenfeld 2009), in promoting this concept to the top tier in constitutional theory. By subjecting this previously vague, amorphous, and loosely used term to rigorous analytical and comparative scrutiny, Jacobsohn revealed its centrality in constitutional thought and practice. Now, a decade later, along with his co-author Yaniv Roznai, Jacobsohn has made a similarly pathbreaking contribution with the concept of constitutional revolution (Jacobsohn and Roznai 2020).

A key issue that arises from considering the two books alongside each other is the relationship between the two concepts. Jacobsohn and Roznai acknowledge this, referring to the 'intriguing association between [constitutional] identity and revolution' (Jacobsohn and Roznai 2020, 106) and do some important and interesting preliminary work in explicating how the two relate to each other. In this chapter, my aim is to further explore this relationship, especially as it illuminates the nature and parameters of constitutional identity. In particular, I address the issues of (1) how and to what extent constitutional revolutions impact constitutional identity, (2) whether they do so in a single or uniform way, and (3) the implications of the broadening of the concept of constitutional revolution in the recent book for the possibility (acknowledged in the first) of the 'substitution of one constitutional identity for another' (Jacobsohn 2010, 49).

4.1 CONSTITUTIONAL IDENTITY

For current purposes, I wish to focus on just three of the many important and fascinating elements of the earlier book. The first is why constitutional identity should become, or be understood as, a central concept in constitutional theory. Although Jacobsohn makes this claim and it permeates the entire project, as far as I am aware he does not explicitly make the case for it or explain why in so many words. Rather, this case is left somewhat implicit, but it seems to me that there are two major reasons, which reflect and express the twin dimensions of the concept as he elucidates it.

One of these reasons is that each constitutionalist system has its own separate and distinct constitutional identity which reflects its particular combination of historical experience, founding ideals, internal and external disharmonies, ordinary politics, evolution, and commitments to the future, regardless of textual commonalities. In this way, constitutional identity rejects the notion of 'generic constitutionalism', based on parchment borrowings or impositions, and affirms the difference side of the sameness–difference methodological divide in comparative law (e.g., Dannemann 2012). Accordingly, the nature and components of constitutional identity ought to be a major focus of theoretical work in constitutional studies and the subject matter of comparative constitutional law is significantly constitutional identities; it is, or should be, what we compare.

The other reason is that constitutional identity is itself central to the key issue of constitutional change and transformation, however brought about. Such change, and especially radical change, is always to or within a particular identity; constitutional identity is *what* changes as a result. These two reasons reflect the twin dimensions of the concept of constitutional identity as Jacobsohn sees it: the distinctness or separateness of each identity (synchronic) and the nature of this identity over time (diachronic).

The second element I wish to highlight is that Jacobsohn appears generally to accept the distinction between national identity and constitutional identity, in that the former is 'rooted more in extra-constitutional factors such as religion and culture than in the language of a legal document' (Jacobsohn 2010, 9) and to reject the 'more encompassing Aristotelian notion of a constitution' (Jacobsohn 2010, 9), which conflates 'the identity of the state with the substance of the constitution…' (Jacobsohn 2010, 8). A country's national identity is continuous through constitutional regime change, even though there are certain specific situations – including 'where the express purpose of the constitution is to separate the future from the past in ways that will have transformative effects on social behavior' – in which 'the distinction between national and constitutional identities is difficult to sustain' (Jacobsohn 2010, 9–10).

The final element of the first book I want to underscore here is the central and recurring framing reference to Lincoln's distinction from his First Inauguration between the people's 'constitutional right' to formally amend the constitution and system of government and their 'revolutionary right' to overthrow it (Jacobsohn 2010, 49, 16, 105, 112). Jacobsohn states that:

> When this [the revolutionary] option is exercised there is no doubt that the goal sought is substitution of one constitutional identity for another (assuming the post-revolutionary regime is a constitutionalist one); less certain is whether the constitutional process can be legitimately used to effect such a change, and whether there are implicit substantive limits to change achieved through procedures enumerated in the document. (Jacobsohn 2010, 16)

Here, in the first book, Jacobsohn already anticipates the 'revolutionary-identity relationship' referenced in the second (Jacobsohn and Roznai 2020, 145). In the remainder of this chapter, I wish to bring these three elements together by exploring how the later focused study on the concept of the constitutional revolution addresses this 'less certain' question, what remains (if anything) of the distinction between the constitutional and revolutionary options, and how it changes or complicates the notion of a new constitutional identity.

4.2 CONSTITUTIONAL REVOLUTION

The overall thesis of the second book is, in many ways, to reject – or at least narrow – the difference between these two Lincolnian options. For it argues that constitutional revolutions span the two and are not limited to the classic 'revolutionary option' of overthrowing the regime by means of an illegal (and usually violent) generic political revolution as an act of the people's constituent power. Rather, conceptually, constitutional revolutions are defined by the extent of change, a paradigm shift in the experience of constitutionalism, and not by how they are brought about (Jacobsohn and Roznai 2020, 19). Accordingly, constitutional revolutions may be, and often are, the result of legal acts, including popular exercise of the 'constitutional option' and change carried out by the peoples' constituted organs of government. Thus, (1) formal amendments to an existing constitution, whether involving direct citizen participation (as in Ireland between 2015 and 2018)[1] or voted on only by elected representatives (as in Hungary in 1989), (2) replacing a constitution through the formal amendment process (as in Hungary in 2011), or (3) transformative judicial interpretation (Israel in 1995), can each result in a constitutional revolution. In the authors' view, both of Lincoln's options can produce the degree of change necessary for a constitutional revolution to take place. In this understanding, political revolutions (resulting in constitutionalist regimes) are one sub-type of the broader concept.

Now, for what it is worth, I continue to think that constitutional revolutions and political revolutions resulting in constitutionalist regimes (what I have referred to as 'revolutionary constitutionalism') are qualitatively different phenomena, even though they can overlap in that both may take place during the same historical event (Gardbaum 2017).[2] So, to call the American or French Revolutions constitutional revolutions is to significantly understate or mis-state what they were. Both may have involved constitutional revolutions, but they were not limited to this or most accurately described as such. The Israeli constitutional revolution of 1995 or the UK one of 1998 are simply not the same type of phenomenon as the Romanian revolution of 1991 or the Tunisian of 2011. The New Deal constitutional revolution

---

[1] For some of the details, see Jacobsohn and Roznai 2020, 254.
[2] Gardbaum 2017, 178–181 includes a discussion of the difference between the two concepts.

and the American Revolution are not accurately or usefully categorized as the same type of event, even though both involved radical legal change.

But the primary question I wish to explore here is what the implications of this broadening of the concept of constitutional revolution are for the notion of the 'substitution of one constitutional identity for another' (Jacobsohn 2010, 16). Is the possibility of a new constitutional identity still limited to the first, revolutionary option or can this be the aim or result of any constitutional revolution, however brought about? Indeed, does the very possibility of a new constitutional identity still exist in, and after, the second book? If not, is this a problem or a significant loss?

Constitutional Revolution is ambiguous on this issue. Unlike *Constitutional Identity*, it does not, to the best of my knowledge, ever refer to a 'new' or 'substituted' identity but rather always to a 'changed' or 'transformed' one. Once again, the association between constitutional identity and revolution is made clear, as the authors state that a constitutional revolution necessarily involves a 'discernible transformation in the substance of a polity's constitutional identity' (Jacobsohn and Roznai 2020, 37), that 'a constitutional revolution is accompanied by critical changes in constitutional identity' (Jacobsohn and Roznai 2020, 15) and that 'a constitutional revolution is a hinge moment in the development of [this] constitutional identity' (Jacobsohn and Roznai 2020, 55). But it is unclear whether such change, transformation, or development may ever include the break and discontinuity of a *new* constitutional identity and, if so, whether in principle any type of, or route to, constitutional revolution may have this result.

If anything, the evidence appears to point towards the very possibility of a new constitutional identity disappearing altogether in *Constitutional Revolution*, insofar as the discussion of the first concept in this book ties it inextricably (although, of course, not exclusively) to the constitutional past. So, notwithstanding the significant change: 'Its [a constitution's] identity, even when undergoing significant transformation, will remain tethered to past conflicts that do not dissipate with the implementation of novel constitutional arrangements' (Jacobsohn and Roznai 2020, 45). Also, 'a constitutional identity is an evolving phenomenon rooted in a disharmony often manifest in the tension between commitments expressive of a nation's past and the determination of those who seek to transcend or modify it' (Jacobsohn and Roznai 2020, 55).

This constitutive, and seemingly inescapable, connection to the past also appears to draw constitutional identity closer to national identity. For just as the latter can never really be new due to its essential connection to history, and is always transformed over time but never replaced, so too does this now appear to be the case for constitutional identity. Hence, perhaps, the authors' reference to the 'national-constitutional identity' (Jacobsohn and Roznai 2020, 267). It may even be that constitutional identity is now conceived as *generally* part of national identity, a sub-set of it, rather than only exceptionally – in certain specific scenarios like the Kemalist constitution in Turkey.

In sum, *Constitutional Revolution* appears to resist the notion of a new constitutional identity as part of its attempt to reject, or reduce the difference between, the two Lincolnian options. By building up the 'constitutional option' as part of the broader concept of a constitutional revolution, the 'revolutionary option' and its seemingly distinctive aspects – including aiming at a new constitutional identity – are downgraded as a sub-type within the overall species.

4.3 DOES THIS MATTER?

If I am correct that *Constitutional Revolution* exhibits scepticism about the possibility of a new constitutional identity, is this a problem? Does the distinction between a new or substituted constitutional identity on the one hand, and a transformed or changed one on the other, matter for any relevant purposes? Is this merely splitting hairs?

I believe that achieving a new constitutional identity is the best way to understand certain constitutional revolutions, especially of the 'new beginnings' (Ackerman 1997) variety, so that we do lose something by denying or rejecting this possibility. Examples would include South Africa after the end of apartheid and the coming into effect of the 1996 constitution; the new democratic Spain after the end of the Franco dictatorship; India after independence; France after 1789; and the Federal Republic of Germany in 1949. These constitutional revolutions did not result in merely a radically changed or transformed constitutional identity; this does not fully capture what they aimed at and achieved. At the same time, a radically changed or transformed constitutional identity seems to me the more precise and accurate way to understand certain other recent constitutional revolutions, such as those in Israel and the United Kingdom since the Human Rights Act 1998. To deny ourselves the possibility of a new constitutional identity, and therefore the distinction between it and a transformed one, strikes me as giving up a category that provides greater precision in describing, understanding, and comparing constitutional revolutions.

There is, moreover, no need to do so. I believe that the thesis of *Constitutional Revolution* is perfectly consistent with the idea of a new or substituted constitutional identity and does not depend on rejecting it. As some of the examples just given indicate, this idea is – like the authors' concept of constitutional revolution – about the extent of change in identity and not how it is brought about. Some 'nonrevolutionary' constitutional revolutions result in a new constitutional identity for a country; this is *not* only the effect of the revolutionary option. Others result in a lesser, but still radical change. It may perhaps be true that a greater number of successful resorts to the revolutionary option achieve a new constitutional identity than through the nonrevolutionary, but this must be discounted by their relatively low success rate.

Here I think it may be helpful to introduce a third relevant type of identity in addition to national and constitutional identity. This is legal identity or culture:

roughly the way a country conceptualizes and experiences law (as well as the distinction between law and politics), organizes its legal concepts, system, institutions, and education, understands and incorporates legal history and change, and makes legal arguments (Roux 2018). Legal identity is narrower than both national and constitutional identity, as it has more specialized concerns, institutions, and personnel. On a spectrum running from breadth of relevant factors to narrowness, legal identity would occupy the opposite pole from national identity, with constitutional identity in between. But legal identity is more like national than constitutional identity in being relatively impervious to replacement and sits closer to it on this second spectrum. Thus, while I have posited that South Africa and Germany acquired new constitutional identities as a result of the constitutional revolutions underlying their current regimes, their legal identities or cultures retained far greater continuity with the past. Of course, constitutional and legal identity overlap, but they are not the same.

Accordingly, I think we can say the following about the 'identity-revolution relationship' (Jacobsohn and Roznai 2020, 145). The two seminal volumes develop illuminating and consistent accounts of the two concepts, and my hope is that this chapter brings them into greater equipoise. Constitutional revolutions always result in radical change to constitutional identity. Some constitutional revolutions, including some that do not involve a political revolution, result in a new or substituted constitutional identity while others transform their existing and continuing one. But like the concept of constitutional revolution itself, this is a matter of the extent of the change and not how it is brought about. In this way, constitutional identity is generally different from national (and, to a slightly lesser extent, legal) identity in that replacement, while still relatively unusual, is a conceptual and practical possibility.

Finally, we are in a position to answer the 'less certain' question raised in *Constitutional Identity* as to whether 'the constitutional process can be legitimately used to effect ... the substitution of one constitutional identity for another' (Jacobsohn 2010, 16). Subject to the authors' account in the new book of how the people may legitimize a constitutional revolution instigated by the constituted powers, the answer is: yes. Constitutional revolutions of all types, and not only the revolutionary overthrow sub-type, may result in a new constitutional identity. Such a new identity still has some engagement with the past – it is not a completely foreign country – but it is essentially an engagement of contrast and rejection rather than of continuity, development, and evolution. It is not the same constitutional order.

In sum, in downplaying the sharp break as an essential or defining feature of constitutional revolutions, the second book appears to do the same for constitutional identity. But, just as Jacobsohn and Roznai's insights and analysis need not deny that some constitutional revolutions do involve a sharp break with the past, so too with constitutional identity.

REFERENCES

Ackerman, Bruce. 1997. 'The Rise of World Constitutionalism'. *Virginia Law Review* 83: 771–797.
Dannemann, Gerhard. 2012. 'Comparative Law: Study of Similarities or Differences?' In *The Oxford Handbook of Comparative Law*, edited by Mathias Reimann and Reinhard Zimmermann, 383–420. Oxford: Oxford University Press.
Gardbaum, Stephen. 2017. 'Revolutionary Constitutionalism'. *International Journal of Constitutional Law* 15: 173–200.
Jacobsohn, Gary. 2010. *Constitutional Identity*. Cambridge: Harvard University Press.
Jacobsohn, Gary, and Yaniv Roznai. 2020. *Constitutional Revolution*. New Haven: Yale University Press.
Rosenfeld, Michel. 2009. *The Identity of the Constitutional Subject: Selfhood, Citizenship, Culture and Community*. Philadelphia: Routledge.
Roux, Theunis. 2018. *The Politico-Legal Dynamics of Judicial Review: A Comparative Analysis*. Cambridge: Cambridge University Press.

5

The Death of Constituent Power

Victor Ferreres Comella

INTRODUCTION

In this essay, I want to suggest that constitutional theory should abandon the picture it has traditionally drawn regarding constituent power. The idea that there exists a sovereign people, endowed with the unlimited power to enact a constitution whenever and however it wishes, should be rejected, for it makes no sense for both conceptual and normative reasons. In particular, a constitutional theory committed to liberal and democratic principles is at war with the notion that the people operate under no normative constraints when they originate a constitution.

The conception that insists on the normative omnipotence of the people as holders of constituent power has traditionally captured the imagination of scholars and politicians alike. Its origins can be traced back to an influential pamphlet by Emmanuel-Joseph Sieyès (1748–1836), "What is the Third Estate," published in January 1789 just before the outbreak of the French Revolution (Sieyès 2003, 133–144). The piece was meant to serve the revolutionary cause of the third estate comprising common citizens. To grasp the historical context of the work, we should recall that the representatives of the third estate gathering in Versailles in 1789 decided to assume the authority to speak for the nation as a whole. On the strength of this assumption, they resolved to enact a new constitution without observing the fundamental rules of the *ancien régime*. In particular, they disregarded the existing division of society into three orders (the clergy, the nobility, and the common people). A Declaration of the Rights of Man and of the Citizen was soon proclaimed by the national assembly, and a constitution was finally adopted in 1791. Sieyès' theory on the *pouvoir constituant* sought to justify the revolutionary actions of the constitutional framers. He contended that the nation carries constituent power, a power that is not subject to any positive law. "There is no reason to be afraid of repeating the fact," he wrote, "that a nation is independent of all forms and, however it may will, it is enough for its will to be made known for all positive law to fall silent in its presence, because it is the source and supreme master of all positive law" (Sieyès 2003, 138).

Similar ideas had been voiced in America around that time. The United States Constitution of 1787 was not enacted into law in accordance with the procedures stipulated in the Articles of Confederation, which required approval by the legislatures of all member states. Instead, the framers decided that the ratification of the Constitution by special constitutional conventions in nine states would be sufficient. By way of defense, the framers appealed to the authority of the people, whose will would be expressed in such conventions. In Federalist No. 40, for example, James Madison argued that "in all great changes of established governments, forms ought to give way to substance" (Hamilton et al. 2000, 253). A rigid adherence to forms "would render nominal and nugatory the transcendent and precious right of the people," announced in the Declaration of Independence, "to abolish or alter their governments as to them shall seem most likely to effect their safety and happiness." Ultimately, what matters is the will of the people: as the new constitution "was to be submitted *to the people themselves*, the disapprobation of this supreme body would destroy it forever; its approbation blot out antecedent errors and irregularities" (Hamilton et al. 2000, 253–254).[1]

The notion that the people possess an unbounded constitution-making power was later invoked by political movements challenging constitutional orders in many countries. Spreading democracy seemed to require the acceptance of this idea.

This idea exhibits serious flaws, however, as I will argue next.

5.1 MORAL CONSTRAINTS ON CONSTITUENT POWER

Let us start with the moral constraints on constituent power. If one is committed to the principles of political morality animating liberal democracies, one must reject the proposition that morality falls silent when a constitution is being framed. Constituent power cannot be understood to occupy a morally indifferent space. Indeed, if we believe that principles of political morality require the state to behave in a certain manner, those principles must do significant work when a constitution designed to govern the state is being discussed.

Interestingly, Sieyès himself explicitly mentioned natural law and morality as a limit on constituent power. "Prior to the nation and above the nation there is only natural law," he wrote (Sieyès 2003, 136). "Morality," he maintained, "is what should regulate all the ties binding men to one another, both in terms of their individual interests and their common or social interest" (Sieyès 2003, 133–134). Sieyès, after all, was a child of the Enlightenment. Liberal principles were part of the basic morality he endorsed. Constitutions at that time, moreover, were conceptually linked to the recognition of fundamental rights and the doctrine of the separation of powers. This connection was explicitly asserted in Article 16 of the French Declaration of the Rights of Man and of the Citizen of 1789, which announced that "any society in

---

[1] Emphasis in the original. For a commentary on Federalist No. 40, see Levinson 2015, 149–151.

which no provision is made for guaranteeing rights or for the separation of powers, has no Constitution."

This Enlightenment natural law tradition led Sieyès and many others to acknowledge that the constituent power of the nation was not unfettered from a moral point of view. Constituent power was indeed bound by political morality.[2] It was only regarding positive law that constituent power could be said to be unlimited, an issue we will discuss later.

Natural law ideas resonate in liberal-democratic constitutions around the world, even if their foundation and specific articulation have changed. The belief in human dignity and the inherent rights of the person is widely shared in constitutional democracies. As Aharon Barak has documented, the vast majority of constitutions expressly mention human dignity (Barak 2015, 49–65). Human dignity appears in constitutional texts as a value to be acknowledged. Its recognition is not supposed to be a matter of choice.

Political philosophers elaborating upon the liberal-democratic tradition have also insisted on the need for constitutions to observe certain principles. John Rawls, for example, distinguishes several stages for constructing political rules. The principles of justice agreed upon by representatives placed in the original position, acting behind a veil of ignorance, are to constrain the actions of constitutional framers subsequently asked to hammer out the basic rules for the polity (Rawls 1971, 195–201). There is no talk here about a morally untrammeled constituent power.

It is certainly true that theories of justice cannot be implemented without a theory of authority, as Jeremy Waldron has emphasized (Waldron 1999). We may agree on certain substantive principles derived from the liberal-democratic normative scheme, but we still face the question as to the best institutional arrangements to specify and secure those principles. We may embrace freedom of speech, say, but this does not yet tell us whether statutes enacted by parliament should be subject to judicial scrutiny on freedom of speech grounds. To this end, we need to engage in an argument about the respective strengths and weaknesses of parliaments and courts when it comes to protecting freedom of speech. Similarly, we need to enter a larger conversation regarding the distribution of authority between the constitutional framers, the ordinary legislature, the courts, and the institutions empowered to amend the constitution. We might conclude, for instance, that under certain conditions of participation and deliberation, the framers of a constitution should have the last word on principles of justice, the consequence being that courts should not be authorized to check the validity of constitutional provisions. But the fact that there may be powerful reasons not to subject a constitution to judicial review in the name of fundamental principles does not entail the consequence, of course, that constituent power is free to disregard them.

---

[2] For a similar point, Roznai 2021, 1391.

It is important to emphasize a particular respect in which constituent power must be deemed to be limited. In a liberal democracy, constituent power must be taken to be one power among others. Such power manifests itself in the enactment of a constitution. It does not go beyond that. It is not entitled, therefore, to interfere with the legislative, executive, and judicial powers, to follow Montesquieu's famous tripartite classification. Indeed, the fact that constituent power ranks higher than ordinary powers does not mean that the former can absorb the latter. Constituent power designs the bodies that will be trusted with the legislative, executive, and judicial functions. We can thus say that these ordinary powers "flow" from constituent power. But they do so, not because they were originally part of constituent power, but because it is the task of constituent power to set up the organization of the state, which entails distributing those ordinary powers among various bodies.

Of course, it would be possible to envisage an assembly wielding all the powers – not only constituent power but all the rest. The assembly would thus be authorized to write a constitution, enact ordinary laws, hear cases as a court of justice, enforce the laws as if it were the executive branch, supply public services as the administration does, etc. This concentration of all powers in a single organ would be a clear breach of the liberal principle of the separation of powers. The distinction between constituent power and constituted powers is itself a manifestation of that principle. Constituent power cannot exercise the powers it institutes. Its task is simply to institute them (Carré de Malberg 2004, 510).[3]

It is interesting to observe, in this connection, that Jean-Jacques Rousseau tied his notion of the general will of the people to the enactment of general and abstract laws. "When I say that the province of the law is always general, I mean that the law considers all subjects collectively and all actions in the abstract; it does not consider any individual man or any specific action," he wrote (Rousseau 1968, 81–82). Objectivity disappears, he observed, when a particular fact or right is being dealt with on a matter that has not been settled by an earlier general rule. This must also be true of constitutional laws ("political laws" or "fundamental laws," as he calls them), which are a type of law, according to Rousseau. This being the case, it would be incoherent for the institution that expresses the general will of the people at the constitutional level to be conferred the additional authority to adjudicate individual disputes.

We can conclude from all this that the unrestricted nature of constituent power cannot plausibly be understood to refer to principles of political morality.

---

[3] Carré de Malberg maintained that the idea that a constitutional assembly can concentrate all the powers is "one of the biggest mistakes committed in France since 1789," (Carré de Malberg 2004, 549). Interestingly, he argued that because only the nation (an abstract entity) is sovereign, no institution can claim to enjoy sovereign power. A constitutional assembly is one institution among many, in spite of the relevance of its mission. The assembly cannot hold all the powers as if it were the nation itself (Carré de Malberg 2004, 550–551). For a discussion of this issue with examples drawn from recent constitutional assemblies, see Colón-Ríos 2020, 226–261.

Is the omnipotence of constituent power a question of legal rules, then? As I will argue next, it is not plausible to maintain that constituent power works out its will in a sphere that is isolated from positive law. Positive law is everywhere, even in the space the nation occupies when it originates a constitution.

5.2 CONSTITUENT POWER AND POSITIVE LAW

To begin with, we need to confront the question of who belongs to the group of people wielding the power to draft a constitution? Sieyès, for example, assumed that only citizens are part of the group; foreigners are to be excluded (Sieyès 2003, 107). We may think there is a moral justification for this restriction, but we obviously need legal rules to specify who possesses the nationality of a given state. There is nothing natural about nationality.

Furthermore, not all citizens can be entitled to participate in constitutional politics (or in ordinary politics, for that matter). There are sound reasons, for instance, for not allowing minors to vote. The question, then, is who counts as a minor, and legal rules must enter the picture to provide an answer, as Sieyès acknowledged (Sieyès 2003, 107).

And what happens when the majority of the population living in a particular territory within the state wishes to secede from it and form a separate state? Is secession authorized? Constitutional law and international law have a part to play in providing an answer to this question. Invoking the sovereignty of the people to decide this issue leads nowhere. Who is the relevant people for purposes of the secession problem? How do we demarcate the relevant boundaries?

Once we have identified the collection of individuals who count as the group we call "the people," procedures are required for the group to convey its will on the constitutional stage. Sieyès suggested that citizens should elect extraordinary representatives, endowed with a specific mandate to frame the constitution. After deliberating on the matter, the vote of the majority of representatives ought to prevail. Sieyès appealed to first principles to justify the superiority of this scheme to alternative ones. There is much to be said, indeed, for the introduction of a degree of specialization in political functions, given the advantages of the division of labor. And there is certainly an argument in favor of majority rule as a voting protocol, an argument based on the principle of equality (and on status quo neutrality), although we may have good grounds to deviate from that rule when a constitution is being discussed. To enhance the stability of the constitution, we may be justified in forcing representatives to seek a broader consensus and meet a supermajority threshold. Furthermore, we may want to submit the constitution to the people for their ratification in a referendum, to strengthen its legitimacy. In any event, whatever arrangements we choose, we must resort to positive law to translate individual votes into collective decisions in accordance with specific electoral and parliamentary procedures.

There is another important set of legal rules operating as constraints on constituent power: those pertaining to international law. The constitution can be regarded as the supreme law of the land, but it can only regulate the sphere of matters that international law accords to each individual state. Constituent power is not beyond the reach of international law. It's a cardinal principle of international law, moreover, that a state cannot invoke provisions of its internal law as justification for its failure to perform a treaty, as article 27 of the Vienna Convention on the Law of Treaties of 1969 proclaims. Domestic constitutions are, of course, part of internal law as far as this principle is concerned.

It should also be noted that citizens are expected to obey the constitution, which is legally binding. How is it possible for the people to be bound by a document they themselves are supposed to have enacted? How can a people bind itself? The answer is that only by way of rules is this possible. As H. L. A. Hart explained, we need to distinguish between citizens acting in their official capacity (as members of the body entitled to enact a constitution) on the one hand, and citizens acting in their private capacity on the other. Citizens in the latter capacity are to obey the constitution enacted by citizens acting in the former capacity. But this distinction between the two capacities requires the existence of legal rules establishing the conditions under which the pertinent official capacity can be exercised (Hart 1961, 74, 78).

So we cannot really dispense with positive law altogether. Constituent power is in the hands of the nation, but the nation is a legal construction. There is no nation inhabiting the state of nature. Only positive law brings the nation into existence for constitutional purposes. And only positive law can allow for the formation and manifestation of the collective will of the nation.

Now, it is true that the legal rules effectively employed to channel the framing of a new constitution may imply a break with earlier law. Such was the case in France in 1789, and in the United States in 1787, to return to the two examples mentioned above. Indeed, a good number of constitutions in different parts of the world were not enacted in compliance with the procedures of constitutional amendment or revision stipulated in the governing constitutions. Sometimes the breach was justified, due to the excessive difficulty of the regular procedures, while other times it was not. The gravity of the breach, moreover, varied. In some cases, only a minor irregularity was committed, while in other instances the most basic norms of the constitutional order were infringed upon. Such legal infractions, however, did not mean the total suspension of the legal system. A new constitution cannot result from actions that are totally detached from the law. As Andrew Arato has argued, legal rules may be violated during the constitution-making process, but it is not possible to violate all of them. A legal vacuum is an impossibility (Arato 2016, 20–21).

After all, the state whose political structure is being altered by means of a new constitutional charter is already there. For a state to exist, a body of legal rules organizing the state must have previously emerged. There is no state without laws. It is true that, in the context of historical processes leading to the establishment of federations, the federal government is a new entity brought to life by means of the constitution. But the political units that get together to form the federation must already exist, and this necessitates the organizing function of positive law.

In sum, the idea that the constituent power of the people is disconnected from positive law is not tenable.

5.3 CONSTITUENT POWER AS A USEFUL METAPHOR

Suppose we agree that the constituent power of the people must be understood to be bound by principles of political morality, and that a core of positive law is needed to make it possible for a nation to exercise that power. Advocates of Sieyès might still rely on pragmatic grounds to rescue the theory that postulates the existence of a sovereign people holding an unlimited constituent power. They could argue that the theory can serve useful purposes on a rhetorical level.

The theory, in particular, might help reinforce the democratic case in favor of certain institutional arrangements we may have good reason to establish and maintain. Even if there are independent normative justifications for such arrangements, the theory of constituent power may be thought to inject a measure of democratic legitimacy into such arrangements to hedge them against potential objections.

Take the issue of judicial review of legislation, for example. Is it acceptable for courts to be given the authority to test the validity of legislation against constitutional norms? A rich debate has developed concerning the democratic deficit of judicial review, as we all know. Arguably, there are sound grounds to support this institution, to better guarantee certain rights and values which may be infringed upon by transient ordinary majorities in parliament. This instrumental justification may look insufficient to some people, however. To alleviate democratic qualms, we may want to secure a stronger democratic warrant for courts to have the power to review laws.

Here enters the theory of the unlimited constituent power of the people. The constitution, we may want to say, documents the will of the nation. Ordinary statutes, in contrast, are the product of legislative bodies, made up of ordinary representatives. If we emphasize the connection between the constitution and popular will, on the one hand, and de-emphasize the link between ordinary statutes and popular will, on the other, judicial review appears to be democratically acceptable. Indeed, when courts strike down an ordinary statute, they can be taken to be preserving the will of the sovereign people against erosion by the legally limited legislative body. Of course courts may make mistakes when interpreting the meaning of the constitutional text, but the important point is that judges are not expected to restrain popular will in exercising legislative review but instead to preserve it.

This argument figures in the Federalist Papers, for example. In Federalist No.78, Alexander Hamilton defends judicial review against the charge that it implies the superiority of the judicial role to the legislative power. According to Hamilton, judicial review "only supposes that the power of the people is superior to both; and that where the will of the legislature, declared in its statutes, stands in opposition to that of the people, declared in the Constitution, the judges ought to be governed by the latter rather than the former" (Hamilton et al., 499). Hamilton acknowledges that sometimes the law that breaches the constitution has been "instigated by the major voice in the community," in spite of which courts should not defer to the legislature. The constitution is still the supreme law: "until the people have, by some solemn and authoritative act, annulled or changed the established form, it is binding upon themselves collectively, as well as individually" (Hamilton et al., 501). The Supreme Court of the United States followed in Hamilton's steps when it ruled in 1803 that the judiciary had the power to disregard unconstitutional laws.[4] The Court portrayed the constitution as the fundamental law laid down by the sovereign people. Judges safeguard the will of the people when they verify the conformity of legislation to the constitution. This democratic understanding of judicial review has been worked out by scholars in recent decades. According to Bruce Ackerman, for instance, when courts strike down a law on constitutional grounds they seek to preserve the considered judgments of the people, expressed in rare "constitutional moments," against erosion by the actions of political representatives in normal times (Ackerman 1991, 261–265).

It is worthy of note that Sieyès was one of the few voices in France sponsoring the introduction of a mechanism for constitutional review of legislation. In 1795, he proposed the institution of a "constitutional jury," a council of wise men selected by the national assembly to check the validity of laws against constitutional precepts (Bredin 1988, 366–369). His proposal was rejected at that time, but it clearly influenced the establishment of a *Sénat conservateur* as the guardian of the constitution in 1799 (Bredin 1988, 476–477, 481–482). Sieyès was a pioneer in this regard. We must remember that it took a long historical period of time for most European countries to allow courts – whether ordinary courts or specialized constitutional tribunals – to control statutes for their constitutional validity.[5]

A related area where appealing to the unlimited *pouvoir constituant* of the sovereign people can help buttress particular institutional arrangements concerns constitutional amendment. Constitutions typically lay down specific procedures for their amendment that are more burdensome than those employed to enact and modify ordinary statutes. Constitutional change may require the approval of a parliamentary supermajority, for example, or the holding of a specific constitutional assembly, or ratification by the people in a referendum.

A case can be built in favor of some measure of constitutional rigidity to guarantee political stability and safeguard rights against legislative override by bare majorities

---

[4] *Marbury v. Madison* 5 U. S. (1 Cranch) 137 (1803).
[5] On the reasons for the reluctance in Europe to embrace judicial review of legislation as practiced in the United States, see Ferreres Comella 2009.

in parliament. This instrumental justification, however, may be considered insufficient to answer democratic worries. At this juncture, an argumentative strategy drawing inspiration from Sieyès can be helpful. It may insist that the amendment power is a legally "constituted" governmental power. All the organs of the state, including those with the ability to alter the constitution, are constitutional creatures of the people. They must accordingly respect the legal bounds set out by the latter. Indeed, if the people have decided that gathering the votes of a simple majority in parliament is not sufficient to modify the constitutional text, democracy requires us to respect that choice.[6]

Constitutions sometimes go further and place certain principles or institutions or rules beyond the reach of the amendment power. An explicit "intangibility or eternity clause" may name certain things that can never be changed. Alternatively, interpreters may read into the constitutional text implicit limitations on the amendment power. A number of basic principles, for example, may be regarded to be so fundamental to the constitution's identity that they are taken to be absolutely entrenched.[7]

Again, there may be instrumental reasons grounding the decision to place substantive restrictions on amendments. These restrictions are open to democratic challenges, however. When facing such challenges, it may be useful to invoke the constituent power of the sovereign people. We can point out, indeed, that there is nothing undemocratic in ensuring observance of the limitations laid down by the constitution. It is the sovereign people, the fountain of all powers, that has created the specific body tasked with the constitutional amendment function. If the people have decided to set out substantive limitations on the amendment power, democracy prescribes that we should comply with that decision.

So the doctrine that assigns an unlimited power to the people in the constitutional arena offers rhetorical resources we can draw on for purposes of building a democratic defense of particular institutional arrangements we may wish to support, even if we believe we already have independent reasons in justification of such arrangements.

On the other hand, the doctrine of the *pouvoir constituant* has its downsides. For one thing, it falsely assumes the existence of a homogeneous people sharing a consistent set of political convictions that get recorded in a constitutional document. By neglecting the existence of rules that make it possible for a people to be constructed as a political unit and for its will to be formed and expressed, the theory tends to present a distorted account of the political realities of constitution-making processes. As a matter of fact, the individuals who make up the political community

---

[6] On the legally constrained nature of the amendment power, see Roznai 2017 and Albert 2019.
[7] In some countries, the judiciary has exercised the power to review the validity of amendments on substantive grounds. For a discussion of this issue, with rich comparative law references, see Jacobsohn 2010.

are widely divergent, and many tensions arise among them. When a constitution is being written, no deep political and social harmony emerges. Important frictions appear. Not surprisingly, the rules and principles finally inserted in the constitutional charter form a complex normative scheme. As Gary Jacobsohn has shown, a constitution can mirror and contribute to the formation and transformation of the political identity of a given society, but this identity is the result of profound disharmonies of various kinds (Jacobsohn 2010).

Another pragmatic disadvantage relates to the task of designing the procedures of constitutional amendment. It is hard, indeed, to define the appropriate avenues for future constitutional change in light of the social and political conditions of a given country. How difficult should it be to alter the constitution? What mechanisms should be required to amend it? Shaping the amendment rules is no easy endeavor. Now, it would be wrong for the framers to relativize the importance of this institutional choice by pointing out that, after all, the sovereign nation can always enter the historical stage to pronounce its will without being bound by existing constitutional rules. The constitutional enterprise cannot succeed if the framers assume the existence of this mysterious subject, entitled to appear at any moment to destroy the constitutional order and start things from scratch. Why worry about amendment rules if constituent power can always impose its will in any manner it chooses?

Of course, the amendment rules may need to be disregarded if they become dysfunctional at extraordinary political moments. But we should count such instances of rupture as failures of the constitutional project, not as the way things are supposed to be in a world inhabited by an omnipotent people. As the European Commission for Democracy through Law (Venice Commission) has declared, the general principle should be stressed that "any major constitutional change should preferably be done according to the prescribed formal amendment procedures."[8] In democratic regimes, in particular, violations of amendment procedures are difficult to justify. As Sergio Verdugo argues, it is understandable that political actors may want to appeal to the unconstrained power of the people when the regime they wish to alter is a tyrannical one. In contrast, "there are fewer reasons to invoke the unconstrained power of the people if the system that we are trying to change already has a reasonable well-functioning democracy" (Verdugo 2023, 33).

It would be a mistake, moreover, to believe that major constitutional changes can only be brought about by way of legal breaches. As Gary Jacobsohn and Yaniv Roznai have explained with many examples drawn from different parts of the world, legal continuity is compatible with the implementation of constitutional transformations of great magnitude. Legal continuity does not entail regime continuity (Jacobsohn and Roznai 2020, 98).

---

[8] See "Report on Constitutional Amendment," adopted by the Venice Commission on 11–12 December 2009, para. 22.

5.4 CONSTITUENT POWER AND THE DEATH OF GOD

There is an obvious parallelism between the traditional doctrine of the unlimited constituent power of the people and theological views.[9] According to religious understandings, God is omnipotent. He freely decides to create the world and chooses the laws the world will be subject to. God can suspend the operation of those laws, through miracles. And He could extinguish them: He could destroy the world and make a new one governed by different laws if He so willed.

A similar image is offered in the constitutional domain through the doctrine of the *pouvoir constituant*. The sovereign nation, it is held, can freely decide to create the governmental structure of the state. It lays down the constitutional rules by which the state must abide, including the rules on constitutional amendment. Because of its sovereignty, the nation can always come back to the political stage and originate a new constitution, disregarding the extant rules governing legal change.

In theological thought, moreover, postulating the existence of an infinite God is important to emphasize the finite nature of the world. In addition, the idea of a morally and intellectually perfect God helps us stress the fallibility of human beings and their institutions. Similarly, in the realm of political thought, assuming the existence of an original, unlimited constituent power permits us to highlight, by way of contrast, the legally constrained nature of both the ordinary legislature and the body vested with the constitutional amendment power.

As noted earlier, the doctrine of the constituent power of the nation can be enlisted to contribute to the defense of constitutional rigidity and judicial review of legislation. We already have independent reasons of an instrumental kind, however, to support these institutional arrangements. Such reasons, I submit, should be deemed sufficient. We do not need to postulate the existence of a legally omnipotent people in the background, as the fountain of all laws, in order to shield those arrangements against democratic censure.

Nietzsche famously said that God is dead. Our civilization has killed God, though we are still not aware of the grave consequences of this action. Nietzsche called for the transfiguration of values. He feared we might enter a nihilist phase once we realized that the traditional source of values had been destroyed.

The theory of constituent power offered by Sieyès in "What is the third estate?" makes no sense, I have argued. A "natural" sovereign nation, operating in a world without legal rules, cannot exist. Positive law is everywhere. We should come to terms with the fact that such a natural, extra-legal nation is dead as a constitutional concept. Fortunately, we have independent grounds to support the institutions we have. Imagining the existence of an extra-legal sovereign is not necessary for

---

[9] As Carl Schmitt wrote, "all significant concepts of the modern theory of the state are secularized theological concepts." Thus, the omnipotent God becomes the omnipotent lawgiver, and the miracle in theology is like the exception in jurisprudence. Schmitt 2005, 36.

justification purposes. In the same way that we can observe the fallibility of human beings without presupposing the existence of God, we can insist on the limited character of the ordinary legislature and of the constitutional amendment power without assuming, by way of contrast, the existence of an omnipotent people that can arise at any time and make a new constitution.

This is not to deny that there may be something special in constitutional moments, in terms of the intensity and extension of popular participation. The authority of the constitution may derive in part from the democratic quality those moments display, as Bruce Ackerman has argued in the American context (Ackerman 1991). But the difference between ordinary politics and constitutional politics is one of degree, not of kind. Importantly, there are always legal rules constructing and limiting the people. A truly sovereign nation is a myth.

The natural and legally unlimited constituent power that Sieyès described in his famous pamphlet is dead. But the institutions that were historically associated with it can survive that death.[10]

REFERENCES

Ackerman, Bruce. 1991. *We the People: Foundations*. Cambridge: Harvard University Press.
Albert, Richard. 2019. *Constitutional Amendments: Making, Breaking, and Changing Constitutions*. Oxford: Oxford University Press.
Arato, Andrew. 2016. *Post Sovereign Constitution Making: Learning and Legitimacy*. Oxford: Oxford University Press.
Barak, Aharon. 2015. *Human Dignity: The Constitutional Value and the Constitutional Right*. Cambridge: Cambridge University Press.
Bredin, Jean-Denis. 1988. *Sieyès: La clé de la Révolution française*. Paris: Éditions de Fallois.
Carré de Malberg, Raymond. 2004. *Contribution à la Théorie Générale de l'État*. Paris: Dalloz.
Colón-Ríos, Joel. 2020. *Constituent Power and the Law*. Oxford: Oxford University Press.
Ferreres Comella, Victor. 2009. *Constitutional Courts and Democratic Values: A European Perspective*. New Haven: Yale University Press.
Hamilton, Alexander, John Jay, and James Madison. 2000. *The Federalist*. New York: The Modern Library.
Hart, H.L.A. 1961. *The Concept of Law*. Oxford: Oxford University Press.
Herzog, Don. 2020. *Sovereignty, RIP*. New Haven: Yale University Press.
Jacobsohn, Gary Jeffrey. 2010. *Constitutional Identity*. Cambridge: Harvard University Press.
Jacobsohn, Gary Jeffrey, and Yaniv Roznai. 2020. *Constitutional Revolution*. New Haven: Yale University Press.
Levinson, Sanford. 2015. *An Argument Open to All: Reading the Federalist in the 21st Century*. New Haven: Yale University Press.
Rawls, John. 1971. *A Theory of Justice*. Cambridge: Harvard University Press.

---

[10] My argument in this piece dovetails with Don Herzog's claim that sovereignty in the classical sense, understood as unlimited, indivisible, and unaccountable authority, does not exist in constitutional states governed by the rule of law. Believing in that kind of authority is like believing in unicorns. "Sovereignty is unicorn government." See Herzog 2020, 259.

Rousseau, Jean-Jacques. 1968. *The Social Contract*. London: Penguin.
Roznai, Yaniv. 2017. *Unconstitutional Constitutional Amendments: The Limits of Amendment Powers*. Oxford: Oxford University Press.
Roznai, Yaniv. 2021. "The Boundaries of Constituent Authority." *Connecticut Law Review* 53 (5): 1381–1408.
Schmitt, Carl. 2005. *Political Theology: Four Chapters on the Concept of Sovereignty*. Chicago: The University of Chicago Press.
Sieyès. 2003. *Political Writings*. Indianapolis/Cambridge: Hackett Publishing Company.
Verdugo, Sergio. 2023. "Is It Time to Abandon the Theory of Constituent Power?" *I.CON, International Journal of Constitutional Law* 21 (1): 14–79.
Waldron, Jeremy. 1999. *Law and Disagreement*. Oxford: Oxford University Press.

6

Constitutional Identity as a Source of Ontological Security

Joanne Wallis

In his landmark book, *Constitutional Identity*, Gary Jacobsohn challenged us to consider what we are doing 'when we invoke the particular attributes or characteristics of a constitution that enable us to identify it as a unique legal and political phenomenon' (Jacobsohn 2010, 2). He presented this as a way to 'help clarify the stakes involved in struggles between the opposing forces of constitutional preservation and change' (Jacobsohn 2010, 2). In this chapter, I consider how Jacobsohn's concept of 'constitutional identity' can 'travel' (Bal 2002) from the discipline of law to that of international relations, with a particular focus on how it can inform analyses of the 'ontological security' of states. The concept of ontological security is used to understand subjectivity and focuses on managing anxiety in the constitution of self-identity. The ontological security of states is important because when a state is ontologically insecure this can challenge its ability to do, act, and be. I illustrate my analysis with examples from my work on constitution making and peacebuilding in Timor-Leste.[1]

As will be illustrated by the Timor-Leste case, my discussion is based on the premise that a constitution – and the constitutional identity it generates – can contribute to creating a sense of ontological (in)security for a state and its people. A constitution can provide answers to fundamental existential questions and help to define a state's self-identity by narrating a sense of biographical continuity and by establishing the institutions and practices that build the routines required to create a protective cocoon for a state's citizenry. I do not overstate a state's capacity to achieve ontological security, and recognise that states always face sources of anxiety, from both within and without – as I demonstrate, constitutional identity can itself become a source of ontological insecurity. My analysis is structured around three aspects of Jacobsohn's conceptualisation of constitutional identity: that identity emerges dialogically; that both continuity and change are critical to constitutional identity; and that disharmony and contingency characterise all constitutional identities. I conclude that Jacobsohn's conceptualisation of constitutional identity provides analytical tools that build on the ontological security scholarship in valuable ways.

[1] This chapter draws on Wallis (2014).

6.1 ONTOLOGICAL SECURITY SCHOLARSHIP

The ontological security scholarship in international relations draws on concepts that have themselves travelled through disciplines, starting in psychoanalysis with the work of R.D. Laing. Laing described an ontologically secure person as one who has a 'sense of his presence in the world as a real, alive, whole, and in a temporal sense, a continuous person' (Laing 1969, 39). Laing proposed that such a person 'will encounter all the hazards of life, social, ethical, spiritual, biological from a centrally firm sense of his own and other people's reality and identity' (Laing 1969, 39). Ontological insecurity will arise when a person needs to 'deal with … anxieties and dangers' which mean that 'identity and autonomy are always in question' (Laing 1969, 42).

The concept of ontological security then travelled to sociology, where Anthony Giddens used it to understand modernity and globalisation. Giddens proposed that to be ontologically secure a person must 'possess, on the level of unconscious and practical consciousness, "answers" to fundamental existential questions which all human life in some way addresses' (Giddens 1991, 47). Those answers will come from that person's reasonably stable sense of 'self-identity', that is, their sense of who they are. A person's self-identity depends on them developing a 'consistent feeling of biographical continuity', based on a 'narrative of the self', that is, 'the story or stories by means of which self-identity is reflexively understood' (Giddens 1991, 53, 243).

Beyond conscious self-identity, a person's ontological security depends on their ability to rely on 'a social normality, a predictability, which then structures their practical everyday interactions as natural, normal, and imbued with common sense' (Croft 2012, 221). This 'natural attitude' 'brackets out questions about ourselves, others and the object-world which have to be taken for granted in order to keep on with everyday activity' (Giddens 1991, 37). Both a person's natural attitude and self-identity are constructed intersubjectively (Browning and Joenniemi 2017). At least part of a sense of social normality is built on 'trust relations' which enable individuals to establish a 'protective cocoon which "filters out" … many of the dangers which in principle threaten the integrity of the self' (Giddens 1991, 54). This sense of trust and social normality create 'temporal and spatial emotional structures' which can enable people to 'make sense of themselves and the world around them' (Kinnvall 2017, 94). This cocoon can be challenged by anxiety, a 'sense that the future will be unlike the past in ways we can hardly conceive of, much less control' (Kinnvall and Mitzen 2020, 245). To manage this anxiety, actors 'seek security and safety in the everyday', through routines and 'maintaining coherent autobiographical narratives' (Kinnvall and Mitzen 2020, 245).

The concept of ontological security then travelled to international relations, where scholars have applied it in three contexts. First, they have analysed the state as a seeker of ontological security in its relations with other states (Lupovici 2012; Mitzen 2006; Zarakol 2010). Second, they have considered how state representatives seek to fulfil particular notions of self-identity, that is, how they tell convincing stories about the self of the state through autobiographical narratives (Steele 2008; Subotic 2016). Third, they have considered how states seek ontological security within their society 'through the cultural and institutional constructs, or everyday narratives, that provide the foundation for individual and group interaction' (Kinnvall and Mitzen 2020, 246). This involves 'narrative engagement', that is, how 'members of a society engage with collective stories of what it means to inhabit a particular political entity, be it a nation-state, a resistance movement, or a political party' (Kinnvall and Mitzen 2020, 246).

6.2 CONSTITUTION MAKING IN TIMOR-LESTE

Few – if any – states or societies can claim to be ontologically secure; questioned historical narratives, conflicting societal groups, contested political institutions, and tensions with other states are common. As Timor-Leste approached formal independence in May 2002, it faced both physical and ontological insecurity. Many Timorese people faced challenges to their physical security arising from low levels of human development and unresolved societal tensions, and the Timor-Leste state had a delicate relationship with its former occupier, Indonesia. But equally challenging was a sense of ontological insecurity, whereby the nascent Timor-Leste state felt 'more unreal than real ... precariously differentiated from the rest of the world', such that its identity and autonomy were in question (Laing 1969, 42) and it did not know 'which dangers to confront and which to ignore' (Mitzen 2006, 345).

While Timor-Leste's experience of Indonesian occupation contributed to its ontological insecurity, this was solidified by the fact that 'Timor-Leste' is a relatively recent construct. For centuries Timor Island (which today consists of Timor-Leste and Indonesian West Timor) was fragmented into small settlements. Although the Portuguese arrived in the sixteenth century, they exerted little control beyond their fortifications until the early twentieth century. Even after Portugal incorporated its half of Timor Island into the Portuguese state in 1951, most Timorese only had infrequent direct contact with the colonial administration (Dunn 2003). After the April 1974 *Revoluçao do Cravos* in Portugal, tensions between Timorese political associations – stoked by an Indonesian disinformation campaign – resulted in civil war, primarily between *Frente Revolucionaria de Timor Leste Independente* (FRETILIN), which favoured immediate independence, and *União Democratica Timorense* (UDT), which advocated autonomy within Portugal before independence. The war was short, and on 28 November 1975, a victorious FRETILIN made a unilateral declaration of independence. In response, on 30 November 1975 (certain) UDT and other Timorese leaders signed the *Balibo Declaration*, which declared the territory's integration into Indonesia. Indonesia used this to justify its invasion on 7 December 1975.

In May 1998, economic collapse forced Indonesian President Muhammad Suharto to resign. His replacement agreed to hold a 'popular consultation' to decide the political future of the territory on 30 August 1999 (UN 1999).[2] After the overwhelming result in favour of independence was announced on 4 September 1999, the Indonesian military and their supporting Timorese militias engaged in a 'scorched earth' campaign (Dunn 2001). On 15 September 1999, the United Nations Security Council authorised the International Force for East Timor (InterFET) to restore peace and security.[3]

On 25 October 1999 InterFET was replaced by the United Nations Transitional Administration in East Timor (UNTAET), which was mandated to build the new state by temporarily assuming sovereign powers.[4] Although civil society groups proposed that an appointed constitutional convention engage in extensive public consultations and then draft the Constitution, the UNTAET-appointed Timorese National Council resolved that it would be made by an elected Constituent Assembly that was not mandated to consult the public. The Assembly was highly partisan, with FRETILIN securing enough seats to dominate decision-making. As the Assembly engaged in only minimal consultation, the impact of the public's views had little impact on the Constitution. This meant that the national narrative it enshrined reflected the partisan preferences of the Assembly, as did its approach to local sociopolitical practices and institutions, which were largely overlooked in favour of highly centralised formal state institutions. Consequently, the Constitution both reflected and generated ontological insecurity, particularly during the first few years of independence. This contributed to a major security crisis in 2006 that led to the collapse of the army, severely destabilised the state, and necessitated an international stabilisation force.

6.3 IDENTITY EMERGES DIALOGICALLY

Jacobsohn reminds us that a constitution 'incorporates more than the specific document itself' (Jacobsohn 2010, 4). Indeed, the '[w]ords on paper, like the physical boundaries of a state, are only an introduction to the determination of identity, which in the end incorporates the beliefs and behaviour of the governed as well as the content of their governing document' (Jacobsohn 2010, 124–125). This means that constitutional 'identity emerges *dialogically*', via an 'engagement between the core commitment(s)' of the constitution and its 'external environment' (Jacobsohn 2010, 7, 13). But that dialogical process occurs within boundaries, as 'certain paths of constitutional development are effectively foreclosed by the traditions and collective mindset of a people' (Jacobsohn 2010, 89). This means that constitutional

---

[2] UN Security Council, S/Res/1236, *On the Situation in East Timor*, 7 May 1999.
[3] UN Security Council, S/Res/1264, *On the Situation in East Timor*, 15 September 1999.
[4] UN Security Council, S/Res/1272, *On the Situation in East Timor*, 25 October 1999.

identity cannot be 'abstracted from the larger historical narrative of which it is a part' (Jacobsohn 2010, 93). Crucially, the dialogical process is intersubjective and relational, an 'interactive process in which a person develops a self in response to an environment consisting of religion, state, family and so on' (Jacobsohn 2010, 107–108).

This dialogical approach to identity formation has parallels in the scholarship on ontological security, which emphasises that 'dialogical self-narratives are linguistically constituted and reconstituted through people's relationships' (Kinnvall 2004, 748). A constitution – and the constitutional identity it generates – can help to create the self-narratives on which a state's natural attitude can rest. That is, their constitutional identity can provide answers for a citizenry to questions about their state and their national identity which can make them sufficiently ontologically secure to operate on a daily basis. This is because a constitutional identity can create institutions of governance and justice that can structure and routinise their everyday interactions and provide mechanisms to resolve their disputes. It can also build a sense of identity through its national narratives and definitions of who qualifies as a citizen that draw sufficient boundaries around a population to allow them to act as a reasonably coherent group.

This dynamic has been evident in Timor-Leste. The Timorese political system was largely treated as 'a *tabula rasa*' by UNTAET (Chesterman 2002, 64), overlooking the local sociopolitical practices that dominated the lives of the almost 90 per cent of the population who lived in rural areas. This approach was continued by the FRETILIN majority in the Constituent Assembly, which was mostly drawn from the diaspora and tended to see the recognition of local tradition and custom as 'bringing back the dark ages'.[5] This was despite a consensus in public consultations in favour of maintaining and recognising pre-existing local sociopolitical practices and institutions, particularly those based at village and hamlet levels (UNTAET 2001). Consequently, the Constitution created a highly centralised government and for the first few years after independence state administrative and justice institutions had little reach beyond the capital, Dili. This undermined the ontological security of many Timorese people, as their predictable social normality – which had already been severely disrupted by twenty-four years of Indonesian occupation as well as the violence that had preceded and followed the 1999 referendum – was not reflected in their Constitution.

But as constitutional identity emerges dialogically, during the first few years after independence a process of engagement occurred between the formal institutions created by the Constitution and the local sociopolitical practices that regulated most Timorese people's lives. This partly occurred through the judiciary deciphering the genome of the Constitution so that it made sense to people. For example, as Timorese judges replaced the international judges employed during the UNTAET

---

[5] Interview with a FRETILIN Member of Parliament, Dili, 11 May 2010.

era, many adopted an approach guided by 'legal pragmatism' (JSMP 2005a; USAID 2007)[6] by informally incorporating customary compensation payments into their sentences and by recognising out-of-court agreements reached through local justice mechanisms that were often favoured by litigants for their legitimacy and efficiency (JSMP 2005b). While this resulted in legal pluralism that could potentially have undermined the rule of law (Grenfell 2013), it was broadly within the boundaries set by the Constitution, which requires the state to 'recognise and value the norms and customs of East Timor that are not contrary to the Constitution' (s. 2(4)). In public consultations held during the constitution-making process, many Timorese expressed support for the continued use of customary law as a complement to state law, particularly in relation to local matters (UNTAET 2001).

Engagement with local sociopolitical practices also helped the dialogical development of constitutional identity in the political and administrative realms. Two years after independence the government introduced a programme of decentralisation to local sociopolitical institutions, including democratic elections for village and hamlet leaders,[7] who were empowered to 'lead activities' in a broad range of areas (Wallis 2012).[8] That dialogical process has continued, with further powers and funding gradually decentralised in the years since (Wallis 2017). Again, this occurred within boundaries set by the Constitution, which committed the state to administrative (ss. 5(1), 71(1), 137(2)) and political (s. 72(1)) decentralisation.

6.4 CONTINUITY AND CHANGE

As noted, the ontological security scholarship holds that self-identity relies on developing a consistent feeling of biographical continuity whereby a person is 'able to sustain a narrative about the self and answer questions about doing, acting, and being' (Kinnvall 2004, 746). This biographical narrative represents the 'story or stories by means of which self-identity is reflexively understood, both by the individual concerned and by others' (Steele 2008, 10).

Early ontological security scholarship in international relations emphasised the importance of the stability of this understanding of self (Mitzen 2006). This has been the most criticised aspect of the scholarship, as it assumed that 'the self already has an identity, with ontological security primarily understood in terms of the preservation and management of identity claims' (Browning and Joenniemi 2017, 40), which can have 'conservative, reactionary political effects' (Kinnvall and Mitzen 2020, 249). Therefore, some early ontological scholarship was said to reduce ontological security to identity preservation, which was problematic because 'attempts to reinforce an established identity can actually at times undermine the actor's sense of

---

[6] Interview with an international governance adviser, 10 May 2010.
[7] *Law on the Election of Suco Chiefs and Suco Councils* No. 2/2004, 2004.
[8] *Decree Law on Community Authorities* No. 5/2004, 2004, ss. 1, 2, and 6.

ontological security' (Browning and Joenniemi 2017, 32). Consequently, there have been calls to analyse 'how subjects become connected to particular identities and why they articulate identity claims in the way they do' (Browning and Joenniemi 2017, 32). This is because ontological security is 'not just a question of stability but also adaptability', that is, an 'openness towards and the ability to cope with change' in a way that does not fundamentally rupture biographical continuity and allows the person to 'locate themselves and routinise their relationships with the world' (Browning and Joenniemi 2017, 32, 35).

Jacobsohn's conceptualisation of constitutional identity offers some answers to these critiques, as while he similarly identifies that 'continuity in consciousness' is 'key to establishing the identity of a person', he goes on to recognise that 'nations, more so than individuals, have multiple and conflicting self-understandings' (Jacobsohn 2010, 104). He also acknowledges that change may be necessary or desirable, particularly if traditional practices are unjust. Therefore, a constitutional identity can have an 'aspirational aspect that is at odds with the prevailing condition of the society within which it functions', by representing 'a mix of political aspirations and commitments that are expressive of a nation's past, as well as the determination of those within the society who seek in some ways to transcend the past' (Jacobsohn 2010, 128, 7). Indeed, some constitutions explicitly seek to 'separate the future from the past in ways that will have transformative effects on social behaviour' (Jacobsohn 2010, 10). This leads Jacobsohn to identify two types of constitutions. The first are *militant*, which represent an 'expression of defiance directed against an existing social structure whose transformation had been deemed desirable by the document's framers' (Jacobsohn 2010, 22). The second are *acquiescent*, which are 'not the proximate source of societal transformation. Fundamental to the identity of these constitutions is a preservative disposition, a commitment to maintain the essential continuity of such structures of societal stability as the church and private property' (Jacobsohn 2010, 23).

In 1999, as the Timorese people began the process of building their independent state, they faced ontological insecurities stemming from the role that some played in supporting (or at a minimum, acquiescing to) the Indonesian occupation, and how these people would be reconciled and live alongside the 'heroes' of the resistance who had fought for the independent state. They also faced anxiety about the relationship between Timor-Leste and its former occupier, Indonesia, particularly whether their independence would be respected. Constructing a historical narrative that could resolve these insecurities and address this anxiety was a major challenge of the constitution-making process. This is because 'securing a "desirable" memory, one that presents the state and the nation as heroes and not villains of some commonly shared and recognisable international story ... is necessary for a state's continuing sense of stability' (Subotic 2018, 298).

The preamble to the Timorese Constitution outlines a biographical narrative that focuses on the 'liberation' of Timor-Leste from 'colonisation and illegal occupation' as the dominant frame of Timorese self-identity. Yet it also emphasises that Timor-Leste will maintain 'privileged ties' with Lusophone countries (s. 8(3)). While this desire to maintain links to a colonial past might seem to contradict the narrative of liberation, it reflects Timor-Leste's desire to distinguish itself from Indonesia. Lusophone culture is seen as an important counter to Indonesia's attempt during its occupation to emphasise Timor-Leste's connections to its territory of West Timor, and to Malay culture more broadly.

But this narrative reflects a selective memory of Timorese history which foregrounds the contribution of FRETILIN to the liberation of Timor-Leste, particularly the older generation who were active during the 1975 civil war and early years of the resistance to Indonesian occupation. References to Lusophone culture also reflect the values of the older generation, who were socialised by the education they received during colonisation to value becoming a 'good Portuguese' and to cut ties with 'barefoot Timorese culture' (Gusmão 2000, 5–6). The identified national symbols, including the flag, name of the state, date of independence, and national anthem, also all prioritise FRETILIN. While a non-FRETILIN Constituent Assembly member admitted that this was 'controversial',[9] a FRETILIN Assembly member argued that FRETILIN was a 'historical truth' that 'could not be denied'.[10] The Constitution therefore missed the opportunity to articulate a biographical narrative that could provide a foundation for different – often conflictual – Timorese groups to interact as citizens of the Timor-Leste state.

This conservative biographical narrative, which sought to preserve and enshrine an exclusionary interpretation of Timorese identity, contributed to physical insecurity, manifested most significantly during the 2006 security crisis discussed below. It also generated ontological insecurity, as younger generations of 'clandestine' resistance supporters, as well as those who supported integration in Indonesia, saw no place for themselves within this narrative. As one descendant of a pro-Indonesia family observed, those who supported integration interpreted this national narrative as implying that they were 'second class to those involved in the resistance'.[11] This autobiographical narrative also overlooked the role of local tradition and custom, which reflected FRETILIN's preference for focusing on anti-colonial struggle. Yet many young Timorese emphasised a more 'indigenous' historiography that acknowledged their cultural unity with West Timor and which offered 'in their view, a truly postcolonial perspective on nationalism' (Leach 2006, 232),[12] although this carried the attendant risks of legitimising Indonesia's cultural justifications for its invasion.

[9] Interview with a former member of the Constituent Assembly and Member of Parliament, Dili, 13 May 2010.
[10] Interview with a former member of the Constituent Assembly and government official, Dili, 2 February 2010.
[11] Interview with a Timorese intellectual, Dili, 12 May 2010.
[12] Interview with a Timorese intellectual, Dili, 12 May 2010.

Therefore, the biographical narrative outlined in the Constitution challenged the formation of a consistent feeling of self-identity amongst Timorese citizens in the years immediately following independence. By privileging a FRETILIN-led narrative of history, the Constitution solidified a societal division between people from the eastern (referred to as *Lorosa'e* in Tetum) and western (*Loromonu*) regions of Timor-Leste. These identities emerged during Portuguese colonisation and became increasingly salient under UNTAET, as they defined political and economic competition (Babo-Soares 2003, 283). A narrative emerged which claimed that *Lorosa'e* were 'heroes' of the resistance to Indonesian occupation, while *Loromonu* were marginalised as Indonesia's 'accomplices' (Trindade and Castro 2007, 12). As the Constitution prioritises FRETILIN's role in the resistance it appeared to support these claims, because FRETILIN is associated with eastern regions. Political leaders instrumentally used the division to rally support, and this was translated into electoral results (Leach 2009).

The division also took institutional form in the security forces. The new army initially consisted of two battalions, one composed primarily of veterans of FRETILIN's armed wing, who identified as *Lorosa'e*, the other comprising new recruits who were overwhelmingly *Loromonu*. The *Policia Nacional de Timor-Leste* (PNTL) initially consisted of several former members of the *Polisi Republik Indonesia* who were characterised as *Loromonu*. Consequently, tensions emerged within – and between – the army and police force. These tensions escalated into a major security crisis in April and May 2006, which was instigated after 159 soldiers, who were reportedly *Loromonu*, alleged that they had been discriminated against and left their barracks to go on strike. After they were dismissed for desertion, they peacefully protested in front of the Government Palace in Dili. The protest attracted a range of disaffected groups, including youths and members of veterans' and security associations. On the last day of the protest, 28 April 2006, violence erupted. As the PNTL was already suffering from numerous institutional weaknesses, it was unable to restore order. Instead, FRETILIN Prime Minister Mari Alkatiri called in the army, many of whom used disproportionate force (UN 2006). These tensions expanded to wider society and necessitated an international stabilisation force. Since the crisis, the privileging of the older generation of FRETILIN (and its armed wing) has had practical consequences, with veterans of the resistance (many of whom had participated in the 2006 security crisis) entitled to very large pension schemes (Wallis 2013, 2019).

The Constitution had purportedly militant intentions, as it sought to create democratic political and justice institutions that would replace local sociopolitical ones. As one FRETILIN MP commented, FRETILIN 'takes seriously' the word 'Revolutionary' in its title, and 'wants to change society, rather than remain in the past'.[13] But it ultimately failed to transcend the past, as it had acquiescent

---

[13] Interview with a Member of Parliament, Dili, 11 May 2010.

consequences that have enabled the older generation of resistance leaders to continue to dominate political power, as their past role in the resistance is so central to the self-identity of the Timor-Leste state.

6.5 DISHARMONY AND CONTINGENCY

Therefore, the Timor-Leste case demonstrates that a constitutional identity can have perverse, damaging, or exclusionary consequences. Analogously, those seeking ontological security tend to 'securitise subjectivity' (Kinnvall 2004, 749), that is, they tend to counter-productively 'assert identity along axes of self and other in ways which achieve ontological security at the expense of those others' (Rossdale 2015, 373). This highlights the need to pay attention to the politics of ontological security-seeking, as the 'narrative on which ontological security rests is a political discourse with political effects' (Rossdale 2015, 374).

Indeed, Jacobsohn argues that 'constitutional disharmony drives the process of identity development and clarification', as it 'generates a dialogical process that may result in changes in identity' (Jacobsohn 2010, 13–14, 326). This disharmony is either 'in the form of contradictions and imbalances internal to the constitution itself', or 'in the lack of agreement evident in the sharp discontinuities that frame the constitution's relationship to the surrounding society' (Jacobsohn 2010, 87). This means that 'the course of constitutional identity is impelled by the discord of ordinary politics within limits established by commitments from the past' (Jacobsohn 2010, 15). Consequently, constitutional identity has a 'contingent quality' (Jacobsohn 2010, 20). Relatedly, more recent ontological security scholarship has argued that 'it is not the content of the biography that counts (which might change dramatically over time), but the identification of the self as a biographically endowed person that aspires for articulation that ultimately matters' (Browning and Joenniemi 2017, 40). Like Jacobsohn, the ontological security scholarship has argued that subjectivity 'needs to be continually claimed, fought for, performed and articulated' in an intersubjective process of 'securing recognition for this from significant others' (Browning and Joenniemi 2017, 42).

In Timor-Leste, disharmony arising both from the biographical narrative outlined in the Constitution and from the political institutions it created, has meant that constitutional identity has been continuously negotiated since independence in 2002. The gradual recognition of local sociopolitical practices and institutions has led to the evolution of political institutions and enhanced the legitimacy and effectiveness of the state (Wallis and Neves 2021). But contests over the national narrative continue, with the older generation of resistance figures denying disharmony and invoking the dominant interpretation of constitutional identity to bolster their domination of high political office and consequently, political power. This has had consequences for the state's ontological security, with the claimed central role of these resistance figures to Timor-Leste's biographical narrative making it difficult for younger generations or those with opposing views to challenge them without risking undermining the identity, and likely stability, of the state.

CONCLUSION

The scholarship on ontological security has mushroomed over the last fifteen years and now makes a major contribution to the international relations literature. Yet that scholarship has not seriously considered how a constitution – and the constitutional identity it generates – can contribute to creating a sense of ontological (in)security for a state and its people by answering fundamental existential questions and helping to define a state's self-identity by narrating a sense of biographical continuity. In turn, while the literature on constitutions and constitution making has considered the role that constitutions can play in state-, nation-, and peacebuilding, it has not deeply analysed their relevance to ontological security. As I have demonstrated, if Jacobsohn's conceptualisation of constitutional identity travels to international relations it can provide valuable analytical tools that can address some of the underdeveloped aspects of the ontological security literature and make clear the important role that constitutions can play.

REFERENCES

Babo-Soares, Dionisio. 2003. Branching from the Trunk: East Timorese Perceptions of Nationalism in Transition. PhD Thesis. Canberra: Australian National University.

Bal, Mieke. 2002. *Travelling Concepts in the Humanities: A Rough Guide.* Toronto: University of Toronto Press.

Browning, Christopher S. and Pertti Joenniemi. 2017. 'Ontological Security, Self-articulation and the Securitization of Identity'. *Cooperation and Conflict* 52 (1): 31–47.

Chesterman, Simon. 2002. 'East Timor in Transition: Self-determination, State-building and the United Nations'. *International Peacekeeping* 9 (1): 45–76.

Croft, Stuart. 2012. 'Constructing Ontological Insecurity: The Insecuritization of Britain's Muslims'. *Contemporary Security Policy* 33 (2): 219–235.

Dunn, James. 2001. *Crimes against Humanity in East Timor, January to October 1999: Their Nature and Causes.* Dili: UNTAET.

Dunn, James. 2003. *East Timor: A Rough Passage to Independence.* Double Bay: Longueville Books.

Giddens, Anthony. 1991. *Modernity and Self-Identity: Self and Society in the Late Modern Age.* Cambridge, UK: Polity.

Grenfell, Laura. 2013. *Promoting the Rule of Law in Post-Conflict States.* Cambridge: Cambridge University Press.

Gusmão, Xanana. 2000. *To Resist Is to Win! The Autobiography of Xanana Gusmão*, edited by Sarah Niner. Richmond: Aurora Books.

Jacobsohn, Gary Jeffrey. 2010. *Constitutional Identity.* Cambridge: Harvard University Press.

JSMP. 2005a. *Judge Applies Customary Law in a Criminal Case, Press Release*. Dili: Judicial System Monitoring Programme, 19 May.
JSMP. 2005b. *The Interaction of Traditional Dispute Resolution with the Formal Justice Sector in Timor-Leste*. Dili: Judicial System Monitoring Programme, November.
Kinnvall, Catarina. 2004. 'Globalization and Religions Nationalism: Self, Identity, and the Search for Ontological Security'. *Political Psychology* 25 (5): 741–767.
Kinnvall, Catarina. 2017. 'Feeling Ontologically (In)secure: States, Traumas and the Governing of Gendered Space'. *Cooperation and Conflict* 52 (1): 90–108.
Kinnvall, Catarina and Jennifer Mitzen. 2020. 'Anxiety, Fear, and Ontological Security in World Politics: Thinking with and beyond Giddens'. *International Theory* 12 (2): 240–245.
Laing, R.D. 1969. *The Divided Self: An Existential Study in Sanity and Madness*. London: Penguin Books.
Leach, Michael. 2006. 'History on the Line: East Timorese History after Independence'. *History Workshop Journal* 61 (1): 223–237.
Leach, Michael. 2009. 'The 2007 Presidential and Parliamentary Elections in Timor-Leste'. *Australian Journal of Politics and History* 55 (2): 219–232.
Lupovici, Amir. 2012. 'Ontological Dissonance, Clashing Identities and Israel's Unilateral Steps Towards the Palestinians'. *Review of International Studies* 38 (4): 809–833.
Mitzen, Jennifer. 2006. 'Ontological Security in World Politics: State Identity and the Security Dilemma'. *European Journal of International Relations* 12 (3): 341–370.
Rossdale, Chris. 2015. 'Enclosing Critique: The Limits of Ontological Security'. *International Political Sociology* 9 (4): 369–386.
Steele, Brent. 2008. *Ontological Security in International Relations*. New York: Routledge.
Subotic, Jelena. 2016. 'Narrative, Ontological Security, and Foreign Policy Change'. *Foreign Policy Analysis* 12 (4): 610–627.
Subotic, Jelena. 2018. 'Political Memory, Ontological Security, and Holocaust Remembrance in Post-communist Europe'. *European Security* 27 (3): 296–313.
Trindade, Jose and Bryant Castro. 2007. *Rethinking Timorese Identity as a Peacebuilding Strategy: The Lorosa'e-Loromonu Conflict from a Traditional Perspective, European Union Technical Assistance to the National Dialogue Process in Timor-Leste*. Dili: GTZ.
UN. 1999. *Report of the Secretary-General: Question of East Timor*. UN Doc. A/53/951-S/1999/513, 5 May.
UN. 2006. *United Nations Independent Special Commission of Inquiry for Timor-Leste*. UN Doc. S/2006/822, 2 October.
UNTAET Constitutional Affairs Branch. 2001. *Constitutional Commission Public Hearings, Executive Summary*. Dili: UNTAET.
USAID. 2007. *Rule of Law in Timor-Leste*. Dili: Freedom House, USAID and the ABA Rule of Law Initiative.
Wallis, Joanne. 2012. 'A Local-liberal Peace Project in Action? The Increasing Engagement between the Local and Liberal in East Timor'. *Review of International Studies* 38 (4): 735–761.
Wallis, Joanne. 2013. 'Victors, Villains and Victims: Capitalising on Memory in Timor-Leste'. *Ethnopolitics* 12 (2): 133–160.
Wallis, Joanne. 2014. *Constitution Making during State Building*. New York: Cambridge University Press.
Wallis, Joanne. 2017. 'Is "good enough" Peacebuilding Good Enough? The Potential and Pitfalls of the Local Turn in Peacebuilding in Timor-Leste'. *The Pacific Review* 30 (2): 251–269.

Wallis, Joanne. 2019. 'Timor-Leste is a Rich Country, but also a Poor One: The Effect and Effectiveness of Public Transfer Schemes'. In *Routledge Handbook of Contemporary Timor-Leste*, edited by Andrew McWilliam and Michael Leach, 124–135. Abingdon: Routledge, 2019.

Wallis, Joanne and Guteriano Neves. 2021. 'Evaluating the Legacy of State-building in Timor-Leste'. *Asian Journal of Peacebuilding* 9 (1): 19–40.

Zarakol, Ayse. 2010. 'Ontological (In)Security and State Denial of Historical Crimes: Turkey and Japan'. *International Relations* 24 (3): 3–23.

7

The Crisis in, and of, Constitutional Identity

Upendra Baxi

INTRODUCTION

Professor Gary Jacobsohn's eminent contributions to the field of comparative constitutional studies (COCOS, my abbreviation) are well known. I first met him in print when was kind enough to send me a manuscript exploring constitutional developments in the USA and Israel, which later became a stellar book, *Apple of Gold* (Jacobsohn 2017). I was privileged to review his work the *Wheel of Law* (Jacobsohn 2006).[1] The third work that influenced me was his germinal *Constitutional Identity* which I partially explore here. Gary Jacobsohn educated us all to be a forerunner in the tradition that has now been excitingly referred to by Professor Zumbansen as comparative transnational constitutional law (Zumbansen 2012).[2] Clarity (of style), courage (revisiting contested discursive meanings and paths), and the craft (of making contingent meanings, unfold here within what some aesthetic theories have named 'chaosmos', a 'disordered order'). He also developed the art of gentle reprimand and chided those who regarded, almost with evangelical enthusiasm, judicial review power and the styles of its representation.[3] In doing so, Jacobsohn always alerted us against (what is now frankly billed as) the 'partisan constitution' (Dani 2013).[4]

---

[1] See also, Baxi 2007. (I went so far as to suggest in 2007 that from a grounded subaltern COCOS perspective) '...all constitutional forms [that] furnish ideologically incomplete narratives and distinctions between liberal vs illiberal constitutionalism today do not overcome the inheritance of the "Third Reich's military constitutionalisms"'.
[2] See, also, Hirschl 2014, 205: '...the pretense that insights based on the constitutional experience of a small set of "usual suspect" settings – all prosperous, stable constitutional democracies of the "global north" – are truly representative of the wide variety of constitutional experiences worldwide, and constitute a "gold standard" for understanding and assessing it.'
[3] In a Festschrift article, Gary J. Jacobsohn and Yaniv Roznai referred to my notion of a judicial 'minirevolution' and could not help gently chiding me for referring to Courts as 'constitutional revolutionaries'! I take the point given the judicial counterrevolution since Justice Aharon Barak in Israel detailed by them. See Roznai and Jacobsohn 2020. See also Mordechay and Roznai 2017.
[4] Referring to new amendments to old constitutions and subsequent developments, a '...partisan constitution' is one whose text emerges 'by entrenching the normative convictions and institutional solutions favored by a contingent political majority, departs from mainstream European constitutional culture and its idea of a "pluralist constitution" (Dani 2013). One may similarly develop a conception of partisan constitutionalism.'

No greater (to adopt a phrase of Jurgen Habermas) than a 'continent of contested conceptions' assails us when thinking of 'constitutional identity', where the self and others stand contrasted by more abstract and collective entities at least at a metatheoretical level. We must learn to ask, with Gary, a basic set of questions: Does each constitution have an identity? Who determines it and how? Does that identity remain fragile (lying in constitutional quicksand) or is it more robust? Do constitutions have basic structures and essential features (or unenumerated rights)? Do the essential features determine the basic structure from time to time, as in the case of India, or does the basic structure – namely the constitutional judicial review (CJR) power and process – decide what they will be? Does the robustness lie there and not at the peripheries of the basic structure? [One is reminded hereof what legendary Karl Lewellyn used to say at Chicago Law School to his first semester law entrants: 'Do not look at what the judges say, but rather look at *what they do with what they say*' (emphasis added)]. How robust, or fragile, then, can the basic structure of a constitution and essential features be? How is all this interpreted? Are we talking about ontology (ways of being) or epistemology (ways of knowing)? Or both? Or something else? What are its perils, and what promises does its quest bring with it?[5]

This crowd of concerns elegantly, and at times tormentingly, present in Jacobsohn's analysis shows how the question of constitutional identity, is thus at once an ontological concern touching the very being of law and epistemological anxiety as there are different ways of arranging and perceiving the limits and divisions of power which may result in changes *in*, and even *of*, change of the entire constitution. Obviously, there is some identity and there are some limits; the discussions raise many concerns about the cross-cutting relations of 'identity' and social 'change' – between who gains what, why, how, and when, through making constitutional social, change decisions and when. And what indeed may be the accumulation of the unintended consequences of social change policies?[6] We may further want to ask: What may be the unintended consequences of theorising 'constitutional identity'?

Of course, the discussion about these issues is less acute, or may not even arise, when the Constitution is said to be authored by God or is divinely revealed. When constitutions are based on and express Divine Will the faithful and the pious have

---

[5] We do not here visit the relation between 'legal' identity and 'constitutional' identity (as in the case of citizen and foreigner). See the interesting discussion by Clarke (2015). And as regards migrants in the European Union state borders, see Murray 2017. The introduction states the main theme succinctly: '…the civilization we know as Europe is in the process of committing suicide and that neither Britain nor any other Western European country can avoid that fate the end of the lifespans of most people currently alive Europe will not be Europe and the peoples of Europe will have lost the only place in the world we had to call home'. For a concise statement of intergroup dynamic see, however, Johnston 2018. See also Carlier, Crépeau and Purkey 2020.

[6] The literature here is immense and spread across all types of human conduct. I highlight here only a couple of recent contributions. The difficulties of unravelling the nature of these consequences and their impact have recently been well illustrated in *Polity* 48:(4): see, especially, Scudder 2016; Sunstein 1994; Parvik and Pollock 2020.

the obligation to 'do or die'. It is blasphemy, and more, to defy His Will. And 'natural law' doctrines only come into play when the constitution is thought to be the product of Divine Reason and God has given the gift of pious reason to humans of owing interpretations only of his reasoned commands. Obviously, then, the celestial sovereignty does not know any limits to His volition; natural law interpretation may only occur when God allows for pious interpretation, and pious interpretation may not change the word of God. This, in brief, is called theocratic constitutionalism.[7] Who may perform pious interpretation is a vexatious question in non-theocratic constitutionalism (Tew 2018).[8] If one moves from the realm of religion to that of spirituality, one may well note Jacobsohn's distinction between constitutional identities provided by a normatively insurrectionary constitution (dynamic) and a more traditional (static) one. Speaking of the Indian constitution, he avers that 'To the extent, however, that the constitutional "soul" in India was intended to be ornery – that is to say, confrontational and militant in relation to the social order within which it was embedded – the Indian case presents an interesting challenge to the dominant theory of identity' (Jacobsohn 2016). One may well ask whether the ornery articulations are more Delphic than ordinary CJR ones as raising questions pertaining to the 'theory of identity'?

Obviously, Jacobsohn adopts 'a deeply constitutive' view of identity' as it re-enacts an understanding of the constitution as the foundation for both legal and social relations within a polity', adopting a saying of Jean-Jacques Rousseau: 'Before examining the act by which a people elect a king, it behoves us to examine the act by which a people is a people. For this act necessarily precedes the other and is the true foundation of society' (Jacobsohn 2010).[9] This quest makes us aware of the disharmony of constitutional law and politics, indicating 'alternative' possibilities. Such 'possibilities', are not fatal to constitutional identity but rather disharmonies [that] retain identifiable characteristics enabling us to perceive fundamental continuities persisting through 'any given regime transformation' [4].[10] Jacobsohn goes further, endorsing Stanley N. Katz's criterion for affirming the presence of

---

[7] See, further, Hirschl 2010. As far as I can tell, it is not germane to Hirschl's work, but the distinction between 'theistic' natural law and secular natural law in itself quite crucial as it entails a contrast between the 'will' and 'reason' of God.

[8] She offers an astonishing narrative of how religion in a constitutional order is introduced through 'less transparent means of constitutional change', through a detailed analysis of the Malaysian judiciary that has made a nominally 'secular' Malaysian constitution into an Islamicist state by acts of interpretation. This is a fascinating narrative of how changes *in* the constitution may in fact be changes *of* the constitutional order. Unconstitutional constitutional amendments are not the only game in town!

[9] See, also, the subsequent magisterial work by Roznai 2017. We do not here dwell on the differences in narrating constitutional identity by Rosenfeld (2012) or with earlier work (Fletcher 1993) but it should suffice here to say that some distinctive sociological and justice views of identity stand here unfolded.

[10] Jacobsohn celebrates 'disharmony' as 'both necessary and troubling', following an interpretation of Rousseau's political thought, in which 'the human good [is viewed] not as 'a unity but as a set of disharmonious attributes or tendencies that must somehow be arranged in a life so as not to tear the human being apart', quoting Marks (2005, 87).

constitutional government: 'Generic constitutionalism consists in a process within a society by which a community commits itself to the rule of law, specifies its basic values, and agrees to abide by a legal/institutional structure which guarantees that formal social institutions will respect the agreed-upon values...'. This would mean a distinction between a general (foundational) identity and a collection of constellations of regimes of dominant interests and governance power. Add to this the fact that Jacobsohn's cross-cultural studies show us that all constitutions are works in progress, complicated by some understandings of the distinction between changes *in* and changes *of*, constitution (Levinson 1995), and we arrive both at the doorstep of complexity and indeterminacy of 'unconstitutional constitutional amendments'.

The 'how' question is best addressed when we look at the agency of normative entities who claim to marshal amending power itself as a constituent power, where the real question is no longer the power to amend but the power to make and unmake a constitution, a power of repeal and total reconstruction. These entities are the state (understood as the leader of the elected party in the legislature and recognised opposition parties), the constitutional courts (which claim a co-equal constituent power) and the people (in whose name the constitution is made or unmade). When any one of these entities stands invoked as wielders of constituent power, compliance with the amending article provides only a thin (as it so happens now, proceduralist) theory of amending power. Legal positivism of the strictest variety endorses proceduralism as justice in the most minimal sense, de-privileging any questions of wisdom, morality, or consequences of decision, whether legislative or judicial. Constituent power, when exercised in the name of the demos or wielded by 'masses', becomes (as Carl Schmitt would call it) an act of 'sovereign dictatorship' against the situation of 'commissariat dictatorship', which merely comprises acts of rectifying an act of amending the constitution so that it works more efficiently (or extends the practical reason of bettering the bad!).

7.1 IDENTITY ENTREPRENEURSHIP

Many anxieties surround 'identity' to which Jacobsohn draws our attention. I have myself drawn attention to the difficulties in pursuing the human right to identity, particularly the distinction between the notion of 'identity' and the notion of practices of identification (POI) – the latter comprising three different, but interrelated human rights: (1) the human right to choose POI; (2) the human right to belong and to contest communitarian identity; and (3) the human right to manage the practices of identity subversion. Human rights discourse gives much attention to the problem posed by primordial and ascribed and achieved identities but perhaps as much also to imposed identities, even to the point of 'imperialism' of human rights, which may be pertinent to a great deal of what Jacobsohn says. The question of relation between agency and structure emerges rather sharply if one were to consider the POI relative to constitutional identity formations.

It may be apposite, perhaps, to invoke Nancy Leong's analysis of 'identity entrepreneurs'. She, of course, offers her argument in the context of 'racial capitalism', a subset of 'identity capitalism'. She describes identity entrepreneurs as those who leverage their 'identity as a means of deriving social or economic value', focusing on 'identity entrepreneurship where, in order to gain social or economic benefits', a member of 'an out-group intentionally makes her identity salient in a manner pleasing to the in-group' (Leong 2016, 1347).[11] How this may extend to 'disharmony' in the making, unmaking, remaking of constitutional identity is a difficult question, more so if constitutional entrepreneurs are oligarchies, who are constitutional elites – who make the constitution and operate it (or flout it with impunity) – and justices and lawyers (including law academics), constitute themselves as a guild, specialising in what Sir Lord Coke identified in the early seventeenth century as 'artificial reason of the law' (Foran 2020, 2022).

Identity entrepreneurship may also be considered at the level of the subject of identity by 'pluralizing both the territorial space [in which] constitutional identity exists and the constitutional subject it interacts' (Gebeye 2023). In a sense, this is what Jacobsohn means by 'constitutional identity' but a fine gloss is placed by Gebeye who engages three levels of identity in African societies: international/supranational, national, and subnational/regional. A dynamic constitutionalism is surely at work, but the dynamic is different than that necessarily implicated in the classical 'liberal' constitutionalism. The cornerstone of African constitutionalism is not '*We, the people*' (the 'singular conception of peoplehood') but '*We, the nations, nationalities and peoples*' (a plural conception); this is best exemplified by the Ethiopian Constitution, 1995. Similarly, 'Nigeria has accommodated Sharia and democracy' (the twelve sharia-implementing states of northern Nigeria), – a kind now named 'Shariacracy' at the 'subnational level although such system was not originally anticipated in its constitution'. The cosmopolitan character of the African Union's (AU) constitutional framework, Ethiopia's conception of plural peoplehood within the prism of We the Nations, Nationalities and Peoples and Shariacracy, constitute 'constitutional identity at continental, national, and subnational levels respectively both in the descriptive sense of encapsulating the fundamental aspects of each constitutional system and inputting additional barriers for constitutional change'. Precisely for these reasons, 'unlike the European Union, the AU has no difficulties in defining itself along the lines of demos as "We the people of Africa" in Agenda 2063' (Gebeye 2023).[12]

On the other hand, Julian Scholtes (although he ultimately critiques it) notes the appropriation and abuse of the concept of constitutional identity by authoritarian

---

[11] She concludes, rather optimistically, that: 'By protecting agency and promoting full information through both legal and social mechanisms, we can help to ensure that out-group identity entrepreneurs consider the consequences of identity entrepreneurship for both themselves and the out-group. In so doing, we can harness identity entrepreneurship as a force for progress toward an egalitarian society.'

[12] The flip side is that Shariacracy may not observe even some or all core human rights.

and populist forces within Europe. Increasingly, 'populist and authoritarian governments have turned their platforms into constitutional project[s]' and 'they have discovered for themselves the notion of constitutional identity as a practical excuse to sidestep transnational legal obligations'. Some 'scholars ... highlight' the concept of constitutional identity as an 'inherently dangerous concept' ... suggesting that it 'ought to be abandoned' for its intended as well as unintended 'violations of the rule of law and other shared European values'.

But Scholtes argues that 'the root problem' is that 'illiberal authoritarianism' in Europe is that 'illiberals and authoritarians will abuse law and constitutional identity to their own ends'. The authoritarian and populist appropriations of constitutional identity must be identified and understood as abuses of the concept (Scholtes 2001, 535–536, 547–555).

However, there is much in the narratives of 'unconstitutional constitutional amendments' that Jacobsohn offers, transcending the more voguish categories of 'constitutional 'borrowings' and constitutional 'transplants' now modified as transfers (Baxi 2013a). On the other hand, 'the big transformation of constitutional identities has already taken place where constitutionalism is 'ever more transcending the boundaries of the nation-state'. Indeed, 'transnational legal regimes, over the past few decades, have gained momentum of their own. They no longer solely derive their legitimacy from states but also impart legitimacy onto them' (Scholtes 2001, 535).

However, Scholtes argues that abandoning altogether the concept of constitutional identity will not 'stop bad-faith actors from colonizing and misusing constitutional discourses in search of legitimacy' and further that the 'authoritarian and populist appropriations of constitutional identity must be understood as abuses of the concept that are identifiably distinct from other uses of constitutional identity' (Gallie, 1956a, 1956b).[13] Hijacking of deeply pluralist concepts to anti-pluralist causes and carrers is scarcely new, although the means and methods may be. At the same time before pronouncing a judgement of abuse, some advertence to what philosophers name as 'essentially contested concepts' is necessary.

No matter how narratives of imposition, adaptation, and globalisation dominate, we understand overall that constitutional identity in multicultural and pluractional societies will always be shaped by indigenous dialogues and pluralist forces in a society, national histories and memories, and practices of domination and resistance of and by the people. I think that this is now a widely shared ground, that Mark Tushnet has called the 'inevitable globalization of the constitutional law' (Tushnet 2009). We may note in passing that we do not have

---

[13] These are concepts, according to Gallie, which entail 'endless disputes about their proper uses on the part of their users' and 'which, although not resolvable by argument of any kind, are nevertheless sustained by perfectly respectable arguments and evidence' (Gallie 1956b, 169). See also, Collier, Hidalgo, and Maciucean, 2006.

many narratives of what the 'Global North' may have overall learnt/unlearnt from the Global South, despite the many worthwhile forays in comparative law and jurisprudence.[14]

It would, perhaps, be a worthwhile exercise to look at the alternate thinking that suggests, perhaps to a deeper pluralism, eschewing substantially the idea of unity of the law. One approach is to think of an innate plurality of normative ends pursued by various social assemblages or groups. This I initially designated as C1 (standing for constitutional text), C2 (constitutional interpretation) and C3 (constitutional theory or ideology) (Baxi 2000); and subsequently dissipated C2–C12 (the varieties of citizen interpretations – starting from constitutional and apex courts to conjoint interpretation by other organs of government and then dissipating further into interpretation made/urged by the media, corporations, social action groups, human rights groups, individual citizens, and all manner of peoples hurt and wounded by law or non-law (Baxi 2013b). This multiplicity of constitutional voices and visions is invariably non- homogenous and this is what Hans Lindahl's notion of 'ought places' in law fully unfolds (Lindahl 2013). Ought places are finite and internal to legal order; and their spatiality occurs in many ways but is always confined to legal and normative spaces of state and law. 'Fault lines' occur in divining the postulated continuity of 'we'-ness – the idea of continuity of legal collective. The faultlines are crucial when these signify a *'broken universality'* of 'legal reciprocity available to a collective. ... *Claims to human rights indirectly evoke the normative blind spot of a collective's normative order'*. Is it then time to rethink the idea of constitutional we-ness altogether, thus fully recognising that all this privileged discourse leads us to its doorstep? (Oklopcic 2018).[15]

---

[14] Hard questions, besides these, remain for comparative law and jurisprudence. Ran Hirschl formulates these raising a series of questions: 'Why is the migration of constitutional ideas happening, and who are its main agents and advocates? Which polities and courts are the most and least receptive to transnational migration of constitutional ideas, and why? Which types of constitutional controversies are most conducive to inter-court borrowing? What makes certain cases canonical in comparative constitutional jurisprudence? What links can be identified between the triumph of democracy, the emergence of an economic and cultural "global village," and the transnational migration of constitutional ideas? What accounts for the variance in scope, nature, and timing of various countries and courts' convergence to the constitutional supremacy model? And what explains the variance among jurisdictions in government implementation or judicial enforcement to similar constitutional rights provisions? He rightly recommends that a 'turn from comparative constitutional law to comparative constitutional studies is as urgently warranted as it is indisputably opportune' (Hirschl 2014, 281).

[15] Oklopcic explores ways in which 'the people' are constructed in social theory and practices of power politics and suggests a refreshing reinterpretation of popular sovereignty, self-determination, constituent power, foundational authority, constitutional self-government, and sovereign equality. The discussion in Chapter 8 ('Constitutional Isomorphs: Beyond Collective Self-Government'), Chapter 9 ('An Isomorphic Pluriverse: Beyond Sovereign People'), and Chapter 10 ('A New Hope: Image Wars and Eutopian Imagination') repay several readings as suggesting a new 'constitutional isomorph'.

REFERENCES

Baxi, Upendra. 2000. 'Constitutionalism as a Site of State Formative Practices'. *Cardozo Law Review* 21: 1183–1210.

Baxi, Upendra. 2007. 'Book Review: Understanding Constitutional Secularism in 'Faraway Places': Some Remarks on Gary Jacobsohn's The Wheel of Law'. *Indian Journal of Constitutional Law* 1: 231–243.

Baxi, Upendra. 2013a. '"Ordering" Constitutional Transfers: A View from India'. In *From Order to Transfer: Comparative Constitutional Design and Legal Culture*, edited by Günter Frankenberg, 189–208. London: Edward Elgar Publishing.

Baxi, Upendra. 2013b. 'Preliminary Notes on Transformative Constitutionalism'. In *Transformative Constitutionalism: Comparing the Apex Courts of Brazil, India and South Africa*, edited by Oscar Vilhena, Upendra Baxi and Frans Viljoen, 19–48. Pretoria: Pretoria University Law Press.

Baxi, Upendra. 2013. *The Future of Human Rights* (3rd ed., Delhi, Oxford University Press, 172–177; the 4th ed., forthcoming, 2024).

Carlier, Jean-Yves, François Crépeau, and Anna Purkey. 2020. 'From the 2015 European "Migration Crisi" to the 2018 Global Compact for Migration: A Political Transition Short on Legal Standards'. *McGill International Journal of Sustainable Development Law & Policy* 16 (1): 35–81.

Clarke, Jessica A. 2015. 'Identity and Form'. *California Law Review* 103 (4): 747–839.

Collier, David, Fernando Daniel Hidalgo, and Andra Olivia Maciucean. 2006. 'Essentially Contested Concepts: Debates and Applications'. *Journal of Political Ideologies* 11 (3): 211–246.

Dani, Marco. 2013. 'The "Partisan Constitution" and the Corrosion of European Constitutional Culture'. *LEQS Paper No. 18/2013*.

Fletcher, George P. 1993. 'Constitutional Identity'. *Cardozo law Review* 14: 736–746.

Foran, Michael. 2020. 'Constitutional Legitimacy, Artificial Reason, and the Common Law'. *Strathclyde Law Blog*. Posted on October 9, 2020. www.strath.ac.uk/humanities/lawschool/blog/constitutionallegitimacyartificialreasonandthecommonlaw/.

Foran, Michael. 2022. 'The Constitutional Foundations of Reasonableness Review: Artificial Reason and Wrongful Discrimination'. *Edinburgh Law Review* 26 (3): 295–320.

Gallie, Walter B. 1956a. 'Art as an Essentially Contested Concept'. *The Philosophical Quarterly* 6 (23): 97–114.

Gallie, Walter B. 1956b. 'Essentially Contested Concepts'. *Proceedings of the Aristotelian Society* 56: 167–198.

Gebeye, Berihun Adugna. 2023. 'The Identity of the Constitutional Subject and the Construction of Constitutional Identity: Lessons from Africa'. *UCL Research Paper Series* 2/2023.

Hirschl, Ran. 2010. *Constitutional Theocracy*. Cambridge: Harvard University Press.

Hirschl, Ran. 2014. *Comparative Matters: The Renaissance of Comparative: Constitutional Law*. Oxford: The Oxford University Press.

Jacobsohn, Gary J. 2006. *The Wheel of Law: India's Secularism in Comparative Constitutional Context*. Princeton: Princeton University Press.

Jacobsohn, Gary J. 2010. *Constitutional Identity*. Cambridge: Harvard University Press.

Jacobsohn, Gary J. 2016. 'Constitutional Identity'. In *The Oxford Handbook of the Indian Constitution*, edited by Sujit Choudhry, Madhav Khosla, and Pratap Bhanu Mehta, 110–126. Oxford: Oxford University Press.

Jacobsohn, Gary J. 2017. *Apple of Gold: Constitutionalism in Israel and the United States*. Princeton: Princeton University Press.

Johnston, Jasper. 2018. *The European Migrant Crisis: Psychology, Conflict, and Intergroup Relations*. Barcelona: United Nations University, Institute for Globalization, Culture, and Migration.

Leong, Nancy. 2016. 'Identity Entrepreneurs'. *California Law Review* 104 (6): 1335–1339.

Levinson, Sanford. 1995. 'How Many Times Has the United States Constitution been Amended? (A) <26; (B) 26; (C) 27; (D) >27: Accounting for Constitutional Change'. In *Responding to Imperfection: The Theory and Practice of Constitutional Amendment*, edited by Sanford Levinson, 13–36. Princeton: Princeton University.

Lindahl, Hans. 2013. *Fault Lines of Globalization: Legal Order and the Politics of A-Legality*. Oxford: Oxford University Press.

Marks, Jonathan. 2005. *Perfection and Disharmony in the Thought of Jean-Jacques Rousseau*. New York: Cambridge University Press.

Mordechay, Nadiv and Yaniv Roznai. 2017. 'Symposium: Constitutional Capture in Israel?' ICON-S-IL, August 23, 2017. www.iconnectblog.com/2017/08/constitutional-retrogression-israel.

Murray, Douglas. 2017. *The Strange Death of Europe: Immigration, Identity, Islam*. London: Bloomsbury.

Oklopcic, Zoran. 2018. *Beyond the People: Social Imaginary and Constituent Imagination*. Oxford: Oxford University Press.

Parvik, Nassim and Anne Pollock. 2020. 'Unintended by Design: On the Political Uses of "Unintended Consequences"'. *Engaging Science, Technology, and Society* 6: 320–327.

Rosenfeld, Michel. 2012. *Identity of the Constitutional Subject: Selfhood, Citizenship, Culture, and Community*. New York: Routledge.

Roznai, Yaniv. 2017. *Unconstitutional Constitutional Amendments: The Limits of Amendment Powers*. Oxford: Oxford University Press.

Roznai, Yaniv and Gary Jacobsohn. 2020. 'Judicial Activism, Courts and Constitutional Revolutions – The Case of Israel'. In *Judicial Review: Process, Power, and Problems: Essays in Honor of Professor Upendra Baxi*, edited by Salman Khursid, Siddarth Luthera, Lokendra Malik and Shruti Bedi, 163–187. Cambridge: Cambridge University Press.

Scholtes, Julian. 2001. 'Abusing Constitutional Identity'. *German Law Journal* 22 (4): 534–556.

Scudder, Molly. 2016. 'Beyond Empathy: Strategies and Ideals of Democratic Deliberation'. *Polity*, 48 (4): 524–550.

Sunstein, Cass R. 1994. 'Political Equality and Unintended Consequences'. *Columbia Law Review* 94: 1390–1412.

Tew, Yvonne. 2018. 'Stealth Theocracy'. *Virginia Journal of International Law* 58: 31–96.

Tushnet, Mark. 2009. 'The Inevitable Globalization of Constitutional Law'. *Virginia Journal of International Law* 49 (4): 985–1006.

Zumbansen, Peer. 2012. 'Comparative, Global and Transnational Constitutionalism: The Emergence of a Transnational Legal-Pluralist Order'. *Global Constitutionalism* 1: 16–52.

PART II

Comparative Perspectives

8

Confucian Constitutional Identity

Ngoc Son Bui

INTRODUCTION

In the conclusion of his influential book *Constitutional Identity*, Professor Gary Jacobsohn discusses the role of Confucianism in the determination of Korean constitutional identity as an example of how the comparative inquiry into constitutional identity can be further explored (Jacobsohn 2010, 338–346). This contribution further considers how Confucian values constitute constitutional identity in three Confucian-influenced countries in Asia: China, South Korea, and Singapore.

Confucianism has its origins in ancient China. It is not a static tradition but has evolved over time with different schools, such as classical Confucianism in the pre-Qin period, Neo-Confucianism under the Ming and Qing dynasties, and New Confucianism in modern China which integrates classical Confucian values with modern Western values. Confucian moral–political principles do not have fixed meanings but acquire novel connotations through interpretative construction in different periods (Yao 2000). The dynamic of Confucianism is the condition for the dynamics of Confucian constitutional identity. Confucian constitutional values are subject to dialogic interpretations.

This contribution considers the role of Confucianism in the formation of constitutional identity in the three Asian countries. It is based on four positions in Professor Jacobsohn's framework for comparative study of constitutional identity: the text as a start; bounded fluidity; the disharmonic invitation; and the balance of internal and external disharmonies.

This contribution argues that Confucian constitutional identity is a part of broader constitutional identity in contemporary China, South Korea, and Singapore. Confucian constitutional identity refers to distinctive constitutional commitments to a harmonious society; a government responsible for collective public good; moral leaders; and relational individuals' familial and social duties. The Confucian commitments are embodied in the formal and/or prescriptive constitutions in the three jurisdictions. The constitutions' Confucian heritages are continuously dynamic.

Disharmony provokes change in Confucian constitutional identity. The change involves not only judicial but also social and political activities.

8.1 CONFUCIAN CONSTITUTIONAL IDENTITY

8.1.1 China

Confucianism is the ideological base for law and the government structure of subsequent dynasties in China (Zhao 2015). Confucian legacies continue to manifest in various aspects of Chinese contemporary society, ranging from meritocratic politics to the Karaoke trade and the 2008 Olympic Games (Bell 2008). The socialist state in China castigated Confucianism during the Cultural Revolution but has recently supported the spread of Confucian values in society (Jiang 2018, 169–170). Xi Jinping said: "Confucianism recorded the Chinese nation's spiritual activities, rational thinking and cultural achievements in building their homeland, reflected spiritual pursuits of the Chinese nation, and provided a key source of nutrition for the survival and continuous growth of our nation" (Xi 2014). He believes that Confucianism "contains important inspirations for solving the troubles facing us today" such as "widening wealth gaps, endless greed for materialistic satisfaction and luxury, unrestrained extreme individualism" (Xi 2014).

China's Constitution is socialist, meaning that it is ideologically defined by fundamental principles of Marxism-Leninism, including the leadership of a communist party, democratic centralism, the national economy, and basic rights regulated by the state. However, it is a "disharmonic constitution."

Internally, China's Constitution includes competing constitutional aspirations: socialist, liberal, and Confucian. Apart from the socialist commitments, the document also incorporates liberal aspirations for human rights, private property, and a market economy. Confucianism also contributes to the internal constitutional disharmony in China. China's Constitution does not explicitly refer to the term "Confucianism," but implicitly expresses Confucian culture. China's constitutional preamble states that the Chinese people "jointly created its magnificent culture." This includes Confucian culture. Moreover, the 2004 constitutional amendment added former Chinese leader Hu Jintao's "Scientific Outlook on Development" to the preamble. One core feature of the Outlook is the view to create a "harmonious society," although this was not explicitly mentioned in the amendment. However, the 2018 constitutional amendment explicitly adds "harmonious" to the preamble as a core constitutional commitment of the Chinese state. Harmony is the key value of the Confucian tradition (Li 2014). For example, to Mencius, along with good timing and advantageous condition, "harmonious people" – meaning different people capable of working together – is the most important thing in human affairs (Li 2006, 587).

Several provisions in the body of China's Constitution echo Confucian values. For example, Article 3 requires the National People's Congress and the local

People's Congresses at all levels to be responsible to the people. This resonates with the Confucian principle of *minben (people-as-basis)*, which considers the people as the foundation of the country and requires the government to be responsible to them (Murthy 2000). Article 45 stipulates that elderly citizens enjoy the right to material assistance from the state and society. This constitutional right echoes the Confucian culture of respecting elderly people. In addition, Article 49 provides that "adult children shall have the obligation to support and assist their parents." This constitutional duty is consistent with the Confucian duty of filial piety. According to Confucianism, "There are three degrees of filial piety, the highest is the honoring of your parents; second is not disgracing them; and the lowest is being able to support them" (cited in Yu 2019, 182).

Externally, China's Confucian constitutional commitments are dissonant with the surrounding society. For example, the constitutional commitment to social harmony is disharmonic with the increasing social unrest (Minzner 2018, 88). The constitutional commitment of a government responsible to the people is at odds with government corruption (Minzner 2018, 80). Social harmony and people-as-basis government are the constitutional aspirations that the Chinese state aims to achieve in the long-term future.

Constitutional disharmony constitutes the condition for the dynamic of Confucian constitutional identity in China. The dynamic involves not judicial interpretation, as courts in China do not have constitutional review power, but rather legislative and discursive activities.

First, the legislature is the place to define Confucian constitutional meanings. For example, to implement the constitutional duty of adult children to support their parents, China enacted a filial piety law called *Law of the People's Republic of China on the Protection of the Rights and Interests of the Elderly* (Yu 2019, 181). Article 1 states that this law aims to "promote the Chinese people's virtues of respecting and providing for the elderly." These are Confucian virtues. The law requires adult children to support their parents financially. Moreover, under the amended version in 2013, the law adds that "family members living apart from the elderly should frequently visit or send greetings to the elderly persons" (Yu 2013). The addition indicates the Confucian moral aspect of filial piety. Thus, with the legislative interpretation, the constitutional duty to filial piety denotes both financial and moral meanings.

Second, Confucian constitutional identity is defined in discursive settings. Intellectual discourse is foundational to the definition of constitutional values (Powell 1993). Chinese intellectuals invocate Confucianism to define a native constitutionalist model known as "Confucian constitutionalism." Discursive construction of Confucian constitutional identity includes both positivist and normative strands. The positivist discourse reconstructs Confucian values and institutions as local constitutionalist qualities. For example, Zhang Qianfan interprets the Confucian concept of *li* (ritual) as higher constitutional norms of the state (Chengyi 2014, 46). The normative discourse expresses aspiration to a new constitutional system in China rooted in Confucian identity. For example, Jiang Qing proposes a Confucian constitutional model featuring three houses: the House of Profound Confucians representing the sacred sources of legitimacy; the House of National Polity representing historical sources of legitimacy; and the House of Common People representing popular sources of legitimacy (Chengyi 2014, 51). Qing's normative discourse indicates an aspiration for a transformation of constitutional identity in China. His constitutional model is exclusively informed by Confucian tradition. It tends to seek a constitutional harmony, without incorporating competing constitutional commitments (such as socialist or liberal ones).

8.1.2 South Korea

The most Confucian location on Earth is the Korean peninsula (Koh 2016, 191), which is due in part to the long stability of the Choson dynasty, the last Confucian government in Korea. Empirical research indicates that Koreans "despite their liberal individualization and diversification in terms of moral and/or religious value, are simultaneously committed to core Confucian values, most notably filial piety, respect for elders, and ritual propriety (*li*)" (Kim 2015,193).

South Korea's Constitution includes a commitment to liberal values, such as fundamental liberal rights, the separation of power, and judicial review by a specialist constitutional court. However, the Constitution also stipulates commitment to traditionalist values. Its Article 9 provides that: "The State shall strive to sustain and develop the cultural heritage and to enhance national culture." While this provision does not explicitly refer to Confucianism, it implies the state's constitutional commitment to promote Confucian culture, an important component of Korean culture.

However, the external constitutional harmony in South Korea is more prominent than the internal one. The formal Constitution's commitments to liberal values are dissonant with the prescriptive, actual constitution which includes commitments to Confucian communitarian values.

The disharmony between liberal and Confucian commitments is the source of the constitutional identity dynamics in South Korea. Given that family is the core institution in a Confucian culture, it is not surprising that the constitutional identity dynamics in South Korea involve the definition of familial values. Professor Jacobsohn has provided a thoughtful account of the Confucian aspect of the constitutional case on the marriage ban between people who have the same family name (Jacobsohn 2010, 342–343).

Another case involves the Confucian-derived family head (*hoju* 戶主) system in South Korea which subjected children and wives to the lead of father and husband. On February 3, 2005, the Constitutional Court in Korea ruled that Articles 778, 781(1), and 826(3) of the Civil Code, which provided for the family head system, contradicted the constitutional principles of human dignity and gender equality stipulated in Article 36(1) of the Constitution (Kim 2016, 118). This ruling led to the abolition of the family head system in South Korea. Sungmoon Kim argues that this case displays two competing commitments. On one hand, the Court attempted to protect liberal constitutional commitments to human dignity and gender equality. On the other hand, "the Court came to the decision of constitutional nonconformity with an important caveat that Confucian values, such as ancestor worship, respect for elders, filial piety, and harmony in family, still cherished by Koreans in the form of public mores, would remain intact, even after the abolition of the family-head system" (Kim 2016, 123).

In another case in 2011 involving a daughter suing her mother for being abused for over forty years, the Korean Constitutional Court upheld the Criminal Procedure Act's provision prohibiting criminal accusation against one's lineal ascendants (Seong-Hak Kim 2015: 61). The dominant opinion wrote that:

> The current provision is based on our historical ideology of "hyo," or the Confucian tradition of filial piety, which imposed on children to duty to take care of the parents or grandparents. According to this tradition, it is a good use for a child to harry harm caused by his or her parents or grandparent. Filing a criminal complaint against one's parents or grandparents is considered as a behavior against morality. (cited in Seong-Hak Kim 2015, 63)

The Court explicitly defends the Confucian value of filial piety.

The dynamic of Confucian constitutional identity in South Korea is not limited to familial issues. The recent presidential impeachment case indicates how the identity of an ideal leader looks from a Confucian point of view. Examining the Korean Constitutional Court's 2017 decision to uphold President Park Geun-hye's impeachment, Kim Sungmoon attributes Confucian ideas to the Court's jurisprudence "characterized by highly moralistic language and style of reasoning" (Kim 2019, 586). The Court's ruling indicates the dissonant commitment to both liberal democratic and Confucian values. In the first instance, the Court reasoned that the legitimacy of the president derives from the people with the delegated power practiced within the Constitution and the law. At the same time, the Court deployed moral reasoning: The president lacked "sincerity" in her public apology, and her conduct revealed "her betrayal of the trust of the people" (Kim 2019, 596). So, the Court tried to demonstrate the president's constitutional and moral violations. Kim concludes that:

> The values that the Court aimed to promote were not limited to liberal democratic values. In fact, it upheld with equal enthusiasm key Confucian values such as benevolence (*ren*), capacity of empathy (*ce yin zhi xin* 惻隱之心), sincerity or faithfulness (*cheng* 誠), and trustworthiness (*xin* 信), although it never mentioned "Confucianism" in so doing or made it its formal task to explicitly promote Confucian values. In a sense, it is by appealing to Confucian values that the Court was able to protect Korea's democratic constitution that is liberal in its formal structure. (Kim 2019, 609)

Kim's argument indicates that the dynamic of Korean constitutional identity involves the disharmony between the formal commitments to liberal constitutional values and the societal commitments to Confucian values. Due to this constitutional dissonance, the legitimacy of the political leader (president) in South Korea does not merely depend on legal foundations (popular elections and the commitments to constitutional protection): It also depends on moral foundations which derive from Confucian values. An ideal political leader, therefore, must exercise public power legally and morally.

8.1.3 Singapore

Singapore, where 75 percent of the population is ethnic Chinese, has been influenced by Confucianism (Tu 1984). Mindy Chen-Wishart demonstrates that "The core values of filial piety and kinship ties remain strong among the Chinese Singaporeans, albeit given new interpretations and expressions in the new social conditions" (Chen-Wishart 2013, 14). Singapore's constitutional identity is defined by the dissonance between the formal commitment to Westminster parliamentarism and the elite's commitment to Confucian communitarianism. While the formal text of the Singapore Constitution provides for a Westminster model of parliamentarian government as the consequence of post-colonial institutional design, the political elite has subscribed to Confucian communitarian values to facilitate nationalism (Tan 2013, 282). Singapore's communitarian constitutional polity holds that the function of the government is to pursue the collective interests of the state and society.

The communitarian ideology of Singaporean constitutional polity is best expressed in the White Paper on Shared Values adopted by the government in 1991 as the "national ideology" to develop "a coherent Singaporean identity" (Government of Singapore 1991). "Although the White Paper states categorically that the Shared Values are not Confucian values, a number of writers have observed that the Shared Values bear strong resemblance to [a] Confucian ideal" (Tan 2012, 454). It contemplates four shared values: "placing society above self, upholding the family as the basic building block of society, resolving major issues through consensus rather than contention, and stressing racial and religious harmony" (Government of Singapore 1991). The paper states that the shared values are shared by all communities in Singapore and not Confucian ethics (Government of Singapore 1991). However, it notes that "[the] Chinese community can draw upon Confucian concepts which form part of their heritage, to elaborate the abstract shared values into concrete examples and vivid stories" (Government of Singapore 1991). The paper illustrates:

> Many Confucian ideals are relevant to Singapore. For example, the importance of human relationships and of placing society above self are key ideas in the Shared Values. The concept of government by honorable men "君子" (junzi), who have a duty to do right for the people, and who have the trust and respect of the population,

fits us better than the Western idea that a government should be given as limited powers as possible, and should always be treated with suspicion unless proven otherwise. (Government of Singapore 1991)

Li-ann Thio considers the White Paper on Shared Values a kind of soft constitutional law as "its communitarian orientation has been judicially endorsed and applied" (Thio 2010, 779). Drawing on several cases such as *Goh Chok Tong v. Chee Soon Juan* and *Lee Hsien Loong v. Singapore Democratic Party*, she demonstrates that the view of government leaders as *junzi* "with internalized standards of moral integrity appears to have influenced the judiciary in shaping the normative assumptions underlying the law on political defamation" (Thio 2010, 778). In addition, as soft constitutional law, the White Paper has operated as "the interpretive matrix through which the balance between competing rights and public goods are struck – helps make sense of the contemporary adjudicatory approach toward fundamental liberties" (Thio 2010, 779). This is illustrated in cases such as *Ong Ah Chuan v. Public Prosecutor* and *Colin Chan v. Public Prosecutor* (Thio 2010, 779).

Singapore's constitutional polity is not exclusively defined by Confucianism. However, the Confucian tradition provides vocabularies, concepts, and values, such as *xiao* (filial piety) and *junzi* (honorable men) to define Singapore's constitutional communitarian identity.

8.2 COMPARATIVE ANALYSIS

8.2.1 *Textual and Prescriptive Constitution*

Professor Jacobsohn argues that the constitutional text is normally an important venue to express constitutional identity (Jacobsohn 2010, 348). The constitutional texts of China, South Korea, and Singapore do not explicitly refer to Confucianism, but Confucian values are implicitly embodied in these texts in some way. The absence of an explicit reference to Confucianism in the constitutional texts is mainly due to value plurality in these countries. In China, there are various sources of normative orders and values (such as Confucianism, Taoism, Islam, etc.), and therefore the Constitution cannot entrench a single tradition. South Korea is a liberal democracy and pluralist society, and hence the constitutional entrenchment of Confucianism is impossible. The lack of an express reference to Confucianism in Singapore's Constitution is also due to the pluralist nature of Singapore society.

However, the cases of China and South Korea indicate that, despite the absence of explicit reference, Confucian values are embodied in the several constitutional provisions on citizens' constitutional duties (China), and the state's constitutional duty to promote national culture (South Korea). In these two cases, the constitutional texts are actually the start to explore the Confucian contributions to the formation of constitutional identity.

Beyond the formal constitutional texts, the Singapore case suggests that textual soft constitutional law or a quasi-constitution (Sheehy 2004, 73), such as the government-authored paper on shared values, can express constitutional identity. This text particularly renders Confucianism a part of Singapore's communitarian constitutional identity.

Constitutional texts are not exclusive sources of constitutional identity. Professor Jacobsohn argues that "constitutional identity involves more than just the official charter of a nation; it incorporates the prescriptive constitution as well, which includes long-standing commitments and sanctioned practices that may be at odds with the language of the document currently in force" (Jacobsohn 2010, 345). Confucianism forms the "long-standing commitments and sanctioned practices" in China, South Korea, and Singapore. Therefore, it is part of the prescriptive constitution in these countries. Confucian values in practice inform how citizens and government in these polities define the meaning of ideal citizens (who should not only be entitled to rights but also required to perform their duties to their families and society); and ideal leaders (who should not only come to power legally but also acquire moral qualities.)

8.2.2 Bounded Fluidity

Professor Jacobsohn states that "the future of constitutional identity is inscribed in its past" (Jacobsohn 2010, 349). Even when a state experiences a constitutional rupture, some shared commitments can survive the rupture (Jacobsohn, 2010, 350). China, South Korea, and Singapore have experienced a rupture in their constitutional development, but the shared Confucian commitments still remain in some ways.

China experienced a constitutional revolution, which presented an institutional rupture from the Confucian dynastic government. In 1911, Sun Yat-sen led a revolution which overturned the Qing dynasty – a Confucian government – and established the Republic of China (ROC). This constitutional revolution, however, does not completely repudiate Confucianism. Confucian values can be found in Sun Yat-sen's republic constitutional doctrine which informed ROC's institutional design (Bui 2016, 159; Ip 2008, 327). Particularly, Sun advanced a doctrine of five powers. Apart from the Montesquian powers, he added two powers (examination and censorship) which derive from the Confucian dynastic institutions of civil examination and Censorate. Sun's five-power doctrine is the ideational base for ROC's 1946 Constitution which is currently enforced in Taiwan. Modeled after Sun's doctrine, this constitution provides for five *yuans* (government branches): legislative, executive, judicial, examination, and supervision (Bui 2016, 174). Thus, the republic constitutional revolution does not present a clean break with the Confucian past. Its continuity of several aspects of the Confucian tradition defines the identity of the new republic constitutional order.

China's communist revolution in 1949 led to the establishment of a new socialist constitutional identity of the People's Republic of China. Socialist constitutional revolution, however, does not lead to a complete rupture with the Confucian past. As indicated above, the Confucian commitments to social harmony, government responsibility, and familial duties are embodied in China's formal and prescriptive constitution.

South Korea's revolutionary constitutional change also presents continuity with its Confucian past. After the democracy movement in 1987, a set of "revolutionary constitutional amendments" were introduced, which facilitated the creation of a new liberal democratic constitutional order (Jacobsohn and Roznai 2020, 72). The new order is defined by generic identities of constitutionalism, such as the separation of powers, individual rights, and constitutional review. However, the revolutionary constitutional change does not completely depart from the Confucian past. The Constitution committed the state to promote national cultural heritage which includes Confucian culture. In addition, while the Korea Constitutional Court is a liberal institution, it has operated in the Confucian soil in a manner of remonstrance which echoes the Confucian institution of Censorate (Ginsburg 2002, 763–799). Formal institutional design may be liberal, but institutional practices continue the Confucian past. Apart from institutional design and practice, as Kim Sungmoon indicated, the Confucian commitments also inform substantive dissonant values of the South Korean constitutional polity.

Singapore's post-colonial constitutional development is considered an "evolution of a revolution" (Thio and Tan 2009). Significant constitutional amendments and changes are regarded as "constitutional moments that defined a nation" (Tan and Thio 2015). Singapore's revolutionary constitutional change, however, is bounded by the Confucian tradition which informed the shared values as quasi-constitutional values with communitarian orientations.

8.2.3 *Disharmonic Invitation*

Professor Jacobsohn demonstrates that "whether by design or by accident the dissonance in a polity's formal constitution functions as a provocation to change…. The judiciary is of course a principal actor in the shaping of constitutional identity, but it is rarely a unilateral actor" (Jacobsohn 2010, 351). The three Asian cases confirm this position. The disharmony between Confucian and competing commitments shapes the dynamics of constitutional identity in these cases, which involve judicial, political, and social activities.

Confucian constitutional identities include the commitments of a government responsible to the collective public good, morally good leaders, and civic duties to the family and society. These Confucian values are dissonant with generic identities of liberal constitutionalism which emphasize a limited government in the name of individual liberty; legally elected leaders; and fundamental rights. The diffusion of liberal constitutionalism in South Korea, a society with a long Confucian tradition, generates the polity's disharmonic constitutional commitments to both liberal and Confucian values. That disharmony provides the base for the dynamics of constitutional identity in South Korea, which involves the interpretive activities of the Constitutional Court. However, beyond the courtroom, different social actors (including social movements) engage in defining the meanings of Korean dissonant constitutional values. The dynamics of the 2016 Candlelight Movement surrounding the impeachment of former Park Geun-hye provides an example.

Confucian constitutional identities are also dissonant with socialist constitutional identities. The former underlines the social harmony ensured by a responsible government, moral leaders, and virtual and talented intellectuals, while the latter stresses class struggle led by a revolutionary communist party as the vanguard body of workers. In addition, Confucian constitutional identities are communitarian, while socialist constitutional identities are statist. The former are concerned with the duties of individuals in broader social relations (ruler and subject, father and son, husband and wife, older and younger brothers, and friends), while the latter focus on individuals' duties to the state. The diffusion of the socialist constitutional model in a Confucian context induces disharmonic commitments to both socialist and Confucian values in socialist China. The dissonance between Confucian and socialist commitments provokes change to China's constitutional identity. As China does not have judicial constitutional review, the change involves formal constitutional amendment, legislative activities, and the public discourse.

Confucian constitutional identities are also disharmonic with Westminster parliamentarism. While the former focuses on the moral legitimacy of leaders and the duties of relational individuals, the latter features the legal–institutional legitimacy of the leader and the rights of autonomous individuals. Decolonial constitutional design in a society with ethnic Chinese as a majority invites disharmonic commitments between Western institutions and Confucian values. The dissonance animates the change to Singapore's constitutional identity with its communitarian orientation. The change involves both judicial interpretation and government discourse.

8.2.4 *External Disharmonies*

Internal disharmony is not the only source of the dynamics of constitutional identity. Professor Jacobsohn reveals that "competing commitments or aspirations internal to a constitution engage each other while concurrently being deployed in a dialectical relationship with energized forces in the larger social order" (Jacobsohn 2010, 353). The three stories in Asia confirm this view.

Formal constitutional commitments are sometimes disharmonic with external surroundings. In China, the formal commitments to constitutional socialism are dissonant with society's Confucian practices. In South Korea, the formal commitments to liberal constitutionalism are at odds with the social adherence to

Confucian mores. In Singapore, the formal commitments to the Westminster system of government are cacophonic with the elite discourse of Asian values (including Confucian values).

External disharmony invites the engagement of the larger society in defining the meaning of the constitutional commitments. In China, intellectuals seek a Confucian constitutional model rooted in national tradition and social practice. In South Korea, feminist movements have engaged in several constitutional cases to define the meaning of gender quality. The political discourse on Asian values in Singapore seeks to define the nation's constitutional identity.

CONCLUSION

Professor Jacobsohn has provided an influential theory of constitutional identity. This contribution is based on his theory to explore how Confucianism defines constitutional identity in three Asian polities: China, South Korea, and Singapore. Confucian constitutional identities include the core commitments to a harmonious society; a government working for the collective public good; moral leaders; and relational individuals' duties to family and the larger society. These Confucian values are embodied in some way in the formal and/or prescriptive constitutions in the three Asian countries. Confucian constitutional commitments are dissonant with liberal and socialist constitutional commitments. This constitutional dissonance provokes change to the constitutional identity of these countries. The change involves not only judicial interpretation but also the social and political construction of constitutional meanings.

REFERENCES

Bell, Daniel A. 2008. *China's New Confucianism: Politics and Everyday Life in a Changing Society*. Princeton: Princeton University Press.
Bui, Ngoc Son. 2016. "Sun Yat-Sen's Constitutionalism." *Giornale di storia costituzionale/Journal of Constitutional History* 32 (2) 157–179.
Chengyi, Peng. 2014. *Chinese Constitutionalism in a Global Context*. London: Routledge.
Chen-Wishart, Mindy. 2013. "Legal Transplant and Undue Influence: Lost in Translation or A Working Misunderstanding?" *International and Comparative Law Quarterly* 62: 1–30.
Ginsburg, Tom. 2002. "Confucian Constitutionalism? The Emergence of Constitutional Review in Korea and Taiwan." *Law & Social Inquiry* 27 (4): 763–799.
Government of Singapore. 1991. "Shared Values (Government Printers)." Available at: https://eresources.nlb.gov.sg/printheritage/detail/016ff3de-843f-4e35-8410-7d6dd3fbb66b.aspx
Ip, Eric C. 2008. "Building Constitutional Democracy on Oriental Foundations: An Anatomy of Sun Yat-sen's Constitutionalism." *Historia Constitucional* 9: 327–339.
Jacobsohn, Gary Jeffrey. 2010. *Constitutional Identity* Cambridge: Harvard University Press.
Jacobsohn, Gary Jeffrey and Roznai, Yaniv. 2020. *Constitutional Revolution*. New Haven: Yale University Press.
Jiang, Yi-Huah. 2018. "Confucian Political Theory in Contemporary China." *Annual Review of Political Science* 21(1): 169–170.

Kim, Sungmoon. 2015. "Public Reason Confucianism: A Construction." *American Political Science Review* 109: 187–200.

Kim, Sungmoon. 2016. *Public Reason Confucianism: Democratic Perfectionism and Constitutionalism in East Asia.* Cambridge: Cambridge University Press.

Kim, Sungmoon. 2019. "From Remonstrance to Impeachment: A Curious Case of 'Confucian Constitutionalism' in South Korea." *Law & Social Inquiry* 44: 586–616.

Koh, Byong-Ik. 1996. "Confucianism in Contemporary Korea." In *Confucian Traditions in East Asian Modernity: Moral Education and Economic Culture in Japan and the Four Mini-Dragons,* edited by Tu Wei-Ming. Cambridge: Harvard University Press.

Li, Chenyang. 2006. "The Confucian Ideal of Harmony." *Philosophy East and West* 56 (4): 583–603.

Li, Chenyang. 2014. *The Confucian Philosophy of Harmony.* London: Routledge.

Minzner, Carl. 2018. *End of an Era: How China's Authoritarian Revival Is Undermining Its Rise.* Oxford: Oxford University Press.

Murthy, Viren. 2000. "The Democratic Potential of Confucian Minben Thought." *Asian Philosophy* 10: 33–47.

Powell, H. Jefferson. 1993. *The Moral Tradition of American Constitutionalism: A Theological Interpretation.* Durham, NC: Duke University Press.

Seong-Hak Kim, Marie. 2015. "Confucianism that Confounds: Constitutional Jurisprudence on Filial Piety in Korea." In *Confucianism, Law, and Democracy in Contemporary Korea,* edited by Sungmoon Kim. London: Rowman & Littlefield International.

Sheehy, Benedict. 2004. "Singapore, Shared Values and Law: Non-East versus West Constitutional Hermeneutic." *Hong Kong Law Journal* 34: 67–82.

Tan, Charlene. 2012. "'Our Shared Values' in Singapore: A Confucian Perspective." *Educational Theory* 62 (4): 449–463.

Tan, Eugene K. B. 2013. "Autochthonous Constitutional Design in Post-Colonial Singapore: Intimations of Confucianism and the Leviathan in Entrenching Dominant Government." *Yonsei Law Journal* 4 (2): 273–308.

Tan, Kevin Y. L. and Li-Ann Thio. 2015. *Singapore: 50 Constitutional Moments That Defined a Nation.* Singapore: Marshall Cavendish Editions.

Thio, Li-ann. 2010. "Soft Constitutional Law in Nonliberal Asian Constitutional Democracies." *International Journal of Constitutional Law* 8 (4): 766–799.

Thio, Li-ann and Kevin Y. L. Tan. 2009. *Singapore. Evolution of a Revolution: Forty Years of The Singapore Constitution.* London: Routledge.

Tu, Weiming. 1984. *Confucian Ethics Today: The Singapore Challenge.* Singapore: Marshall Cavendish Academic.

Xi, Jinping. 2014. "Xi Jinping's Speech in Commemoration of the 2,565th Anniversary of Confucius' Birth." *China & US Focus Library,* September 24, 2014. http://library.chinausfocus.com/article-1534.html.

Yao, Xinzhong. 2000. *An Introduction to Confucianism.* Cambridge: Cambridge University Press.

Yu, Hua. 2013. "When Filial Piety Is the Law." *New York Times,* July 7, 2013. www.nytimes.com/2013/07/08/opinion/yu-when-filial-piety-is-the-law.html.

Yu, Lüxue. 2019. "Filial Support Obligations under Singapore, United States, and Chinese Law: A Comparative Study." *Frontiers of Law in China* 14 (2): 164–192.

Zhao, Dingxin. 2015. *The Confucian-Legalist State: A New Theory of Chinese History.* Oxford: Oxford University Press.

9

'(A-)Religious & Democratic' Militant Dual Constitutional Identities and the Turn to Illiberalism

The Case of France

Eugénie Mérieau

INTRODUCTION

This chapter seeks to expand Gary Jacobsohn's concept of 'dual constitutional identity', which he defined as follows: 'The identity of a constitution represents an amalgam of generic and particularistic elements consisting of certain attributes of the rule of law that are the necessary condition for constitutional governance, and the specific inheritance that provides each constitution with its unique character' (Jacobsohn 2006, 374). In particular, this chapter will look at dual constitutional identities referring to both 'democracy' – the generic element – and religious identity – the 'specific inheritance that provides each constitution with its unique character'. The obvious case study is Israel, whose 'dual constitutional identity' is 'Jewish and democratic' but other, less obvious cases include Thailand, whose constitutional identity refers to both Buddhist Kingship and democracy, and France, a 'secular democracy' – secularism being here apprehended as one specific form of religion.

In this short paper, I am not aiming to 'trace causal links among pertinent variables' in order to 'substantiate or refute testable hypotheses' (Hirschl 2005, 125). Instead, following Gary Jacobsohn's own methodology, I engage in what Ran Hirschl calls 'concept formation through multiple description[s]' by using the 'most difficult case', France, long established as a democracy and a country in which religion is believed to play a minimal role. France has a 'dual constitutional identity' whereby both constitutive elements of identity are in tension with one another. This type of constitutional identity relies on a common set of mechanisms derived from militant democracy to protect the state religion from real or imagined threats from minorities – and doing so in the name of democracy rather than in the name of religion: bans/dissolution of political parties, eternity clauses and states of emergency.

What is constitutional identity and how to locate it? This chapter identifies constitutional identity as being based on four elements located in the Constitution (in the material sense): first, the self-definition of the state as written into the Constitution; second, the judicial definition of the state's constitutional identity as articulated in constitutional case law and jurisprudence; third, the elements of the state's identity that are specifically protected by tools of militant democracy such as eternity clauses and bans on political parties or groupings, either mentioned in the Constitution, or other laws. Lastly, constitutional identity reveals itself in the framework of the state of exception, which specifically targets communities deemed to pose a threat to the state's identity.

If specific constitutional values are given pre-eminence over others, one may find them in amendment rules. As Richard Albert states, 'amendment rules are one of the sites where constitutional designers may express a polity's constitutional values, both to the persons who are nominally or actually bound by its terms, and externally to the larger world' (Albert 2013, 225). Eternity clauses protect 'core' or 'deeply constitutive' constitutional dispositions from amendment. The study of unconstitutional constitutional amendments by Yaniv Roznai documents the extent to which these meta-constitutional norms can in fact exist even in the absence of explicit eternity clauses, and be applied as such by Constitutional Courts (Roznai 2017). Bans on political parties are the 'mirrors' of eternity clauses, in that they work upstream to protect constitutional identity from contestation, by suppressing the very possibility that challenges to constitutional identity be even voiced in the public sphere and become a political issue (Weill 2017). Finally, the framework of the state of exception is also a good marker of constitutional identity in that it is a response to the state's perception of what is constitutive of an existential threat.

To exist, identity needs alterity as much as territory needs frontiers. In political terms, this means that for constitutional identity to exist, there needs to be 'constitutional exclusion' of the communities representing a form of 'constitutive' alterity. These excluded communities must not be fully excluded though: they must remain present to cement national identity and grant legitimacy to the state's permanent reaffirmation of its identity. Unamendability clauses, bans on political parties and the framework of the state of exception all work towards that very end. Such political rationality, the *raison d' état*, focuses, at the very least, on ensuring territorial integrity and maintaining the form of the state, but also, in cases of 'dual constitutional identities', in defending a specific religion and the worldview and politics associated with it. Two parallel trends occur across jurisdictions characterized by 'dual constitutional identities': the progressive constitutionalization of eternity clauses (and bans on political parties) on the one hand, and the progressive constitutionalization of the state of emergency or exception, on the other hand.

As 'dual constitutional identities' produce and reproduce exclusion while adhering to democracy, the characterization of these states as democratic or undemocratic is often highly contested. France, whose history of emergency legislation is one of the longest in the world – and which has been under a state of emergency for almost five years until 2021– is increasingly referred to as a flawed democracy (The Economist 2022). France has adopted an (a)religious constitutional identity that is contested by a significant minority population, who also happen to be excluded from the protection of constitutional guarantees as they live, in various forms, under a state of emergency.

This chapter will identify and examine France's contested formation of constitutional identity, by giving a brief overview of the interrelated developments concerning eternity clauses and bans on political parties and associations on the one hand, and the use of the state of exception on communities excluded from the state's definition of national identity on the other hand.

French constitutional identity was formed during the French Revolution and 'fixed' during the Third Republic. It was during the Third Republic indeed that both the republican character of the French regime was definitively adopted and that the separation of Church and State (laïcité) was officially affirmed and implemented.

9.1 FRANCE'S CONTESTED FORMATION OF A REPUBLICAN AND LIBERAL-DEMOCRATIC CONSTITUTIONAL IDENTITY

Launching the French Revolution, the Tiers-Etat proclaimed itself a constituent assembly and started to work on drafting a constitution. Its preamble, the 1789 Declaration of the Rights of Man and Citizen declared, among others, freedom of religion as well as democracy to be the founding principles of the new constitutional order. While drafting the first Constitution, the Constituent Assembly first passed a martial law, to be used and implemented on the Champ de Mars in July 1791 to repress the protesters eventually calling for a republic. The Constitution was finally adopted in September 1791, installing a constitutional monarchy with Louis XVI as its constitutional monarch. The following century saw a succession of political regimes, oscillating between monarchies/empires and republics, but whose constitutions all relied on various types of states of exception usually in the form of martial law (Mérieau 2019).

The First Republic was proclaimed in 1792, the second in 1848. Both were short-lived and ended with a Bonapartist military coup, in 1799 by Napoleon and 1851 by Louis-Napoleon, respectively. Both republics had a fully developed Constitution, complete with their own versions of martial law. In between the two republics, the traditional form of constitutional monarchy returned for about thirty years, from 1814 to 1848. This was the time of the conquest of Algeria, started in 1830 under the 'July Monarchy', and formally ended eighteen years later in 1848, under the Second Republic. While the First Republic had proclaimed formal equality for all Frenchmen, the Second Republic denied that the French Constitution applied to the newly acquired French colonies. Article 106 of the Constitution of the Second Republic stated that the legal order applicable to the colonies should differ from metropolitan France – the 'empire of the French Constitution' did not apply in French colonies.

Eventually, in 1870, Louis Napoleon Bonaparte lost to the Prussians in Sedan and abdicated putting an end to the Second Empire. The Republic was once again proclaimed, the third iteration of it. Yet no consensus as to the form of regime France should take emerged. In the political vacuum created by Napoleon the Third's abdication and the uncertainty over the choice of political regime, the Commune, a revolutionary uprising calling for communalist self-government, was proclaimed at the Paris City Hall in March 1871.

In Versailles, where the government and assembly had been displaced, monarchists and republicans were forced into a circumstantial alliance to end the Commune. They chose Adolphe Thiers, a royalist, but elected 'head of the executive', to lead the counter-revolution in Paris. Martial law was declared – and would last three years. But the compromise was so tenuous that it was impossible, without ruining the royalist–republican alliance, to adopt a formal constitution and settle the form of the regime. The National Assembly issued the following statement: 'The National Assembly, holder of sovereign power, considering that it is necessary, while waiting for a decision on the institutions of France, to address the necessities of government, decrees: M. Thiers is the head of the executive power of the French Republic.'

This statement made clear that while the regime was officially that of a republic, it was not definitively decided yet and a monarchical restoration was still possible. Adolphe Thiers, from the outset, stated in Parliament that the question of the political regime was to be left for later. The lack of a constitution was part of the strategic ambiguity deemed necessary in order to set up a stable government to restore order and put an end to the Commune through military intervention, and also to pursue the colonial conquest. Among the monarchists and the republicans, there was indeed another consensus on the topic of foreign policy and in particular on the need to pursue colonial conquest for the aggrandizement of France. Adolphe Thiers sent the military to the streets of Paris to repress the Commune, which ended in massive bloodshed, while pursuing the violent 'pacification' of Algeria.

Notwithstanding the return to order and stability in Paris, the successive 'constitutional' laws, the Rivet Law in 1871, the de Broglie Law in 1873, and the law on the 'septennat' (seven-year term for the Presidency) in 1873, while defining the powers of M. Thiers, now called 'President of the Republic', did not settle the issue of the form of the regime. Monarchists, divided between the 'legitimists' and the 'Orléanists', were still waiting for their respective preferred monarch to take the Presidency and turn it into a throne.

But in the following years, this possibility slowly faded away. In 1875, three laws were adopted which created the constitutional framework of the Third Republic. In particular, the Wallon Amendment, for the first time, referred to the Presidency without referring to M. Thiers; and stated that the President of the Republic was to be 'elected' by Parliament for seven years, and could be re-elected. Interestingly, this amendment, which tilted the Third Republic towards a republican government – and is now often considered to be the date of birth of the republican tradition in

France – was adopted with a majority of only one vote: 353 votes in favour to 352 votes against it. Notable here was the role of the elected representatives from the French colonies, including Algeria, who voted in a strong majority for the Republic – without them, the fate of France would have been quite different.

Yet, if a first stone was set, the regime type would not be fully settled until the Presidency and Parliament were to be held by republicans rather than monarchists. It would be fully settled after a major political crisis, called the crisis of 16 May 1877. During this crisis, the president, Mac Mahon, a monarchist, who had succeeded to Thiers, revoked his prime minister. This was read as a monarchist interpretation of the Constitution. The Assembly rebelled against the president, and Mac Mahon responded with a dissolution of the legislature. New elections were held, and the republicans won. Mac Mahon had to abide by a republican reading of the Constitution, whereby the prime minister is responsible before Parliament, not before the head of state. Mac Mahon finally resigned.

The new president, Jules Grévy, announced to the House that he would not use the weapon of dissolution, a monarchist attribute, and that he would also not consider the prime minister to be responsible before him. The parliamentary, republican interpretation of the Constitution would be called the 'Grévy Constitution' and be dated 1879. The same year, Parliament decided to return, together with the government, from Versailles to Paris, a strong symbol of the end of the 'wait' for monarchical restoration. Five years later, in 1884, it voted the following constitutional amendment: 'the republican form of government cannot be the object of a revision proposal'. The 1884 constitutional amendment settled the fate of France for good: France was now firmly a republic, and a return to monarchy would be unconstitutional. Once again, elected representatives from the colonies helped secure the republican nature of the French government.

As the regime type was settled, the liberal character of the state had to be affirmed. Unlike with former republican constitutions, the Constitution of the Third Republic had no catalogue of rights. Major laws had to be passed to give rights and liberties to the people. Most French landmark liberal laws were passed during the Third Republic, such as the Law on Freedom of the Press (1881), the Law on Freedom to form Trade Unions (1884), the Law on Freedom of Association (1901) and, perhaps the most distinctive of all, the Law on the Separation of Church and State (1905). This law defined the principle of laïcité as follows: 'Article 1: The Republic ensures freedom of conscience. It guarantees the free exercise of religious office under restrictions in the interest of public order; Article 2: The Republic does not recognize, give salaries nor subsidize any religion.'

Yet, at the same time, France was using religion – Islam – as a main discriminating factor in denying rights and liberties to Muslims in the colonies and imposing on them a permanent state of emergency. Muslims were part of a specific legal category, created in 1865, of 'Indigenous subject' (as opposed to the category of 'French citizen'). In Algeria, notably, it had established a legalized state of dictatorship where all executive, legislative and judicial powers were vested in the hands of a governor. In 1881, the French Parliament adopted a law on the status of the Indigenous population in the colonies, the infamous 'Code of the Indigénat' which, unlike its name suggests, had nothing of a code but was a set of miscellaneous pieces of legislation: they denied Indigenous 'subjects' rights granted under the French Constitution and the French civil code. Instead, governors were given the right to order internment, forced labour, deportation and sequestration of Indigenous population at will. These executive orders could not be challenged before any court.

Many of these legal tools and techniques were re-used when the Third Republic officially dissolved into a Nazi state in 1940, through constitutional means. The dual legal system – the Code of Indigénat – was only formally abolished with the Fourth Republic in 1946. But the Fourth Republic was short-lived, and a new version of an anti-Muslim State of Siege, renamed State of Emergency for pragmatic reasons, declared in Algeria in 1955, gave birth to the current, Fifth Republic.

9.2 THE FIFTH REPUBLIC AND STATES OF EMERGENCY: THE ANTI-MUSLIM COLONIAL CONTINUUM

The new State of Emergency Law was designed to apply to the 'others' of the Republic, most notably Muslims from Algeria. It was adopted in 1955 to deal with what was called at the time 'events' in French Algeria. It was later used on French territory per se, targeting specific populations of Algerians, most notably in 1961–1962. In the 1980s, it was enforced in various French colonies: New Caledonia (December 1984), the islands of Wallis and Futuna (October 1986), and French Polynesia (October 1987). Thus, until the end of the 1980s, the emergency law had been declared only to apply to French colonies and their populations.

This changed – to a limited extent – in 2005 when it was declared in the suburbs of Paris. The 'colonial' continuum was undeniable though as populations subjected to the emergency law in the suburbs were mostly immigrants and sons and daughters of immigrants, especially from Algeria. In November 2015, following the terrorist attack on the Bataclan in Paris, a state of emergency was declared nationwide, targeting the 'radicalized' Muslim population. The emergency decree empowered the Minister of the Interior and his representatives at the local level to pronounce house arrests and house searches without prior judicial authorization, to forbid circulation and gatherings, to order places of gatherings to be closed, to dissolve groupings and associations and to close down mosques.

In December 2015, it was attempted to constitutionalize the emergency law and create a new article in the French Constitution. The draft article 36-1 – Article 36 being the constitutionalization of the 1878 version of Martial Law – also entailed a provision stripping bi-nationals – often second- or third-generation immigrants from Algeria – of their French nationality if they had been convicted of terrorism-related offences. This draft provision yielded massive opposition and the entire proposal was finally relinquished before it could be examined by the Constitutional Council.

With the exception of the latter proposal, use of the emergency law was found constitutional and legal by the courts, be it the constitutional, administrative or civil courts. Although the emergency law authorizes the declaration of a state of emergency for a maximum period of twelve days, it was in continued use for two years, from 2015 to 2017. The Constitutional Council and the Council of State issued several decisions related to the six renewals of the state of emergency – always to find them justified (Hennette-Vauchez 2018). In late October 2017, to mark the two-year anniversary, the Ministry of Interior published its key numbers: 4,469 house searches, 754 house arrests, nineteen mosques shut down.[1] In total, these measures led to only six prosecutions – which accounts for less than 0.5 per cent of the number of people put under house arrest.

Finally, in November 2017, the state of emergency was lifted. Instead, a law 'against terrorism' was enacted, which enshrined the dispositions of the 1955 *état d'urgence* into the criminal code,[2] making the emergency permanent. Most notably, the possibility to order house raids and searches without judicial authorization and to restrict freedom of movement of individuals, also without judicial authorization, made its way into 'ordinary' criminal law. This 'migration' was found to be constitutional by the Constitutional Council.[3]

9.3 THE PRACTICE OF MILITANT CONSTITUTIONAL IDENTITY: ETERNITY CLAUSES AND BANS ON POLITICAL PARTIES AND ASSOCIATIONS

The 1884 eternity clause, protecting the 'republican form of government', was enshrined in the 1958 Constitution (Art. 89-5). The question of what exactly the republican form of government refers to is open to interpretation. Is the secular character of the Republic (*'laïcité'*) part of the republican form of government? As Article 1 of the Constitution states, France is a Republic 'with adjectives': 'France is an indivisible, secular, democratic and social Republic'. In fact, there is little doubt as to the inclusion of *'laïcité'* (secularism) as a defining part of French constitutional identity, together with indivisibility and democracy.

---

[1] Available here: www.interieur.gouv.fr/Actualites/L-actu-du-Ministere/Bilan-de-l-etat-d-urgence.
[2] Loi n° 2017-510 du 30 octobre 2017 renforçant la sécurité intérieure et la lutte contre le terrorisme, JORF 31 October 2017.
[3] Constitutional Council, Decision n° 2021-822 DC, 30 July 2021 Loi relative à la Prévention d'Actes de Terrorisme et au Renseignement.

On three occasions, the French Constitutional Council seemed to acknowledge some form of supra-constitutionality: in 1971, it included the preamble of the Constitution into the formal Constitution, giving constitutional status to many grand principles such as those derived from the 1789 Human Rights Declaration;[4] in 1982, it creatively identified what it called 'constitutional objectives' and included them in the by-then-already-inflated-Constitution (called the 'constitutional block');[5] and in 2006 it stated that the transposition of EU directives into French Law could not violate 'principles inherent in French constitutional identity'.[6] These three unexpected developments seem to signal that the Council may already accept, without recognizing it, French constitutional identity, defined as 'the republican form of government' as forming the basis of 'supra-constitutional' principles that must be defended against constitutional revision, even when such constitutional revision stems from the need to conform to EU law.[7]

Interestingly, these three major revolutions in the case law of the French Constitutional Council have to do with public order. As for 1971, it included the 1789 Declaration on the Rights of Man and Citizen whose Article 10 of the 1789 Declaration of the Rights of Man stated limits to freedom of religion: 'No one shall be disquieted on account of his opinions, including his religious views, provided their manifestation does not disturb the public order established by law.' The 1982 'discovery' of constitutional objectives also dealt with 'public order' as being the first and foremost duty of the state, to be balanced with that of preserving the pluralism of the media. Finally, the 'constitutional identity' mentioned in 2006 was defined for the first time in 2021 as being the existence of a public administrative police force in charge of maintaining public order. Militant constitutional identity is the defence of 'public order', whose contours are precisely the state's self-proclaimed identity.

Public order is also the main justification for bans on political parties. The French Constitution does not expressly mandate political parties to adhere to 'the republican form of government'. Article 4 of the Constitution states that 'political parties and political groupings must respect the principles of national sovereignty and democracy'. However, this prohibition is explicit in legislation governing political parties. A political party is an association, whose status is based on the 1901 Law of Association; Article 3 states that 'any association founded on an illicit cause or object, contrary to the laws, to good morals, or that would aim to cause harm to the integrity of the national territory, or to the republican form of government is void and without effect'.[8] Throughout the Third, Fourth and Fifth Republics, independentist political parties and associations in the French colonies were dissolved

---

[4] Constitutional Council, Decision n° 71-44 DC, 16 July 1971 Liberté d'Association.
[5] Constitutional Council, Decision n° 82-141 DC, 27 July 1982 Loi sur la Communication Audiovisuelle.
[6] Constitutional Council, Decision, n° 2006-540 DC, 27 July 2006 Loi relative au Droit d'Auteur.
[7] Constitutional Council, Décision n° 2021-940 QPC, 15 October 2021 Société Air France.
[8] Loi du 1er juillet 1901 relative au contrat d'association, JORF 2 July 1901.

on this basis. In its current version, Article L212-1 of the Code of Interior Security empowers the government to dissolve groupings if their 'object or action leads to violating the integrity of the national territory or to harm by force the republican form of government'.

Following the landmark dissolution of the Committee against Islamophobia in France (CCIF) in 2020[9] and other Muslim associations, several French pro-Palestinian associations are now in the process of administrative dissolution. Yet in spite of calls to dissolve the Party of the Indigenes of the Republic, the only political party representing the interests of the Muslim community (from former French colonies specifically, in particular, Algeria), no administrative dissolution has been launched, perhaps because it never participated in elections and made it clear it never intends to do so.

In 2021, a new law against 'Islamic separatism' targeting the Muslim community in France, provided a tightened framework on associations and made their dissolution easier. Initially named the 'Law against Separatism' and aiming to 'work against those who want to break away from the Republic and wish to live under their own laws, not those of the Republic', the 'Law on the Values Comforting the Principles of the Republic'[10] amended both the 1901 Law on Associations and Article L212-1 of the Code of Interior Security. Associations are now required to sign a 'contract of republican engagement' before they can access public funding or have rights to file cases in courts; this contract binds them to adhere to secularism.

The law was found to be constitutional by the Constitutional Council,[11] which censored only a clause prohibiting the stay on French territory of foreigners whose actions were deemed 'unrepublican', the Constitutional Council finding this unspecified 'unrepublicanism' to be too vague. Here, the Constitutional Council merely indicated to lawmakers the need to define 'unrepublicanism'. In any case, this law tentatively linked together *'laïcité'* and the republican form of government, paving the way for the inclusion of secularism in the legal definition of the 'republican form of government'.

In recent years, pieces of legislation targeting Muslims in the name of *'laïcité'* have all been found constitutional: examples include the 2004 law prohibiting the wearing of religious signs in school[12] and the 2010 law prohibiting full face covering in public spaces.[13] In the summer of 2016, however, the 'burkini bans', issued en masse by mayors on the beaches of Southern France, were found, in majority – but

---

[9] Décret du 2 décembre 2020 portant dissolution d'un groupement de fait, JORF 3 December 2020.
[10] Loi n° 2021-1109 du 24 août 2021 confortant le respect des principes de la République, JORF 25 August 2021.
[11] Constitutional Council, Décision n° 2021-823 DC, 13 August 2021 Loi confortant le respect des principes de la République.
[12] Loi n° 2004-228 du 15 mars 2004 encadrant, en application du principe de laïcité, le port de signes ou de tenues manifestant une appartenance religieuse dans les écoles, collèges et lycées publics, JORF 16 March 2004.
[13] Loi n°2010-1192 du 11 octobre 2010 interdisant la dissimulation du visage dans l'espace public, JORF 12 October 2010. Constitutional Council, Decision n. 2010-613 DC, 7 October 2010 Loi interdisant la dissimulation du visage dans l'espace public.

not all – to be unlawful by the administrative courts.[14] This was the exception and the Council of State later reversed its stance. During the summer of 2022, it ruled that the authorization of a burkini in a municipal swimming pool was unlawful, stating that authorizing the burkini was in breach of the very principle of *laïcité*. This judgment had been issued in the framework of a new administrative procedure of emergency, created by the 2021 Law against Separatism, called the '*déféré-laïcité*', allowing the prefect to ask the administrative court to suspend any decision of a municipal council for suspicion of a breach of *laïcité*.

In 2023, the Ministry of Interior launched a series of attacks against human rights associations involved in the defence of minorities, such as the League of Human Rights, created in defence of Captain Dreyfus, a Jewish army officer wrongly condemned of treason during the Third Republic; in the year 2020, the Ministry of Higher Education and Research launched an investigation into the 'Islamo-leftism' that was 'proved to be growing like "cancer" in French universities'. These various measures are demonstrative of the illiberal turn taken by France in recent years – in fact, illiberalism perhaps is in the very fabric of French constitutional identity. When it is 'dormant' instead of 'militant', democracy can thrive, but when it becomes militant, then democracy is at risk.

CONCLUSION: (ACCIDENTAL) DISHARMONIC CONSTITUTIONS OR (BUILT-IN) EXCLUSIONARY CONSTITUTIONALISM?

French constitutional scholars like to deny the existence of a French constitutional identity. Recognizing it would amount to acknowledging the existence of supra-constitutional norms, and this would put constitutional scholars from the dominant positivist school at unease. For a long time, resistance was strong. But just like the global expansion of judicial power, France cannot be fully insularized from global trends. From the 2000s onwards, the French Constitutional Court has started to use the expression 'constitutional identity',[15] without defining its contours. In the 2020s, it has started to give some content to it – public order, linked to secularism.

This chapter has claimed that constitutional identity needs to be understood in light of the regulation of constitutional alterity, in particular through the tools of militant democracy and the state of emergency. In the 'most difficult' case under scrutiny, the apex court acts as the guardian of a type of militant democracy that protects a specific, ethno-religious, type of democracy. This chapter strongly agrees with Rivka Weill that 'the unamendability doctrine and the ban on extremist political parties are complementary tools that rest upon similar theoretical justifications'(Weill 2017): namely, the strategic construction of alterity and enmity to build and preserve

---

[14] Council of State, ord. 402742, 26 August 2016.
[15] Constitutional Council, Decision n° 2006-540 DC, 27 July 2006 Loi relative au droit d'auteur.

identity. The militant protection of constitutional identity is a Schmittian political tactic: it aims to portray those excluded from the state's protection as 'unpatriotic', 'internal enemies'. Based on the democratic trajectory of the case of France, it appears that constitutional identities tying a religious (or secular) identity to democratic principles and giving their courts the tools of militant democracy to police constitutional faith may threaten the very foundations of democracy.

REFERENCES

Albert, Richard. 2013. 'The Expressive Function of Constitutional Amendment Rule'. *McGill Law Journal* 59: 225–281.
The Economist 2022. www.eiu.com/n/campaigns/democracy-index-2022/
Hennette-Vauchez, Stéphanie. 2018. 'The State of Emergency in France: Days Without End?' *European Constitutional Law Review* 14: 700–720.
Hirschl, Ran. 2005. 'The Question of Case Selection in Comparative Constitutional Law'. *The American Journal of Comparative Law* 53: 125–156.
Jacobsohn, Gary. 2006. 'Constitutional Identity'. *The Review of Politics* 68: 361–397.
Mérieau, Eugénie. 2019. 'French Authoritarian Constitutionalism and Its Legacy'. In *Authoritarian Constitutionalism: Comparative Analysis and Critique*, edited by Günter Frankenberg and Helena Alviar Garcia, 185–208. Cheltenham: Edward Elgar Publishing.
Roznai, Yaniv. 2017. *Unconstitutional Constitutional Amendments, The Limits of Amendment Powers*. Oxford: Oxford University Press.
Weill, Rivka. 2017. 'On the Nexus of Eternity Clauses, Proportional Representation, and Banned Political Parties'. *Election Law Journal* 16: 237–246.

CASES AND LEGISLATION

Constitutional Council, Decision n° 71-44 DC, 16 July 1971, Loi complétant les dispositions des articles 5 et 7 de la loi du 1er juillet 1901 relative au contrat d'association.
Constitutional Council, Decision n° 82-141 DC, 27 July 1982, Loi sur la communication audiovisuelle.
Constitutional Council, Decision, n° 2006-540 DC, 27 July 2006, Loi relative au droit d'auteur et aux droits voisins dans la société de l'information.
Constitutional Council, Decision n° 2010-613 DC, 7 October 2010, Loi interdisant la dissimulation du visage dans l'espace public.
Constitutional Council, Decision n° 2021-822 DC, 30 July 2021, Loi relative à la prévention d'actes de terrorisme et au renseignement.
Constitutional Council, Decision n° 2021-823 DC, 13 August 2021, Loi confortant le respect des principes de la République.
Constitutional Council, Décision n° 2021-940 QPC, 15 October 2021 Société Air France
Council of State, ord. n° 402742, 26 August 2016.
Council of State, ord. n° 464648, 21 June 2022.
Loi du 1er juillet 1901 relative au contrat d'association, JORF 2 July 1901.
Loi n° 2004-228 du 15 mars 2004 encadrant, en application du principe de laïcité, le port de signes ou de tenues manifestant une appartenance religieuse dans les écoles, collèges et lycées publics, JORF 16 March 2004.

Loi n° 2010-1192 du 11 octobre 2010 interdisant la dissimulation du visage dans l'espace public, JORF 12 October 2010.

Loi n° 2017-510 du 30 octobre 2017 renforçant la sécurité intérieure et la lutte contre le terrorisme, JORF 31 October 2017.

Loi n° 2021-1109 du 24 août 2021 confortant le respect des principes de la République, JORF 25 August 2021.

10

Constitutional Identity in Bangladesh

Complexity and Contestations

Ridwanul Hoque

INTRODUCTION

Scholars tend to characterize states in terms of their identity (Rosenfeld 2012). For Jacobsohn (2010), a constitution acquires an identity through experience and out of a dialogic interaction between a nation's past and its aspired future. Embedded in this idea is the attribute of adaptability of constitutional identities. Jacobsohn (2010, 13) argued for a 'more fluid concept of identity, in which constitutional assertions of self-definition are part of an ongoing process entailing adaptation and adjustment as circumstances dictate'. I will revert to the relevance of this theorizing later for a better understanding of Bangladesh's imperfect and ambivalent constitutional identity.

When a state is born through a revolution, as was the case for Bangladesh, its national identity may be diffused into the constitution's identity. However, the merging of Bangladesh's constitutional identity and national identity was not that easy. The merging was rather problematic, with the constitutional identity being deficient in recognition of multiple nationalisms.

Bangladesh's Constitution was adopted on 4 November 1972 (with effect from 16 December 1972). The founding identities of the Constitution were *secularism, democracy, socialism,* and *Bengali nationalism*. These identities began to change in 1975 when the country abandoned democracy for one-party authoritarianism. There was no constitutional government from August 1975 to December 1990, when the Constitution had been drastically changed to incorporate *Bangladeshi nationalism*, redefine *socialism*, replace *secularism* with the *principle of absolute trust in Almighty Allah*, and adopt Islam as the state religion. In 2011, the Constitution was further amended to restore 'secularism' but without shunning the state religion, and to qualify collective Bengali nationalism with individual Bangladeshi nationalism.

In this chapter, I will analyze Bangladesh's constitutional identity from the perspectives of its foundation, change, and contestation. I will also relevantly reflect on that identity's congruence with or divergence from the national identity of Bangladesh.

10.1 BANGLADESH'S CONSTITUTIONAL IDENTITY

At its founding moment, Bangladesh was swayed with a sense of collective identity and constitutional patriotism instead of 'national identities' (Peters 2002). Bangladesh's independence from Pakistan in 1971 is said to be a clear rejection of Jinnah's 'two-nation theory' based on which British India was partitioned into two states: Pakistan (Muslim majority) and India (Hindu majority). Instead, Bangladesh arguably fought for its independence based on linguistic Bengali nationalism, to which the framers of the Constitution took an integrationist/assimilative approach. A demand for constitutional recognition of various non-Bengali ethnic nationalisms was outrightly rejected, which led to the assimilation of other nationalities.

The Proclamation of Independence of 10 April 1971 (effective 26 March 1971), the country's first and interim constitution, chose democracy as the means of governance and declared the normative goals of 'equality, human dignity and social justice'.[1] When the Constitution was adopted, its identity came to be crystallized as a secular, socialist-democratic instrument based on Bengali nationalism. This formulation can be seen, to borrow from Jacobsohn (2010), as a connection between the nation's (historical) past and aspirations for the future. This identity formulation can also be explained as a progression from, and a derivative of, the identity of 'equality, human dignity, and social justice' under the Proclamation of Independence.

10.1.1 The Four Identity Principles

The preamble of the 1972 Constitution declared that 'the high ideals of nationalism, socialism, democracy and secularism' would be the 'fundamental principles of the Constitution' because those ideals 'inspired our heroic people to dedicate themselves to, and our brave martyrs to sacrifice their lives in, the national liberation struggle'.

The formulation of this preambular language is interesting in that it claims that the four ideals had either been in popular practice at the time of Bangladesh's independence or they were what the people aspired to. At the time of constitution making (Hoque 2021), there was little time for an intense debate on the four identity principles. However, there were contestations in the Constituent Assembly about secularism, socialism, and Bengali nationalism. Democracy was an uncontested identity principle because the constituent people unequivocally aspired to a democratic system.

Branded as 'high ideals', the four identity principles are fundamental state policy principles that guide state governance but are not judicially enforceable. The non-justiciability of fundamental principles of state policy may be misread for the idea of judicial incapacity to enforce democracy or secularism. However, because of the

---

[1] For the Proclamation see the Constitution, seventh schedule.

doctrine of basic structure,[2] these four identity principles are enforceable basic features or the essential core of the Constitution (Hoque 2018).

As this chapter shows, these constitutional identity markers are contested and are in constant adaptation. Before dealing with the notion of contested identities, I will first present a narrative of the four identity principles as adopted during the founding of the Constitution.

10.1.1.1 Nationalism

The first foundational principle was 'nationalism', more specifically Bengali nationalism, which was inseparable from the people's identity. As Hossain (2013, 141) argued, nationalism 'represented an assertion by the people of their identity, which evolved during its historical struggle into the right to their language, culture, traditions and history'. As Hossain (2013, 141) continued, '...the people of Bangladesh had emphasised that they were exercising their right to self-determination to create a [nation-state]. [...] Now that Bangladesh had been established as a nation-state, and was recognised as such by the world, their national identity could no longer be questioned'.

Accordingly, the founding Constitution adopted an assimilative approach to citizenship and nationalism by declaring that the citizens would be known as 'Bangalees' (Art. 6) and the nation as 'Bangalee' (Art. 9). It provided that the identity of the Bangalee nation is derived from its language and culture and that the nation's 'unity and solidarity' shall be the basis of Bangalee nationalism (Art. 9). Moreover, 'Bengali' (currently 'Bangla') was accorded the status of the state language (Art. 3), thereby diminishing the status of other languages. As Bangladesh is nationalistically, linguistically, and culturally plural, these provisions are exclusionary of many peoples who are not Bangalee and/or have their own native languages. The non-recognition of other nations (and languages) in the Constitution, along with the exclusionary politics, was a serious blow to inclusive constitutionalism.

10.1.1.2 Socialism

The framers wanted to give distinct meaning to socialism, to be attained through a democratic process and by establishing a 'socialist society, free from exploitation' (Constitution Drafting Committee Report 1972, 2617). Article 10 imposed a duty on the state to establish a 'socialist economic system' with a view to attaining a just and egalitarian society. Several other provisions enacted state policy principles in aid of socialism. Article 20, for example, establishes that everyone would have the right to work and be paid according to their work, while prohibiting the enjoyment of 'unearned incomes'.

---

[2] *Anwar Hossain Chowdhury v Bangladesh* (1989) BLD (Special) 1.

In both the Constitution Drafting Committee and the Constituent Assembly, 'socialism' was intensely debated. In the concluding session of the Assembly on 4 November 1972, Bangabandhu Sheikh Mujibur Rahman (Bangabandhu), the leader of the House, reiterated that socialism in Bangladesh was to be realized progressively and it was to be compliant with the country's social 'climate' (Halim 2014, 962). Accordingly, the Constitution kept room for affirmative state actions for various minority groups ('any backward section of citizens') for their 'advancement' or 'representation' (Arts. 28(4) and 29(3)). However, no positive duty for the realization of the socialist goal was enacted. Whether, or to what extent, socialism has been realized in Bangladesh since independence remains a major question today.

10.1.1.3 Democracy

The Constitution (Art. 11) declared that Bangladesh 'shall be a democracy in which fundamental human rights and freedoms and respect for the dignity and worth of the human person shall be guaranteed'. Article 11 also warranted effective participation by the people through their elected representatives in administration. Democracy would co-exist with socialism. As Bangabandhu reaffirmed, 'We want such a democracy that would promote social welfare and protect the suffering masses of this country and the exploited people from the exploiters' (Halim 2014, 961).

Bangladesh adopted a system of parliamentary democracy, with the principle of collective governmental responsibility to Parliament. To entrench democracy, the founding Constitution underscored the need for a system of fair, free, and multi-party elections, by establishing an 'independent' Election Commission. There are no specific provisions for political parties except that the elections are required to be contested on a party line. The Constitution, however, defined a political party and prohibited those organized along religious lines, that is, for the 'abuse of religion for political purposes' (Art. 12).

10.1.1.4 Secularism

The Constitution established secularism as one of the fundamental state principles. Article 12 stated that secularism shall be realized by the elimination of: 'communalism', 'the granting by the State of political status in favour of any religion', 'the abuse of religion for political purposes', and 'any discrimination against, or persecution of, persons practising a particular religion'. Article 38 of the Constitution, in line with the secular identity, banned religion-based politics in the sense that any association 'for the purposes of destroying the religious, social and communal harmony among the citizens' would be anti-constitutional. However, Art. 41 guaranteed the right to freedom of religion to every citizen or religious community or denomination.

Secularism, thus, was originally envisioned as a system in which the state would not favour any religion, the political parties would not be operated on a religious basis, and the citizens would have the freedom to practise their chosen religion.

10.1.2 Complexity, Destruction, and Contestation of Constitutional Identities

Since independence, the identity of the Bangladesh state or its Constitution has remained continuously contested. The confusion about national identity began during the British Raj. The Muslims of Bengal reportedly braced for a Muslim identity during the later years of colonial rule. However, once Pakistan emerged as a separate state they preferred to be identified more as Bengali than Muslims (Anisuzzaman 2000, 45). Today, Bangladesh 'remains a deeply fragmented nation – fragmentation to which the politics of identity continues to contribute' (Anisuzzaman 2000, 63). The cultural Bengali identity and the religious orientation of the Muslims are the most contested identities (Bhardwaj 2011; Riaz 2016; Hashmi 2022). According to a historical account of Bangladesh's identity formation, there are three streams of political philosophy about national identity: (i) Islamic, (ii) secular, and (iii) nationalist (territorial/linguistic) (Hassan 2004, 189).

Again, given this narrative, there is a lack of conciliation among these streams. While the extreme right and religion-based forces seek to attain the Islamic philosophy/identity, the Awami League, the party under whose leadership the war of liberation was fought, believed in socialism, secular identity, and Bengali nationalism. By contrast, the Bangladesh Nationalist Party, a post-1975 party, is a staunch follower of Islamic identity and Bangladeshi nationalism as opposed to Bengali nationalism.

All four high ideals noted above, including democracy, became subject of constitutional change in the mid-1970s. In particular, the principles of socialism, nationalism, and secularism were changed or shunned by regimes following the 1975 coup, while democracy remained substituted by authoritarianism during those regimes.

10.1.2.1 Democracy, Constitutional Replacement in 1975, and the Path to Authoritarianism

The Constitution (Fourth Amendment) Act 1975, enacted during the regime of Bangabandhu Sheikh Mujibur Rahman, Bangladesh's founding leader, replaced the system of parliamentary democracy with a one-party authoritarian rule overnight. The Amendment turned the judiciary into a subservient state organ by making the judges removable at the wish of the President, suspended many civil rights, and curtailed press freedom. The Fourth Amendment, thus, drastically changed the basic structure of the Constitution by replacing its democratic identity with constitutional dictatorship (Choudhury 1995, 45).

Shortly after the constitutional replacement, President Sheikh Mujibur Rahman was assassinated on 15 August 1975. Then followed successive military regimes until the nation's re-embracement of democracy in 1991. Although democracy as a constitutional principle was not replaced by military regimes, the nation remained an autocratic state from 1975 to 1990. Despite its transition to democracy in 1991, Bangladesh's democratic decline or backsliding (Riaz 2021) in recent years has led to a remarkable distortion of its democratic constitutional identity. Particularly since the general election of 2014, which was avoided by all major opposition parties, Bangladesh started transitioning to autocracy and, in the aftermath of a massively rigged election in 2018 (Riaz 2020), the country has turned out to be a truly hybrid regime (Riaz and Parvez 2021). The 7 January 2024 election, again, has been a one-party election, with major oppositions boycotting.

10.1.2.2 Socialism: The Road Not Taken

Socialism was a contested identity too. There was an intense debate in the Constituent Assembly over whether socialism was to be the state's policy and whether democracy and socialism could go hand in hand. Rahman (1974, 16) considers Bangladesh's political philosophy of socialism through democracy as an internal contradiction from the perspective of Marxist-Leninist theory. Socialism as a constitutional identity seems to be appearing suddenly. Before independence, socialism was hardly present in social discourse, although the Awami League's student wing demanded a socialist state in the early 1960s, and some prominent party leaders in March 1971 urged Bangabandhu to pursue revolutionary socialism along with democracy (Maniruzzaman 1975, 896).

As noted above, Bangabandhu in his 4 November speech underscored a society-specific version of socialism in Bangladesh, to be realized progressively through democratic processes. Scholars observe that the history of the Constitution suggests that socialism in 1972 was meant to be the progressive realization of 'the economic and social rights of the people' and not the 'radical' redistribution of ownership of property (Sabera and Rahman 2023). Social and economic rights under the Constitution are, however, not enforceable human rights. Rather, they are judicially non-enforceable state policy principles. For that reason, the lone opposition member in the Constituent Assembly, Suranjit Sengupta, critiqued the Constitution as anything but a socialist document.

The Constitution provided for the nationalization of private companies and businesses, the expropriation by the state of private property, and an unenforceable principle of prohibition of unearned income. During the time of one-party rule in 1975, socialism was sought to be achieved via compulsory cooperative societies. However, Bangladesh has never sincerely attempted to realize the goal of socialism but has rather leaned toward a free economy.

In the post-1975 years, the first military ruler redefined socialism to have meant economic and social justice. Chowdhury (2011, 188) thinks that the 'socialistic inspirations of the revolutionary leadership were in marked distinction with the free-market[,] de-regularized economy professed by the erstwhile Pakistani military elite [and later by the military administration] in Bangladesh'. As Chowdhury

(2011, 188) continued, the military establishment was in no way comfortable with a socialist Constitution. The military ruler in the mid-70s indeed privatized many state-owned entities. In present-day Bangladesh, socialism remains a rather forlorn identity, and the connotational goal of social justice is becoming increasingly obliterated.

10.1.2.3 Contested Nationalism

The concept of national or constitutional identities in effect remains vague everywhere, especially in a plural, multi-national society (Faraguna 2016). When India gained independence in 1947 from the British, the territory of what is now Bangladesh went to Pakistan based on the so-called two-nation theory (Ahmed 1997), spearheaded by the Pakistan Muslim League under Mohammed Ali Jinnah, which argued for Indian partition (independence) on a Hindu–Muslim divide. Leaders from Bangladesh supported the Pakistan movement, although one of the great leaders during the time of British India, Huseyn Shaheed Suhrawardy, rejected Jinnah's two-nation theory in 1946 as an imperialist approach (Jalal 1985, 185). Ironically, when Bangladesh attained its liberation from the Pakistani regime, its independence was based on a clear rejection of religion-based nationality in favour of linguistic nationalism and a secular 'Bengali' identity (Huq 2018) advocated by the party that led the independence movement, the Awami League.

The contentions that pivoted around Bengali nationalism are historically rooted in religion-based politics, which dates to the pre-independence era but strongly exists in today's Bangladesh. Region-based political parties and groups and the Bangladesh Nationalist Party are staunch supporters of religion- and territory-based Bangladeshi nationalism, while the Awami League supports Bengali nationalism based on language, culture, and secularism.

Some scholars think that adopting Bengali nationalism as a national identity for a Muslim-majority nation was a contradictory step in constitution making (Karim 2015). By contrast, Anisuzzaman (1995) argues that despite the Hindu–Muslim identity divide, a collective Bengali identity emerged and contributed to the founding of Bangladesh. Although the ethnic Bengali identity is centuries old, the political Bengali identity is relatively new, prominently figuring in the late 1940s in the demand for Bangla as Pakistan's state language. As Riaz (2016, 186) poignantly notes, 'Generally speaking, two contesting identities and their political articulations have dominated the political landscape for the past [50] years. These two identities are ethnic and religious, that is the Bengali and Muslim identities, respectively. [...] The binary framing of the debate conceals the complexity of national identity formation and identity politics.'

I will return to this issue of contested Bengali nationalism later. Now, how the hegemonistic approach to nationalism at the time of constitutional founding led to the exclusion of non-Bengali nationalisms should be considered. The exclusionary

Bengali nationalism (Hoque 2017) excluded Indigenous communities from 'We, the people of Bangladesh'. The framers of the Constitution consciously dismissed the demand of Indigenous peoples for recognition. In the Constituent Assembly, the only elected representative of Chittagong Hill Tracts (CHT), Manobendra Narayan Larma, objected to Bengali nationalism as the only identity and expressed his dismay at the absence of a minority protection clause in the draft Constitution. He stated that the Constitution 'did not reflect the hopes and aspirations of the tribal population' (Constituent Assembly Debates, vol 2, 536). To press their demand, a delegation of Indigenous peoples led by Mr Larma met Bangabandhu and demanded that their autonomy be protected constitutionally and that a legislature for CHT be established (Khan and Rahman 2012, 72–83). These demands were summarily rejected on the grounds of being against national sovereignty and Bengali nationalism.

When the Constitution was adopted, all citizens were declared to be known as 'Bangalees' (Art. 6) and 'Bangla' was declared the state language. This aggressive assimilative Bengali identity may have arisen from the wartime mandate in 1971 that ultimately subsumed and delegitimized all other identity claims (Yasmin 2014). Bangladesh thus began a troublesome constitutional journey with an assimilative or integrational approach to Indigenous autonomy and identity, rather than an accommodative or inclusive approach (McGarry, O'Leary, Simeon 2008, 41).

The post-1975 military ruler, General Ziaur Rahman, thought that the secularist-nationalist identity was against the Muslim identity of the nation. Zia amended the Constitution by a military decree to replace 'Bengali nationalism' with 'Bangladeshi nationalism', arguing that the terminology of 'Bangladeshi' will include all citizens. This phase in Bangladesh's political history marks an official contestation of nationalism. The new Bangladeshi nationalism had a purported objective of including all non-Bengali nations, but there is still some form of othering embedded in the binary of Bengalis and Bangladeshis (van Schendel 2000). Indeed, nothing was done constitutionally to acknowledge the distinct nationalities of non-Bengali/Indigenous peoples. Bengali was still the one and only state language.

The Fifteenth Amendment to the Constitution (2011) introduced a balanced position between the two forms of nationalism: recognizing Bangalee (Bengali) nationalism as collective nationalism while providing that the individual national identity of a citizen is 'Bangladeshi' (Art. 6).

10.1.2.4 Secular v Religious Identity

Although the country began its journey on a secular basis of nationhood, Islam soon became an 'important component' (Mohsin 2004) socially and politically. Hashmi (2022, 276) thinks that the emergence of Bangladeshi did not destroy the two-nation theory, but rather the Bangladeshi Muslims' 'growing sense of insecurity' vis-à-vis Indian dominance is at the core of Islamic identity that began to consolidate in the post-1975 period.

One of the intensely debated subjects during the constitution-making was whether it was politically correct to adopt secularism as a founding principle. One or two members urged for some recognition of Islam along with the principle of secularism. Earlier, the Awami League's manifesto of the 1970 election, based on which Bangladesh emerged as an independent nation, promised that, if voted to power, the party would not make any laws against Islamic principles. Aware of Islam as the religion of the majority, thus, the framers were cautious in constitutionalizing secularism. Bangabandhu reassured that secularism would not equate to the 'absence of religion', but rather have the function of eliminating communal politics and exploitation of the people in the name of religion (Hossain 2013, 142–143). As he emphasized in his concluding speech in the Assembly, secularism was 'to prevent the use of religion as a political tool' (O'Connell 1976, 69).

Nevertheless, it was a drastic decision to incorporate secularism in the Constitution, especially because the majority of the people were known for their Muslim identity (Hashem 2010), and, importantly, the secular identity was adopted quite hastily. Secularism appears to be the most contested identity marker. Kabeer (1991, 55) believes that it was a 'fusion of Bengali culture and humanist Islam' that inspired the 'Bengali Muslims' to fight for independence in 1971, while Rashiduzzaman (1994, 58–59) thinks that Islam was 'an unyielding political identity' in Bangladesh that was impossible to ignore. For Karim (2015), secularism as a value was imposed by the ruling Awami League. By contrast, Anisuzzaman (1993) thinks that secular identity began to form before Bangladesh's birth, while Khondker (2010, 188 and 210) believes it 'has a future as long as democratic norms of tolerance and pluralism are strengthened'.

The contestation between secularism and the Muslim identity emerged quite seriously immediately after the emergence of Bangladesh. The first martial law regime (20 August 1975–30 May 1981) began a process of Islamization of the Constitution after the assassination of Bangabandhu. In 1977, General Zia replaced secularism with the principle of 'absolute trust and faith in Almighty Allah'. Further later, the second military ruler, General HM Ershad, made Islam the state religion via the Eighth Amendment to the Constitution (7 June 1988). The two military rulers made these changes to gain political legitimacy (Hakim 1998) from the support of the majority, the Muslims.

After the introduction of state religion, several civil society organizations, professional bodies, and lawyers began a movement against the demolition of the secular identity of the state. Several constitutional challenges to the Eighth Amendment's state religion clause were filed in 1988. Despite the protests, and although 'the people did not ask for these changes', 'the majority accepted them willingly' (Anisuzzaman 2000, 63).

The country transited to democracy in 1991, but subsequent years record a history of an increasing trend of politicization of Islam. Even the secular Awami League once made a coalition with, and sought support from, religion-based political parties, both registered and unregistered (Lorch 2019; Rahman 2023). Political Islam

(Riaz and Fair 2015) has since become an entrenched reality, so much so that the Awami League government, when restoring the principle of secularism in 2011, kept Islam as the state religion.

Following a favourable court decision,[3] the government in 2011 brought about the Fifteenth Amendment to reinstate 'socialism' and 'secularism' in their original form and to introduce the concept of 'Bangladeshis' along with Bengali nationalism. Interestingly, 'alongside the principle of secularism, the state religion clause has been kept intact albeit with new wordings' (Hoque 2018, 13).

The co-existence of state religion and secularism seems to be a contradictory idea in an ordinary sense.[4] However, when seen in the context of confrontational politics over national identity, this co-existence seems to be 'a uniquely skilled tool to navigate through competing claims of identity' (Hoque 2018, 14) and 'politically and constitutionally desirable' (Billah 2014). This desirable contradiction is compatible with the pluralist frame of diverse faiths and religions in society. This can also be explained by Jacobsohn's (2010, 13) view that constitutional identity is subject to adaptation and adjustment 'as circumstances dictate'. As Menski (2015, 23) argued, there is 'simply no contradiction in a Muslim-dominated country to have [an] explicit commitment to Islam written into ... the national Constitution, provided that this same Constitution also contains strong and effective mechanisms for religious and other minorities'.

In recent years, therefore, the binary of secular and Islamic identity has somewhat been compromised with a recalibrated secular identity standing alongside the state religion. In this context, it was not surprising that, following the restoration of secularism, the government affirmed it was not going to ban religion-based political parties or that the Supreme Court refused to hear a challenge to the constitutional status of Islam (Hoque 2016).

CONCLUSIONS

Bangladesh's founding constitutional identities have remained contested since their adoption in 1972. The identity of Bengali nationalism was exclusionary, and the secular identity was hegemonic in that it was not adopted through a wider deliberative process.

Of the four elements of the constitutional identity, none is in its original form today. Present-day Bangladesh stays far separated from constitutional democratic politics and is currently based on populism and an authoritarian developmental goal (Muhammad 2020). The founding vision of socialism appears to be empty political rhetoric, despite certain positive socialist schemes and state affirmative actions.

---

[3] See *Khondker Delwar Hossain v Bangladesh Italian Marble Works Ltd* (2010) 62 DLR (AD) 298 (invalidating the Fifth Amendment that abolished secularism).
[4] See further Bhuiyan (2022); Rahman (2023); Huq (2018).

The secular identity was abandoned in 1977 by the military regime based on their political intention to garner support from the majority Muslims. This abandonment was probably prompted by the failure of what Hashmi (2022, 36) calls the 'socialist-secular-Bengali nationalist' government of the founding leader in 1975. Secularism was restored in 2011, only to stay along with Islam as the state religion. This approach to reconciling the conflicting identities of secularism and state religion is probably congenial for constitutional durability and national political stability. However, the time has not yet come to judge the success or futility of this attempt or Bangladesh's embracement of 'Islamo-secularism'(Chowdhury 2022).

While Bengali nationalism has been retained as an identity marker, the 'Bangladeshi' identity for the citizens has also been introduced. Nevertheless, the social and political behaviour of the state and non-state forces continue to indicate a chasm in the multi-ethnic, multi-religious fabric of society. Constitutional equality, therefore, remains elusive for all sorts of minorities in Bangladesh.

A sensible conclusion is that Bangladesh's constitutional identity is either in crisis or in a state of continuous construction as a result of the crisis of identity politics that remained before, during, and in the aftermath of the founding of the nation.

REFERENCES

Ahmed, Akbar. 1997. *Jinnah, Pakistan and Islamic Identity: The Search for Saladin*. London: Routledge.

Anisuzzaman, M. 1993. *Creativity, Reality and Identity*. Dhaka: International Centre for Bengal Studies.

Anisuzzaman, M. 1995. *Identity, Religion, and Recent History: Four Lectures on Bangladesh Society*. Calcutta: Maulana Abul Kalam Azad Institute of Asian Studies.

Anisuzzaman, M. 2000. 'The Identity Question and Politics'. In *Bangladesh: Promise and Performance*, edited by Rounaq Jahan, 45–63. Dhaka: University Press Limited.

Bhardwaj, Sanjay K. 2011. 'Contesting Identities in Bangladesh: A Study of Secular and Religious Frontiers'. Asia Research Centre Working Paper, no. 36. London: LSE. www.lse.ac.uk/asiaResearchCentre/_files/ARCWP36-Bhardwaj.pdf.

Bhuiyan, Md Jahid Hossain. 2022. 'The Contested Concept of Secularism and Bangladesh'. *American Journal of Comparative Law* 6, no. 3: 399–448.

Billah, SM Masum. 2014. 'Can "Secularism" and "State Religion" Go Together?' In *Human Rights and Religion*, edited by Mizanur Rahman and M.R. Ullah, 32. Dhaka: ELCOP.

Choudhury, Dilara. 1995. *Constitutional Development in Bangladesh: Stresses and Strains*. Dhaka: University Press Limited.

Chowdhury, M. Jashim Ali. 2011. 'Claiming a "Fundamental Right to Basic Necessities of Life": Problems and Prospects of Adjudication in Bangladesh'. *The Indian Journal of Constitutional Law* 5: 184–208.

Chowdhury, Rokeya. 2022. 'From "Secular" to "Islamo-Secular" Bangladesh'. PhD thesis, McGill University.

Constituent Assembly Debates, 2 vols. 1972. Dhaka: Parliamentary Secretariat.

Faraguna, Pietro. 2016. 'Taking Constitutional Identities Away from the Courts'. *Brooklyn Journal of International Law* 41, no. 2: 491–578.

Hakim, Muhammad A. 1998. 'The Use of Islam as a Political Legitimization Tool: The Bangladesh Experience, 1972–1990'. *Asian Journal of Political Science* 6, no. 2: 98–104.
Halim, Muhammad A. 2014. *Bangladesh Constituent Assembly Debates* (in Bangla). Dhaka: CCB Foundation.
Hashem, Ferhana. 2010. 'Elite Conceptions of Muslim Identity from the Partition of Bengal to the Creation of Bangladesh, 1947–1971'. *National Identities* 12, no. 1: 61–79.
Hashmi, Taj. 2022. *Fifty Years of Bangladesh, 1971–2021: Crises of Culture, Development, Governance, and Identity*. London: Palgrave McMillan.
Hassan, M. T. 2004. 'Constitution of Bangladesh, Politics and Nationality: A Philosophical Analysis' (in Bangla). *Chittagong University Journal of Law* 9: 185.
Hoque, Ridwanul. 2016. 'Constitutional Challenge to the State Religion Status of Islam in Bangladesh: Back to Square One?' *I-Connect: International Journal of Constitutional Law* blog, May 27, 2016. www.iconnectblog.com/2016/05/islam-in-bangladesh.
Hoque, Ridwanul. 2017. 'Inclusive Constitutionalism and the Indigenous People of the Chittagong Hill Tracts in Bangladesh'. In *Indian Yearbook of Comparative Law 2016*, edited by M. P. Singh, 217–248. New Delhi: Oxford University Press.
Hoque, Ridwanul. 2018. 'Eternal Provisions in the Constitution of Bangladesh: A Constitution Once and for All?' In *An Unconstitutional Constitution?: Unamendability in Constitutional Democracies*, edited by Richard Albert and Bertil E. Oder, 195–229. Cham, Switzerland: Springer.
Hoque, Ridwanul. 2021. 'The Making and Founding of Bangladesh Constitution'. In *Constitutional Foundings in South Asia*, edited by Kevin Y. L. Tan and Ridwanul Hoque, 91–120. Oxford: Hart Publishing.
Hossain, Kamal. 2013. *Bangladesh: Quest for Freedom and Justice*. Dhaka: University Press Limited.
Huq, Eusef Robin. 2018. 'The Legality of a State Religion in a Secular Nation'. *Washington University Global Studies Law Review* 17, no.1: 244–265.
Jacobsohn, Gary J. 2010. *Constitutional Identity*. Cambridge, MA: Harvard University Press.
Jalal, Ayesha. 1985. *The Sole Spokesman: Jinnah, the Muslim League and the Demand for Pakistan*. Cambridge: Cambridge University Press.
Kabeer, Naila. 1991. 'The Quest for National Identity: Women, Islam, and the State'. *Feminist Review* 37: 38–58.
Karim, L. 2015. 'In Search of an Identity: The Rise of Political Islam and Bangladeshi Nationalism'. http://web.uvic.ca/~anp/Public/posish_pap/Karim.pdf.
Khan, Borhan Uddin and M. M. Rahman. 2012. *Protection of Minorities: Regimes, Norms and Issues in South Asia*. Newcastle upon Tyne: Cambridge Scholars.
Khondker, Habibul Haque. 2010. 'The Curious Case of Secularism in Bangladesh: What Is the Relevance for the Muslim Majority Democracies?' *Totalitarian Movements and Political Religions* 11, no. 2: 185–201.
Lorch, Jasmin. 2019. 'Islamization by Secular Ruling Parties: The Case of Bangladesh'. *Politics and Religion* 12, no. 2: 257–282.
Maniruzzaman, Talukder. 1975. 'Bangladesh: The Unfinished Revolution?' *The Journal of Asian Studies* 34, no. 4: 891–911.
McGarry, John, Brendan O'Leary, and Richard Simeon. 2008. 'Integration or Accommodation? The Enduring Debate in Conflict Regulation'. In *Constitutional Design for Divided Societies: Integration or Accommodation?*, edited by S. Choudhry, 41–88. Oxford: Oxford University Press.
Menski, Werner. 2015. 'Bangladesh in 2015: Challenges of the Iccher Ghuri for Learning to Live Together'. *University of Asia Pacific Journal of Law & Policy* 1, no. 1: 9-32.

Mohsin, Amena. 2004. 'Religion, Politics and Security: The Case of Bangladesh'. In *Religious Radicalism and Security in South Asia*, edited by S. P. Limaye, M. Malik and R.G. Wirsing, 467–488. Hawaii: Asia-Pacific Center for Security Studies.

Muhammad, Anu. 2020. 'From "Socialism" to Disaster Capitalism'. *The Daily Star*, November 25, 2020. www.thedailystar.net/opinion/news/socialism-disaster-capitalism-2012313.

O'Connell, Joseph T. 1976. 'Dilemmas of Secularism in Bangladesh'. *Journal of Asian and African Studies* 11, no. 1–2: 64–81.

Peters, Bernhard. 2002. 'A New Look at "National Identity". How Should We Think about "Collective" or "National Identities"? Are There Two Types of National Identities? Does Germany have an Ethnic Identity, and Is It Different?' *European Journal of Sociology* 43, no. 1: 3–32.

Rahman, Md. Anisur. 1974. 'Priorities and Methods for Socialist Development of Bangladesh'. In *The Economic Development of Bangladesh within a Socialist Framework*, edited by E.A.G. Robinson and Keith Griffin, 16–26. London: Palgrave MacMillan.

Rahman, Muhammad R. 2023. 'Secularism and Islam as the State Religion: Conflict or Coexistence?' In *A History of the Constitution of Bangladesh: The Founding, Development, and Way Ahead*, edited by Ridwanul Hoque and Rokeya Chowdhury, 58–73. London: Routledge.

Rashiduzzaman, M. 1994. 'Islam, Muslim Identity and Nationalism in Bangladesh'. *Journal of South Asian and Middle Eastern Studies* 18, no. 1 (Fall): 36–59.

Report of the Constitution Drafting Committee, Bangladesh Gazette, Extraordinary, 12 October 1972, Dhaka ('Constitution Drafting Committee Report 1972').

Riaz, Ali. 2016. *Bangladesh: A Political History Since Independence*. London and NY: I.B. Tauris.

Riaz, Ali. 2018. 'More Than Meets the Eye: The Narratives of Secularism and Islam in Bangladesh'. *Asian Affairs* 49, no. 2: 301–318.

Riaz, Ali. 2020. 'Voting in a Hybrid Regime: Explaining the 2018 Bangladeshi Election'. *Asian Politics & Policy* 12, no. 2 (May): 251–252.

Riaz, Ali. 2021. 'The Pathway of Democratic Backsliding in Bangladesh'. *Democratization* 28, no. 1: 197.

Riaz, Ali. and C. C. Fair. 2015. *Political Islam and Governance in Bangladesh*. London: Routledge.

Riaz, Ali. and S. Parvez. 2021. 'Anatomy of a Rigged Election in a Hybrid Regime: The Lessons from Bangladesh'. *Democratization* 28, no. 4: 801–820.

Rosenfeld, Michel. 2012. 'Constitutional Identity'. In *The Oxford Handbook of Comparative Constitutional Law*, edited by M. Rosenfeld and A. Sajo, 756–775. Oxford: Oxford University Press.

Sabera, T. and Naveed M. Rahman. 2023. 'Justice as Fairness and the Constitution of Bangladesh'. In *A History of the Constitution of Bangladesh: The Founding, Development, and Way Ahead*, edited by Ridwanul Hoque and Rokeya Chowdhury, chapter 13, 209–223. London: Routledge.

van Schendel, Willem. 2000. 'Bengalis, Bangladeshis and Others: Chakma Visions of a Pluralist Bangladesh'. In *Bangladesh: Promise and Performance*, edited by Rounaq Jahan, 65–106. Dhaka: University Press Limited.

Yasmin, Lailufar. 2014. 'The Tyranny of the Majority in Bangladesh: The Case of the Chittagong Hill Tracts'. *Nationalism and Ethnic Politics* 20: 116–132.

11

Clashing Identities?

Traditional Authority and Constitutionalism in Africa

Heinz Klug

INTRODUCTION

In his pathbreaking book, *Constitutional Identities*, Gary Jacobsohn not only elucidates the role of constitutional identities but also envisions the co-existence of "seemingly irreconcilable visions of national identity" within a constitutional order (Jacobsohn 2010, 272). Instead of these conflicting visions undermining the constitutional order Jacobsohn finds that "[d]isharmony is endemic to the constitutional condition" (Jacobsohn 2010, 271) and he argues it "is critical to the development of constitutional identity" (Jacobsohn 2010, 5). Thus, through an extraordinary range of comparative cases, the book demonstrates how contestation over constitutional identity, through the existence of disharmonic elements, is both central to how constitutional identities evolve and shape constitutional politics (Jacobsohn 2010, 13–15). The challenge, as Jacobsohn acknowledges, comes from those elements within the constitutional order that stand in contradiction to the very essence of the constitutional order itself.

As Jacobsohn argues in his conclusion, the disharmonic constitution remains a bounded constitution, at least at its core. He notes that while "[m]uch of the mutability of constitutional identity is traceable to the disharmony within the constitution, ... the strands that constitute the tension in this disharmony also set limits on the nature of the change engendered" (Jacobsohn 2010, 350). This vision Jacobsohn acknowledges stands in contra-distinction to the idea of tensions that might culminate "in a rupture of constitutional continuity" (Jacobsohn 2010, 88). Yet, he argues, "even in cases of radical transformation, the shaping of new constitutional identity is never simply a matter of 'reflection and choice'" (Jacobsohn 2010) and is thus by implication imbued to a degree with the constitutional history, politics, and to an extent, identity, that preceded the rupture. Short of such rupture, the disharmonies in the constitutional order are, from Jacobsohn's perspective, productive to an evolving constitutional identity. What then are the limits of the disharmonic constitution and what might be said about disharmonic elements that seem to pose an existential threat to a democratic constitutional order yet remain significant and legitimate aspects of the social order?

Exploring this question in the context of African constitutionalism more broadly, this chapter asks whether the continued existence and even incorporation of forms of governance that explicitly contradict the founding values of a constitution are simply disharmonic or do they pose a direct threat to the continued existence of a constitutional order? If the latter, then we might ask whether making a distinction between those social and constitutional elements that are simply disharmonic, and thus productive elements of a constitutional order, and those that might pose a fundament threat to the constitutional order, might not produce a more sustainable constitutionalism. In sub-Saharan Africa "traditional authority" exists in many forms, including through institutional recognition in many constitutions whose founding values include democracy and human rights. While there is debate over both the nature of democracy and the content of human rights in Africa, the assumption in this chapter is that traditional authorities, at least in the form of institutionalized governance structures, represent either a disharmonic element within or an existential threat to democratic and liberal constitutions.

In this chapter, the general term "traditional authorities" refers to a particular set of institutions that participate in different forms of governance or hold authority and enjoy the loyalty of communities across the African continent. At the same time, it is important to note that traditional authority is more properly understood as a source of social authority that extends far beyond any specific institutions. In his extraordinary "Biography of an African Community, Culture, and Nation," historian Kwasi Konadu demonstrates that traditional authority may be located in relationships, biographies and histories that extend far beyond our "traditional" notions of such institutions (Konadu 2019). It is thus important to acknowledge that the constitutional recognition and incorporation of "traditional authorities" which is the focus of this chapter, does not claim to include all the diverse sources and forms of social and even political authority that exist in African communities, or for that matter, sociologically in all human communities, "traditional" or "modern" across the globe.

Despite this caveat, this chapter will focus on the place of traditional authority inside and outside formal constitutions and explore whether the persistence of traditional authority, as a form of recognized and unrecognized social power, is either a disharmonic element within African constitutional orders or an existential threat to African constitutional orders that claim to be based on democracy and the recognition of human rights. To explore this question the chapter will first explain the different constitutional responses to traditional authority across sub-Saharan Africa. Second, the chapter will explicate the different roles that traditional authorities play within the framework of post-colonial constitutions across Africa. Third, it will explore the relationship between traditional authority and constitutional identity in the African post-colony before concluding with a discussion of whether traditional authorities may be considered, in Gary Jacobsohn's terms, a disharmonic element providing a constructive dynamic in the formation of constitutional identities or if, alternatively, they might, especially in their colonially reconstructed form, be an existential threat to the sustainability of democratic constitutionalism in sub-Saharan Africa?

11.1 TRADITIONAL AUTHORITIES AND AFRICAN CONSTITUTIONS

Across sub-Saharan Africa, traditional authorities remain a fact of life in many countries (Logan 2013). A recent *Afrobarometer* public attitude survey, documenting views on governance from across Africa, confirms the continued relevance of institutions of traditional authority on the continent (Afrobarometer Round 7, 2016–2018). The survey included two questions asking respondents about their trust in leaders and to evaluate the performance of leaders, including traditional leaders (Afrobarometer Round 7, 2016–2018). On the question of trust, 55.8 percent of respondents indicated that they trusted traditional leaders either "somewhat" or "a lot" while only 15.9 percent stated that they trusted them "not at all."[1] When it came to the question of performance, 61.4 percent either "approved" or "strongly approved" the performance of traditional leaders, while only 25.6 percent either "disapproved" or "strongly disapproved" of how they "performed their jobs over the past twelve months."[2] These results, while at a high level of generality, make it clear that whatever institutional role they might have, traditional authorities enjoy the confidence of a significant percentage of the African population.

Repeated waves of political and constitutional reconstruction have swept across sub-Saharan Africa since the waning of colonialism (Young 2012). While distinct in form and substance, each of these waves has sought, in different ways, to address the existence of traditional authority. While sovereign sub-Saharan African states reflect nearly fifty different post-colonial histories, there are several distinct alternatives in the ways they address the existence of traditional authority. First, there is a division reflecting the colonial experiences of direct and indirect rule. Direct colonial rule either incorporated traditional leaders into the bureaucratic system of the colonial state or simply expected local authorities to deliver resources, often by delegating authority to the private sector (Young 1994, 103–105). Indirect rule by contrast recognized the existence of traditional leaders and institutions and brought them into the colonial constitutional order so long as they remained loyal to the colonial state (Young 1994, 107–113). As Mahmood Mamdani argues, the essence of the colonial state lies in its institutional segregation, creating what he terms a "bifurcated state" (1996, 16–18), which took on a particularly racial character in

---

[1] Responses to the question: How much do you trust each of the following, or haven't you heard enough about them to say? Traditional leaders (Afrobarometer Round 7, 2016–2018).
[2] Responses to the questions: Do you approve or disapprove of the way that the following people have performed their jobs over the past twelve months, or haven't you heard enough about them to say? Your traditional leader (Afrobarometer Round 7, 2016–2018).

the context of settler-colonialism. Extending this analysis to the post-colonial state, Mamdani sees the state resting on a specific mode of rule reflected in the continued division between state and traditional authority and the interaction of a rural-urban division that is both geographic and institutional – producing a decentralized despotism in the colonial era and requiring for the project of democratization a transcendence of the "dualism of power around which the bifurcated state is organized" (Mamdani 1996, 301).

Second, in the post-colonial era, several newly independent states explicitly excluded traditional authorities from their new constitutional orders and sought to suppress them on ideological or political grounds. Thus, several African constitutions make no mention of traditional authorities at all, even at the local level. For example, the Constitution of Senegal, like many former French colonies, simply provides for democratically elected local governments, stating that "territorial collectivities constitute the institutional framework of the participation of the citizens in the management of public affairs" and that "[t]hey administer themselves freely by assemblies elected by universal direct suffrage" (Constitution of Senegal 2001, Art. 102). Apart from these former French colonies, whose constitutions embrace the French constitutional tradition, there are countries such as Kenya and Tanzania which, through different historical processes, seem to have disentangled traditional and formal state authority so that their constitutions recognize customary law or indigenous legal traditions but have incorporated this legal pluralism into the formal legal system and provide no recognition or role for traditional authorities as separate institutions. In the case of Kenya, the incorporation of traditional authorities into the colonial bureaucracy carried over into the post-colonial state so that traditional authorities do not play a formal role in governance, although they retain influence in rural communities (Rohregger et al. 2021). Tanzania, by contrast, explicitly abolished tribal chieftaincies at independence and a recent study on accountability indicates that while local government institutions compete with societal associations for legitimacy, traditional authorities have little influence, especially when compared to religious organizations (Lawson and Rakner 2005). Interestingly, in the case of Tanzania, customary law was incorporated into the formal legal system even as separate customary law courts were disbanded. A recent study found that even though traditional chieftaincy structures do not play a role, "other authorities relying on customary or informal norms and sources of authority such as clan leaders, village elders, religious authorities or self-help groups mediate the relationships between the state and citizens" (SDC 2015, 3).

The absence of any constitutional recognition of traditional and cultural authorities does not mean that such institutions do not exist in a society. Systems of legal pluralism, whether based on religious law or other informal rule-bound orders, exist in all societies. However, the failure to recognize these sources of social authority becomes salient for governance and constitutional legitimacy when these alternative sources of governing authority have as much or even more legitimacy than the formal constitutional order. This difficulty was evident in cases where newly independent African states either attempted to formally abolish the institution of chieftaincy or simply excluded traditional authorities from the arena of governance. In some cases, states were forced to backtrack and recognize traditional authorities after periods of conflict or concern that local government could not effectively govern without their participation. Both Angola and Mozambique adopted independence constitutions that provided no recognition of traditional authorities yet in the post-Cold War wave of democratization both countries reversed course and now explicitly recognize traditional authorities in their constitutions. This re-emergence of traditional authorities and indigenous law in the context of democratization (Ubink 2008) is especially significant in contexts where efforts to build local alternatives – such as the attempt to build community-controlled courts and popular justice in Mozambique (Sachs and Welch 1990) – were undermined by armed civil conflict.

Finally, there were those constitutions that from independence provided a specific institutional role for traditional authorities at either the national, regional, local, or multiple levels of government (Constitution of Uganda 1995, Art. 32(2); Constitution of Lesotho 1993, Chapter V, Sec. 44–53; Constitution of Eswatini 2005, Chapter II. Monarchy, Sec. 4–13 and Chapter XIV, Traditional Institutions Sec. 227–35; and, Constitution of Botswana 1966, Part III, Sec. 77–85). Significantly, despite formal constitutional recognition, the powers granted to traditional authorities at either the national or regional levels of government are mainly advisory, even when the issues they are empowered to address directly affect the interests of traditional authorities and the cultural communities they represent. Even when they are granted more direct governance powers as part of the formal local government structures, these are often dependent on national or regional government support given the control over legislative and budgetary authority that is generally held by those higher levels of government. This formal distribution of power does not, however, reveal the significance of cultural- and community-based power exercised by traditional leaders. This is most clearly demonstrated by the ability of traditional leaders to deliver votes to political parties during elections, especially in rural areas. As a result, it is evident that even dominant political parties, such as the African National Congress in South Africa and the Zimbabwe African National Union in Zimbabwe, have passed laws to empower traditional authorities to gain their cooperation in delivering electoral support in rural areas.

11.2 WHAT ROLES FOR TRADITIONAL AUTHORITIES IN POST-COLONIAL CONSTITUTIONS?

Constitutional clauses recognizing traditional authorities vary in both the form of the recognition and the roles assigned or implied by that recognition. On the one end of the spectrum, are those constitutions that guarantee the state's recognition of traditional authorities and specify the role they will play in the polity. At the other extreme are those who simply acknowledge their existence or specify that they must play no role in the political process at all. A striking example of the guarantee of traditional authority is the Constitution of Ghana which states that "[t]he institution of chieftaincy, together with its traditional councils as established by customary law and usage is hereby guaranteed" (Constitution of Ghana 1992, Art. 270(1)). It then proceeds to deny the national legislature any authority to intervene in these institutions by stating that "Parliament shall have no power to enact any law which" either "(a) confers on any person or authority the right to accord or withdraw recognition to or from a chief for any purpose whatsoever, or (b) in any way detracts or derogates from the honour and dignity of the institution of chieftaincy" (Constitution of Ghana 1992, Art. 270(2)(a) and (b)). The constitution then establishes regional houses of chiefs that select a national house of chiefs with broad authority over matters pertaining to the chieftaincy and appellate jurisdiction, to be exercised by a Judicial Committee of the National House of Chiefs, "in any cause or matter affecting chieftaincy which has been determined by the Regional House of Chiefs in a region, from which appellate jurisdiction there shall be an appeal to the Supreme Court, with the leave of the National House of Chiefs, or the Supreme Court" (Constitution of Ghana 1992, Art. 273(1)).

In addition to guaranteeing the institution, the Constitution of Ghana ensures the economic independence of these institutions by both protecting stool lands and providing for the allocation of a portion of the proceeds from these lands to both sustain the stool and the traditional authority. Art. 267 of the Constitution first states that "[a]ll stool lands in Ghana shall vest in the appropriate stool on behalf of, and in trust for the subjects of the stool in accordance with customary law and usage" (Constitution of Ghana 1992, Art. 267(1)) and then specifies that after "[t]en percent of the revenue accruing from stool lands" is paid "to the office of the Administrator of Stool Lands to cover administrative expenses" (Constitution of Ghana 1992, Art. 267(6)) the remaining revenue is to be divided proportionately, with "twenty-five percent to the stool through the traditional authority for the maintenance of the stool in keeping with its status; twenty percent to the traditional authority; and fifty-five percent to the District Assembly, within the area of authority of which the stool lands are situated" (Constitution of Ghana 1992, Art. 267(6)(a)(b) and (c)). The significance of stool land as a resource base for traditional authority is secured by another constitutional provision that ensures that it remains distinguished from any land market by providing that "[s]ubject to the provisions of this Constitution, no interest in, or right over, any stool land in Ghana shall be created which vests in any person or body of persons in freehold interest howsoever described" (Constitution of Ghana 1992, Art. 267(5)).

While many other African constitutions valorize and recognize roles for traditional authorities, they rarely provide the detailed protection seen in the Ghanaian Constitution and usually subject the role of traditional authorities to legislative determination. Take, for example, the Constitution of Mozambique which provides that "[T]he State shall recognise and esteem traditional authority that is legitimate according to the people and to customary law" (Constitution of Mozambique 2004, Art. 118(1)). It then subjects this guarantee to legislative control by providing that the "[s]tate shall define the relationship between traditional authority and other institutions and the part that traditional authority should play in the economic, social and cultural affairs of the country, in accordance with the law" (Constitution of Mozambique 2004, Art. 118(2)). Other constitutions provide even less guarantees or definition of the role that traditional authorities might play in governance. The South African Constitution, for example, recognizes the "institution, status and role of traditional leadership, according to customary law" (Constitution of South Africa 1996, Sec. 211(1)), but then states with less promise that "National legislation may provide for a role for traditional leadership as an institution at a local level on matters affecting local communities" (Constitution of South Africa 1996, Sec. 212(1)). The only explicit command is that the "Courts must apply customary law when that law is applicable subject to the Constitution and any legislation that specifically deals with customary law" (Constitution of South Africa 1996, Sec. 211(3)). The Constitution of Chad simply acknowledges that "traditional authorities are the guarantors of use and custom" (Constitution of Chad 2018, Title XIV, Art. 217) and that they "concur in the control of populations and support the action of the Autonomous Collectivities" (Constitution of Chad 2018, Art. 219).

In addition to recognition, some of the constitutions that provide a role for traditional authorities also attempt to restrict the scope of their role in society, most often attempting to limit their political influence by specifically denying or restricting them from participating in partisan politics. On the one hand, this may be viewed as an attempt to hold these authorities above the political fray as symbols of social coherence; however, there is also a clear indication that constitution makers have attempted to separate the social and political authority of traditional authorities from electoral politics at both the national and sub-national levels. While the Ghana Constitution provides some of the most explicit constitutional guarantees for traditional authorities, the constitution also defines a chief as a "person, who, hailing from the appropriate family and lineage, has been validly nominated, elected or selected and enstooled, enskinned or installed as a chief or queen mother in accordance with the relevant customary law and usage" (Constitution of Ghana 1992, Sec. 277) and explicitly prohibits a chief from being "active in party politics" (Constitution of Ghana 1992, Sec. 276(1)). Furthermore, it provides that any chief wishing to participate in politics by "seeking election to Parliament shall abdicate his stool or skin" (Constitution of Ghana 1992, Sec. 276(1)); however, it does allow chiefs to "be appointed to any public office for which he is otherwise qualified" (Constitution of Ghana 1992, Sec. 276(2)). Most sub-Saharan African constitutions that recognize traditional authorities do not explicitly prohibit chiefs or traditional authorities from political engagement; however, the definition of their role in giving advice to the legislature to being represented on various bodies from land boards to local government implicitly shapes the political realm in which these institutions are expected to operate.

How central then are traditional authorities to the constitutional orders of sub-Saharan African states? The answer to this question lies first in our conception of the relationship between the formal provisions of a constitution and the actual distribution of power in a society and, more specifically, how we understand the power that traditional authority may wield, whether it is constitutionally recognized or not. The recognition of traditional authorities in South Africa's 1996 Constitution and the continuing debates over their role: whether in the repeated attempts to pass constitutionally valid national legislation; in actual legal and political struggles over their assertion of authority (Holomisa 2011); in relation to land rights (Ntsebeza 2005); negotiations over mining rights (Manson and Mbenga 2014); or in constitutional cases over the interpretation of customary law, reveals the complexity and enduring character of this issue. A wealth of research since 1994 in South Africa has explored the historical, political, social, and economic consequences of the resurgence of traditional authority within the country's new constitutional order (Ntsebeza 2005; Oomen 2005). While the Constitutional Court has repeatedly adopted progressive interpretations of customary law (Bhe 2005; Shilubana 2007), others have argued that government policy has promoted the emergence of a "neo-traditionalism" that has facilitated more conservative constructions of traditional authority (Zenker 2018, 243–263). The survival and even resurgence of traditional authority within the constitutional order, whether formally recognized or not, is based on a combination of the ability of traditional authorities to leverage their political and economic resources (Gibbs 2014) as well as the "fact that many South Africans derive meaning from their African roots, values and customs, including some elements of culture that traditional authorities claim to embody" (Anslie and Kepe 2016, 32). It is this combination of formal recognition, political mobilization, and what Barbara Oomen described as "the constitutive effects of cultural rights legislation" (Oomen 2005, 241) that informs the constitutional identities of many post-colonial states.

11.3 TRADITIONAL AUTHORITY AND CONSTITUTIONAL IDENTITY IN THE POST-COLONY

Approximately 52 percent of the forty-eight sub-Saharan national constitutions explicitly include traditional authorities in their institutional structures. If we include both institutional recognition as well as the inclusion of customary or indigenous law as a source of law, whether in the regular courts or as the law applied in dispute management institutions under the auspicious of traditional authorities, the number goes up to approximately 64 percent of constitutional orders in sub-Saharan Africa. In addition, there is evidence that in some African countries, traditional authorities are held in such high esteem that they have significant political and economic influence even if they have no formal recognition or role in the constitutional order. However, in a few cases, such as Tanzania, their status in society does seem to have been eclipsed by new political and social institutions.

Furthermore, the status of traditional authorities in those constitutional orders in which they have been formally incorporated varies dramatically both across and within these societies. This variation seems to correlate with their access to public and private resources in addition to political authority. Studies on the role of traditional authorities in post-apartheid South Africa indicate that the political and economic status of these authorities has to a large degree depended on their relative access to specific resources or political arrangements. For example, the Royal Bafokeng Nation, in 2007, were "the largest single shareholder in the world's second largest platinum producing company" (Manson and Mbenga 2014, 143) while the late Zulu king, Goodwill Zwelitini kaBhekuzulu, was made the sole trustee of the Ingonyama Trust under whose control all the 'communal' and state lands of the former KwaZulu Bantustan were placed (Centre for Legal Studies (CLS), Rural Women's Action Research Program 2015).

Whether traditional authorities are recognized or not, a large group of sub-Saharan African constitutions recognize customary or indigenous law as a valid source of law within their constitutional orders. While usually subject to the constitution, or explicitly subject to the rights of women, the recognition of indigenous law is not always correlated with the inclusion of indigenous institutions or traditional authorities. If in some cases traditional authorities are recognized as having jurisdiction to decide matters brought before them under indigenous law, this is only constitutionally recognized in a minority of African constitutions. Instead, if indigenous law or custom is considered a source of law, jurisdiction over its enforcement and development is often located in the ordinary courts. In the case of former British colonies where common law took root, both indigenous law and common law are made subject to the constitution, even when constitutional supremacy is not enshrined. For example, in Uganda, the constitution states that "Laws, cultures and traditions which are against the dignity, welfare or interest of women or other marginalized group ... or which undermine their status, are prohibited by this Constitution" (Constitution of Uganda 1995, Sec. 32(2)).

CONCLUSION

Jacobsohn argues that constitutions include disharmonious elements that reflect tensions within the constitutional order, and that constitutional conflict within the parameters of these elements produces ever-changing yet uniquely specific constitutional identities. The multiplicity of ways in which traditional authorities are recognized and incorporated into sub-Saharan African constitutions provides an expansive example of such elements and a broad canvas upon which to explore how disharmonious elements within these constitutions might impact constitutional identities across the continent. While Jacobsohn recognizes that in some cases a constitutional identity may include a concerted attempt to preclude significant social forces, such as the long attempt to maintain a purely secular constitution in Turkey, the case of traditional authorities in Africa provides another option that may be viewed as either a challenge or supplement to the theory of constitutional identity. Even if many African constitutions do include some recognition of traditional authorities, there are many other African constitutions that make no mention of traditional authorities at all. In these cases, we might consider whether the presence in society of social institutions that continue to play a significant role in the governance of people's lives, may, if not recognized, also impact constitutional identities. To the extent that these are simply symbolic institutions, they may not have much effect on constitutional identity, but where they command significant social loyalty and are looked to for both specific governing functions as well as legitimacy, they may provide a completely alternative source of identity. This alternative identity may merely be supplemental to the constitution but at times it has clearly served as more than a symbolic alternative, even undermining the authority of those attempting to govern under the formal constitution.

Where African constitutions recognize traditional authorities, the significance of this recognition to the question of constitutional identity will depend in part on whether recognition is purely symbolic or if the constitutions grant significant power and protection to these institutions. However, Mahmood Mamdani warns that whether embraced symbolically, as protectors of culture, trustees of community lands, or as integral parts of governance in the new constitutional order, these institutions are a "non-racial legacy of colonialism [which] needs to be brought out into the open so that it may be the focus of public discussion" (Mamdani 1996, 4). It is this warning and the complicated history and interaction between colonial rule and traditional authorities that raises the possibility that these institutions are not merely elements of constitutional disharmony in democratic constitutions but rather pose an existential threat to the fundamental values of democracy and human rights these constitutions formally embrace.

Alternatively, when it comes to the formal inclusion and recognition of traditional institutions within African constitutions, we might ask whether their presence represents an embrace of constitutional diversity and the multiplicity of identities that James Tully argues is a necessary response to demands for constitutional recognition (Tully 1995). This constitutional embrace of traditional authority and institutions would, however, raise the question of whether these new constitutional orders will simply reproduce and legitimize polities that would continue to reflect what Mamdani has identified as a bifurcated state of despotic rural versus urban democracy in the post-colony? If, however, we adopt Jacobsohn's approach and simply identify the constitutional incorporation of traditional authority as elements of constitutional disharmony integral to the shaping of constitutional identities, then we might imagine that the struggle for recognition and democratic participation within

African constitutional orders will continue to evolve a variety of constitutional identities depending on the specific history of each country.

The challenge, however, is to confront Martin Chanock's observation that African constitutional orders seemed to have too often "floated meaninglessly above the societies for which they have been designated, until the bubble bursts in outbreaks of violence" (Chanock 2010, 127). This observation, which is congruent with Mamdani's critique of the bifurcated state and the failure of constitutionalism to gain legitimacy on the African continent, was reflected famously in Okoth-Ogendo's view that Africa has "constitutions without constitutionalism" and in the contributions by other African academics at the Harare Conference on 'State and Constitutionalism in Africa' in May 1989 (Shivji ed. 1991). However, in more recent times we have seen an increasing number of democratic elections and peaceful transitions in power and a constitutional resilience that offers a glimpse of an alternative trajectory for constitutionalism in Africa.

Acknowledging the challenges to constitutionalism in Africa, Berihun Adugnu Gebeye has recently argued, in his book *A Theory of African Constitutionalism*, that "constitutionalism will not take root in Africa unless it takes into account African values and realities in both its normative articulation and institutional design" (2021, 69). Even as this statement reflects Martin Chanock's observation that top-down constitution making in Africa results in "the writing of increasingly complex constitutions, with increasingly sophisticated institutions and rights guarantees" that have failed to gain legitimacy (Chanock 2010, 127), Gebeye suggests that a syncretic understanding of African constitutionalism "supplies us with the theoretical foundations and practical tools for its future diagnosis, improvement, and consolidation by piercing the veils of the legal centralist and legal pluralist paradigms." While Gebeye's vision would recognize traditional authority as a disharmonic element in the struggle for constitutional identity in Africa, it remains a question whether this disharmony is a less productive element and might indeed be an existential threat to the forms of democratic constitutionalism espoused in the formal constitutions of many African states today.

REFERENCES

Afrobarometer Round 7. 2016–2018. Available at: https://afrobarometer.org/.

Ainslie, Andrew, and Thembele Kepe. 2016. "Understanding the Resurgence of Traditional Authorities in Post-Apartheid South Africa." *Journal of Southern African Studies* 42 (1): 19–33.

Chanock, Martin. 2010. "Constitutionalism, Democracy and Africa: Constitutionalism Upside Down." *Law in Context* 28(2): 126–144.

CLS. 2015. "Land Rights Under the Ingonyama Trust, Rural Women's Action Research Programme." Available at: www.cls.uct.ac.za/usr/lrg/downloads/FactsheetIngonyama_Final_Feb2015.pdf.

Gebeye, Berihun Adugna. 2021. *A Theory of African Constitutionalism*. Oxford: Oxford University Press.

Gibbs, Timothy. 2014. *Mandela's Kinsmen: Nationalist Elites and Apartheid's First Bantustan*. Johannesburg: Jacana Media.
Holomisa, Phathekile. 2011. *A Double-Edged Sword: A Quest for a Place in the African Sun*. Johannesburg: Real African Publishers.
Jacobsohn, Gary. 2010. *Constitutional Identity*. Cambridge: Harvard University Press.
Konadu, Kwasi. 2019. *Our Own Way in This Part of the World: Biography of an African Community, Culture, and Nation*. Durham, NC: Duke University Press.
Lawson, Andrew and Rakner Lise. 2005. "Understanding Patterns of Accountability in Tanzania, Final Synthesis Report." Available at: www.gsdrc.org/docs/open/doc98.pdf.
Logan, Carolyn. 2013. "The Roots of Resilience: Exploring Popular Support for African Traditional Authorities." *African Affairs* 112 (448): 353–376.
Mamdani, Mahmood. 1996. *Citizen and Subject: Contemporary Africa and the Legacy of Late Colonialism*. Princeton: Princeton University Press.
Manson, Andrew and Bernard K., Mbenga. 2014. *Land Chiefs Mining: South Africa's Northwest Province Since 1840*. Johannesburg: University of the Witwatersrand Press.
Ntsebeza, Lungisile. 2005. *Democracy Compromised: Chiefs and the Politics of Land in South Africa*. Cape Town: HSRC Press.
Oomen, Barbara. 2005. *Chiefs in South Africa: Law, Power & Culture in the Post-Apartheid Era*. Oxford: James Currey.
Rohregger, Barbara, Katja Bender, Bethuel Kinyanjui Kinuthia, Ester Shuring, Grace Ikua and Nicky Pouw. 2021. "The Politics of Implementation: The Role of Traditional Authorities in Delivering Social Policies to Poor People in Kenya." *Critical Social Policy* 41 (3): 404–425.
Sachs, Albie and Gita Honwana Welch. 1990. *Liberating the Law: Creating Popular Justice in Mozambique*. London: Zed Press.
SDC (Swiss Agency for Development and Cooperation). 2016. "Case Study 2: Insights on Customary and Informal Authorities in Iringa Region." Available at: www.ids.ac.uk/download.php?file=files/dmfile/Tanzaniacasestudy.pdf.
Shivji, Issa G. (ed). 1991. *State and Constitutionalism: An African Debate on Democracy*. Harare: Southern Africa Political Economy Series (SAPES) Trust.
Tully, James. 1995. *Strong Multiplicity: Constitutionalism in an Age of Diversity*. Cambridge: Cambridge University Press.
Ubink, Janine. 2008. *Traditional Authorities in Africa: Resurgence in an Era of Democratization*. Leiden: Leiden University Press.
Young, Crawford. 1994. *The African Colonial State in Comparative Perspective*. New Haven: Yale University Press.
Young, Crawford. 2012. *The Postcolonial State in Africa: Fifty Years of Independence, 1960–2010*. Madison: University of Wisconsin Press.
Zenker, Olaf. 2018. "Land Restitution (Old and New) Neotraditionalism and the Contested Values of Land Justice in South Africa." In *Pursuing Justice in Africa: Competing Imaginaries and Contested Practices*, edited by Jessica Johnson and George Hamandishe Karekwaivanane, 243–263. Athens: Ohio University Press.

CASE LAW

Bhe v Magistrate, *Khayelitsha* 2005 1 SA 580 (CC).
Shilubana v Nwamitwa 2009 2 SA 66 (CC).
MM v MN 2013 4 SA 415 (CC).

12

Imposed Revolution?

"August Revolution," "Imposed Constitution," and the Identity of the Constitution of Japan

Keigo Komamura

INTRODUCTION: DISHARMONY AND IDENTITY

Every identity depends on the identities of others. In other words, every identity could be constituted and discerned only when it is placed in a dialogic or intersubjective context.[1] Identity does not stand alone as an isolated status in a vacuum. Meanwhile, it is certainly widely shared that no identity must be given or imposed by others. Arguably, identity needs a compensatory pair consisting of two contrasting perspectives to discern it, such as the intersubjective and autonomous perspectives as mentioned above, the contextual and universal ones, the past and future ones, and so on.

Contrasting sometimes destabilizes self-mastery, brings about disharmony to identity, or even drives us into self-entrenchment. In moments of identity crisis like those, however, there would be a possibility for identity to not just weaken but also reinforce or reshape its substance. As for *constitutional* identity, Gary J. Jacobsohn observes, "constitutional disharmony is critical to the development of constitutional identity, even as it may make more challenging the task of establishing the specific substance of that identity at any given point in time" (Jacobsohn 2000, 4). (Constitutional) disharmony is not a destructor but a driving force for the development of (constitutional) identity.

Then, what kind of prism will constitutional identity be clarified through?

In the first place, most basically, constitutional identity is articulated through the complementary pair of universalism and particularism. Based upon a specific political community or nation-state, in most cases, constitution is a system of the interplay of the universal (e.g., ideas of fundamental or human rights, international order, and peace, etc.) and the particular (e.g., its own history, culture, and tradition, etc.).

---

[1] Michel Rosenfeld observes, "Delimiting different models of constitution-making is particularly useful in as much as it casts light on alternative ways of handling the relationship between pre-constitutional, constitutional, and extra-constitutional identities. ... Each of these models casts the relationship between self and other in a different light" (emphasis added) (Rosenfeld 2010, 149–150).

Identity of the Constitution of Japan   151

Therefore, constitutional identity is defined and shaped according to a twofold resonance of universalism and particularism.[2]

In the second place, horizontal comparison and vertical comparison are relevant here. As Michel Rosenfeld correctly points out, "the relationship between constitutional and extra-constitutional identity varies *from one country to another*, and even *within the same country over time* due to evolution, revolution, or reform" (emphasis added) (Rosenfeld 2005, 3). Two types of analysis are suggested here: horizontal and vertical. Vertical analysis is particularly relevant for the identity of the Constitution of Japan because, as seen later, the rhetoric of "revolution" played a major role in theoretical justification of Japan's new constitution. Constitutions "cannot be thought of exclusively as the purely internal expression of a polity" within the same country over time because constitution making and identity-building after revolution, war, or radical reformation often "requires a break with the past," thus setting the latter regime against the former regime (Rosenfeld 2010, 203). Vertical and diachronic analysis is useful to verify if a revolutionary reformation is successfully accomplished or unsuccessfully unfinished, and success or failure of identity-building of a new constitution can be traced by comparison with the identity of the previous regime.

These complementary pairs as analysis devices – the universal and the particular, the horizontal and the vertical – would inflict 'disharmony' on the constitutional identity of the country. As mentioned, however, constitutional disharmony is critical to a moment of truth for constitutional identity.

In this chapter, the observation explored above will be applied to the case of the Constitution of Japan established in 1946. As is probably well known, the Constitution of Japan built its postwar identity by *negating* the preceding constitution, the Constitution of the Empire of Japan (aka the Meiji Constitution) of 1889. This *revolutionary* event, however, produced two disharmonious factors to the new constitution: internal and external.

First, the internal disharmony, as discussed in detail later, lies in the fact that the enactment of the new constitution disconnected the new regime from the old *in substance*, but kept them connected *in procedure*. The "August Revolution" theory, which was proposed as an idea to resolve this dissonance, will be examined by vertical comparison in the next Section. Second, the external disharmony gave rise to the "imposed constitution" problem. The enactment of the new constitution in Japan took place within the international legal framework of the time, triggered by Japan's defeat in World War II. This process was seen as a kind of external coercion, and conservative forces in particular have been critical of the new constitution, arguing that it was imposed by the

---

[2] "[T]he nation-state or at least some nation-states devoted to the essential tenets of constitutionalism, such as France and the United States" may have nurtured "a working balance" between universalism and particularism (Rosenfeld 2000, 1225 and 1228). Instead of "the traditional dichotomy of particularism and universalism," Sergio Dellavalle reforms political identity through a new bridging framework of "extending particularism" and "contextualizing universalism" (Dellavalle 2018, 776).

United States, and have used it as a flag of argument for constitutional revision in the hands of the Japanese people. This chapter will explore the "imposed constitution" issue by horizontal comparison between the international framework and domestic order.

12.1 AUGUST REVOLUTION

12.1.1 *Constitution Making as an Implementation of the Potsdam Declaration*

The modernization of Japan began in 1868 when the Meiji Restoration opened the country after a long-term isolation. The 1889 Meiji Constitution used the Constitution of Prussia as its model and introduced a system of constitutional monarchy. However, subsequent history unfolded with the rise of militarism, the deification of the emperor, and thought control by State Shintoism, which dragged the country into World War II.

Japan was to lose the war in the end. The Allied Powers issued the Potsdam Declaration[3] on July 26, 1945, and pressed Japan to surrender.

The "terms" the Potsdam Declaration called for include the following: complete disarmament of the Japanese military forces (Section 9), punishment of "all war criminals" (Section 10), "revival and strengthening of democratic tendencies" (Section 10), establishing "respect for fundamental human rights" such as "freedom of expression, of religion, and of thought" (Section 10), and establishment of "a peacefully inclined and responsible government" (Section 12). These demands were to fundamentally reform the Meiji regime, in other words, the Declaration made total reforms of the Meiji Constitution inevitable. The political leaders and high officials of the Department of Army resisted accepting the Declaration immediately because it did not refer explicitly to what happened to the emperor system. As the closure of war approached, the Japanese Government and its army still stubbornly persisted in protecting the "national polity" (*kokutai*) in which the emperor could retain his sovereign power and authority through all eternity.

The Cabinet debated the terms the Declaration requested in an intensive but sluggish way. It did not make any progress. After the two atomic bombings in Hiroshima and Nagasaki, however, Prime Minister Suzuki finally decided to ask the emperor if it was permissible to accept the Potsdam Declaration and then end the war. The emperor immediately replied in the positive. Thus, the Declaration was accepted on August 14, and WWII ended on August 15, 1945. This is how the constitutional reform began.[4]

---

[3] For full text of the Declaration, see National Diet Library (2003).
[4] Historical descriptions of the process of making the Constitution of Japan in this chapter are mainly based on the following literatures: Koseki 1997; Sato 1962–1994; Takaanagi, Otomo and Tanaka 1972. *See also* Komamura 2010 for details of historical facts about the arguments explored in this chapter.

12.1.2 A Legal Contradiction in Legitimacy of the Constitutional Reform

General Douglas MacArthur, the Supreme Commander for the Allied Powers (SCAP) who was granted full authority for occupation, arrived in Japan on August 30. General Headquarters (GHQ), whose mission was to implement the demands of the Potsdam Declaration under SCAP's directives, was set up on October 2. MacArthur met with the leaders of the Japanese Government and urged them to transform the nation in accordance with the Declaration. In the meetings, he said in a certain military tone, "the Japanese Constitution must be revised" (Koseki 1997, 9). However, the Japanese Government initially either dismissed or disregarded these requests and assumed that *partial revisions* of the Meiji Constitution would suffice. General MacArthur noticed their reluctance and concluded that the government of Japan had neither willingness nor capacity to implement the Potsdam Declaration. In the following months, the constitutional reform process went through various dramatic steps, and eventually, it was implemented and realized using the *revision procedure* in Article 73 of the Meiji Constitution.

The birth of the Constitution of Japan fundamentally changed, almost completely denied, the Meiji Constitution in a true sense. In order to implement the demands of the Potsdam Declaration, the emperor retreated from being a sovereign to a symbol, and sovereignty was placed in the hands of the people. The military was disarmed, and militarism was replaced by pacifism (the renunciation of war in Article 9). The list of basic human rights has become remarkably more extensive and abundant than the former constitution. At the same time, however, these great changes brought about a legal contradiction in the legitimacy of the new constitution, because dramatic reforms were carried out in the form of "revision" of the Meiji Constitution using its revision procedure in Article 73.[5] If the meaning of *revision* or *amendment* is taken literally and seriously, the newborn constitution should just be an *adjustment* or *modification* of the old one. But in reality, the new one rejected the former one. In other words, the new constitution denied its continuity with the Meiji regime *in substance*, but still maintained continuity with it *in its procedure*.

12.1.3 Miyazawa's August Revolution Theory

Professor Toshiyoshi Miyazawa, a prominent constitutional law scholar of the time who was a member of the governmental task force to initiate the reforms, proposed the "August Revolution" theory as a solution to the paradox (Miyazawa 1967, 375–400).

---

[5] In fact, in the latter stages of the drafting process, the call for the establishment of a Constitutional Assembly became temporarily stronger. But this idea was immediately rejected by the Cabinet and MacArthur because they need to complete revision quickly. See Koseki 1997, 148–149.

The main points of the theory are as follows. Acceptance of the Potsdam Declaration in August 1945 brought *"a revolution"* to Japan. The Declaration required Japan to carry out a series of reforms such as transferring from Imperial sovereignty to popular sovereignty, from theocracy to democracy, and from militarism to pacifism. This revolutionary event, Miyazawa states, radically changed the fundamental premise (*konpon tateme*) of the Meiji Constitution. To be sure, the Meiji Constitution still remained the same and its governmental structure was still working right after August 15 but the Declaration changed *"the basic meaning and premise"* of the Meiji Constitution. Metaphorically speaking, Miyazawa's theory comes down to this: Even though the shape and appearance of the body is exactly the same, it has become completely different at the cellular level due to exposure to the flash of the revolution.

The August Revolution theory assumes that there are legal limits to constitutional revision. First, constitutional revision cannot change the fundamental premise because the revision itself is legitimized by that premise. Second, as far as the Meiji Constitution is concerned, it is a fundamental premise that the emperor governs based on his divine will (divine sovereignty), and this cannot be altered by the revision clause. Miyazawa states that it is "a logical suicide" or "a legal incompetency" for the constitution to change that premise by its own procedure (Miyazawa 1967, 382). Accepting the Potsdam Declaration, however, generated the August Revolution which removed those limits from the revision procedure. Thus, the establishment of the new constitution using the procedures of the old constitution was *logically and legally justified through the metaphor of revolution*. Continuity with the previous regime was denied, but this was not caused by the establishment of the new constitution itself, but, earlier than that, by the acceptance of the Potsdam Declaration.

12.1.4 *Implications of the August Revolution Theory*

The August Revolution theory represents too much of a conceptual solution to a question that might be problematic only when viewed from a theoretical interest in law. In any event, there was no real revolution at all. However, even today, legal theorists in Japan still rely on this theory when discussing the legitimacy of constitution making. So, I would like to elicit the implications of the August Revolution theory from the perspective of constitutional identity. If Miyazawa's theory is right, the August Revolution transformed not just the fundamental premise of the constitution but also the constitutional identity.

12.1.4.1 The Potsdam Declaration as a New Source of Normative Authority

First, a new constitutional identity for Japan was forged and shaped by the Potsdam Declaration. According to what the August Revolution theory suggests, it was the

Potsdam Declaration, not the new constitution itself, that brought about the revolution in Japan. The enactment of the new constitution was merely the implementation of the Declaration. Miyazawa argued that because the August Revolution transformed "the fundamental premise changed" of the Meiji Constitution and the "fundamental premise" thus became the basis for new legitimacy, it was possible to establish a completely new constitutional system using the old revision procedure. However, this far-fetched explanation is still incomprehensible. Rather, it should be seen that the August Revolution established the Potsdam Declaration as *a new source of normative authority* on which postwar Japan should rely after its defeat, and the Meiji Constitution was deprived of its authoritative status and turned into a wreck, a cast-off skin, or debris.

In this way, the path to the mission of postwar Japan can be understood as a process of implementing the international promises made in the Declaration, the new authoritative legitimacy for Japan *beyond* the Constitution of Japan.

12.1.4.2 The August Revolution as an Unfinished Revolution

Second, in fact, the August Revolution does not necessarily seem to have completely cut off the previous regime. Indeed, the August Revolution brought about a fundamental shift from "divine sovereignty" to "popular sovereignty." However, this only denied the theocracy and rejected the emperor's status as a sovereign, not the emperor system itself. The emperor system itself survived in the new constitution as a symbolic one (Article 1 of the new constitution).

On this point, Miyazawa wrote as follows: "This revolution did not necessarily abolish the emperor system, nor did it promise its abolition" (Miyazawa 1967, 384).[6] Although the August Revolution denied continuity with the Meiji system, it can be said that continuity with the Meiji system was maintained in a narrow sense insofar as the emperor system itself (albeit a symbolic one) remained. What does this mean for postwar Japan? Miyazawa offers the following outlook.

> As a result of the rejection of theocracy and the recognition of popular sovereignty, the basis of the emperor system was said to be the will of the people, and depending on this, the possibility – the theoretical possibility – of abolishing the emperor system was given. This is because the will of God, which was the basis of the emperor system, is said to be eternal and unchanging, but the will of the people is never eternal and unchanging. (Miyazawa 1967, 386)

The August Revolution is an unfinished revolution. It gives Japan a chance to search for ways in which the elements of modern constitutionalism and Japan's unique cultural institutions could coexist.

---

[6] Insofar as it did not, Miyazawa states, it could be said that the national polity was maintained if the theory of the national polity allowed for an emperor system without sovereign power (Miyazawa 1967, 385).

12.2 IMPOSED CONSTITUTION?

The revolutionary trait of the Constitution of Japan is, after all, derived from the Potsdam Declaration. But was the new constitution enacted in the *correct manner* as mandated by the Declaration? Session 12 of the Potsdam Declaration demanded that "a peacefully inclined and responsible government" shall be established in accordance with "the freely expressed will of the Japanese people." Was the constitution making implemented by "the freely expressed will" of the Japanese people?

12.2.1 A Brief Story of the Process of Making the Constitution of Japan

On October 11, 1945, MacArthur met with Kijuro Shidehara, the newly appointed prime minister, to provide a suggestion on "liberalization of the Constitution." The Shidehara Cabinet was not in favor of constitutional reform; however, it set up a task force called the Constitutional Problem Investigation Committee, aka *the Matsumoto Committee* after its chairman, Joji Matsumoto, in order to initiate just research of the constitution, not its revision. The Matsumoto Committee did not recognize what the Potsdam Declaration really required of Japan. They just made small amendments to the Meiji Constitution and created conservative drafts.

On the other hand, on December 16, 1945, at the Moscow meeting, the Allied Powers reached an agreement to form the Far Eastern Commission (FEC) (comprising thirteen victorious nations, including China and the Soviet Union). This brought a radical change in how the occupation of Japan should be carried out. From February 26 of the following year, FEC was to start activities which would inevitably constrain the power and authority of SCAP in regard to the reformation of the constitution. Against a background of the Allied Powers' moves to curtail his authority and of the ongoing Cold War, MacArthur needed to quicken constitutional reforms.

MacArthur was very lucky because, on February 1, 1946, the *Mainichi* newspaper disclosed and criticized the draft proposal of the Matsumoto Committee. The draft was too conservative and not significantly different from the Meiji Constitution. At this moment, MacArthur started writing the GHQ draft and completed it in around ten days.

On February 13, Courtney Whitney as Chief of Government Section at the GHQ, met Matsumoto and the Minister for Foreign Affairs Shigeru Yoshida to inform them that the Japanese plan they had previously submitted was "wholly unacceptable," and then handed over the GHQ draft in place of Japan's. At that time, GHQ allegedly stated that accepting the draft prepared by them was the only way to protect the emperor, and this is said to have made a strong impression on the Japanese side.[7]

---

[7] The SCAP record recounts what Whitney told them: "As you may or may not know, the Supreme Commander has been unyielding in his defense of your Emperor against increasing pressure from

The debate about "imposed constitution" originated from this event. Finally, on February 22, the Cabinet decided to accept the GHQ draft as a springboard for constitutional reform.

12.2.2 Imposed Constitution?

These stories may infer that drafting the new constitution itself was due to *external interference*. In the case of Japan, however, the constitutional change occurred as a result of the acceptance of the Potsdam Declaration and its implementation. By accepting the Declaration, the Japanese Government agreed to transform the previous regime. Of course, this acceptance was not a "voluntary choice." In a situation where one is faced with a choice between "dead or alive," choosing the latter is not a voluntary choice. Since the defeat of the war was "imposed" by the violence of war (i.e., the two atomic bombings), there is no such thing as a *voluntary defeat*.

In short, the defeat was imposed, and then the Declaration was imposed too. Since the Declaration thus imposed demanded to make a new constitution, the Japanese Constitution is inevitably an imposed constitution. Rather, the question is whether it is *legitimately* imposed or not.

12.2.3 MacArthur's Authorities to Take Direct Action

The action taken by MacArthur and GHQ on February 13 was not only to reject the Matsumoto Committee draft but also to impose the so-called GHQ draft on the Japanese Government. How could MacArthur have taken such a powerful step? In fact, MacArthur was given a great deal of authority in the early stage of the occupation. The establishment of an organization to jointly manage the occupation policy was considerably delayed due to the lack of coordination among the Allied Powers (between the U.S. and the Soviet Union in particular), and the occupation of Japan was basically left to the United States, or, more precisely, to the State-War-Navy Coordinating Committee (SWNCC), and to SCAP (MacArthur) and GHQ who were stationed in Tokyo, at least provisionally.

The Basic Initial Post-Surrender Directive approved by SWNCC on November 1, 1945, enlisted powers given to SCAP to implement the Potsdam Declaration as long as SCAP respects the free will of the Japanese people. In paragraph 5 a, however, it reads "At all times, however, and in all circumstances you are empowered yourself

the outside [FEC] to render him subject to war criminal investigation. ... But, gentlemen, the Supreme Commander is not omnipotent. He feels, however, that the acceptance of the provisions of this new Constitution [the GHQ draft] would render the Emperor practically unassailable...." (Takayanagi, Otomo and Tanaka 1972, 326–329). Matsumoto interpreted these remarks as "MacArthur does support the Japanese Emperor, and this draft constitution is the only way of protecting *the person of the Emperor* from those who are opposed to him" (emphasis added) (Ashida 1986, 76).

to take *direct action* if and to the extent that Japanese authorities fail satisfactorily to carry out your instructions" (emphasis added). So it would be a legally possible interpretation that the Matsumoto draft failed to carry out MacArthur's instructions satisfactorily, and Whitney handed over the GHQ draft as *a direct action*.

If the directive is interpreted in this way, the imposition of the GHQ draft could be legally justified. MacArthur initially entrusted the Japanese Government with the task of reforming its own constitution, but he regarded the Matsumoto Committee's conservative draft as not satisfactorily meeting the demands of the Declaration. If the issuance of the Potsdam Declaration were the August Revolution, the imposition of the GHQ draft on February 13 could be called the "February Revolution," which called for the second (true) acceptance of the Declaration.[8]

12.2.4 *February* Coup d'État: *MacArthur vs. FEC*

However, direct action was *not officially* taken because, at this point, MacArthur had already lost his authority to revise the Meiji Constitution.

Three months prior, on December 16, 1945, at the Moscow conference, the foreign ministers of the United Kingdom, the United States, and the Soviet Union reached an agreement to form the FEC consisting of thirteen victorious nations, the highest-level body with decision-making authority over SCAP (see Section 12.2.1).

The chain of command, with the FEC at its apex, was as follows. Policies decided by the FEC were sent through the U.S. government as orders to MacArthur and GHQ. According to "Terms of Reference of the Far Eastern Commission and the Allied Council for Japan" of December 27, 1945, the victorious nations of the United States, Britain, China, and the Soviet Union had the right to veto the occupation policy of Japan, while the U.S. government was given the power to issue "interim directives" in the state of emergency, which could be used to enforce MacArthur's occupation policy (Koseki 1997, 68–69). Of course, the interim directives did not include changing Japan's constitutional system or radically reorganizing the administration of the occupation, and the FEC reserved the right to review MacArthur's occupation policies. Yet, despite this legal framework, MacArthur tried to proceed with his occupation policy at an increasing pace.

On January 29, an envoy from the predecessor organization of the FEC arrived in Tokyo from the U.S. and told MacArthur that the FEC had been established and its first meeting would be held on February 16. During the conversation, when the subject turned to constitutional reform, MacArthur responded as follows: "The constitutional reform has been taken out of my hands by the Moscow Agreement. When I gave the first instructions on the constitutional reform, I had the authority

---

[8] Shoichi Koseki, a constitutional historian in Japan, calls this event as "a second defeat 'imposed' on Japan," or "Japan's second surrender" (Koseki 1997, 98, 109).

to do so. But now I am not giving any instructions or orders. I only give suggestions" (Koseki 1997, 75–76). Thus, MacArthur was aware that he had no authority over the reform of Japan's constitutional system, but from another point of view, the fact that the FEC would not initiate its activities until February 16 means that MacArthur could proceed with the reform until then. He and GHQ's moves were swift. As mentioned earlier, the *Mainichi* newspaper scooped the Matsumoto Committee draft on February 3, and the draft prepared by GHQ in around ten days was "imposed" on the Japanese Government on February 13, just three days before the February 16 FEC's first meeting.

Earlier I proposed a legal interpretation that the imposition of the draft constitution by GHQ could be understood as a legitimate "direct action" based on the directives of the SWNCC, but this idea needs to be corrected. MacArthur was already without authority to reform the constitution when the FEC was created, and he himself was clearly aware of this. Nevertheless, he boldly pushed for the enactment of a new constitution with the Japanese Government. This was not a legitimate direct action, but a military betrayal of the FEC, by which I mean MacArthur's February *coup d'état*.

12.2.5 A Legitimately Imposed Constitution

However, this "February *coup d'état*" was ultimately a great success. The GHQ draft was accepted by the Japanese Government and debated in the Imperial Diet. The U.S. State Department as well as the FEC tried to stop him, but MacArthur only emphasized the merits of the draft. Rather, the FEC decided to closely monitor the ongoing constitutional debate and, in fact, became involved in the process itself, pushing for the introduction of a civilian clause to counter the partial amendment to the original draft of Article 9 (war renunciation clause), an amendment that foreshadowed Japan's future rearmament. In any event, the new constitution was eventually enacted.

On October 17, 1946, immediately after the draft of the new constitution had passed the Imperial Diet, the FEC decided on two measures: (a) the new constitution should be submitted to a national referendum immediately after its enactment,[9] and (b) the FEC should examine the new constitution within two years of its enactment. MacArthur strongly resisted the FEC's proposal because it undermined the authority of the new constitution. The FEC tried to conduct a review, and several proposals to rewrite the new constitution were made by participating countries. But that scheme sparked a backlash from the Japanese Government and the public. In the end, the FEC's scheme was never actualized and faded away. The FEC was abolished in 1952 with the entry into force of the Peace Treaty.

---

[9] This measure was not realized. If it had been, the postwar debate on the "imposed constitution" would have taken on a very different aspect.

In light of the above, it can be said that MacArthur's February *coup d'état* was finally approved *ex post facto* by the FEC. The illegal imposition was complemented by the international frameworks of the time, or more precisely, by obtaining *ex post facto approval* under such frameworks. In the end, it would be fair to say that the Japanese Constitution was imposed as a matter of fact, however, it was a legitimate imposition.

CONCLUSION: THE IDENTITY OF THE CONSTITUTION OF JAPAN

The revolutionary nature of the Constitution of Japan of 1946 lies in the nature of the Potsdam Declaration. As for a revolutionary impact, the latter is original but the former is only derivative.

It was not the new constitution itself that brought down the Meiji regime and subverted the Meiji Constitution, but rather the defeat in war and the resulting acceptance of the Potsdam Declaration. The new constitution was enacted as an implementation of the task of state transformation demanded of the Japanese Government by the Declaration. And since the Declaration was *imposed* on Japan by the victors of World War II as a condition for its surrender, it is quite natural for us to recognize that the new constitution was also *imposed* on Japan.

The question truly worth asking is whether it was *legitimately* imposed. As discussed above, the enactment of the new constitution, pushed by MacArthur, was almost a *coup d'état* that deviated from the international legal framework of the time, but it was legally complemented by finally obtaining *ex post facto* approval by the legitimate authority holder, the FEC. If this observation is correct, then it is not productive to continue to criticize the MacArthur-led new constitution as an "imposed constitution" by the argument of ignoring the true constitutional constituent, "We the People of Japan."[10] Rather, we should consider what the implications of the August Revolution in 1945 could have for us now and ask how to apply them to our postwar commitment to the Constitution of Japan. The following two points might be important.

First, as may be easily understood, the assumption that the Constitution of Japan was due to the implementation of the Potsdam Declaration means that this

---

[10] The theory of imposed constitution assumes that the boundaries of "We the People" are fixed at the time the constitution is initiated or in the process of enactment of it, and that they are granted the status of constitutional authorship (the status of constituent power). Challenging this proposition, Chaihark Hahm and Sung Ho Kim correctly state that "for constituent people does not, and cannot, have a pre-existing fully formed identity or boundary prior to constitutive constitutional politics" and "the people's identity and boundary arise through complex negotiations during the founding process vis-à-vis external forces and past legacies" (Hahm and Kim 2015, 65). They also correctly argue that "We the People" are "formed as they make a constitution, rather than pre-existing or presiding over any putative constituent moment" (Hahm and Kim 2015, 8).

declaration was the source of the constitution's legitimacy. And this has another meaning. It implies that the Declaration constitutes the limit of constitutional revision of the constitution. Even if the constitution is to be revised in the near future, the Potsdam Declaration and the principles of modern constitutionalism enshrined in it cannot be changed. If a revision that rejects any elements of the Declaration is realized, it would be a revision beyond its limit. In other words, it would be not a revision but a revolutionary project of the creation of a different constitution.

Second, the August Revolution of 1945 was an unfinished revolution. Indeed, the Constitution of Japan denied the sovereignty of the emperor in the Meiji Constitution, but the emperor system itself survived as a symbolic one. As Miyazawa's view introduced in Section 12.1.4.2 suggests, the question of how to reconcile the two different characteristics of the popular sovereignty newly introduced and the symbolic emperor system is an issue open to future generations. Should we build a fine balance between norms and culture? Should we create a new Japan that is thoroughly modernized by abolishing the emperor system at all? Or should we revert to the Meiji system with the emperor as the sovereign?

As Gary J. Jacobsohn suggests, once again, disharmony is not just a good thing for constitutional identity but rather even an integral part of it (Jacobsohn 2000, 3–7). The tension between popular sovereignty and the emperor system is a disharmony internalized in the Constitution of Japan. It is not something that should be eliminated but is indeed an integral part of Japan's constitutional identity. The revolution of 1945 that brought about this tension is an unfinished project, but it is difficult to make an easy prediction as to whether the tension will disappear or become a dormant volcano awaiting its next eruption.

REFERENCES

Ashida, Hitoshi. 1986. *Ashida nikki*. Vol. 1. Tokyo: Iwanami Shoten.
Dellavalle, Sergio. 2018. "Squaring the Circle: How the Right to Refuge Can Be Reconciled with the Right to Political Identity." *International Journal of Constitutional Law* 16 (3): 776–805.
Hahm, Chaihark and Sung Ho Kim. 2015. *Making We the People: Democratic Constitutional Founding in Postwar Japan and South Korea*. Cambridge: Cambridge University Press.
Jacobsohn, Gary Jeffery. 2000. *Constitutional Identity*. Cambridge: Harvard University Press.
Komamura, Keigo. 2010. "Legitimacy of the Constitution of Japan: Redux." *Reischauer Institute of Japanese Studies (Harvard University): Constitutional Revision Research Project*. https://projects.iq.harvard.edu/crrp/publications/legitimacy-constitution-japan-redux.
Koseki, Shoichi. 1997. *The Birth of Japan's Postwar Constitution*, translated by Ray A. Moore. Boulder: Westview Press.
Miyazawa, Toshiyoshi. 1967. *Kenpô no genri (The Principles of Constitution)*. Tokyo: Iwanami Shoten.
National Diet Library. 2003. "Birth of the Constitution of Japan." *National Diet Library Gallery*. www.ndl.go.jp/constitution/e/etc/co6.html.

Rosenfeld, Michel. 2000. "Comment: Huma Rights, Nationalism, and Multiculturalism in Rhetoric, Ethics, and Politics: A Pluralist Critique." *Cardozo Law Review* 21: 1225–1242.

Rosenfeld, Michel. 2005. "The Problem of 'Identity' in Constitution-Making and Constitutional Reform," Benjamin N. Cardozo School of Law Jacob Burns Institute for Advanced Legal Studies, Working Paper 143.

Rosenfeld, Michel. 2010. *The Identity of the Constitutional Subject: Selfhood, Citizenship, Culture, and Community*. London and New York: Routledge.

Sato, Tatsuo. 1962–1994. *History of the Japanese Constitution-Making*. Vols 1–4. Tokyo: Yuhikaku.

Takayanagi, Kenzo, Ichiro Otomo, and Hideo Tanaka. 1972. *The Process of the Enactment of the Japanese Constitution*. Vol. 1. Tokyo: Yuhikaku.

13

India

A Constitution in Search of an Identity

Gautam Bhatia

The Indian Constitution was drafted over three years, between 1947 and 1950. It had a shifting membership, that ranged between 389 and (after the partition of India) 299 members, elected or nominated under varying sets of rules. The Constituent Assembly was thus a "polyphonic" drafting body (Nigam 2004). In the last seventy years, it has been amended 105 times (an average of more than once a year). Some parts of the Constitution arguably form mini-Constitutions of their own: for example, Part IX, which deals with devolved government, has forty-six sub-clauses (Articles 243A to 243ZT) — longer than many national Constitutions! — and lays out a detailed administrative structure for local government. The Sixth Schedule, which governs the administration of certain indigenous areas, has twenty sections that — together — create a uniquely modified parliamentary structure of governance, complete with emergency powers. Any account of Indian constitutional identity must therefore grapple with the length, complexity, and diversity of concerns and functions that underpin the document.

13.1 IDENTITY AS A CONTESTED TERRAIN

Indeed, one might even begin by questioning whether it makes sense to attribute an "identity" to a document of such length, breadth, and bewildering array of detail. A survey of judicial and scholarly treatment of the issue appears to answer in the affirmative. The starting point is the 1973 judgment of the full bench of the Indian Supreme Court, *Kesavananda Bharati v Union of India*.[1] In *Kesavananda*, a seven to six majority held that the Indian Constitution had an unamendable "basic structure." The basic structure was pegged at a level of high abstraction: Basic features included democracy, secularism, the rule of law, equality, federalism, and judicial independence (to name a few). In subsequent decisions, the Court came to explicitly frame the basic structure in the language of constitutional identity:[2] According

---

[1] Kesavananda Bharati v Union of India (1973) 4 SCC 225.
[2] Minerva Mills v Union of India (1980) 3 SCC 625.

to the Court, an "amendment" was no longer an amendment if the document being amended was denuded of its "identity."

The basic structure, then, looms large over any discussion of Indian constitutional identity. Scholars have, in tandem, tended to locate constitutional identity in the sweeping phrases of the Constitution's Preamble, and in its chapters on fundamental rights and directive principles (Parekh 2008).

However, it is this very sweeping and abstract character of the basic structure that raises challenges for constitutional identity. In a characteristically thoughtful and illuminating essay, Gary Jacobsohn – in whose honor this Festschrift has been written – notes that elements of the basic structure are of two types: constitutive of *constitutionalism* (e.g., the rule of law, separation of powers, or judicial independence), and constitutive of substantive *political* commitments (secularism) (Jacobsohn 2015). Jacobsohn notes that the content of the latter category is deeply contested: The meaning of secularism has been the subject of conflict from the beginning of the Republic, a conflict that has played out in courts, in legislatures, and – often with destructive consequences – in politics (Jacobsohn 2015). For Jacobsohn, thus, constitutional identity is dynamic, constantly informing – and informed by – democratic politics.

In this sense, while it is correct to say that "secularism" is a part of Indian constitutional identity, it is also questionable how much meaning this really carries, as the term "secularism" is something of a floating signifier. Jacobsohn correctly notes that when we ask ourselves what "secularism" really means, the answer necessarily takes us outside the realm of the Constitution and of judicial decisions interpreting the Constitution.

Admittedly, there have been attempts of late (including by the present author) to ground some of these concepts in a constitutional history of political and social transformation (Bhatia 2019).[3] However, as the judicial pushback to the judgment of the Supreme Court in *Indian Young Lawyers' Association* – which sought to accord the concept of secularism a transformative character by taking the side of intra-group religious dissenters against social authority – shows, there is no widespread agreement over whether – and how – the Indian Constitution has a transformative identity.[4] The historical record itself is undoubtedly patchy, with the period leading up to the framing of the Constitution revealing no clear consensus on the transformative character of the Constitution.[5]

"Secularism" is not the only aspect of substantive constitutional identity whose shifting and contested character makes it difficult to pin down. Consider "equality."

---

[3] See, e.g., Navtej Johar v Union of India (2018) 10 SCC 1; Indian Young Lawyers' Association v State of Kerala (2019) 11 SCC 1; Government of the NCT of Delhi v Union of India (2018) 8 SCC 501.
[4] The judgment – that held that women worshippers had a constitutional right to access a certain temple – is presently in suspended animation after a different bench of the Court changed its own rules regarding the review of decided cases in order to "refer" it for reconsideration to a larger bench.
[5] For discussion, see the essays in *The Indian Constituent Assembly: Deliberations on Democracy* (Udit Bhatia ed., Routledge 2017).

In the course of its history, the Supreme Court has repeatedly altered its views about what equality means and requires. This has played out primarily through litigation over the scope and interpretation of the Constitution's affirmative action provisions (Constitution of India, Art. 15(4), 16(4)). The Court has moved from a formal, color/caste-blind version of equality, to a more substantive version that views affirmative action as a part of fulfilling the mandate of equality, and then yet again to a somewhat hybrid version that sees the purpose of equality as finding the right balance between the claims of "merit" and the claims of affirmative action (Bhatia 2022; Sitapati 2015). As with "secularism," the Court's decisions have not happened in a political vacuum, but in the context of political struggles over the meaning of "equality," struggles that have included, for example, disputes over the range and character of groups that are entitled to affirmative action.

The fluid nature of this account of constitutional identity is further evident when we consider the fact that in the forty-nine years since the *Kesavananda Bharati* decision, the basic structure doctrine has been invoked to strike down constitutional amendments in only a handful of cases. If, indeed, the basic structure is where constitutional identity lies, then it is a rather accommodative identity, which can assimilate, for example, departures from the one-person-one-vote principle[6] and significant alterations to its affirmative action provisions[7] without (in the Supreme Court's opinion) meaningfully departing from its democratic or egalitarian character. This once again raises the question of whether constitutional identity – if articulated in this fashion – has any real conceptual purchase. Perhaps the best we can do – with Jacobsohn – is to acknowledge that our conclusions about Indian constitutional identity can be tentative at best, and accurate at a certain point of time but subject to the push-and-pull of constitutional politics outside and inside the courtroom.

13.2 UNDERSTANDING CONSTITUTIONAL IDENTITY THROUGH THE LENS OF POWER

Discussions around transformative constitutionalism – thus far – have been limited to Jacobsohn's second conception of constitutional identity: substantive political commitments. Here is where a further problem arises: Together, the fundamental rights and directive principles chapters of the Indian Constitution comprise around 10 percent of the Constitution itself. Now of course, this is not dispositive: it might just be that 10 percent of the constitutional text is more fundamental to its identity than the other 90 percent. Certain Constitutions, indeed, seem to create an inbuilt hierarchy: The Constitution of Kenya, for example, "entrenches" certain provisions by making them more difficult and onerous to amend (Constitution of Kenya 2010,

---

[6] R.C. Poudyal v Union of India, AIR 1993 SC 1804.
[7] M. Nagaraj v Union of India, (2006) 8 SCC 212.

Chapter XVI). That said, however, a version of constitutional identity that appears to leave out 90 percent of the Constitution deserves a closer look.

In this context, I would suggest that the Constitution ought to be understood not so much as a document of *rights and responsibilities*, but as a document about the *allocation and distribution of power*. Understanding constitutional identity through the lens of power allows us to read the Constitution as a whole, while also including the elements of the basic structure discussed above. Indeed, I would suggest that the chapters on fundamental rights and directive principles (those that come up most often in discussions around constitutional identity and the basic structure) are best understood as *one* of multiple ways in which the Constitution speaks of, and to, power.

I suggest that under the Constitution the question of power is considered along the following axes (both through the text and through silences): Should power be *distributed* or *concentrated*? *Unitary* or *federal*? *Direct* or *representative*? Vested in *electoral* or "*guarantor*" (i.e., fourth branch) institutions? Vested in the *state* or the *People*? Should it be *homogenous* or *plural*? While some of these axes are captured in the first category of Jacobsohn's typology (basic features integral to *constitutionalism* rather than *a* particular constitutional history), not all of them are. I suggest, therefore, that in articulating Indian constitutional identity, we need to move beyond just the basic structure and its components; in addition, we should understand Indian constitutional identity by paying close attention to how the constitutional text, judicial decisions, and constitutional politics deal with the question of power.

My argument here is as follows: *First*, as a document for regulating power, the Indian Constitution is in tension with itself. There are elements of the Constitution that articulate a vision of power that is *homogenous, concentrated, and unitary*, exercised predominantly through *representative, electoral* institutions, and within the framework of the *state*. The observation is not new: As both Aditya Nigam and Uday Mehta have observed, a number of imperatives at the time of the founding resulted in the drafting of a Constitution that was primarily *Statist* in character, with ideas of nationhood subordinated to the state (Mehta 2007; Nigam 2004). *However*, at the same time – both explicitly and through silences and implications – the Constitution undermines or interrogates its own dominant register by also advocating for *plural, distributed*, and *federal* forms of power, where both the *People* and *guarantor institutions* play a role in addition to – and often to constrain – electoral institutions, and where the state is not – in the last analysis – the sole repository of power. It is in this way that I argue that the Constitution is in tension with itself – one might even say, in something of an identity crisis!

This tension creates a terrain of contestation and a set of interpretive choices. Formally, this contestation is to be resolved through the judicial branch – primarily, the Supreme Court of India. My *second* argument, then, is that when faced with interpretive choices between the two visions of power outlined above, the Indian Supreme Court, for the most part, has chosen the former at the expense of the latter.

The *centralizing drift* – as I call it – which is already latent within the constitutional text and structure has been further accelerated and entrenched by the jurisprudence of the Supreme Court. This brings us to a point where – to go back to Jacobsohn's framing – the "dynamic identity" of the Indian Constitution has gradually crystallized in different forms of centralized power. It is important to note that this was not inevitable, but the product of conscious judicial choice. It follows from that, of course – although this will not be part of this chapter – that it is not irreversible either: The purpose of showing that things need not have been this way is to also show that they *need not be this way in the future*.

To chart out the Supreme Court's trajectory on each of the axes of power mentioned above would require a monograph. In this chapter, I shall limit myself to two issues. First, I shall summarize how the Constitution maps out the power relations flagged above. Second, I shall take one axis along which power is divided – the federal axis – as a fuller illustration for the argument above, and consider one important judgment – *State of West Bengal v Union of India* – which dealt with questions around the federal allocation of power. Through a discussion of the issues raised in the case, I will attempt to show how the Court was faced with clear choices with respect to constitutional identity and power, and to interrogate the reasoning underlying the choices that the Court *did* make. This is, obviously, illustrative, but it also gestures to the fuller form of the argument and lays the groundwork for its future development.

13.3 AXES OF POWER UNDER THE INDIAN CONSTITUTION

The Constitution contemplates a parliamentary and federal governance structure, existing at two levels: the center ("union") and the several states. It is trite to say that the Indian Constitution is "biased" toward the center: In the domains of law-making, finance, and administration, the union is granted far greater powers than the states. Scholars have pointed to various – complementary – reasons for the federal "bias" of the Constitution, from the independence-era, need to construct a national political economy (Tillin 2021, 161), to concern for minorities' well-being under state governments more prone to capture by entrenched local power (Kholsa 2020), to fears of secession (Mehta 2007).

While these reasons are reflected in the provisions outlined above, where – in certain domains – state power is evidently subordinate to union power – neither they nor the provisions themselves, are exhaustive of the full gamut of power relations between the union and the states. Nor do these reasons amount to an interpretive approach to how these power relations *should* be understood in the absence of an explicit regulating provision. Thus, a profusion of terminology – that India is an "asymmetric" federation, a federation with a unitary "bias," or a "quasi-federation" – ultimately obscures more than it reveals. To the extent that it indicates the existence of provisions explicitly in the Constitution, it is rather banal; to the extent that it indicates how the relationship between the union and the states *should* be understood in other cases, it says nothing at all. It is here, however, that judgments such as *State of West Bengal v Union of India* – which we shall consider in the next section – become important. In these judgments, the Supreme Court has repeatedly held that constitutional silences ought to be interpreted *in favor of the union*: that is, in a dispute between union power and state power, where the constitutional text is not completely determinative, the Constitution's pre-existing "tilt" toward the union justifies an interpretation in favor of the union. Over the years, this has therefore led to a further entrenchment of power in the union.

Furthermore, the relationship between the center and the states is not uniform. At the time of Independence, the state of Jammu and Kashmir – by virtue of the manner of its accession to the Indian Union – was guaranteed its own Constitution and a degree of autonomy (Article 370). The position of Jammu and Kashmir has often been articulated as an exception that proves the rule that the Constitution envisages a *homogenous* federation. Once again, a careful reading of simply the bare text of the Constitution demonstrates that the situation is more complicated. The Constitution's Fifth and Sixth Schedules set up a detailed governance structure for "Scheduled Areas" and "Scheduled Tribes"; the Sixth Schedule, in particular – as noted above – resembles almost a mini-Constitution in its attention to legislation, administration, and adjudication. Throughout the Constitution itself, various provisions envisage special structures in certain autonomous districts within the State of Assam; and over the years, additions to Article 371 have created a situation where as many as twelve states are the beneficiaries of "special provisions," ranging from affirmative action in certain areas to immunity from certain federal legislation dealing with civil or personal laws. The dominant, homogenous register of the Indian federation, thus, is faced with a counterpoint of federal *pluralism*. In this context, however, over the years, whenever the constitutional status of Jammu and Kashmir vis-à-vis the Indian Union has come into question at the Supreme Court, the Court's interpretations have supported a gradual erosion of state autonomy.[8] The culmination of this history is the effective abrogation of Article 370 in 2019, a challenge to which is pending before the Supreme Court at the time of writing, thereby creating an effective fait accompli that further undermines constitutional pluralism.

At the union level itself (and replicated at the level of the states), the horizontal distribution of power follows the parliamentary model, with its familiar blurring of the line between the legislature and the executive. *In theory*, a number of checks and balances exist to avoid the growth of an imperial presidency (or, in India's case an imperial prime minister-ship). These checks and balances are familiar: bicameralism with an Upper House that represents the states and has veto powers over all legislation (other than money bills), and collective cabinet responsibility. At the

---

[8] See, e.g., Sampat Prakash v State of Jammu & Kashmir, AIR 1970 SC 1118; Mohd Maqbool Damnoo v State of Jammu & Kashmir, AIR 1972 SC 963.

same time, however, the Indian Constitution also explicitly constitutionalizes rule by decree: When Parliament is not in session, the Council of Ministers can advise the president to pass "Ordinances" that have the "force and effect" of law (Dam 2013). While it is evident that Ordinances are *meant* to be limited to emergencies, there is no *explicit* limitation placed upon the president's ordinance-making power, other than a requirement of parliamentary ratification on the next convening of the House. Although in recent years the Supreme Court has interpreted constitutional ambiguities and silences to *limit* the concentration of power within the union executive, rather than to expand it, it has not framed its judgments in terms concrete enough to be enforceable, or to act as an effective check on the executive.[9] For example, despite a 2017 judgment of the Supreme Court seeking to limit Ordinances, there has been no perceptible change in political practice since that time.

The role of the People, and of guarantor institutions, as counterpoints to electoral institutions, is perhaps a reflection of the Indian Constitution's dated character. Other than the mandatory recitation in the Preamble ("We the People..."), the People are more or less totally off-stage. Amending power, for example, is entirely the prerogative of the legislature under Article 368, with no scope for public participation. Unlike other, more recent Constitutions, the concept of public participation itself finds no mention in the constitutional text. Similarly, and unlike more recent Constitutions, the Indian Constitution does not have a fleshed-out conception of a fourth branch or guarantor institutions. The Constitution does envisage an Election Commission with a degree of independence from the political executive when it comes to removal or varying of service conditions; appointments, however, remain in the hands of the union executive,[10]; and there are similar provisions for a comptroller and auditor general.

At first blush, therefore, the Constitution appears to set out a classical vision of public power being exercised solely through the representative bodies selected through the electoral route. However, a journey beyond the constitutional text reveals a more complex story. Public participation and fourth branch institutions have become part of the Indian legal landscape in the form of *legislation*, but what is particularly crucial is that such legislation has invariably been justified on the basis that it is giving *effect* to existing constitutional rights. Thus, public participation is integral to the scheme of the 2007 Forest Rights Act and is explicitly understood as giving effect to the fundamental rights to life and livelihood of indigenous and other forest-dwelling peoples. Similarly, the Information Commission – a classic example of a fourth branch institution – has been established under the Right to Information Act, which – in turn – was enacted on the understanding that it was implementing

---

[9] Krishna Kumar Singh v State of Bihar, (2017) 3 SCC 1.
[10] Very recently, the Supreme Court has put in place an alternative mechanism of appointment, to hold the field until Parliament passes a law on the subject of the appointment of election commissioners.

the fundamental right to information (itself derived from the fundamental right to freedom of speech and expression).[11] In comparative constitutional theory, the concept of constitutional statutes – or "super-statutes" – is not unknown. Arguably, therefore, while public participation and fourth branch institutions were not integral to constitutional identity in the Indian Constitution *as enacted*, to return to Jacobsohn once again, they are *now* a part of an evolving, dynamic constitutional identity tied to redistribution of power away from the union executive. Or, at the very least, that is one plausible way of understanding constitutional evolution in this domain; at this point in time, along this axis, the resolution of constitutional identity remains open.

Let us finally come to the state itself. The topic of fundamental rights and directive principles has been studied in great detail, and I do not intend to rehearse those studies here. Put briefly, the fundamental rights chapter contains a series of broadly worded clauses that allow for the restriction of rights for a range of state interests, ranging from "public interest," "decency or morality," and "public order" (Kannabiran 2004). At the heart of the restrictions regime is Article 22, which – almost uniquely among democratic Constitutions – expressly authorizes administrative detention without trial. The history of Article 22 is a contested one, with the Constituent Assembly Debates arguably creating the space for a narrow and restricted reading; judicial interpretation, however, has almost uniformly refrained from reading in any limitations – other than bare procedural ones – upon the state's power of administrative detention. The upshot of this has been a blurring between the "state of exception" and the "state of normalcy" in India's criminal justice system, with the latter gradually – and incrementally – subsumed within the former (Singh 2007). While Article 22 constitutes the textual foundation for this blurring – writing in, as it does, a permanent state of exception into the Constitution text itself – it is a series of judicial choices that have ensured that the dynamic evolution of this piece of Indian constitutional identity has been *toward* centralization of power (in this case, within the state, at the expense of the citizen, rather than the other way around).

The above discussion sacrifices a degree of complexity for the sake of brevity. That said, the point can be summed up as follows: The identity of the Indian Constitution can be best thought of in the language of power, and how power is allocated, distributed, and contained. A study of the Constitution reveals that constitutional identity has both a dominant and a non-dominant register. The dominant register understands power as being concentrated, homogenous, unitary, vested in electoral and representative institutions, and exercised through the state. The non-dominant register counters the dominant one with a vision of power that is distributed, plural, federal, has space for the People and non-electoral institutions, and constrains the state. The former is more explicitly visible on the surface of the Constitution, but the latter is equally present, if somewhat submerged. This makes the Constitution a terrain

[11] State of MP v Raj Narain, AIR 1975 SC 865.

of contestation with respect to the question of identity, and indeed, ensures that constitutional identity is not given but rather, *constructed* through a series of interpretive choices. The primary vehicle of making – and articulating – those interpretive choices is the judiciary, and a study of its record indicates that in most (but not all cases), the judiciary has contributed to – or at least, failed to stop – a centralizing drift within constitutional identity, or – in other words – further entrenchment of the dominant register at the cost of the non-dominant.

13.4 ILLUSTRATION: *STATE OF WEST BENGAL V UNION OF INDIA*

State of West Bengal v Union of India was decided by a six-judge bench of the Supreme Court in 1962.[12] The key issue in the case was whether the union could acquire property owned by a state (the State of West Bengal), for the purposes of coal prospecting and development. The State of West Bengal argued that it could not, inter alia, because under the federal scheme, *sovereignty* was shared between the union and the states. Consequently, the non-consensual acquisition of property of the latter by the former was not allowed.

By a majority of five to one, the Supreme Court rejected this argument. The majority judgment rested its reasoning on a particular historical story of Indian federalism. Unlike – for example – the USA, the Indian Union had not been formed out of independent states coming together and voluntarily ceding a part of their sovereign power to a federation. Rather, the "legal theory" on which the Indian Constitution was based was a "withdrawal" of powers to the People, and their subsequent decision to distribute it among the union and the states. The majority then noted that the scheme of the Constitution evidently established union supremacy in important respects. That being the case, the majority held that "to imply limitations on that power on the assumption of that degree of political sovereignty which makes the States coordinate with and independent of the Union, is to envisage a Constitutional scheme which does not exist in law or in practice."[13]

An examination of the majority's opinion reveals, however, that what passed as a matter-of-fact retelling of Indian constitutional history – and the consequences that apparently flowed logically from that history – actually entailed a series of interpretive choices. To start with, the historical story that Indian federalism differed from American federalism because – apparently – provincial units had no meaningful independent existence at the time of the framing of the document has become a near-article of faith in any account of Indian federalism. Like many other articles of faith, however, it fails to stand up to a modicum of serious scrutiny. The history of the evolution of responsible government in colonial India – starting with constitutional

---

[12] State of West Bengal v Union of India 1964 SCR (1) 371.
[13] State of West Bengal v Union of India 1964 SCR (1) 371.

reforms in 1909 – *begins* with the establishment of provincial legislatures, with a (limited) central legislature making a substantially later appearance on the scene (Elangovan 2019). "Provincial autonomy" was a serious political issue all through the late-colonial period; and perhaps most importantly, a substantial portion of the Constituent Assembly was nominated via the provincial legislatures; indeed, as any superficial survey of the Constituent Assembly Debates reveals, individual speakers spoke as *representatives of their respective provinces*.[14] There is, therefore, no warrant to hold that provincial identity was negated – or subordinated into a larger, unitary identity – at the time of the framing of the Indian Constitution; if anything, the history of the framing asks us to draw the opposite inference.

It is then equally easy to see how the majority's interpretive choice continued on the path to privileging the historical story that it told. As flagged above, the fact that the Indian Constitution has a number of provisions encoding union supremacy over state power is an objective fact. The often-unacknowledged debate, however, is *what follows from that*. One argument might be that these provisions only go to show that union supremacy is a part of constitutional *identity* and that, therefore, any interpretive doubt ought to be resolved in favor of the union. The *other* interpretation, however, is that by specifically setting out the provisions where union power was meant to prevail, the framers of the Constitution were making explicit the *federal* principle: namely that, unless *explicitly* stated that union power was to prevail, the Constitution would have to be interpreted with a view to devolution of power, or – in other words – with a view toward ensuring that state sovereignty would continue to be preserved unless *expressly* ceded to the union via the Constitution. The historical story told by the majority enabled it to present the former interpretive argument as simply a natural corollary of what Indian federalism (or, at a more abstract level, Indian constitutional identity) *was*; as we have seen, however, it was an interpretive choice, the nature of which becomes clearer once the full historical story is told.

That the majority were making an interpretive choice becomes even clearer when we consider the dissenting opinion of Subba Rao J. Noting that there was no reason to consider the very particular American historical experience as constituting the default for what federalism *should* be, Subba Rao J adopted the second interpretation flagged above: that what a plain reading of the Constitution revealed was that where it was so intended, the union was *expressly* vested with supremacy in certain departments, but that in other departments, the states and the union were to be treated as equal sovereigns. Subba Rao J justified this by telling an alternate historical story of Indian federalism, one that I hinted at above:

> Historically, before the advent of the Constitution, there were different Provinces enjoying in practice **a fair amount of autonomy and there were innumerable**

[14] In the Constituent Assembly Debates, a speaker's name is immediately followed by the name of the province that he or she is representing (if applicable).

States with varying forms of government ranging from pure autocracy to guided democracy. There were also differences in language, race, religion etc. ... in those circumstances our Constitution adopted a federal structure with a strong bias towards the Centre....[15]

Subba Rao J, thus, advanced a normative and historical understanding of the Constitution according to which the *distribution* or dispersal of power through the polity was a fundamental tenet of constitutional identity – as the Constitution was committed to holding together a diverse and plural society – and that federalism was one way of achieving that goal. Based upon this, he went on to hold that the non-consensual taking of state property was beyond the power of the union government.

The debate between the majority and the dissent in *State of West Bengal v Union of India* thus demonstrates how questions of constitutional identity are tangled up with questions of power. Constitutional identity is shaped around how power is distributed, wielded, and contained, and involves courts having to make a series of interpretive choices that starkly affect how the Constitution speaks to, and of, power. *State of West Bengal v Union of India* is one example of how those choices came to be made.

CONCLUSION

In this essay, I have attempted to interrogate – and expand – discussions around Indian constitutional identity. Judicial and scholarly discourse often associates Indian constitutional identity with the "basic structure." Following Gary Jacobsohn, I have argued that identity, as articulated through the basic structure, is best understood as dynamic and contested at any time, rather than concrete and unchanging. I have also argued that the basic structure does not tell the complete story of Indian constitutional identity. That story needs us to understand the Indian Constitution through the lens of power, and how the Constitution organizes power relations. Here too, we find constitutional silences and a crucial role for the judiciary in defining and articulating constitutional identity. A study of constitutional identity through the lens of power reveals – broadly – a "centralising drift" that is present both in the constitutional text and in judgments interpreting the text. While the "centralising drift" might be a dominant feature of Indian constitutional identity at the present moment, it is important to remember that as in its more substantive avatar, this version of constitutional identity, too, is contested, revisable, and always open to transformation.

I offer a quick provocation, by way of conclusion. Is there a link between the evolution of these two strands of constitutional identity – the strand of power and the strand of substantive political commitments? In an overlapping intellectual enterprise, Roberto Gargarella has convincingly argued that centralization and concentration of power tend to make the effective implementation of a substantive bill of rights

---

[15] State of West Bengal v Union of India 1964 SCR (1) 371 (emphasis supplied).

more difficult (Gargarella 2013). To be sure, the argument is historical, not conceptual, and can be tested by looking at the historic trajectory of constitutionalism in a particular jurisdiction. While a detailed analysis is beyond the scope of this essay, one can flag a few observations as an opening into further investigation: Constitutional identity's centralizing drift does appear to be accompanied by a gradual erosion of the substantive elements of the basic structure; while there have been moments of pushback,[16] the overall trend appears to be toward a dilution of basic features that were meant to keep a *substantive* check on power, alongside the centralizing drift.[17] A detailed investigation about the link between the two, however, is for another day.

REFERENCES

Bhatia, Gautam. 2019. *The Transformative Constitution*. New Delhi: HarperCollins India.
Bhatia, Gautam. 2022. "Equality under the Indian Constitution." In *Imagining Unequals, Imagining Equals*, edited by Ulrike Davy and Antje Fluchter, 231–255. Bielefeld: Bielefeld University Press.
Dam, Shubhankar. 2013. *Presidential Legislation in India*. Cambridge: Cambridge University Press.
Elangovan, Arvind. 2019. *Norms and Politics: Sir Benegal Narsing Rau in the Making of the Indian Constitution, 1939–1950*. Oxford: Oxford University Press.
Gargarella, Roberto. 2013. *Latin American Constitutionalism, 1810–2020: The Engine Room of the Constitution*. Oxford: Oxford University Press.
Jacobsohn, Gary. 2015. "Constitutional Identity." In *The Oxford Handbook of the Indian Constitution*, edited by Sujit Chaudhry et al., 110–127. Oxford: Oxford University Press.
Kannabiran, K.G. 2004. *The Wages of Impunity: Power, Justice, and Human Rights*. Hyderabad: Orient BlackSwan.
Kholsa, Madhav. 2020. *India's Founding Moment: The Constitution of a Most Surprising Democracy*. Cambridge: Harvard University Press.
Mehta, Uday. 2007. "Indian Constitutionalism: Articulation of a Political Vision." In *From the Colonial to the Postcolonial: India and Pakistan in Transition*, edited by Dipech Chakrabarty, Rochona Majumdar, and Andrew Sartori, 13–30. Oxford: Oxford University Press.
Nigam, Aditya. 2004. "A Text without an Author: Locating Constituent Assembly as Event." *Economic and Political Weekly* 39 (21): 2107–2113.
Parekh, Bhikhu. 2008. "The Constitution as a Statement of Indian Identity." In *Politics and Ethics of the Indian Constitution*, edited by Rajeev Bhargava, 43–58. Oxford: Oxford University Press.
Singh, Ujjwal Kumar. 2007. *The State, Democracy, and Anti-Terror Laws in India*. Thousand Oaks: Sage Publications.
Sitapati, Vinay. 2015. "Reservations." In *The Oxford Handbook of the Indian Constitution*, edited by Pratap Bhanu Mehta, Madhav Khosla, and Sujit Chaudhry, 720–742. Oxford: Oxford University Press.
Tillin, Louise. 2021. "Building a National Economy: Origins of Centralised Federalism in India." *The Journal of Federalism* 51 (2): 161–185.

---

[16] For example, S.R. Bommai vs Union of India, (1994) 3 SCC 1, on the subject of secularism.
[17] For example, the Supreme Court's "Ayodhya" judgment in the context of secularism, and the upholding of civil-rights-infringing "special statutes" in the context of the rule of law, to take just two examples.

CASES AND LEGISLATION

State of West Bengal v Union of India 1964 SCR (1) 371.
Prakash v State of Jammu & Kashmir, AIR 1970 SC 1118.
Mohd Maqbool Damnoo v State of Jammu & Kashmir, AIR 1972 SC 963.
Kesavananda Bharati v Union of India (1973) 4 SCC 225.
MP v Raj Narain, AIR 1975 SC 865.
Minerva Mills v Union of India (1980) 3 SCC 625.
R.C. Poudyal v Union of India, AIR 1993 SC 1804.
S.R. Bommai v Union of India, (1994) 3 SCC 1.
M. Nagaraj v Union of India, (2006) 8 SCC 212.
Krishna Kumar Singh v State of Bihar, (2017) 3 SCC 1.
Government of the NCT of Delhi v Union of India (2018) 8 SCC 501.
Navtej Johar v Union of India (2018) 10 SCC 1.
Indian Young Lawyers' Association v State of Kerala (2019) 11 SCC 1.

PART III

American Constitutionalism and Constitutional Identity

14

"This Is (Not) Who We Are"

Reflections on 1619 and the Search for a Singular Constitutional Identity[*]

Sanford Levinson

[A] constitution acquires an identity through experience, [but] this identity exists neither as a discrete object of invention nor heavily encrusted essence embedded in a society's culture requiring it to be discovered. Rather, identity emerges dialogically and represents a mix of political aspirations and commitments that are expressive of a nation's past, as well as the determination of those within the society who seek in some ways to transcend that past. It is changeable but resistant to its own destruction, and it may manifest itself differently in different settings. (Jacobsohn 2006).

> Do I contradict myself?
> Very well then I contradict myself,
> (I am large, I contain multitudes.)
>   Walt Whitman, *Songs of Myself*, 51

I structure my remarks around what has become a common trope in the United States following the occurrence of some embarrassing event or release of information. Political leaders often wish to reassure us that "this is not who we are." (Know Your Meme n.d.). Former President Obama was especially fond of the phrase. Back in 2007, while attempting to drum up support in Iowa, he attacked the way that this country finances medical services "paid for by the skyrocketing premiums that come from the pockets of the American people. This is not who we are." Torture, which was by most assessments widely used during the Global War on Terror, was, according to then-President Obama in 2010 "contrary to who we are." So prevalent was Obama's use of the mantra that it apparently became a ready source of parody in a variety of political cartoons. One should recognize the affinity between the trope and Chico Marx's comment to Groucho Marx in *Duck Soup*, "Who you gonna

---

[*] An earlier version of this essay was prepared for presentation at the "Madison Schmooze" on October 15, 2021, the topic of which was the 1619 Project. As always, I have benefited from suggestions by Mark Graber.

believe, me or your lying eyes?" Mark Graber has cited to me another great unrecognized theorist, Bill Parcells, the Super Bowl-winning coach of the New York Giants. "You are," according to Parcells, "what your record says you are." Wishing that one were a champion does not in fact make one so. And a record of villainy cannot be erased by a performative utterance equivalent to the statement "the person you saw doing those things is not the real me."

To be sure, on occasion, we might wish to accept the proffered description of one's "true" identity if the challengeable behavior in question is indeed a genuine one-off, attributable to some explanation, with suitable remorse, and consequent forgiveness under the general rubric "to err – once – is human." It would truly be dreadful to be judged – and to judge others – by reference to what are genuinely singular events in an otherwise exemplary life. Who among us would want to be judged on the basis of what we did as teenagers? But even if singularity is relevant, surely it does matter if the behavior was recurrent – and not attributable to teenage irresponsibility. And perhaps this is true of institutions, including countries, as well. All institutions are subject to the phenomenon of the "rotten apple" who misbehaves and violates what are proffered to be the institutions' values (often, of course, spelled out in documents called "constitutions"). But, of course, the "rotten apple" metaphor presumes that the rest of the apples are exemplary and the one "rotten apple" a genuine exception.

Anyone embarking on writing a biography – or a national or even institutional history – must decide whether the aim to is determine some "essential truth" about the subject – to peel the onion (or bite into the apple) and find the core reality underneath – or, instead, to present what might be viewed as the equivalent of a picaresque novel, in which the subject undergoes a variety of challenges and makes a number of decisions without, however, truly revealing who they "really are." Life then becomes "one damned event after another," with no narrative arc genuinely joining them save the disparate experiences of the subject. Indeed, if one is sufficiently post-modernist, one might find the search for an "essential self," whether regarding an individual or, even more likely, a country, to be a fool's errand. During my graduate school days long ago, one of the raging controversies involved the search for the "American national character." I dare say that today we are far less likely to suggest that the complex reality of the United States can be reduced to seeming attributes that we are all (or at least enough of us) expected to share. But that modesty has not prevented confident assertions about who "we are" (or "are not") by politicians and those who would try to shape public opinion.

Consider in this context a 2021 article from *The New York Times* entitled "Alabama Begins Removing Racist Language From Its Constitution." Whatever its legal (in) validity, there apparently remains a great deal of language in that state's constitution – the longest in the United States – "that was intended to enshrine white supremacy" (Mzezewa 2021). One of the proponents of removing the offending language is Representative Merika Coleman, the assistant minority leader in the Alabama

House of Representatives. According to the *Times*, "Ms. Coleman wants the reputation of Alabama as intolerant and racist to change. 'Collectively, we are not those folks that were celebrating the birthday of the K.K.K.,' she said. 'That's not who we are.'" No doubt she is correct if the antecedent of "we" are her fellow African-Americans or even contemporary Alabamans publicly willing to identify themselves as Democrats. But, alas, it is not crystal clear even today that all Alabamans are united behind repudiating white supremacy and adopting a more "woke" understanding of contemporary American pluralism.

So now we come to what Americans know as "the 1619 Project" and how exactly we should assess some of the angry responses it has elicited. The reference is to a full issue of the Sunday *New York Time* Magazine that included a number of essays, including a long introduction by Nicole Hannah-Jones, arguing that America as we know it today really began in 1619, when the first enslaved persons arrived at Jamestown, Virginia.[1] American slavery quickly became highly racialized, and the argument is that the ideology of white supremacy underlying the American version of chattel slavery became in effect part of the deep DNA of American thought. This included the Constitution drafted by delegates many of whom owned slaves, including George Washington and James Madison, for starters. Hannah-Jones acknowledges that some positive change has occurred, but ascribes most of the change to Black agency rather than to a common historical narrative that emphasizes the immanent norms embedded in the U.S. Constitution (and the importance of what have disparagingly been termed "white saviors" who, by embracing those purported norms, brought justice to oppressed Black people). Relatively little optimism is expressed about America's future inasmuch as it continues to be led disproportionately by privileged whites (who choose to ignore what has come to be called "white privilege" generated by the structures based on white supremacy). The Project was designed to generate discussion, and it most certainly did.

Critics include not only the right-wing denizens who fabricated Donald Trump's "1776 Report" (The President's Advisory 1776 Commission 2021), which was quickly withdrawn and repudiated by the incoming Biden Administration, but also a number of distinguished and politically liberal (white) historians who signed a collective letter chastising *The New York Times* for its purported excesses (New York Times 2019).[2] For the former, "who we are" is announced in the Declaration of Independence, "one people" dedicated to certain eternal truths, including the proposition that "all men [and, presumably, all humankind] are created equal." That

---

[1] See Hannah-Jones, Roper, Silverman and Silverstein 2021, a greatly extended version of the original *Times Magazine*. Apparently the Jamestown ship included indentured servants as well as enslaved persons, though slavery (and, of course, the slave trade) quickly became established as a primary source of plantation labor.

[2] For a fine overview of the controversy, see Serwer 2020. See also the recent essay by Hochschild 2023 (reviewing The Hillsdale College 1776 Curriculum and the six-part documentary series, "The 1619 Project," hosted by Hannah-Jones).

Thomas Jefferson himself was a slaveholder takes second place to the ostensible commitment to human equality. The signatories of the latter are considerably more sophisticated and nuanced in their understanding of American history, but they are equally censorious of the bleak attribution of national identity set out by Hannah-Jones in her introduction to the Project.

One signatory was Princeton historian Sean Wilentz, whose book *No Property in Man* is built around the reassuring statement by the slaveholding James Madison, at the Philadelphia Convention itself, that the Constitution did not recognize "property in man." This failure to do so – this constitutional silence that was interpreted as speaking mightily for those who wished to listen – formed the basis of much so-called "anti-slavery constitutionalism," though it was never in fact endorsed by Madison himself. In any event, Wilentz and his compatriots denounce as a canard the proposition that the Constitution was in fact a *pro-slavery* document. Wilentz certainly does not deny that slavery was in significant ways protected by the Constitution; what he challenges is the view that this is the *only* thing one might say about the Constitution's relation to America's "peculiar institution." The historians' letter states that "the [1619] project asserts that the United States was founded on racial slavery, an argument ... proclaimed by champions of slavery like John C. Calhoun." It "ignores," though, Lincoln's "agreement with Frederick Douglass that the Constitution was, in Douglass's words, 'a GLORIOUS LIBERTY DOCUMENT.'"

Of course, this Douglass being evoked is what might be called the "later" (or, at least, mid-career) Douglass, who had repudiated his earlier commitment to the belief of William Lloyd Garrison and Wendell Phillips that the Constitution was indeed a "covenant with death and an agreement with hell" (Phillips 1845). Phillips published in 1845 a tract on the Constitution as a "pro-slavery compact," largely based on the relatively recently released papers of James Madison (and after, of course, Joseph Story's opinion for the Court in the 1842 case *Prigg v. Pennsylvania*, which should have stilled any doubts on that point). In *Prigg*, Story, who undoubtedly was privately repulsed by slavery, nevertheless felt it his duty, as a loyal constitutionalist, to uphold the iniquitous Fugitive Slave Law of 1793 instantiating the duty of states to return such fugitives to their home states and their "masters." Story had written a plaintive letter to a friend at the time of *Prigg*: "You know full well that I have ever been opposed to slavery. But I take my standard of duty as a judge from the Constitution" (Cover 1975, 119). Perhaps especially relevant to this essay is Phillips's statement: "What the Constitution may become a century hence, we know not; we speak of it *as it is*, and *repudiate it as it is*" (Phillips 1845). That is, its record should speak for itself.

We might, of course, agree to disagree and accept the proposition, which is surely true, that the Constitution is susceptible to multiple readings concerning the issue of slavery, as is true, for that matter, of any of the basic controversies that have structured American constitutional debate, up to and including secession. It might be pro-slavery, as argued by Calhoun and Phillips; it might be anti-slavery, as presented by Lysander Spooner and later, Douglass. Perhaps it is worth noting that Robert Cover, in his magisterial *Justice Accused*, described this latter position as "utopian"; it did, after all, receive no support from anyone who might be described as within the "mainstream" of legal or, even more certainly, judicial opinion.

But lest one suggest that there is a singular Dworkinian "right answer" to the question about constitutional support for, or opposition to, chattel slavery, one can turn instead to Illinois Senator Stephen A. Douglas, who suggested that the Constitution might simply be neutral or indifferent; he might well have said that "we the (white) people of each given state have complete freedom, under the theory of local popular sovereignty, to decide whether Black human beings should be enslaved."[3] Some Americans were suitably appalled by that idea; others found it compelling. So perhaps "who we are" is irredeemably schizoid instead of singular! Just as there was much interest in the mid-twentieth century in "split personalities" and "the three faces of Eve," so it might be the case that a given country's "constitutional identity" is irredeemably split, as with Dr. Jekyll and Mr. Hyde.

In any case, our response to the 1619 Project and its critics is in part a way of affirming what we think is the "true" identity of the United States – and thus, in some sense of us ourselves, assuming we are, in fact, members of the American sociopolitical community – over time and even today. If we accept the validity of the 1619 argument, then, in Mark Graber's words, "this would entail [that] the United States cannot be what Gary Jacobsohn describes as an acquiescent constitutional order. We cannot claim [that] adherence to the best values of our past will be sufficient to get us out of all difficulties, that a faithful commitment to the Declaration is all we need. Instead, we need a new order that rejects fundamental features of our past." Jacobsohn himself is fully aware that many constitutions bespeak a desire to be *preservationist*. But there can also be a repudiation of a discredited history. These are contingent, rather than necessary, aspects of any given constitution.

There may be, of course, profound political problems in actualizing the desired repudiation; this is surely part of the history of India (or Turkey) since 1947 or 1924. Although, at the least, one might point to an unequivocal narrative arc in those

---

[3] Perhaps it is worth noting that the plea of many contemporary critics of *Roe v. Wade* that the decision as to permitting abortion should be left up to the states, because the Constitution, correctly understood, is "neutral" about the goodness or evil of abortion (or reproductive choice), a version of Douglas's embrace of "popular sovereignty." As with slavery, though, perhaps the central problem is that what was called "the federal consensus" could not successfully maintain itself. Only four years after Lincoln supported its explicit textual endorsement in the proposed "Corwin Amendment" in his First Inaugural Address, he avidly supported the Thirteenth Amendment that abolished slavery throughout the country. Similarly, there appears to be avid support within the United States for the "nationalization" of either of the two contending positions and little reason to believe that supporters of either would truly accept the possibility that states would either "legalize murder, i.e., the killing of innocent fetuses," or oppress women by what the Thirteenth Amendment calls the "involuntary servitude" of being forced to carry fetuses to term.

constitutions as to what might count as success. But what of the United States Constitution, which seems at once to combine both preservationist *and* transformational aspects? A preamble announcing a commitment to "establishing justice" and securing a "more perfect Union" certainly seems at odds with a constitutional text that, among other things, protects the international slave trade for twenty years, until 1808, and grants slave states extra seats in the House of Representatives (and, indirectly, in the Electoral College that selects presidents, who in turn nominate justices to the Supreme Court) by counting enslaved persons as part of the denominator for representation. And, of course, there was the Fugitive Slave Clause that served as the basis of Story's capacious notion of "implied powers" of Congress to safeguard what some called the "peculiar institution" of chattel slavery.

It has therefore been argued, most recently in a remarkable book by University of Pennsylvania law professor Kermit Roosevelt, that the United States Constitution must become more self-consciously transformationist, like the South African Constitution or the 1947 Indian Constitution (Roosevelt 2022). What this means, according to Roosevelt, is that we must give up what he calls the myth of continuity that allows us to valorize the American past and claim, altogether misleadingly, that we are simply following the dictates of, say, the Declaration of Independence, which has, as if by magic, become incorporated into the Constitution itself drafted eleven years later. Jacobsohn himself has written about "aspirational constitutionalism" based fundamentally on the Declaration (Jacobsohn 1984), which Lincoln himself had pronounced the "apple of gold" for which the Constitution was merely an ornamental frame (Jacobsohn 1994). Roosevelt, on the other hand, proclaims that we must liberate ourselves from the Declaration, which will simply not do the work necessary to support the needed transformation. For him, the true beginning of what might become a genuinely admirable America is the aftermath of the slaughter of 750,000 Americans (including would-be Confederates) between 1861 and1865 and the addition to the Constitution, in a highly irregular process that scarcely conforms with the Amendment procedures set out in Article V, of the so-called Reconstruction Amendments.[4]

Roosevelt's critique, it should be noted, is similar to Justice Thurgood Marshall's famous dissent in 1987 from the conventional celebration of the Bicentennial.[5] He declared that he did not "find the wisdom, foresight, and sense of justice exhibited by the Framers particularly profound. On the contrary, the government they devised was defective from the start, requiring several amendments, a civil war, and momentous social transformation to attain the system of constitutional government, and its respect for the individual freedoms and human rights, we hold as fundamental

---

[4] This non-conformity is, of course, the basis of Bruce Ackerman's remarkable studies of American constitutional development under the general title of *We the People*.

[5] Remarks of Justice Thurgood Marshall at The Annual Seminar of the San Francisco Patent and Trademark Law Association, May 6, 1987, reprinted as Marshall 1987.

today" (Marshall 1987). The Reconstruction Amendments might be worth celebrating, but as for the Constitution of 1787, definitely not. Marshall found none of his own identity as an American patriot in that document. There is no truly "usable past," at least before the late 1860s, that will help to provide us with a proud future.

Nikole Hannah-Jones's introductory essay to the 1619 Project as originally published in the *Times* clearly contained some disputable assertions, including the premise that support for the American Revolution – which, incidentally, I now insist on labeling "the American secession from the British Empire" – was significantly affected by the fear that our British masters were on the verge of abolishing slavery in America. Although it seems foolish to ignore the potential effect of Lord Dunmore's assurances that any enslaved persons who enlisted in the Loyalist cause would receive their freedom, it also seems to be an overstatement to suggest that, say, the farmers in New Hampshire consciously risked their lives and sacred honor in order to preserve Washington's plantation at Mount Vernon. It is worth noting, though, that iconoclastic University of South Carolina historian Woody Holton has indeed suggested that "Whites' fury at the British for casting their lot with enslaved people drove many to the fateful step of endorsing independence," (Berkin et al. 2021), and he has apparently been sending out extensive tweets offering evidence for his somewhat idiosyncratic view (@woodyholtonusc, September 1, 2021). Needless to say, Holton has in turn received vigorous pushback from a number of distinguished historians of the Colonial and Revolutionary (or secessionist) period. All of this amply vindicates the Faulknerian view that the past, at least for Americans, never truly becomes Hartley's "foreign country" in which things are done differently; instead, the past remains indelibly stamped on the contemporary consciousness of "true Americans," whether distinguished American historians or ordinary citizens.

So, no one should view this as "merely" an intra-mural fight among professional historians. Nothing less than our national heritage, and self-definition, is thought to be at stake among its participants. This is what makes the subject of "constitutional identity" both so interesting and important on the one hand, and potentially volatile, perhaps even dangerous, on the other. Many of us recognize this double-edge when thinking or writing about, say, Victor Orbán and his explicit defense of an "illiberal" Hungary devoted to restoring a particular kind of nationalist identity. The same is true of those Jews like myself (and, it should be noted, Gary) who are distinctly unhappy with the brand of nationalism now apparently triumphant in Israel. Not surprisingly, this has led to some vigorous debates even among Jews about the basic tenets of Zionism, which is all about defining the identity of the modern Jewish people. But the problems posed by the search for identity are more universal.

Those writing "national histories," especially if they involve the "Founders," are inevitably trying to shape our national self-understanding, whether one of sheer pride in our accomplishments and likely future or one instead of perhaps newly realized shame about important aspects of our past that continue to shape our present and, unless rectified, our future.

It might be useful to compare the standards that are being applied to proponents of the 1619 Project with those applied to others who answer the "who we are" question in a presumptively more politically satisfying way. The "1619ers" are of course making the extremely uncomfortable claim that the answer to the national identity question for most of "us" is "white supremacists," both then and now. "We" who are white males, in particular, can be accused of manifesting a non-benign ignorance about the realities of "white privilege" in explaining not only the past but the structural circumstances that help to account for "our" own "meritorious" successes at present and that of our privileged children in the future.[6] For obvious reasons, most of "us" have a strong interest in rejecting that description, not least because it can be read to make hopeless any genuine attempts to rectify what presumably *all* of "us" would concede is a lamentable history of racially structured enslavement, followed by an equally racially structured period of Jim Crow in the South and other forms of discrimination throughout the rest of the country.

Structuralist or "systemic" arguments are especially problematic if they suggest, basically, that there is no way out of a truly unfortunate, even dire, situation. We sometimes refer to critics of our polity as "prophets," without, perhaps, paying full attention to the fact that the great Hebrew prophets saw no short-run ameliorative paths for the Jewish people. Their deviation from the path set out by God would inevitably lead to destruction and exile; it was too late for "repentance" to avert the severe Divine decree discerned by the prophets. Understandably, we prefer more optimistic prophets who, even as they criticize our injustices, also present reassurance that we can exercise our agency to "bend the arc of history toward justice" and therefore escape the consequences of an untreated national illness. "What is to be done about America's history of racial subordination?" we might well ask, and the deepest structural accounts might suggest that the answer is "Nothing. It is far too late." There may be multiple explanations for Frederick Douglass's apostasy from his initial Garrisonianism, but one possibility is the elemental recognition that successful political campaigns usually rest on a kind of optimism that suggests that there is at least *something* valuable that ordinary citizens can do, beginning with voting into office compatible candidates. It may well be that we do not, and should not, hold political activists to the highest standards of "truth," inasmuch as certain notions of "the truth" may simply be too hard to bear. For a country to be told that it is terminally ill is not likely to be a winning political strategy.

One might well ask, though, what most of this discussion has to do with "us," that is, the likely readers of the essays in this book and those who justifiably wish to celebrate Gary Jacobsohn's remarkable career. So, perhaps I should paraphrase

---

[6] This is a theme as well of Michael Sandel's recent book (2020), which I reviewed (Levinson 2021).

Frederick Douglass, and his great question about "What to the Slave is the Fourth of July?" What, we might ask to the legal academy, is the 1619 Project? Is it of primary, perhaps even exclusive, interest to professional historians or public intellectuals, or does it affect what we do as well in our professional roles? As law professors, we tend to be fixated on opinions of the United States Supreme Court. But, of course, that does not free us from deciding about the extent to which the justices are (or are not) "reliable narrators" of our national past and whether their handiwork deserves close to the same "veneration" that is thought by many (though not by me) to be correctly directed at the Constitution itself. This is especially important inasmuch as justices – who are, after all, at the apex of the American political elite – have every incentive to offer comforting versions of our history and, more particularly, the role that "the rule of law" (and, even more particularly, the opinions of the Court itself) have played in creating what the Court undoubtedly offers as a legal history that one can take genuine pride in. Every day is "Law Day" or "Constitution Day" to members of the Supreme Court eager to reinforce the legitimacy of the existing constitutional order in the eyes (and hearts) of the citizenry.

One will often find, especially after World War II, Supreme Court opinions suggesting that racial discrimination, because "odious to a free people," is not central to understanding our constitutional order. Thus, wrote Chief Justice Warren in *Loving v. Virginia*, "Over the years, this Court has consistently repudiated '[d]istinctions between citizens solely because of their ancestry' as being 'odious to a free people whose institutions are founded upon the doctrine of equality.' *Hirabayashi v. United States*, 320 U. S. 81, 100 (1943)." I suppose it all depends on what one means by "over the years." Surely it is telling that the cited precedent for this 1967 assertion is a 1943 case that in fact upheld an ancestry-based curfew during World War II and then was used to justify the "ethnic cleansing" that took Japanese resident aliens and their often American-citizen children to what one justice described as "concentration camps." Warren, as Attorney General of California at the time, scarcely covered himself with glory with regard to expressing even the slightest sympathy for the injustices being visited upon Japanese nationals (because American law prohibited them from becoming citizens) and their native-born Japanese-American children (like Gordon Hirabayashi and Fred Korematsu themselves). But even if one overlooks those embarrassing "facts of the case," we might still take notice of literally hundreds of cases, including that appropriately known as the *Chinese Exclusion Case*, that suggest that American judges were altogether comfortable with distinctions based exclusively on ancestry or race. And to this story, of course, one must add the lamentable treatment of Indigenous Nations and their members. Ironically or not, Warren's understanding of the foundation of our institutions is altogether congruent with that of the Trumpistas who authored the 1776 Report. After all, they didn't deny the existence of slavery or *Korematsu*; they simply declared that it didn't represent "who we are."

Warren was not a fool when he wrote the Court's opinion in *Loving*, any more than was John Jay, when writing *Federalist No. 2* and proclaiming to his readers his pleasure in the purported fact that "Providence has been pleased to give this one connected country to one united people – a people descended from the same ancestors, speaking the same language, professing the same religion, attached to the same principles of government, very similar in their manners and customs…." This was preposterous, as one suspects that Jay himself recognized even as he was writing these lines in 1787. After all, he lived in a state that, among other things, had translated the text of the 1787 Constitution into Dutch so that those living upstate from New York City (nee "New Amsterdam") could read the document they were being asked to ratify (Levinson 2016). And, of course, Jay was undoubtedly fully aware that slavery was fully legal in New York, as would remain true until 1827. But it was obviously politically useful to proclaim that the new and yet unratified Constitution was written for a basically homogeneous, even if spread-out country, rather than a congeries of "peoples" who might well not be expected to unite all that easily into a single country with a greatly enhanced national government.

Perhaps Hannah-Jones *should* have been more precise in her argument about the linkage between *Somerset*, Dunmore, and support for the American secession. But then one might well say that justices of the Supreme Court should also be more accurate in their own delineations of American history. Consider Joseph Story's omission in *Prigg* of certain important facts as to the status of Elizabeth Morgan's children, who were also kidnapped and sent South. Or consider even *Brown v. Board of Education*, which is nearly unteachable in 2023 inasmuch as it conveys no useful information at all as to exactly why seventeen states, including Kansas, required racially separated schools, not to mention the fact that it is also doctrinally a mess in terms of its definition of "segregation." Warren had made a deliberate decision to avoid any language that white Southerners might view as truly critical (or "hostile"). And perhaps he was correct in his political judgment. But his decision was scarcely without consequences, which continue to this day.

When we design syllabi for our courses, we are inevitably constructing a portrait of America and of the Supreme Court's role in shaping our country. It is our own national identity that is under scrutiny, strict or otherwise, which makes teaching "American constitutional law" in the United States an altogether different enterprise from teaching comparative constitutional law. There is, I believe, an inescapable "politics" contained within any syllabus devoted to teaching one's own constitution to students who are expected to be the "next generation" in a continuing saga of constitutional and national development. I certainly find this to be true for courses examining the United States Constitution.

We are most inclined to recognize this with regard to the endless debates about "methods of interpretation" and whether the Constitution should be treated as "living" or, as Justice Scalia suggested, "dead." To be sure, these are interesting and important, but they can also be orthogonal to considering the overall role that the Court has played in shaping our polity and, more precisely, whether that role has been constructive or lamentable. Or, perhaps, we might conclude, as Mark Tushnet has suggested, that most of what the Court does is really "noise," of no great import one way or the other to the actual development of the country. Thus we have the endless debate not only about what *Brown* "really means" but also, and at least as importantly, whether *Brown* really explains much at all about the post-1954 developments in the United States.

It is quite fascinating to read some of the testimony submitted to President Biden's commission that was charged with the task of considering "reforms" of the Supreme Court. In particular, younger "progressives" seem to be reverting to an earlier, pre-Warren, understanding of the Court in which it was viewed as hopelessly aligned with forces of reaction, including giving fairly consistent aid and comfort to the forces of white supremacy as well, of course, as the owners of property as against the claims of the exploited. Thus Harvard law professor Niko Bowie testified that "as a matter of historical practice, the Court has wielded an antidemocratic influence on American law, one that has undermined federal attempts to eliminate hierarchies of race, wealth, and status" (Bowie 2021). Lest one be overly reassured by his emphasis only on "federal attempts," just think, for example, of the Court's decisions that invalidated voluntary desegregation programs in Seattle and Louisville, not to mention its tortured jurisprudence with regard to state-adopted programs of affirmative action.

Perhaps, for whatever reason, including the pressures of international events and the Cold War, the post-War Court was, for a couple of decades, a devotee of racial justice, though even here it is essential to recognize that Harry Truman deserves more credit than he usually receives at law schools for not only desegregating the armed forces, but also for running (and winning) in 1948 on a clear platform of "civil rights." In any event, to my own surprise, Felix Frankfurter and James Bradley Thayer appear to have developed new admirers from the left, with concomitant support as well for what is often called a thin "political constitution" rather than a much thicker one enforced by the judiciary. Who today really takes seriously Ronald Dworkin's assurances that the judiciary is the "forum of principle"? Or, perhaps, if it is accurately described as such, the "principles" are more likely to be congruent with Herbert Spencer's than with Dworkin's.

It is possible, of course, that one might simply denounce the contemporary Court by comparing it (or them) invidiously to the presumptively far more enlightened Warren-Brennan Court. But if one believes there is even a modicum of truth to the 1619 analysis, then it is obviously naïve to believe that all would be well if only Democrats could pack the Court with whoever might count as the progressive analog to Neil Gorsuch or Amy Coney Barrett. *That* ostensible "cure for what ails us" as a constitutional polity assumes, among other things, that America stands ready to be guided by the opinions of the justices. The most notable such suggestion was surely enunciated, with notable lack of success, in the plurality opinion of Justices O'Connor, Kennedy, and Souter in *Casey*, regarding abortion, which is the closest modern analog to the debates about slavery.[7] Its authors seemed to suggest that American citizens had a duty to accept the Court's resolution of the abortion controversy as determinative. They were obviously unsuccessful in that regard.

And, of course, the United States is certainly not "exceptional" in experiencing a fundamental debate about the legitimacy of judicial oversight in defining fundamental attributes of the country – or, perhaps more tellingly, "nation." That is, is a polity simply a collectivity of the persons who happen to live within it, or does it instantiate what might be called a "national project" of a purportedly singular "people"? One sees in contemporary Israel what I personally regard as the unfortunate, even vitriolic, denunciation of the legacy left by former President of the Supreme Court Aharon Barak, who among other things could be regarded as a "founding father" of the purported "constitutional revolution" in Israel in the 1990s (Kingsley 2023). A highlight of a seminar on comparative constitutionalism that Gary and I gave together was reading the sharp debates between Barak and Mishael Cheshin about the meanings of the Israel Basic Laws and the role of judges in taking responsibility to create a particular constitutional identity. If Barak reminds Americans of Earl Warren, then Cheshin is certainly a worthy successor to Felix Frankfurter, the liberal (in politics) advocate of "judicial restraint" (Snyder 2022). And no one can read the contemporary acrimonious debates between the supporters of the so-called "reforms" backed by the Netanyahu government and the opponents who are marching in the streets against them without realizing that the struggle is very much over the nature of Israeli identity in all respects, both as regards the role of the non-Jewish minority within Israel and concerning as well the relationship between secular and Orthodox Jews even within the ostensible majority.

To the degree that the authors of the 1619 Project, unlike the Hebrew prophets, offer any treatment plan for overcoming the deep structures of our national past, it presumably requires extremely deep therapy and perhaps the political equivalent of chemotherapy. To be sure, it would be nice to read more progressive opinions, but not, perhaps, if the price were the maintenance of either a "veneration" for the existing Constitution or for the version of judicial supremacy embraced by the Court in the post-War era. Perhaps a fitting conclusion is that whether or not we are interested in 1619, 1619 is interested in us, whatever our own wishes in the matter. And, given the world-historical importance of enslavement and the slave trade, one suspects that the issues raised by that Project will have what might be called "penumbras and emanations" across the entire world.

---

[7] Planned Parenthood of Southeastern Pa. v. Casey, 505 U.S. 833, 865–866 (1992).

REFERENCES

Berkin, Carol, Richard D. Brown, Jane E. Calvert, Joseph J. Ellis, Jack N. Rakove, and Gordon S. Wood. 2021. "On 1619 and Woody Holton's Account of Slavery and the Independence Movement: Six Historians Respond." *Medium*, September 7, 2021. https://medium.com/@RichardDBrownCT/on-1619-and-woody-holtons-account-of-slavery-and-the-independence-movement-six-historians-respond-b43369ad52d7.
Bowie, Nikolas. 2021. "The Contemporary Debate over Supreme Court Reform: Origins and Perspectives." *Presidential Commission on the Supreme Court of the United States*, June 30, 2021. www.whitehouse.gov/wp-content/uploads/2021/06/Bowie-SCOTUS-Testimony-1.pdf.
Cover, Robert. 1975. *Justice Accused*. New Haven: Yale University Press.
Graber, Mark A. 2021. Email to Sanford Levinson, Wednesday, October 6, 2021 10:28:19 PM
Hannah-Jones, Nikkole, Caitlin Roper, Ilena Silverman, and Jake Silverstein, eds. 2021. *The 1619 Project: A New Origin Story*. New York: One World.
Hochschild, Adam. 2023. "History Bright and Dark." *New York Review of Books*, May 26, 2023. www.nybooks.com/articles/2023/05/25/history-bright-and-dark-hillsdale-1776-curriculum-1619-project/.
Holton, Woody (@woodyholtonusc). 2021. "The book version of the #1619 Project appears in 76 days. 1 of its central claims – that colonial whites' rage at the Anglo-African alliance pushed them toward Independence – has been disputed." *Twitter*, September 1, 2021. https://twitter.com/woodyholtonusc/status/1433162494571335685?lang=en.
Jacobsohn, Gary Jeffrey. 1984. *The Supreme Court and The Decline of Constitutional Aspiration*. Pennsylvania: Rowman and Littlefield.
Jacobsohn, Gary Jeffrey. 1994. *Apple of Gold: Constitutionalism in Israel and The United States*. Princeton: Princeton University Press.
Jacobsohn, Gary Jeffrey. 2006. "Constitutional Identity." *The Review of Politics* 68 (3): 361–397.
Kingsley, Patrick. 2023. "He's 86 and Long Retired. Why Are Israelis Protesting outside His Home?" *The New York Times*, May 5, 2023. www.nytimes.com/2023/05/05/world/middleeast/aharon-barak-israel-judicial-overhaul.html.
Know Your Meme. n.d. "This Is Not Who We Are." https://knowyourmeme.com/memes/this-is-not-who-we-are.
Levinson, Sanford. 2016. "What One Can Learn from Foreign-language Translations of the U.S. Constitution." *Constitutional Commentary* 31: 55–70.
Levinson, Stanford. 2021. "Exhortation, Transformation, and Politics Comment on M. Sandel's The Tyranny of Merit." *American Journal of Law and Equality* 1: 117–131.
Marshall, Thurgood. 1987. "The Constitution's Bicentennial: Commemorating the Wrong Document?" *Vanderbilt Law Review* 40 (6): 1337–1342.
Mzezewa, Tariro. 2021. "Alabama Begins Removing Racist Language from Its Constitution." *The New York Times*, September 19, 2021. www.nytimes.com/2021/09/19/us/alabama-constitution-racist.html.
The New York Times. 2019. "Letter to The Editor – We Respond to the Historians Who Critiqued The 1619 Project." Published December 20, 2019. www.nytimes.com/2019/12/20/magazine/we-respond-to-the-historians-who-critiqued-the-1619-project.html.
Phillips, Wendell. 1845. *The Constitution a Pro-slavery Compact: Selections From the Madison Papers*. New York: The American Anti-Slavery Society.
Roosevelt, Kermit. 2022. *The Nation That Never Was: Reconstructing America's Story*. Oregon: Blackstone Publishing.

Sandel, Michael. 2020. *The Tyranny of Meritocracy*. New York: Farrar, Straus and Giroux.
Serwer, Adam. 2020. "The Fight Over the 1619 Project Is Not About the Facts." *The Atlantic*, December 23, 2020. www.theatlantic.com/ideas/archive/2019/12/historians-clash-1619project/604093/.
Snyder, Bradley. 2022. *Democratic Justice: Felix Frankfurter, The Supreme Court and The Making of The Liberal Establishment*. New York: W. W. Norton & Company.
The President's Advisory 1776 Commission. 2021. "The 1776 Report." https://trumpwhitehouse.archives.gov/wp-content/uploads/2021/01/The-Presidents-Advisory-1776-Commission-Final-Report.pdf.
Wilentz, Sean. 2028. *No Property in Man: Slavery and Antislavery at the Nation's Founding* (Harvard University Press).

15

Constitutional Aspirationalism Revisited

Justin Buckley Dyer

INTRODUCTION

"Five score years ago," Martin Luther King proclaimed in his most famous speech, "a great American, in whose symbolic shadow we stand today, signed the Emancipation Proclamation" (Carson and Shepard 2002, 81). The backdrop of King's speech was an imposing monument of a magnanimous Abraham Lincoln seated behind a Grecian colonnade that resembled the ancient Parthenon. From there, King looked out onto the National Mall connecting the Lincoln Memorial and the Washington Monument. A quarter million people had gathered in the heat of August for the March on Washington for Jobs and Freedom, and the mall was filled with hope.

King's initial dating by score evoked the language of the King James Bible as well as the cadences and biblical allusions of Lincoln's political rhetoric. Five score years before King shared his dream of racial justice in America, Lincoln began his most famous speech, delivered at the dedication of the cemetery in Gettysburg, by pointing back "Four score and seven years" to a time when, through the crucible of war, "our fathers brought forth on this continent, a new nation, conceived in Liberty, and dedicated to the proposition that all men are created equal" (Basler 1953, 23).

In his speech, King also appealed to the Declaration of Independence and to its self-evident truths. "In a sense we've come to our nation's capital to cash a check," he proclaimed.

> When the architects of our republic wrote the magnificent words of the Constitution and the Declaration of Independence, they were signing a promissory note to which every American was to fall heir. This note was a promise that all men, yes, black men as well as white men, would be guaranteed the unalienable rights of life, liberty, and the pursuit of happiness. (Carson and Shepard 2002, 82)

The American people had defaulted on that promissory note, and King pleaded with urgency that the United States finally "make real the promises of democracy." After holding up the principles of the Declaration as a standard and an aspiration, King found America's commitment to those principles wanting as he gave voice to the "legitimate discontent" of those who steadfastly maintained hope in the promise of America. In King's retelling, on that occasion and for that audience, the pathology of American racism was at odds with American ideals, and he pushed his fellow citizens to live up to the principles of the founding rather than to jettison those principles and begin anew (Carson and Shepard 2002, 82–83).

King's appeal to Lincoln on the occasion of the March on Washington served the political purpose of enlisting the sacred symbols and narratives of American politics in the cause of civil rights while pushing for passage of the major civil rights legislation that President Kennedy had proposed just weeks before on June 19, 1963 – a date full of significance for those who had long celebrated it as a day of jubilee. Kennedy's assassination nearly five months later left Lyndon Johnson at the helm with the urgency of crisis in the air. Johnson pushed hard in the coming months for the congressional passage of the Civil Rights Act, something that came to fruition on July 2, 1964, 188 years to the day of the formal vote for independence by the Continental Congress.

In his remarks upon signing the Civil Rights Act, Johnson – as King had done before him – pointed back to the Declaration of Independence that had laid out for the Continental Congress the principles that justified independence, revolution, and war. Johnson's remarks, written as a kind of civic catechism, foregrounded the tension between principle and practice that had long been true of American civic life:

> We believe that all men are created equal. Yet many are denied equal treatment.
> We believe that all men have certain unalienable rights. Yet many Americans do not enjoy those rights.
> We believe that all men are entitled to the blessings of liberty. Yet millions are being deprived of those blessings – not because of their own failures, but because of the color of their skin. (Johnson 1964)

Like others at critical junctures in American history, Johnson drew on the ideas and ideals of the American founding to provide a goal, a standard, and an aspiration for the American constitutional order.

15.1 ASPIRATIONS AND DISHARMONY

The idea of constitutional aspirations developing within a disharmonic constitutional order has been a core theme of Gary Jacobsohn's work, beginning with his 1983 article "'On This Question of Judicial Authority': The Theory of Constitutional Aspiration," and developed at length a few years later in his book *The Supreme Court and the Decline of Constitutional Aspiration*. Taking Frederick Douglass and Abraham Lincoln as his models, Jacobsohn maintains that Douglass' searing 1852 rebuke of American hypocrisy in an Independence Day oration "anticipated Abraham Lincoln's position in the debates with Stephen A. Douglas that the Declaration and the Constitution were intended, in part, as a statement of ideals or fundamental principles, to be achieved as part of a process of progressive realization" (Jacobsohn 1988). Douglass, Jacobsohn notes, argued that the principles of the founding unsettled the debate over slavery. With the founders, Douglass insisted, "nothing was 'settled' that was not right. With them, justice, liberty, and humanity were 'final'; not slavery and oppression." (Foner 1999, 192; Jacobsohn 1988). America's hypocrisy was to be condemned, but not America's principles. Douglass declared to his audience that the Declaration of Independence was the "ring-bolt to the chain of your nation's destiny" and that it contained the nation's "saving principles," principles that were the solution to the problem of slavery and oppression (Foner 1999, 191).

Those very principles were the ones that divided Lincoln from his old legislative colleague Alexander Stephens. In December of 1860, before Stephens' "Cornerstone Speech" and before Lincoln's own inauguration, the president-elect from Illinois wrote to Stephens: "You think slavery is right and ought to be extended; while we think it is *wrong* and ought to be restricted. That I suppose is the rub. It certainly is the only substantial difference between us." In reply, Stephens urged Lincoln to do what he could to save the Union. "A word fitly spoken by you now, he concluded, would be like 'apples of gold in pictures of silver'" (Basler 1953, 161).

Stephens' allusion to Proverbs 25:11 – *A word fitly spoken is like apples of gold in pictures of silver* – stayed with Lincoln and provoked a deeper meditation on the nature and character of the Union that he and Stephens both wished to preserve. In an unpublished fragment, dated January 1861, Lincoln reflected:

All this is not the result of accident. It has a philosophical cause. Without the *Constitution* and the *Union*, we could not have attained the result; but even these, are not the primary cause of our great prosperity. There is something back of these, entwining itself more closely about the human heart. That something, is the principle of 'liberty to all' – the principle that clears the path for all – gives *hope* to all – and, by consequence, *enterprize*, and *industry* to all.

The *expression* of that principle, in our Declaration of Independence, was most happy, and fortunate. *Without* this, as well as *with* it, we could have declared our independence of Great Britain; but *without* it, we could not, I think, have secured our free government, and consequent prosperity. No oppressed, people will *fight*, and *endure*, as our fathers did, without the promise of something better, than a mere change of masters.

The assertion of that *principle*, at *that time*, was *the* word, *'fitly spoken'* which has proved an 'apple of gold' to us. The *Union*, and the *Constitution*, are the *picture* of *silver*, subsequently framed around it. The picture was made, not to *conceal*, or *destroy* the apple; but to *adorn*, and *preserve* it. The *picture* was made *for* the apple – *not* the apple for the picture.

So let us act, that neither *picture*, or *apple* shall ever be blurred, or bruised or broken.

That we may so act, we must study, and understand the points of danger. (Basler 1953, 169)

Lincoln had previously laid out how he understood those points of danger at the 1858 Illinois Republican Party Convention, where he had been nominated as the Republican Party candidate for the U.S. Senate in a race against the Democratic incumbent, Stephen Douglas. In what became known as his "House Divided Speech," he alluded to the Gospels when he famously said that a "house divided against itself cannot stand" (Basler 1953, 461). Although he did not expect the house to fall, he said, he did think "it will cease to be divided. It will become all one thing or all the other" (Basler 1953, 67).

The reason the house would not go on permanently half slave and half free is because of the irreconcilable conflict between the principles of the American founding – that we are all created equal and endowed by our creator with unalienable rights and that the just powers of government are derived from the consent of the governed – and the way the institution of slavery flagrantly opposed those principles. In light of the founding affirmation of natural equality, natural rights, and government by consent, the institution of slavery stood as a contradiction and a scandal. That is why Douglass called these ideas America's "saving principles" and considered them, with a plea, as the "ring-bolt to the chain" of America's destiny. The realization of those principles in American public life may have been part of America's destiny but it was not inevitable, and this realization would be practically impossible if the principles of the Declaration failed to hold sway over the public mind. Americans were hypocrites, Douglass righteously maintained, but it was better for them to hypocritically betray decent principles than to become principled despots. The tension between principle and practice held out hope for a future harmonization that further approximated justice.

In 1858, when Lincoln gave his "House Divided" speech, the immediate way in which the conflict between principle and practice manifested in American politics was in the debate over the principle of popular sovereignty in the federal territories and the question of whether the states admitted from those territories should give sanction to the institution of slavery, thereby allowing it to expand its influence culturally and politically. Senator Stephen Douglas, professing that he did not personally care one way or another about slavery, had authored the Kansas-Nebraska Act in 1854, signed by President Franklin Pierce, that allowed settlers in those territories to choose whether to protect slavery within their borders. When combined with the Supreme Court's 1857 decision in *Dred Scott v. Sandford*, which held that the Constitution explicitly protects the right of citizens to own and traffic in human property in the federal territories, Lincoln saw the trend toward (and the likelihood of) the nationalization of slavery.

The president at the time of the decision, James Buchanan, said just days before the case was handed down that he would, in common with all good citizens, submit to the Supreme Court's decision, whatever it happened to be (French 1857, 292). Lincoln looked at this, surveyed the political landscape, and then accused Pierce, Douglas, Buchanan, and Chief Justice Roger Taney of putting together the machinery that would extend slavery across the nation. The house would cease to be divided and in the process, the American people would repudiate their own founding principles. "We shall *lie down* pleasantly dreaming that the people of *Missouri* are on the verge of making their State *free*; and we shall *awake* to the *reality*, instead, that the *Supreme* Court has made *Illinois* a *slave* state," Lincoln warned. (Basler 1953, 467). And so, Lincoln's speech was in an important sense about keeping the house divided – at least for a time, until there could be a just resolution of the crisis.

What Lincoln called for was a political effort by Republicans to "meet and overthrow the power of that dynasty," and the first step was to remove Stephen Douglas from the Senate. In Lincoln's understanding, there was much more at stake in that race, and the issues it represented, than ordinary politics. As he said in the seventh and final debate with Douglas during their 1858 Senate campaign, when you cut through everything, the issue ultimately came down to the question of whether slavery is right or whether it is wrong. "That is the real issue," he said.

> That is the issue that will continue in this country when these poor tongues of Judge Douglas and myself shall be silent. It is the eternal struggle between these two principles – right and wrong – throughout the world. They are the two principles that have stood face to face from the beginning of time; and will ever continue to struggle. The one is the common right of humanity and the other the divine right of kings. It is the same principle in whatever shape it develops itself. It is the same spirit that says, "You work and toil and earn bread, and I'll eat it." No matter in what shape it comes, whether from the mouth of a king who seeks to bestride the people of his own nation and live by the fruit of their labor, or from one race of men as an apology for enslaving another race, it is the same tyrannical principle. (Basler 1953, 315)

That Senate race, and the centrality of the Supreme Court's *Dred Scott* decision to the celebrated debates between Lincoln and Douglas, raised for Lincoln the important question of judicial authority.

15.2 THAT EMINENT TRIBUNAL

In response to Douglas' accusation that he was courting anarchy by opposing the Supreme Court's decision in *Dred Scott*, Lincoln clarified that he was "opposed to that decision in a certain sense, but not in the sense which [Douglas] put on it." He would not protest the outcome of the case as it pertains to the parties in the case, Lincoln insisted, but he likewise would not adopt the reasoning and underlying principles of the decision "as a political rule" that would guide the citizen, the legislator, or the executive in future policymaking (Basler 1953, 516). Were he to be elected as the next Illinois senator and a vote should come up in the Senate about barring slavery from the federal territory, Lincoln averred, he would vote for that bill despite the ruling of the Supreme Court in *Dred Scott* (Basler 1953, 495).

From here, we know how the story ends: Douglas maintained his Senate seat in 1858, but Lincoln bested him in a four-way presidential race two years later. Lincoln's sectional victory in the Electoral College provoked southern angst, prompting the plea from Alexander Stephens that Lincoln might say a word fitly spoken for the occasion that would appear to the southern states like an apple of gold in a frame of silver. That word, however, was never spoken, at least not the word the Old South had wanted to hear, and, as Lincoln later reflected in his Second Inaugural Address, "the war came" (Basler 1953, 332). There were many reasons for that war – economic and geopolitical – but it was marked foremost by deep and irreconcilable differences of principle that revolved around whether slavery would be treated as right or wrong. In Lincoln's speeches, writings, and reflections toward the end of the war, he offered a powerful, extended meditation on the meaning and tragedy and hope of America considering its original promise and original sin.

At the war's beginning, however, Lincoln was still focused on this question of judicial authority, and he was not the only Republican thinking about the role of the judiciary in a constitutional republic. Rep. John Bingham, who would later be one of the primary architects of the Fourteenth Amendment, offered one meditation on this topic that foreshadowed Lincoln's First Inaugural Address. "If the Supreme Court is to decide all constitutional questions for us," Bingham declared on the floor of Congress in 1860,

> Why not refer every question of constitutional power to that body not already decided, before acting upon it? I recognize the decisions of that tribunal as of binding force only as to the parties to the suit, and the rights particularly involved and passed upon. The Court has no power in deciding the right of Dred Scott and his children to their liberty, to decide, so as to bind this body, that neither Congress, nor a Territorial Legislature, nor any human power, has authority to prohibit slavery in the territories; neither has that tribunal power to decide that five million persons, born and domiciled in this land, "have no rights which we are bound to respect."[1]

In March of 1861, on his inauguration as president and with the impending secession of the southern states, Lincoln offered a similar reflection on judicial authority in a regime of self-government. "If the policy of the Government upon vital questions, affecting the whole people is to be irrevocably fixed by decisions of the Supreme Court," Lincoln warned, "the people will have ceased to be their own rulers, having to that extent practically resigned their government into the hands of that eminent tribunal" (Basler 1953, 268).

15.3 THE THEORY OF CONSTITUTIONAL ASPIRATION

A constitution of aspiration – a frame of silver around an apple of gold – is incompatible with judicial finality. In Lincoln's hands, Jacobsohn observes, "the provisions of

---

[1] John Bingham (R-OH), *Cong. Globe*, 36th Congress, 1st session (April 24, 1860), H. 1839.

the constitution incorporated an aspirational content that was accessible not only to judges but to other public officials whose first obligation was to advance the cause of the principles defined by this content." (Jacobsohn 2003, 142). During a short stop at Constitution Hall en route to Washington DC for his swearing-in as president, Lincoln told a Philadelphia audience that he "never had a feeling politically that did not spring from the sentiments embodied in the Declaration of Independence" (Basler 1953, 240). "In speaking at the place where both the Declaration and the Constitution had been composed," Jacobsohn notes, "Lincoln was giving voice to the most pervasive theme in all of his political reflections, the inextricability of those two founding documents" (Jacobsohn 1993, 3; Jacobsohn 2021, 83).

Lincoln's statesmanship during the crisis of the house divided offers central lessons for our understanding of constitutional aspirationalism and the role of the judiciary in American constitutional politics. First, the Supreme Court is a teacher, and the Court's unique institutional design ensures that through the adjudication of discrete controversies, the Court also contributes to the constitutional construction and maintenance of a polity (Jacobsohn 2003, 251). This judicial responsibility demands judicial statesmanship or the prudent application of constitutional principles to concrete circumstances. Much of modern jurisprudence, however, is built on a pragmatic rejection of constitutionally determined ends in favor of results-oriented flexibility with respect to constitutional principles. This comes to bear, most saliently, on the modern philosophical rejection of the natural rights tradition (Jacobsohn 1977).

With the rejection of the natural rights tradition – a rejection that is associated especially with Oliver Wendell Holmes Jr. and his successors – there was a simultaneous detachment among twentieth-century scholars and judges from the idea of constitutional aspiration, which depended in its Lincolnian formulation on the rational cogency of the doctrine of natural rights that served as the explicit lodestar for the American Revolution and the early state constitutions (Jacobsohn 1988). That lodestar was, for Lincoln, the apple of gold around which the U.S. Constitution was the frame of silver. "Thus for Lincoln," Jacobsohn notes, "constitutional meaning was scarcely imaginable without the Declaration as ultimate source of interpretive guidance." (Jacobsohn 1993, 3–4). The Constitution took on meaning in light of the animating principles of the Declaration of Independence, and fidelity to the Constitution entailed fidelity to the purposes for which the Constitution came into existence.

Those principles provided the aspirations of the constitutional order. As Lincoln put it in his debates with Douglas, the Declaration's idea of equal creation in natural rights was meant to be "a standard maxim for free society, which should be familiar to all, and revered by all; constantly looked to, constantly labored for, and even though never perfectly attained, constantly approximated and thereby constantly spreading and deepening its influence, and augmenting the happiness and value of life to all people of all colors everywhere" (Basler 1953, 406). Chief Justice Roger Taney's opinion in the *Dred Scott* decision moved decisively against these aspirations by offering a racially ascriptive and parochial interpretation of the natural rights teaching of the Declaration of Independence – excluding those of African descent from any claim to natural equality and insisting the founders meant only that all North American subjects of the British crown were equal to all other subjects of the British crown – and asserting that the Constitution protected the right of all citizens to own and traffic in human property in the common lands of the federal territory.

With this move, "Taney had failed to understand how the aspirations of the Constitution defined Americans as a people," Jacobsohn notes as a summary of Lincoln's position, "and thus his ruling obligated other actors – principally Congress – to mount a political challenge to it" (Jacobsohn 2010, 105). Lincoln's theory of constitutional aspiration, Jacobsohn concludes, "is incompatible with the idea that the Supreme Court exercises an interpretive monopoly over the document" (Jacobsohn 2010, 106; Jacobsohn and Roznai 2020, 267–268). The Court may play a pedagogical and constitutive function in the American order, but it is neither the only nor the ultimate constitutional interpreter. To insist otherwise, Lincoln memorably claimed in his First Inaugural Address, would be to resign our government into the hands of that eminent tribunal.

Martin Luther King Jr. is a modern heir to this Lincolnian vision, a man in whose "persuasive account [the founders'] intentions encompassed more than the achievement of what was immediately possible" (Jacobsohn 1988, 1–2; Jacobsohn 2010, 106, 146; Jacobsohn 2021, 88–90; Jacobsohn and Roznai 2020, 267–268). And in Frederick Douglass, Lincoln's contemporary ideological ally, one finds a man who recognized the truth and justice of the principles of the Declaration even as he lamented America's shameful hypocrisy and racial violence. In anticipation of Lincoln's position in the 1858 Illinois Senate debates, Jacobsohn observes, Douglass nonetheless proclaimed that there "is consolation in the thought that America is young" (Foner 1999, 189; Jacobsohn 1988, 1). This consolation came from a hope that America might yet live up to the "saving principles" of the Declaration of Independence. "Stand by those principles," he admonished an audience in a famous commemoration of Independence Day, "be true to them on all occasions, in all places, against all foes, and at whatever cost" (Foner 1999, 191).

15.4 CONSTITUTIONAL ASPIRATIONALISM REVISITED

Jacobsohn's hopeful interpretation depends on highlighting the constitutive role of what he calls "eighteenth-century principles of natural right" (Jacobsohn 1988, 2010, 105). Those are the principles that infuse the Declaration of Independence and provide aspirational content to our fundamental law; they are the apple of gold around which the Constitution is the frame of silver. Jacobsohn's understanding of constitutional aspiration, growing out of Lincoln's biblical metaphor of an apple of gold, is, however, in tension with many of the recent revisionist interpretations of the American political tradition.

Scholars associated with critical race theory have argued that liberal ideals, derived from eighteenth-century enlightenment philosophy, deceptively mask power hierarchies and advance racial interests (Mills 1997). Other scholars maintain that the liberal tradition, however we understand its virtues or liabilities, does not provide the core aspiration of the American order. In a classic article, Rogers Smith argues instead that "American politics is best seen as expressing the interaction of multiple political traditions, including *liberalism, republicanism,* and *ascriptive forms of Americanism,* which have collectively comprised American political culture, without any constituting it as a whole" (Smith 1993, 549–566). Drawing out these implications for the notion of constitutional aspiration, Mark Graber concludes that "Racist and other ascriptive ideologies are as rooted in the American political tradition as liberal, democratic, and republican ideals" (Graber 2006, 83).

"The problem with this view," Jacobsohn contends, "is that it makes an erroneous inference from the presence of a disharmonic constitutional tradition. It assumes that a conflicted constitutional tradition enables all sides to the conflict to make a plausible claim to speak *for* the constitution" (Jacobsohn 2010, 105; Jacobsohn 2021, 88). But, according to Jacobsohn, that interpretive posture is untenable. It relegates to one tradition among many what has been the central animating aspiration of the constitutional order among its most compelling interpreters. In the account, Jacobsohn associates with Martin Luther King Jr. and Frederick Douglass before him, "*We the People* was unable (and in many cases unwilling) contemporaneously to extend the justice of the Constitution to all those who fell under its sway, but the posterity of the excluded would in due course see their promised constitutional entitlement fulfilled with or without the help of the Court" (Jacobsohn 2010, 106).

The lead essay for the *New York Times'* 1619 Project, published in August 2019, entered this fray by offering a reinterpretation of American history that identified the American founding with the early importation of enslaved people at Jamestown rather than the signing of the Declaration of Independence in Philadelphia. There is much in this interpretive project that is at odds with Jacobsohn's understanding of U.S. constitutional identity and aspiration. The essay downplays Lincoln's contributions to emancipation and flattens him into a committed opponent of black equality, for example (Hannah-Jones 2019, 20). It locates the genesis of the American Revolution in the colonists' purported desire to protect the institution of slavery from British interference (Hannah-Jones 2019, 18). And its claim that "Anti-black racism runs in the very DNA of this country, as does the belief, so well articulated by Lincoln, that black people are the obstacle to national unity," seems to call into question whether there is anything left to be salvaged of Lincoln's apple of gold metaphor (Hannah-Jones 2019, 21).

And yet underneath these surface-level tensions there is something hopeful that unites Nicole Hannah-Jones' project with Jacobsohn's body of work. "[D]espite being violently denied the freedom and justice promised to all," she writes, "black Americans believed fervently in the American creed. Through centuries of black resistance and protest, we have helped the country live up to its founding ideals" (Hannah-Jones 2019, 16). Our founding ideals are true, she insists, because black Americans have struggled to make them true (Hannah-Jones 2019, 14). The contributions of black Americans, in other words, were central to the realization of our core national ideals and aspirations. At this deeper level, there is an implicit convergence on the idea of a fundamental or core constitutional identity that is drawn out over time by actors with agency in the constitutional drama. As Jacobsohn has shown, this theoretical insight about constitutional identity is not unique to the United States, and the theory of constitutional aspiration is not discredited by the mere existence of competing aspirations or traditions within the same political order. "All of this building and repudiating, incorporating and negating," Jacobsohn observes, "is consistent with the primacy of particular aspirations within an ongoing dynamic of disharmonic contestation" (Jacobsohn 2010, 107).

Our constitutional interpretations and our ongoing project of writing, and rewriting, the narratives of our constitutional history continue to implicate questions central to scholarship on the theory of American constitutional aspirationalism. That scholarship takes Lincoln, Douglass, and King as its central interpretive protagonists and the Declaration of Independence as its central interpretive motif. The unitive theme is the principle of equal liberty to all – the apple of gold – which Douglass admonished his fellow citizens to hold on to as their "saving principles" (Buccola 2016, 53). This vision buoyed Douglass after the war, after Lincoln's death, and after emancipation. While some were still talking about schemes for black colonization or for the maintenance of a racially segregated and hierarchical civil society, Douglass envisioned a multiracial republic celebrating our "composite nationality" under a "Government founded upon justice, and recognizing the equal rights of all men" (Buccola 2016, 218–219). Such was a precursor to King's dream that one day America "will rise up and live out the true meaning of its creed," a bold vision built on the principles of natural equality and human dignity and connected deep in the taproot of American ideals. Such a vision offers hope that those principles might yet be our shared principles, part of an American tapestry woven together from past and present that provides our central constitutional aspiration.

REFERENCES

Basler, Roy P., ed. 1953. *Collected Works of Abraham Lincoln*. New Brunswick, NJ: Rutgers University Press.

Buccola, Nicholas, ed. 2016. *The Essential Douglass: Selected Writings and Speeches*. Indianapolis: Hackett Publishing.

Carson, Clayborne and Kris Shepard, eds. 2002. *A Call to Conscience: The Landmark Speeches of Dr. Martin Luther King, Jr.* New York: Grand Central Publishing.

Foner, Phillip, ed. 1999. *Frederick Douglass: Selected Speeches and Writings*. Chicago: Lawrence Hill Books.

French, Jonathan, ed. 1857. *The True Republican: Containing the Inaugural Addresses ... of All of the Presidents of the Unites States from 1789 to 1857*. Philadelphia: J.B. & Smith Company.

Graber, Mark A. 2006. *Dred Scott and the Problem of Constitutional Evil*. New York: Cambridge University Press.

Hannah-Jones, Nicole. 2019. "Our Democracy's Founding Ideals Were False When They Were Written. Black Americans Have Fought to Make Them True." *New York Times*, August 4, 2019. www.nytimes.com/interactive/2019/08/14/magazine/black-history-american-democracy.html?mtrref=www.google.com&gwh=0EDDC383885BCB24C8E9B85B48E2D28E&gwt=regi&assetType=REGIWALL.

Jacobsohn, Gary J. 1977. *Pragmatism, Statesmanship, and the Supreme Court*. Ithaca, NY: Cornell University Press.

Jacobsohn, Gary J. 1988. *The Supreme Court and the Decline of Constitutional Aspiration*. Lanham, MD: Rowman & Littlefield Publishers.

Jacobsohn, Gary J. 1993. *Apple of Gold*. Princeton, NJ: Princeton University Press.

Jacobsohn, Gary J. 2003. *The Wheel of Law*. Princeton, NJ: Princeton University Press.

Jacobsohn, Gary J. 2010. *Constitutional Identity*. Cambridge, MA: Harvard University Press.

Jacobsohn, Gary J. 2021. "Was Abraham Lincoln a Constitutional Revolutionary?" *Constitutional Studies* 7: 77–91.

Jacobsohn, Gary J. and Yaniv Roznai. 2020. *Constitutional Revolution*. New Haven, CT: Yale University Press.

Johnson, Lyndon. 1964. "Remarks Upon Signing the Civil Rights Bill." *Miller Center*. https://millercenter.org/the-presidency/presidential-speeches/july-2-1964-remarks-upon-signing-civil-rights-bill.

Mills, Charles W. 1997. *The Racial Contract*. Ithaca, NY: Cornell University Press.

Smith, Rogers. 1993. "Beyond Myrdal, Tocqueville, and Hartz: The Multiple Traditions in America." *American Political Science Review* 87(3): 549–566.

16

The Constitution at War with Itself

Race, Citizenship, and the Forging of American Constitutional Identity

George Thomas

INTRODUCTION

"The question is simply this: Can a negro, whose ancestors were imported into this country, and sold as slaves, become a member of the political community formed and brought into existence by the Constitution of [the] United States, and as such become entitled to all the rights, and privileges, and immunities, guarantied [sic] by that instrument to the citizen?"

To this question, Chief Justice Roger Taney, in *Dred Scott v. Sandford* (1857), gave a resounding "No." For Taney, *citizens* and "people of the United States" were synonymous terms. And Blacks, free or enslaved, were not part of the people of the United States who brought the Constitution into being. Rather, they were "beings of an inferior order, and altogether unfit to associate with the white race." He continued "and so far inferior, that they had no rights which the white man was bound to respect" (Finkelman 1997, 58, 61).

Taney's opinion lives in infamy. And yet, rather than simply being wrong, we might better understand *Dred Scott* as part of a disharmonic struggle prior to the Civil War that was central to forging American constitutional identity as we now know it. We too easily pass over disharmonic struggle, underplaying how "constitutional disharmony is critical to the development of constitutional identity" (Jacobsohn 2010, 4). The disharmony has long been evident. Begin in 1619 with the importation of enslaved Blacks into Virginia, the very year Virginia also created a charter of self-government (Fehrenbacher 1978, 11). Jump to 1776, when the Declaration of Independence proclaimed that "all men were created equal," while all thirteen states allowed the enslavement of Blacks by law. Turn to 1787, when James Madison worked to ensure that the Constitution would not acknowledge property in man, even while it gave an extraordinary advantage in representation to those states that protected this very property in man. Slavery and self-government, slavery and liberty, and slavery and equality have been featured together from the beginning. They are entwined in powerful ways. This allowed both proslavery and antislavery understandings of the Constitution to grow together, building off of one another over time.

This chapter focuses on Gary Jacobsohn's articulation of constitutional disharmony as central to forging constitutional identity. It does so by looking at the place of Black citizenship prior to the Civil War. While there are powerful arguments that the Constitution could be seen as antislavery, even while it allowed for slavery to persist where it already existed, those who were antislavery did not give much thought to the place of Blacks within the constitutional order – particularly not to the question of Black citizenship. Events like the second Missouri crisis of 1820–1821 forced the issue of Black citizenship onto the polity, requiring constitutional actors to wrestle with questions that were not clear, or easily answered, by way of constitutional text. Following Jacobsohn, identity is forged over time. This offers an important contrast to more prevalent approaches – most notably originalism – that too often try to dissolve constitutional disharmony. Thinking in terms of constitutional disharmony we can better understand constitutional actors as constructing constitutional meaning rather than drawing out latent meaning. If, as Jacobsohn argues, "the document reflects a purpose and design that, even if not always explicitly manifest, ought to have a decisive bearing upon the course of constitutional development," it was because political actors constructed constitutional meaning in a manner that made it so (Jacobsohn 1986, 103).

The first part of this chapter notes the disharmony within the constitutional order regarding slavery. The second section turns to the second Missouri crisis of 1820–1821 to illustrate the "dialogical articulation" of competing understandings of the Constitution over the question of Black citizenship. The third and fourth sections examine how these conflicted understandings, reaching back to the founding generation, sought to construct constitutional identity in a way that would ultimately overcome the disharmony. In the final section, I suggest the Civil War amendments, framed as part of the disharmonic conflicts over Black citizenship, cement one understanding of constitutional identity, while destroying others, and are best understood as a second founding.

16.1 SLAVERY AND CONSTITUTIONAL DISHARMONY

As Sean Wilentz frames it in *No Property in Man*, "the paradox—of a Constitution that strengthened and protected slavery yet refused to validate it—created what have been perceived as the Constitution's confounding ambiguities over slavery. It encouraged the spread of antislavery and proslavery understandings of the Constitution that, though helpful in gaining the Constitution's ratification, could not co-exist forever" (Wilentz 2018, 22). If American ideas pointed to equality and antislavery, American political institutions empowered slavery and thereby perpetuated a brutal and violent inequality. At the Constitutional Convention, James Madison called slavery "the most oppressive dominion ever exercised by man over man" (Farrand 1966, 1:135).

Given this, Madison "thought it wrong to admit in the Constitution the idea that there could be property in men" (Farrand 1966, II: 417). Madison worked to make sure that the Constitution did not explicitly admit this idea even while political institutions empowered the proslavery position, giving its voice more weight in constitutional terms than it would have had absent the three-fifths compromise and the Electoral College. While leading founders tended to think of slavery as an evil in tension with the idea of self-government, even among those who never owned an enslaved person, slavery was by and large met with silence. Antislavery constitutional arguments from the founding generation rely, by and large, on an understanding of the "founders' intent." The idea that leading founders were opposed to slavery, defending it, when they did, as a necessary evil. The crucial point, from this perspective, is that we should recognize that it was wrong – that it was, at root, at odds with the principle of self-government and equality. But this understanding does not get us very far in thinking about Black equality or Black citizenship. To use Jacobsohn's terms, the Constitution *acquiesced* to slavery in powerful ways. Beyond sentiments against it, it is not at all clear that the Constitution as originally understood sought to transform social attitudes about slavery. What Jacobsohn has called "militant" constitutionalism, where a constitution actively seeks to transform social attitudes, bringing them in line with constitutional aspirations, seems altogether absent in the original Constitution (Jacobsohn 2010, 217). In fact, if we follow the now fashionable notion of "original meaning," that is, the idea that the Constitution should be understood as it was by those who ratified it, the antislavery position is likely to be even weaker. Don Fehrenbacher captures this: "The meager evidence available suggests that a systematic poll in 1776 would have produced considerable disagreement on the question of whether black men were included in the philosophy of the Declaration" (Fehrenbacher 1978, 18)

The difficult work of antislavery constitutionalism had to be taken up by others. Efforts to shape our conception of who was part of the people began almost immediately. Shortly after the Massachusetts Constitution of 1780 was ratified, Elizabeth Freeman challenged her status as an enslaved human being. She appealed to the Declaration of Independence and the newly formed Massachusetts Constitution, authored by none other than John Adams. She argued that the Massachusetts Constitution of 1780 pronouncement that "all men are born free and equal" was at odds with slavery even if the Massachusetts Constitution did not say anything in particular about slavery (or women). She won in the Massachusetts Supreme Judicial Court, beginning a chain of cases that would ultimately abolish slavery in that state (Jones 2020, 16). These efforts were part of the backdrop in which the Constitution of 1787 was framed. But the founding generation did little to further the cause of antislavery in constitutional terms, let alone to speak to the position of Blacks within the polity. This question was at the heart of the second Missouri crisis.

16.2 THE MISSOURI CRISIS AND DIALOGICAL ARTICULATION

When Missouri came into the Union in 1820, it was as part of the well-known compromise that sought a balance between slave states and free states while also prohibiting slavery in the Louisiana Purchase territory north of Missouri's southern border. But once admitted to the Union, Missouri created a second constitutional crisis when it prevented "free negros and mulattoes from coming to and settling in [the] State, under any pretext whatsoever" (Wiecek 1977, 123). The issue was whether prohibiting free Blacks from entering the state deprived them of their rights as citizens under Article IV, which guaranteed that "the citizens of each state shall be entitled to all the Privileges and Immunities of Citizens in the several states." This forced onto Congress, as William Wiecek argues, the question: "What was the place in America for the black person who was not a slave?" Were free Blacks citizens of their states? Citizens of the United States? Did they have rights of citizenship under Article IV?

Some northern representatives argued that Missouri's Constitution violated Article IV because it excluded free Black citizens. If Blacks were citizens in Massachusetts, then they had the rights of citizenship, like white citizens, to enter Missouri and enjoy the privileges and immunities of citizenship. As a representative from New York insisted, "free negroes and mulattoes are citizens." And as "citizens of the United States [they] have a right peaceably to pass through, or reside in, any part of the United States" (Annals 1820–1821, 571). This sentiment was echoed by a representative from Massachusetts, who insisted that excluding free Blacks from citizenship was at odds with the Constitution. Other northern representatives argued that it was not for the states to pick and choose which citizens from other states they would recognize as citizens: If state constitutions could exclude "any man who is a citizen of another state in this Union, then it is impossible to reconcile that [state] constitution to the Constitution of the United States" (Annals 1820–1821, 530).

Southerners denied that free Blacks were citizens. Article IV, often referred to as the Comity Clause, did not apply to free Blacks, because they were not part of the citizenry and never had been. As one southern representative argued, the Constitution "was framed by the States respectively, consisting of the European descendants of white men; that it had a view to the liberty and rights of white men; that, with regard to all this colored class, it was a description of people whom that Constitution did not mean to meddle with" (Annals 1820–1821, 550). Charles Pinckney, who had been at the Constitutional Convention in 1787, where he posited that slavery was "justified by the example of all the world," argued that the privileges and immunities clause only applied to whites (Farrand 1966, II: 371). Indeed, he denied Blacks were ever contemplated in terms of citizenship:

> ...at the time I drew that constitution, I perfectly knew there did not exist such a thing in the Union as a black or colored citizen, nor could I then have conceived it possible such a thing could ever have existed in it; nor, notwithstanding all that is said on the subject, do I now believe one does exist in it. (Annals 1820–1821, 1134)

Pinckney overreached. Not only did he falsely claim to be the author of Article IV, but to say that Black citizenship was not contemplated when the Constitution was framed and ratified is not quite the same as saying it could never exist. Constitutional provisions may entail obligations on later generations that were never contemplated by those who framed and ratified them. But Pickney was right that Black citizenship did not come up in 1787–1788 when the Constitution was framed and ratified. In a similar fashion, those who point to the antislavery thinking dominant among leading founders also overreach. To say that the Constitution is, in essence, antislavery, itself a contention open to dispute, is quite different from saying the Constitution recognized Black citizenship. Writing largely about other elements of the Missouri crisis, Madison confessed that the framers and ratifiers did not have clear ideas about the issue. Madison's logic applies even more powerfully to Black citizenship (Madison 1819). Those who framed and ratified the Constitution did not think about these issues or problems – they did not anticipate, nor could they, what history would unfold: "The Missouri antagonists, when faced with the question 'What answer does the Constitution give to our problem?' would have had to answer 'None,' if they had been frank" (Wiecek 1977, 114).

Or at least no clear answer without resorting to deeper, and conflicted, understandings of the principles that underlie the Constitution. The Missouri crisis forced the question of Black citizenship onto the polity. Did the Constitution rest on the idea of republican self-government for white men only? Did it invite a constitutional polity that, resting on the Declaration's insistence that all men are created equal, included Blacks as citizens? The citizenship question was a narrower question situated in larger debates about the place of slavery in the American constitutional order. But answering this question forced a larger reckoning with the nature of the Constitution's commitments where the participants in the conflict articulated antagonistic understandings of constitutional identity.

The Missouri crisis brought out champions of the Declaration's promise, including Black Americans who in the wake of the Missouri Compromise claimed the promise of equality and demanded the rights of citizenship. Black Americans like David Walker appealed to the Declaration and its self-evident truth that all men are created equal to claim the rights of citizenship. Frederick Douglass insisted that Blacks were part of "We the People" who ratified the Constitution: "We, the people—not we, the white people" (Douglass 1857). Changes in our understanding of citizenship and belonging – on what equality demanded of us – have been a central feature of our disharmonic Constitution.

This included the difficult labor of working out what self-government, liberty, equality, and citizenship entailed. Their antagonists also began to articulate a clearer vision of these issues, denying that Blacks were part of the constitutional people in any meaningful sense. In making their arguments, the various participants rooted particular textual clauses, like the Comity Clause, in larger constitutional understandings that frequently reached back to the founding. These debates carried forward over the next four decades. Northern states like Indiana and Ohio also excluded free Blacks from entering their states. Southern states began to require that free Black seamen, often lawfully serving the United States, be imprisoned while their ships were in port so as not to "contaminate" their slaves. These seamen had done nothing wrong but were temporarily imprisoned because of their race. President John Quincy Adams thought such acts were unconstitutional. President Jackson, and his Attorney General Roger Taney, defended the constitutionality of such acts. Indeed, as attorney general, Taney insisted on a point he would later make as Chief Justice: Blacks were "not looked upon as citizens by the contracting parties who formed the Constitution. They were evidently not supposed to be included by the term citizens" (Finkelman 1997, 56). This question culminated in *Dred Scott* where Taney would deepen and clarify his position, drawing on the founding generation to exclude Blacks from the American constitutional order, inscribing white citizenship as central to constitutional identity.

16.3 CONSTRUCTING CONSTITUTIONAL IDENTITY

When Taney stated in *Dred Scott* that Blacks could not be citizens of the United States and were forever excluded from the terms of the social compact, he was constructing constitutional meaning – and identity – based on the idea of a white man's republic. Alternative understandings had existed from the time of the founding. Taney, in this sense, overstated the case that Blacks had "never been regarded as a part of the people or citizens of the state" (Finkelman 1997, 58). As justices Benjamin Curtis and John McLean argued in dissent, Blacks had acted as citizens in several states at the time of the revolution and the founding of the Constitution. Yet no less than Taney, Curtis and McLean were rooting their arguments in underlying ideas about the natural state of freedom that would necessarily apply to Blacks who were not slaves. But, as Mark Graber argues, Taney was right in insisting that free Blacks "were not even in the minds of the framers of the Constitution" (Graber 2006, 48). The Constitution did not clearly speak to citizenship and what the privileges and immunities of citizenship might entail, let alone to whether free Blacks could be citizens. Such questions were not discussed, or even thought about, in the framing and ratifying of the Constitution. There was no ready understanding to be had on this question.

Conflicted understandings were inherent in the Constitution itself, and so political actors were building out constitutional meaning based on underlying assumptions. Both sides had plausible cases and evidence on their side. While Taney's opinion in *Dred Scott* has become infamous, it captures viable strands of constitutional thinking from the founding generation. To be sure, Taney misleadingly insisted that the Constitution *firmly* and *expressly* recognized property in man, when at best it surreptitiously acknowledged it. But when he turned to originalist understandings regarding how the people who ratified the Constitution thought of citizenship for free Blacks, articulating something like original public meaning, he had a powerful case. Only a handful of states, as the dissenting justices pointed out, treated free Blacks as citizens. And even they treated free Blacks as *unequal* citizens. In 1793, federal law only allowed whites to become naturalized citizens. If we are asking what the meaning of citizenship is circa 1789, the average understanding at the time would almost certainly support this contention. The fact that the dissenting justices could point to a few states that provided for Black citizenship, did not overcome the force of this objection. Rather, the dissenting justices argued that given that there were free Blacks at the time of the revolution and founding, they ought to be considered as part of the people who framed and ratified the Constitution. There was historical evidence for this contention, but it, too, was conflicted. The larger argument rested on ideas about natural freedom and equality that were being worked out. As Justice McLean argued in dissent, "being born under our Constitution and laws, no naturalization is required, as one of foreign birth, to make him a citizen. The most general and appropriate definition of the term citizen is 'freeman'" (Finkelman 1997, 101). Being born a freeman, according to McLean, makes one a citizen. Justice Curtis similarly argued that all free persons born "on the soil of a State" are citizens of that state and by the force of the Constitution, citizens of the United States (Finkelman 1997, 112).

Yet ascriptive ideas of citizenship that excluded Blacks also represented a powerful strand of thought and law from the founding on. Even those who were antislavery countenanced racial subordination by law. More liberal understandings of citizenship emerged, and those articulating such ideas argued that a commitment to self-government, liberty, and equality commanded Black citizenship. Such appeals to the Declaration's principles can also be seen as efforts to reframe, perhaps transform, the Constitution.

16.4 TRANSFORMING THE CONSTITUTION AT "WAR WITH ITSELF"

When Taney wrote that those who authored the Declaration could not have meant to include Blacks in its terms, that it was a statement for white men, he was almost certainly distorting the understanding of those who put the Declaration forward *to fit his constitutional argument* in 1857. Ironically, it's not clear that Taney needed to do this. To say, as an abstract proposition, that all men are created equal, did not speak to the more specific claim of whether Blacks were citizens in constitutional terms. And yet taking this step was crucial in attempting to cast the Constitution as creating a polity for whites that excluded Blacks: "The unhappy black race were separated from the white by indelible marks, and laws long before established, and were never thought of or spoken of except as property" (Finkelman 1997, 63).

Also turning to the Declaration, Taney's antagonists like Fredrick Douglass and Abraham Lincoln were pointing to the fact that there was an axiomatic disharmony between slavery and the Declaration's insistence that all men are created equal. Placing the natural equality of human beings as central to reading the Constitution, slavery would ultimately have to go. The document would have to shed slavery and "work itself pure" (Jacobsohn 2003, 65).

The debate over the Declaration became a debate about how to think of constitutional identity. As Douglass put it, exquisitely capturing the notion of disharmony, the Constitution was "at war with itself" (Douglass 1857). It embraced both liberty and slavery. Douglass famously turned to the Declaration in "What to the Slave is the Fourth of July?": America was "false to the past" in perpetuating the "great sin" of slavery (Douglass 1997, 125). Douglass was unstinting in his criticism of America's "revolting barbarity and shameless hypocrisy," but he also began to frame his own argument as a defense of the Constitution as read through the lens of the Declaration's "saving principles." Douglass claimed and acted as a citizen. Insofar as Blacks were people, they were not only part of the actual "We the People" who created the Constitution and were entitled to the benefits it ordained and established but they were also part of the future "We the People" the Constitution must embrace to be true to itself.

Douglass held that the "Constitution, as well as the Declaration of Independence, and the sentiments of the founders of the Republic, give us a platform broad enough, and strong enough, to support the most comprehensive plans for the freedom and elevation of all the people of this country, without regard to color, class, or clime." Indeed, Douglass insisted "The Constitution knows all the human inhabitants of this country as 'the people'" (Douglass 1857). Douglass proceeded to quote Taney's take on the Declaration at length, calling it a "devilish perversion of the Constitution, and a brazen misstatement of the facts of history" (Douglass 1857). Douglass insisted on the antislavery elements from the founding generation, even while disregarding the intent of the founders to preserve slavery. Reading the text of the Constitution by way of the Declaration's "saving principles," Douglass positioned them as essential to America's "yet undeveloped destiny." It was this destiny that Douglass was trying to create, drawing on the past to reframe the Constitution as currently understood. In his effort, Douglass was joining other abolitionists, White and Black alike, who contended that the Constitution's text and principles should take priority over the fact that its framers had compromised with slavery. If Taney had constructed the Constitution in proslavery terms, that was a corruption of the text and the history that should be resisted. In constructing an antislavery Constitution, Douglass sought to "make that instrument bend to the cause of freedom and justice" by reading its text in light of its antislavery principles (Douglass 1860, 156).

Lincoln, also intent on resisting *Dred Scott*, turned to justices Curtis and McLean to point out that Blacks were in fact part of the people who declared independence and made the Constitution. In New Hampshire, Massachusetts, New York, New Jersey, and North Carolina, free Blacks were voters who "had a hand in making the

Constitution" (Lincoln 2012). They were, from the beginning, part of "we the people" even if in other states they were denied citizenship and, worse, held in human bondage. Lincoln went on to what he viewed as the essential point: The condition of Blacks was worse in 1857 than at the time of the founding in the minds of their fellow citizens (Lincoln 2012, 113). Taney's own words, drawn from 1819, partly support this position. As an attorney representing an abolitionist, Taney noted that every "lover of freedom" will hope for the eradication of slavery when we can point to the language of the Declaration "without a blush."

Like Douglass, Lincoln positioned the Declaration as central – its stated commitment to the principle that all men are created equal was the true principle, now degraded. He spoke in clearly aspirational terms: Those who wrote the Declaration

> ...mean simply to declare the right, so that enforcement of it might follow as fast as circumstances should permit. They meant to set up a standard maxim for free society, which should be familiar to all, and revered by all; constantly looked to, constantly labored for, and even though never perfectly attained, constantly approximated, and thereby constantly spreading and deepening its influence, and augmenting the happiness and value of life to all people of all colors everywhere. (Lincoln 2012, 115)

The principle was placed in the Declaration for *future use*. According to Lincoln, the Declaration "contemplated the progressive improvement in the condition of all men everywhere" (Lincoln 2012, 115).

Flowing from his reading of the Declaration, Lincoln avowed a liberal understanding of human equality – and, ultimately, citizenship – rejecting the idea of republican government rooted in racial caste. Yet this was, much like Taney's, a constitutional construction that sought to shape our understanding of constitutional identity. In doing so, Lincoln built on generations of antislavery constitutionalism that sought to subvert – indeed, destroy – the plausible proslavery readings that found some footing in the original Constitution.

The founding generation may have put these ideas in motion, but just what they entailed was not fixed at an imagined moment of founding. Questions around these ideas remain with us. The founders' commitments included obligations with regard to racial equality – among other things – they could not have anticipated or even comprehended. The unkept promises of the Declaration may well act as the touchstone for future generations working from first principles, but just what a commitment to these principles entails is something that has been constructed along the way – in a dialogical conflict – and often against the particulars of history. This work not only continues, but it is a never-ending part of maintaining a constitutional order set in motion more than two centuries ago. Arguments like Lincoln's to restore America to its foundations, to a nation *dedicated to the proposition* that all men are created equal, are efforts to return to something real, but that never *actually* existed – only the promise of it did. And it was from this reading of the founding that Lincoln, Douglass, and abolitionists who offered an antislavery reading of the Constitution were trying to create a constitutional order that reflected the best understanding of the founding.

If Taney's reading of the founders made them worse than the actual history suggests, "disingenuously writing as if he thought public opinion in the founding period sadly more benighted than his own," Lincoln's liberal aspirationalism made the founding generation better (Smith 1997, 267). Jacobsohn positions Lincoln's understanding of natural right, with its aspiration to human equality, as central to the Constitution's meaning. But it is Lincoln who is imputing these goals onto the Constitution. Lincoln is engaged in shaping constitutional identity in a manner that requires the repudiation and negation of Taney's ascriptive understandings (Jacobsohn 2010, 107). As Harry Jaffa wrote long ago in his study of the Lincoln-Douglas debates, the founders' "principle included the Negroes in 'all men,' but the Negroes' rights did *not* impose corresponding duties upon the white masters." Thus, "when Lincoln said that the policy of the Founding Fathers was to place the institution of slavery where the public mind might rest in the belief that it was in course of ultimate extinction, he was also stretching their attitude to fit *his* theory rather than theirs." Lincoln offered "a creative interpretation, a subtle preparation for the 'new birth of freedom'" (Jaffa 1959, 318).

Thomas Jefferson's set of promises in the Declaration were taken by Douglass and Lincoln to entail the end of slavery (whether Jefferson himself saw it this way) and succeeding generations have understood this to entail a commitment to a multiracial vision of citizenship (whether Lincoln himself saw it this way). "When one wishes to keep the promises the Founders committed the nation to, one always discovers that the exigencies of history unfold new demands out of those concepts, demands our generation has almost inevitably failed" (Burt 2013, 4). The commitment to human equality was a commitment to something many founders did not necessarily comprehend in its particulars. Lincoln's insistence on this point, in ending slavery and delivering emancipation, was also a commitment, whether he conceived of it that way, to racial equality and full citizenship.

Yet all of this is premised on the idea that the Constitution rests on principles put forward in the Declaration: that to be a self-governing republic requires human liberty and equality that cannot tolerate racial caste. Arguments along these lines begin from the founding and continue through Lincoln's new birth of freedom. But they are constitutional constructions developed by political actors as part of a dynamic process that forges constitutional identity. And if they create constitutional meaning from particular histories, they also seek to repudiate alternative understandings of constitutional identity. Jacobsohn helps us understand how disharmony shapes constitutional meaning and identity even if constitutional actors build on particular traditions to do so. Constitutional identity is not preordained but something constructed by participants like Douglass and Lincoln.

16.5 THE CORE OF CONSTITUTIONAL IDENTITY

In the American context, the dialogical conflict I have focused on culminated in formal constitutional amendments. For many who framed the Fourteenth Amendment, it rested on and restated the essential principles of the Declaration, inscribing them into constitutional text. The Civil War amendments can be seen as a radical reconstitution of the American people, which were deeply influenced by antislavery constitutionalism. These amendments amount to a second founding that decisively broke from elements of the first founding and remade the Constitution. Yet, from another perspective, it can also be seen as the fulfillment of the promise of the first Constitution that required the dissolution of some inherited understandings and the elevation of others. Even in the latter scenario, which would read the Fourteenth Amendment as a fulfillment of the first founding, we need to highlight that it is a profound correction to the flaws of the Constitution of 1787. It was enough of a correction that we can think of it as a second founding that profoundly improved on the first. This second founding was not latent in the original document, even if the Constitution rested on ideas that opened up the necessity of remaking the Constitution. Inscribing the principles of the Declaration into constitutional text, the Fourteenth Amendment decisively settled the previously contested question of Black citizenship.

Yet the second founding highlights another disharmony Jacobsohn speaks to – the gap between constitutional ideals and practice. The Fourteenth Amendment, to truly constitute Americans as a people, would require reshaping the people, transforming social attitudes about racial equality to realize the aspirations of the amendment. The clear meaning of the amendment was evaded within a decade of its ratification, paving the way for its subversion at least with regard to race. Even with the revolutionary nature of the second founding, there was a century-long struggle, which persists to this day, to live up to its terms. Disharmony remains an inescapable feature of America's constitutional order.

REFERENCES

Annals of Congress, 16th Congress, 2nd Session, 1820–1821.
Burt, John. 2013. *Lincoln's Tragic Pragmatism: Lincoln, Douglas, and Moral Conflict*. Cambridge: Harvard University Press.
Douglass, Frederick. 1857. "Speech on the Dred Scott Decision." https://teachingamericanhistory.org/document/speech-on-the-dred-scott-decision-2/.
Douglass, Frederick. 1997. *Narrative of the Life of Frederick Douglass: An American Slave, Written by Himself*, edited by William Andrews and William McFeely. New York: Norton & Company.
Douglass, Frederick. 2004. "The Constitution of the United States: Is It Pro-Slavery or Anti-Slavery? (1860)." In *Antislavery Political Writings, 1833–1860*, edited by C. Bradley Thompson, 144–156. New York: Routledge.

Farrand, Max. 1966. *Records of the Federal Convention of 1787*, I–II. New Haven: Yale University Press.
Fehrenbacher, Don E. 1978. *The Dred Scott Case: Its Significance in American Law and Politics*. New York: Oxford University Press.
Finkelman, Paul. 1997. *Dred Scott v. Sanford: A Brief History with Documents*. Boston: Bedford Books.
Graber, Mark. 2006. *Dred Scott and the Problem of Constitutional Evil*. New York: Cambridge University Press.
Jacobsohn, Gary J. 1986. *The Supreme Court and the Decline of Constitutional Aspiration*. Totowa: Rowman and Littlefield Publishers.
Jacobsohn, Gary J. 2003. *The Wheel of Law: India's Secularism in Comparative Constitutional Context*. Princeton: Princeton University Press.
Jacobsohn, Gary J. 2010. *Constitutional Identity*. Cambridge: Harvard University Press.
Jaffa, Harry V. 1959. *Crisis of the House Divided*. Chicago: University of Chicago Press.
Jones, Martha. 2020. *Vanguard: How Black Women Broke Barriers, Won the Vote, and Insisted on Equality for All*. New York: Basic Books.
Lincoln, Abraham. 2012. *The Writings of Abraham Lincoln*, edited by Steven B. Smith. New Haven: Yale University Press.
Madison, James. 1819. "Letter to Robert Walsh, Jr." November 27, 1819. https://founders.archives.gov/documents/Madison/04-01-02-0504.
Smith, Rogers. 1997. *Civic Ideals: Conflicting Vision of Citizenship in U.S. History*. New Haven: Yale University Press.
Wiecek, William. 1977. *The Sources of Anti-Slavery Constitutionalism in America, 1760–1848*. Cornell University Press.
Wilentz, Sean. 2018. *No Property in Man: Slavery and Antislavery at the Nation's Founding*. Cambridge: Harvard University Press.

17

Constitutional Identity, Constitutional Politics, and Constitutional Revolutions

Mark A. Graber[*]

Professor Gary Jacobsohn is fond of Abraham Lincoln's "apple of gold" metaphor. Referring to Thomas Jefferson's claim in the Declaration of Independence that "all men are created equal," (Jefferson 1975, 235) the Illinois Republican wrote:

> The assertion of that *principle* at *that time*, was *the* word, *"fitly spoken"* which has proven an "apple of gold" to us. The *Union* and the *Constitution*, are the *picture* of *silver*, subsequently framed around it. The picture was made, not to *conceal*, or *destroy* the apple, but to *adorn*, and *preserve* it. The *picture* was made *for* the apple – not the apple for the picture (emphasis in original) (Lincoln 1953, 169).[1]

Jacobsohn's book on constitutionalism in Israel and the United States is entitled *Apple of Gold*. The above quotation introduces the text and is on the back cover of the hardback edition (Jacobsohn 1993, 3; Jacobsohn 2021, 83). Jacobsohn, in the preface to his *Constitutional Identity*, declares, "I was particularly taken with Lincoln's appropriation of the biblical metaphor of an "apple of gold" framed by a "picture of silver" to understand the role of antecedent principles in constituting a polity that had been compromised at its very inception by practices antithetical to those principles" (Jacobsohn 2010, 15).

The "apple of gold" metaphor suggests that constitutional politics has, at most, an instrumental relationship to the constitutional commitments that form the core of a nation's constitutional identity. Lincoln maintained that Americans were constitutionally committed to abolishing slavery eventually. In another speech Jacobsohn is fond of quoting, the person who would become known as the Great Emancipator declared that the Declaration of Independence "meant simply to declare the *right*, so that that the *enforcement* of it might follow as fast as circumstances should permit" (Lincoln 1953b, 83). The Union and Constitution of the United States were means

---
[*] Much thanks to Gary Jacobsohn for conversations over my academic lifetime, to Yaniv Roznai and Ran Hirschl for their forbearance and advice, and to the other contributors to this volume for their sterling insights on constitutional identity.

[1] The Declaration of Independence was the "apple of gold." Slavery was the "apple of discord" (Lincoln 1953a, 88).

to that end, not independent sources of constitutional identity. Lincoln, at least Jacobsohn's Lincoln, never asserted a constitutional commitment to a presidential system of governance or to a bicameral legislature.[2] American constitutional identity was constituted by the equality and rights commitments made by the Declaration of Independence, not by the governing structures and powers established by the Constitution of the United States.

Politics matters and matters considerably. "[A] constitutional identity," Jacobsohn and Yaniv Roznai maintain in *Constitutional Revolution*, "is something to be realized" (Jacobsohn and Roznai 2020, 270). Elsewhere, Jacobsohn states, "identity emerges dialogically" (Jacobsohn 2010, 7). Constitutional texts initiate processes of fundamental change. *Constitutional Revolution* states, "the act of including specific constitutional language about identity in a document has at the moment of inclusion only aspirational significance, ... it affirms a commitment and a direction" (Jacobsohn and Roznai 2020, 270). Politics is the means by which regimes fully develop constitutional identities. Jacobsohn and Roznai assert, "if the promise embodied in such language is actively pursued in a manner that over time renders the parchment constitutional identity a lived reality, then we can speak of a constitutional revolution" (Jacobsohn and Roznai 2020, 270).

Constitutional politics matters and matters considerably because, as Jacobsohn famously observes, constitutions and constitutional politics are disharmonic. He writes, "tradition rarely presents itself neatly as the harmonious gift from the past, rather it comes to us encumbered with the discordant strands of a complicated history" (Jacobsohn 2010, 19). History offers different paths for national development. National constitutions contain strands that support different constitutional aspirations. Established constitutional institutions interfere with the achievement of settled constitutional commitments. Many people reject constitutional commitments or are not prepared to honor them fully in the present. Constitutional revolutionaries working within a disharmonic constitutional order need politics as well as guns. They must strengthen the strands of constitutional life that are consistent with their constitutional visions and increase the number of citizens prepared to act immediately on that vision.

That "[t]he *picture* was made *for* the apple—*not* the apple for the picture" suggests two possible instrumental relationships between constitutional commitments and constitutional politics. The point of constitutional politics is to achieve certain aspirations, but constitutional politics is not structured in ways that privilege desired outcomes. Lincoln thought elected officials should be guided by the maxim, "all men are created equal," but he never suggested any political institution established by the Constitution of the United States was designed to favor antislavery policies. Alternatively, constitutional politics is structured for the purpose of achieving constitutional aspirations.

---

[2] For my claim that Lincoln was constitutionally committed to some version of majoritarianism, refracted through constitutional institutions that he understood were not perfectly majoritarian, see Graber 2006, 179–184.

Ran Hirschl's influential "hegemonic preservation" thesis maintains that the point of new constitutional processes that empower judiciaries is to maintain constitutional commitments to neo-liberalism and secularism (Hirschl 2004, 2010).

Constitutional politics has three other, more constitutive relationships with constitutional identity. A particular constitutional politics may constitute constitutional identity. *Schneiderman v. United States*,[3] the *Carolene Products* footnote,[4] and John Hart Ely's *Democracy and Distrust* (Ely 1980) maintain that the United States is constitutionally committed to resolving questions concerning fundamental values by robust democratic processes. Whatever the political process churns out, the *Carolene Products* footnote suggests, is consistent with the constitutional identity of the United States as long as that process meets certain democratic standards and does not discriminate against "discrete and insular minorities."[5] A particular constitutional politics might be the constitutionally prescribed means for elaborating inherited constitutional commitments. Constitutional reformers design constitutional processes that empower and privilege the sympathetic, people they believe will share, implement, and develop faithfully their constitutional vision. The persons responsible for the Fourteenth Amendment to the Constitution of the United States thought Sections Two and Three would structure constitutional politics in ways that would guarantee to the extent humanely feasible that Republicans for the foreseeable future controlled the meaning of the Thirteenth Amendment's constitutional ban on slavery (Graber 2023). A particular constitutional politics might be the constitutionally prescribed means for determining constitutional commitments. Constitutional designers faced with a dispute over fundamental principles may design a process that permits warring political movements to make their contested constitutional visions the official law of the land only under certain political conditions. The Constitution of the United States established political institutions that the Federalist framers thought would allow for the emancipation of slaves only when a substantial part of the South endorsed antislavery policies (Graber 2006, 105–106).

This essay explores different relationships between constitutional identity and constitutional politics. One purpose is descriptive. The first five sections briefly discuss the five relationships between constitutional identity and constitutional politics laid out in the previous paragraphs. The more fundamental goal is to undermine the "apple of gold" metaphor as a device for thinking about constitutional regimes. Constitutional politics in most constitutional regimes is as constitutive of constitutional identity as the substantive principles announced in such documents as the Declaration of Independence.

Process and substance can rarely be fully disaggregated when thinking about constitutionalism, constitutional politics, constitutional identity, and constitutional

---

[3] *Schneiderman v. United States*, 320 U.S. 118 (1943).
[4] *United States v. Carolene Products Co.*, 304 U.S. 144, 152–153 n.4 (1938).
[5] *United States v. Carolene Products Co.*, 304 U.S. 144, 152–153 n.4 (1938).

revolutions (Graber 2013, 212–215). Constitutional democracies are typically dedicated to substantive ends and certain democratic processes for achieving, elaborating, and determining those ends. Walter Murphy and his co-editors regard the simultaneous commitment to human dignity and majoritarianism as the defining characteristic of a constitutional democracy (Murphy et al. 2003, 43–59). When constitutional politics is entwined with a particular constitutional identity, changing the structure of the constitutional politics often changes the basic constitutional aspirations of a regime. When regimes commit to a particular process for elaborating or developing constitutional identities, changes in the process alter the constitutional identity of that regime as much as changes in the substantive aspirations that regime is dedicated to achieving. One cannot tell the story of the rise and fall of commitments to racial equality in the United States without telling the story of the rise and fall of the constitutional politics that constitutional actors thought would bring about greater racial equality in the United States.

17.1 CONSTITUTIONAL POLITICS AS PURE POLITICS

The "apple of gold" metaphor treats constitutional politics as neutral grounds for realizing constitutional aspirations. Constitutional aspirations guide and inspire political actors. Lincoln maintained that Thomas Jefferson and his political associates "meant to set up a standard maxim for free society, which should be familiar to all, and revered by all; constantly looked to, constantly labored for, and even though never perfectly attained, constantly approximated, and thereby constantly spreading and deepening its influence, and augmenting the happiness and value of life to all people of all colors everywhere" (Lincoln 1953b, 406). Constitutional institutions are indifferent to such aspirations. They are justified on other grounds and provide no advantages to those persons who best articulate the constitutional ethos. Lincoln never mentioned any constitutional process that he believed facilitated emancipation or strengthened the national commitment to the principles asserted by the Declaration of Independence.

Lincoln celebrated what he believed to be American constitutional aspirations. He hailed free state constitutions for "declar[ing] the wrong of slavery" (Lincoln 1953c, 438). He praised the framers for regarding human bondage "*as an evil not to be extended, but to be tolerated and protected only because of and so far as its actual presence among us makes that toleration and protection a necessity*" (emphasis in the original) (Lincoln 1953c, 535). Future generations of Americans, Lincoln thought, would be inspired by the framing example, even as he acknowledged that the eighteenth-century founders of the United States did not create a republic that fully lived up to the principles announced by the Declaration of Independence. He declared,

> The assertion that "all men are created equal" was of no practical use in effecting our separation from Great Britain; and it was placed in the Declaration, nor for that, but for future use. Its authors meant it to be, thank God, it is now proving

itself, a stumbling block to those who in after times might seek to turn a free people back into the hateful paths of despotism. They knew the proneness of prosperity to breed tyrants, and they meant when such should re-appear in this fair land and commence their vocation they should find left for them at least one hard nut to crack. (Lincoln 1953b, 406)

Constitutional revolutions, Lincoln's framers recognized, unfold over time (Jacobsohn and Roznai 2020, 15). Transformation is a multigenerational project. Americans at any particular time might not finish the task, but as the Jewish proverb goes, they were not free to refrain.

The constitutional barriers Lincoln's framers established to the spread of human bondage were ideological rather than political. When Lincoln insisted "the framers of the Constitution intended and expected the ultimate extinction of that institution," (Lincoln 1953d, 492), the emphasis was on "expected." His Federalist framers gave government the power to weaken slavery, but they did not take any steps to fashion a government likely to exercise that power. The Illinois Republican never celebrated any provision in Article I, Article II, or Article III for privileging electoral coalitions or political movements committed to making antislavery policies. Lincoln did not claim that state equality in the Senate augmented the power of free states or that long terms of office might induce some southern representatives to be more supportive of antislavery policies than a majority of their constituents. Constitutional institutions were neutral between those who thought toleration and protection of slavery remained a necessity and those who favored polities that might quicken the end of human bondage in the United States. The constitutional commitment to the ultimate extinction of slavery rested entirely on Americans remaining committed to the Declaration of Independence. Americans who became more tolerant of slavery would not find the constitutional politics established in 1787 "one hard nut to crack."

Politics matters in this Lincolnian account of constitutional identity but as an instrument rather than as constitutive of constitutional identity. Jacobsohn's Lincoln, Martin Luther King, and other participants in constitutional revolutions made political choices when engaging in constitutional politics. Lincoln and his political allies created a political party. King relied on civil disobedience. The American constitutional identities these political leaders forged were constituted by their commitments to abolishing slavery and racial equality, not by the changing political tactics that their political movements employed in service of that constitutional identity.

17.2 CONSTITUTIONAL POLITICS AS CONSTITUTIONAL

James Wilson suggested a stronger connection than Lincoln offered between constitutional commitments and constitutional politics when the leader of Pennsylvania Federalists claimed that constitutional provisions permitting Congress to ban the international slave trade would facilitate the "ultimate extinction of slavery." J. Wilson informed the Pennsylvania-ratifying convention that the constitutional permission to ban the international slave trade laid "the foundation for banishing slavery out of this country" (Jensen 1976, 463). J. Wilson did not rest content asserting that the Constitution left a path open for Americans to strike a deadly blow against human bondage. He expressed confidence that the Constitution structured politics in ways that increased the probability that Congress would ban the international slave trade in 1808. Congressional control of national expansion would likely increase antislavery strength in the national government. J. Wilson observed, "the new states which are to be formed, will be under the control of Congress in this particular; and slaves will never be introduced among them" (Jensen 1976, 463). These new free states, in turn, would buttress congressional majorities in favor of banning the international slave trade.

Ran Hirschl's hegemonic preservation thesis captures this instrumental relationship between constitutional politics and constitutional commitments. He maintains, "when their policy preferences have been, or are likely to be, increasingly challenged in majoritarian decision-making arenas, elites that possess disproportionate access to, and influence over, the legal arena may initiate a constitutional entrenchment of rights and judicial review in order to transfer power to supreme courts" (Hirschl 2004, 12). The "constitutional entrenchment of rights and judicial review" are not two separate political actions, the first concerned with constitutional commitments and the second concerned with constitutional politics. Persons seeking to strengthen constitutional identities combine new constitutional expressions of their fundamental values with new political processes designed to achieve their constitutional aspirations.

Constitutional politics as constitutional accepts the instrumental relationship between constitutional institutions and constitutional commitments suggested by the "apple of gold" metaphor. J. Wilson and Hirschl regard constitutional politics as a means for achieving constitutional commitments, not as the commitments themselves or processes for elaborating the nature of those commitments over time. Their accounts differ from Lincoln's in that they maintain that framers structure constitutional politics in ways conducive to achieving independent constitutional commitments. Both Lincoln and J. Wilson agreed that the power to ban the international slave trade after twenty years expressed a constitutional commitment to ending slavery (Lincoln 1953e, 22). Lincoln focused on the expressive value of that provision. His Article I favored neither emancipation nor bondage. J. Wilson's Article I created a constitutional structure biased in favor of congressional decisions banning the international slave trade after twenty years.

17.3 CONSTITUTIONAL POLITICS AS CONSTITUTIONAL IDENTITY

The Supreme Court of the United States in *Schneiderman v. United States* offered an understanding of American constitutional identity in which the regime's most fundamental constitutional commitment was to a particular form of constitutional politics. The issue in that case was whether William Schneiderman committed perjury in his application for American citizenship when he swore he was "attached to the principles of the Constitution of the United States."[6] Schneiderman "believed in the essential correctness of the Marx theory as applied by the Communist Party of the United States,"[7] but claimed that Marxism was consistent with American constitutionalism. Six justices on the Supreme Court of the United States agreed. Justice Frank Murphy's majority opinion asserted,

> Article V contains procedural provisions for constitutional change by amendment without any present limitation whatsoever except that no State may be deprived of equal representation in the Senate without its consent. This provision and the many important and far-reaching changes made in the Constitution since 1787 refute the idea that attachment to any particular provision or provisions is essential, or that one who advocates radical changes is necessarily not attached to the Constitution.[8]

Schneiderman was attached to the principles of the Constitution because he believed that Article V was the appropriate vehicle for any constitutional change. He was American as long as he was committed to playing by the constitutional rules for amendment.

Politics is all there is in *Schneiderman*'s notion of constitutional identity. Americans, Murphy indicated, have no common substantive commitments and are not constituted by any substantive commitments. What unites the United States is a commitment to certain processes for reform. Americans play by the constitutional rules for constitutional change, whether those rules require winning elections or passing constitutional amendments. No amendment would work a fundamental change in that constitutional regime, except a constitutional amendment abandoning Article V or perhaps state equality in the Senate.

Footnote four of *United States v. Carolene Products* captures *Schneiderman*'s conception of constitutional identity grounded in commitments to a particular form of constitutional politics. Justice Harlan Fiske Stone's majority opinion insisted that the Constitution empowered democratically elected officials with the authority to make fundamental value choices.[9] What legislatures could not do was "restrict those political processes which can ordinarily be expected to bring about repeal of undesirable legislation" or discriminate against "discrete and insular minorities."[10] Democratic relativism was the foundation of constitutional identity in this regime (Purcell 1973). Substantive values independent of the democratic process need not apply.

Constitutional commitments to democratic processes are common. Jacobsohn and Roznai discuss the importance of democracy to constitutional identity in India

---

[6] *Schneiderman, supra* note 4, 132.
[7] *Schneiderman, supra* note 4, 127.
[8] *Schneiderman, supra* note 4, 137.
[9] *Carolene Products Co., supra* note 5, 152–154.
[10] *Carolene Products Co., supra* note 5, 152–153.

and Israel (Jacobsohn and Roznai 2020, 143–223). Commitments to democracy may go far beyond majority rule. John Hart Ely in *Democracy and Distrust* urged courts to place limits on popular attempts to curb speech, deny access to the ballot, and discriminate against racial minorities (Ely 1980, 73–179). Constitutional interpretation, in his view, "should focus not on whether this or that substantive value is unusually important or fundamental, but rather on whether the opportunity to participate either in the political processes by which values are appropriately identified and accommodated, or in the accommodation those processes have reached, has been unduly constricted" (Ely 1980, 77).

Consociational regimes ground constitutional identity in constitutional politics, Constitutions in consociational regimes ensure that different social groups have at least veto power over national policy (Lijphart 2012). Many include commitments to federalism that enable national minorities to exercise considerable authority in places where they are local majorities. The Constitution may grant minorities the legislative seats necessary to block bills they believe are hostile to those interests. What unites consociational polities, if often tenuously, is a common understanding that groups with very different values have good reason to share the same civic space. A constitutional identity that emphasizes processes that enable people to satisfice is more stable than constitutional identities that celebrate the values of one group while denying authoritative status to the values of others.

17.4 CONSTITUTIONAL POLITICS AS ELABORATING A CONSTITUTIONAL IDENTITY

The members of the Thirty-Ninth Congress who framed the Fourteenth Amendment yoked American constitutional identity to the Republican party. Senator Henry Wilson of Massachusetts on March 2, 1866, asserted, "No political party in any country or in any age has fought on a plain so lofty, or achieved so much for country, republican institutions, the cause of freedom, of justice, and of Christian civilization."[11] The main point of the Fourteenth Amendment, Representative Thaddeus Stevens of Pennsylvania declared in the speech that opened debate on Reconstruction, was to "secure perpetual ascendancy to the party of the Union ... so as to render our republican Government firm and stable forever."[12] Constitutional reform was necessary because, under the Constitution of December 1865, former Confederate states might obtain thirty-seven members of the House of Representatives and thirty-seven votes in the Electoral College for disenfranchised persons of color. This slavocracy bonus would enable the antebellum Jacksonian coalition of slaveholders and doughfaces to regain control of the national government. The result would be "[t]he oppression of the freedmen, the reamendment of their state constitutions, and the

---

[11] *Congressional Globe*, 39th Cong., 1st Sess., App., p. 142.
[12] *Congressional Globe*, 39th Cong., 1st Sess., App., p. 74.

reestablishment of slavery."[13] Apportionment reform would alleviate this threat by placing the South in a dilemma. Former Confederate states would either enfranchise persons of color, which would "continue the Republican ascendancy,"[14] or have their representation reduced by almost forty percent, which would "render them powerless for evil."[15]

H. Wilson and Stevens regarded constitutional politics as an instrument for elaborating constitutional commitments rather than merely as an instrument for achieving them. The Republican Constitution of 1866 was committed to making persons of color equal citizens of the United States. Republicans disagreed among themselves over what made persons of color equal citizens of the United States. Some maintained equal citizens of the United States could be educated in separate schools. Others disagreed (McConnell 1995). Some maintained equal citizens of the United States, at least equal male citizens, had the right to vote and hold office. Others disagreed (Benedict 1974). The Fourteenth Amendment would ensure that Republicans determined the content of the constitutional commitment to equality (Graber 2023). Republicans would determine what constituted slavery, not former slaveholders. The American constitutional identity H. Wilson and Stevens forged was one whose fundamental commitment was to a Republican party majority articulating the constitutional commitments to anti-slavery and racial equality. Republicans would rule, no matter which horn of the dilemma impaled former slaveholders.

Political actors rarely kick the can down the road when making constitutional decisions without making any attempt to structure constitutional development. They use such words and phrases as "liberty," "equality," and "due process" that they are aware are subject to different interpretation. Republicans in 1866 studiously avoided clarifying whether the Constitution empowered Congress to enfranchise persons of color throughout the nation. Nevertheless, constitutional framers typically do not leave the elaboration of their constitutional revolution to an entirely uncertain future. Rather, following Wilson and Stevens, they structure constitutional institutions so that the unfolding of their constitutional commitments will be determined by persons with specific beliefs, capacities, and interests. Republicans would control the constitutional commitment to equality, not former slaveholders, white supremacists, or northern Democrats. The American constitutional identity that Wilson, Stevens and their political allies forged was one in which the future success of the Republican Party was entwined with the future constitutional commitment to the principles laid out in the Declaration of Independence. No fixed endpoint existed, only a commitment to the persons who would determine how a shared commitment would guide constitutional development.

---

[13] *Congressional Globe*, 39th Cong., 1st Sess., App., p. 74.
[14] *Congressional Globe*, 39th Cong., 1st Sess., App., p. 74.
[15] *Congressional Globe*, 39th Cong., 1st Sess., App., p. 74.

17.5 CONSTITUTIONAL POLITICS AS DETERMINING A CONSTITUTIONAL IDENTITY

The Federalist framers fashioned a constitutional commitment to a particular form of constitutional politics as the legitimate process for establishing more substantive commitments. A bisectional constitutional politics formed the core of American constitutional identity in 1787 (Graber 2006, 96–109). If population flowed as the Federalist framers expected, the North would control the Senate and the South would control the House of Representatives. The United States would develop a greater antislavery or proslavery identity only when that identity enjoyed substantial support in both regions of the country. Whether American constitutional identity would be antislavery or proslavery was left to constitutional politics, but to a constitutional politics self-consciously structured to determine the conditions under which the United States would become a regime committed to human freedom or human bondage. Revolutionary changes in the substantive strands of American constitutional identity would be brought about by strict adherence to political strands of American constitutional identity.

This bisectionalism was a basic principle or feature of the original constitutional order. George Washington warned Americans against sectional parties in his farewell address. He described "the danger of parties in the States, with particular reference to the founding of them on geographical discriminations" (Washington 1896, 218). Stephen Douglas spoke for the *"ancien régime"* when he began his first debate with Lincoln by declaring, "Prior to 1854 this country was divided into two great political parties, known as the Whig and Democratic parties. Both were national and patriotic, advocating principles that were universal in their application" (Douglas 1953, 2). Douglas understood that the national political parties that came of age in the 1830s and 1840s were constructed to ensure that national policy had strong support in all sections of the United States. If national party competitions between Jeffersonians/Jacksonians and Federalists/Whigs "are suppressed," Martin Van Buren feared, "geographical divisions founded on local interests, or what is more, prejudices between free and slaveholding states, will inevitably take their place" (Hofstadter 1969).

A regime committed to a form of constitutional politics for determining substantive constitutional commitments differs from a regime in which a form of constitutional politics is the fundamental constitutional commitment. *Schneiderman*, the *Carolene Products* footnote, and *Democracy and Distrust* are animated by a commitment to democratic relativism (Purcell 1973). Constitutional identity is rooted in a commitment to fair democratic processes because no objective basis exists in moral philosophy or the Constitution for determining substantive constitutional values. The persons responsible for the Constitution of 1787 were not democratic relativists. Most believed the immorality of slavery was an objective truth. A few believed slavery was justified by natural law (Kaminski 1995). The constitutional identity they forged emphasized a process for determining objective constitutional truths. A shared constitutional identity rooted in bisectionalism would determine whether more substantive strands of American constitutional identity would move in a proslavery or antislavery direction.

The "constitutionalized framework" for constitutional revolutions is part of the inherited constitutional identity of the regime. Constitutional politics is an object of political competition and not simply the battlefield on which struggles over constitutional identity take place. The Constitution of 1787 abandoned the rules for constitutional revolutions set out by the Articles of Confederation. A more recent proposal for a new Constitution of the United States abandons the rules for constitutional revolutions set out by the Constitution of 1787 (The Delegates of The Democracy Constitution n.d.). That proposed constitution sets out an integrated set of provisions that announce substantive constitutional aspirations, provisions that structure constitutional politics, and provisions that establish a framework for future constitutional revolutions. No neat line in that constitution, in the Constitution of 1787, or in other national constitutions separates commitments to constitutional politics from commitments to substantive values.

Consider thickened, progressive, cosmopolitan constitutional democracy, some version of which describes important strands of constitutional identity throughout much of the constitutional democratic world. Such regimes are committed to robust political freedoms, broadly shared commercial prosperity, inclusiveness, secularism, and, perhaps, international law (Graber 2018, 666). The populist challenge to thickened, progressive cosmopolitan, constitutional democracy is taking place on all these fronts. Populist autocrats limit speech rights while adopting policies that favor persons of certain ethnicities and religions (Graber 2018, 673–678). Treating some elements of thickened, progressive, cosmopolitan, constitutional democracy as the constitutional identity of a regime while regarding others as mere means, fails to grasp how in contemporary constitutional democracies, commitments to robust political freedoms, broadly shared commercial prosperity, inclusiveness, secularism, and, perhaps, international law form an integrated whole.

CONCLUSION: ENTWINING CONSTITUTIONAL POLITICS AND CONSTITUTIONAL IDENTITY

Stephen Elkin observes that a constitutional regime consists of a set of ideals, a set of institutions designed to achieve those ideals, and a people who share the ideals and understand how to operate the institutions (Elkin 2001, 1948). The constitutional identity of a regime is forged by the interaction of ideals, institutions, and people. While different elements of constitutional identity are predominant in distinctive regimes, no one element is the mere frame that was made for the apple and no one element is the apple to which the frame is a mere instrument. Constitutional politics is as constitutive of constitutional identity as the constitutional ideals and the constitutional people who, through constitutional politics, struggle to affirm, create, modify, or abandon various constitutional commitments and aspirations.

Constitutional revolutions occur in regimes when changes in ideals, institutions, or the people transform how ideals, institutions, and the people interact. Lincoln and his political allies entrenched a constitutional commitment to abolishing slavery by building on the revolutionary changes the founders of the American party system made to the way political institutions operated in the United States. Martin Luther King and his political allies entrenched a constitutional commitment to racial equality by building on the revolutionary changes the Republican framers made to who constituted the people of the United States. Potential revolutionary changes in the place of reproductive freedom, racial equality, and immigration in the contemporary American constitutional identity are enmeshed in the increased diversity of the American people and unprecedented political polarization. These revolutionary changes in who constitutes the American people and how the American people engage in politics fuel the bitter struggles over constitutional ideals that play out in national elections, legislative debates, and judicial decisions. From an Aristotelian regime perspective, diversity and polarization are as constitutive of contemporary American constitutional identity as the more progressive or more populist constitutional ideals that are fought over in contemporary constitutional politics. Future revolutionary changes in the United States and in other regimes will likely be constituted by similar fundamental changes in national ideals, national institutions, and the people who share those ideals and operate those institutions.

REFERENCES

Benedict, Michael Les. 1974. *A Compromise of Principle: Congressional Republicans and Reconstruction 1863–1869*. New York: W.W. Norton & Company.

Douglas, Stephen A. 1953. "Mr. Douglas's Speech: First Debate with Stephen A. Douglas at Ottawa, Illinois." In *Collected Works of Abraham Lincoln*. Vol. 3, edited by Roy P. Basler. New Brunswick: Rutgers University Press.

Elkin, Stephen L. 2001. "The Constitutional Theory of the Commercial Republic." *Fordham Law Review* 69 (5): 1933–1968.

Ely, John Hart. 1980. *Democracy and Distrust: A Theory of Judicial Review*. Cambridge: Harvard University Press.

Graber, Mark A. 2006. *Dred Scott and the Problem of Constitutional Evil*. New York: Cambridge University Press.

Graber, Mark A. 2013. *A New Introduction to American Constitutionalism*. New York: Oxford University Press.

Graber, Mark A. 2018. "What's in Crisis? The Postwar Constitutional Paradigm, Transformative Constitutionalism, and the Fate of Constitutional Democracy." In *Constitutional Democracy in Crisis?* edited by Mark A. Graber, Sanford Levinson, and Mark Tushnet. New York: Oxford University Press.

Graber, Mark A. 2023. *Punish Treason, Reward Loyalty: The Forgotten Goals of Constitutional Reform After the Civil War*. Lawrence: University Press of Kansas.

Hirschl, Ran. 2004. *Towards Juristocracy: The Origins and Consequences of the New Constitutionalism*. Cambridge: Harvard University Press.

Hirschl, Ran. 2010. *Constitutional Theocracy*. Cambridge: Harvard University Press.

Hofstadter, Richard. 1969. *The Idea of a Party System: The Rise of Legitimate Opposition in the United States, 1780–1840*. Berkeley: University of California Press.

Jacobsohn, Gary Jeffrey. 1993. *Apple of Gold: Constitutionalism in Israel and the United States*. Princeton: Princeton University Press.

Jacobsohn, Gary Jeffrey. 2010. *Constitutional Identity*. Cambridge: Harvard University Press.

Jacobsohn, Gary Jeffrey. 2021. "Was Abraham Lincoln a Constitutional Revolutionary?" *Constitutional Studies* 7: 77–91.

Jacobsohn, Gary Jeffrey and Yaniv Roznai. 2020. *Constitutional Revolution*. New Haven: Yale University Press.

Jefferson, Thomas. 1975. "The Declaration of Independence." In *The Portable Thomas Jefferson*, edited by Merrill D. Peterson. New York: Penguin Books.

Jensen, Merrill ed. 1976. *The Documentary History of the Ratification of the Constitution*. Vol. 2. Madison: State Historical Society of Wisconsin.

Kaminski, John P. ed. 1995. *A Necessary Evil? Slavery and the Debate Over the Constitution*. Madison: Madison House Publishers.

Lijphart, Arend. 2012. *Patterns of Democracy: Government Forms and Performance in Thirty-Six Countries* (2nd ed.). New Haven: Yale University Press.

Lincoln, Abraham. 1953. "Fragment on the Constitution and the Union." In *Collected Works of Abraham Lincoln*. Vol. 4, edited by Roy P. Basler. New Brunswick: Rutgers University Press.

Lincoln, Abraham. 1953a. "Speech at Bloomington, Illinois." In *Collected Works of Abraham Lincoln*. Vol. 3, edited by Roy P. Basler. New Brunswick: Rutgers University Press.

Lincoln, Abraham. 1953b. "Speech at Springfield, Illinois." In *Collected Works of Abraham Lincoln*. Vol. 2, edited by Roy P. Basler. New Brunswick: Rutgers University Press.

Lincoln, Abraham. 1953c. "Address at Cooper Institute, New York City." In *Collected Works of Abraham Lincoln*. Vol. 3, edited by Roy P. Basler. New Brunswick: Rutgers University Press.

Lincoln, Abraham. 1953d. "Speech at Chicago, Illinois." In *Collected Works of Abraham Lincoln*. Vol. 2, edited by Roy P. Basler. New Brunswick: Rutgers University Press.

Lincoln, Abraham. 1953e. "Speech at New Haven, Connecticut." In *Collected Works of Abraham Lincoln*. Vol. 4, edited by Roy P. Basler. New Brunswick: Rutgers University Press.

McConnell, Michael W. 1995. "Originalism and the Desegregation Decisions." *Virginia Law Review* 81 (4): 947–1140.

Murphy, Walter F., James E. Fleming, Sotirios A. Barber, and Stephen Macedo. 2003. *American Constitutional Interpretation* (3rd ed.). New York: Foundation Press.

Purcell, Edward. 1973. *The Crisis of Democratic Theory: Scientific Naturalism and the Problem of Value*. Lexington: University Press of Kentucky.

The Delegates of The Democracy Constitution. n.d. "A New Constitution for the United States." *Democracy: A Journal of Ideas. A New Constitution for The United States: Democracy Journal*.

Washington, George. 1896. "Farewell Address." In *A Compilation of the Messages and Papers of the Presidents, 1789–1897*, edited by James D. Richardson. Washington: Government Printing Office.

18

American Constitutional Exceptionalism, Constitutional Identity, and Democracy

Miguel Schor

INTRODUCTION

The United States is an odd comparative case. It has an old constitution and strong, contemporary ideological forces resist global trends (Farber 2007). When comparative constitutionalists study the United States, they write about American exceptionalism. All polities undoubtedly are exceptional, but the claim of American exceptionalism has a "historical pedigree and intensity that other national exceptionalisms lack" (Graber 2018, 458). In the first of the Federalist papers, Hamilton (1788) argued, "It seems to have been reserved to the people of this country, by their conduct and example, to decide the important question whether societies of men are really capable of establishing good government from reflection and choice, or whether they are forever destined to depend for their political constitutions on accident and force." The historian Gordon Wood (1998, 614) writes, "The Americans of the Revolutionary generation believed ... they [had] demonstrated to the world how a people could diagnose the ills of its society and work out a peaceful process of cure." In contemporary America, claims of constitutional exceptionalism became intertwined with arguments advanced primarily by politicians over American democracy (Ceaser 2012).

This chapter claims that Gary Jacobsohn (2018) made a seminal contribution to the American exceptionalism literature in *A Lighter Touch: American Constitutional Principles in Comparative Perspective* by tying the idea of constitutional identity to the question of democratic survival. Jacobsohn provocatively argues that contrary to the conventional view that the United States is the paradigmatic example of a nation built on constitutional values, the Constitution applies with a "lighter" touch than is the case with many of our peer democracies. The United States, unlike many contemporary democracies, has not embraced the idea that certain foundational commitments are unamendable (Ackerman 1991, 6–33; Roznai 2017)[1] or that

---

[1] The one exception is that Article V of the Constitution provides that "no State, without its Consent, shall be deprived of its equal Suffrage in the Senate."

constitutional values may limit the competition for power (Issacharoff 2015; Schor 2021). At the core of the American constitutional project is the idea that the preservation of representative government is up for constitutional grabs. The question Jacobsohn raises is whether this lighter touch might prove problematic were the American Constitution to undergo a stress test.

This chapter illuminates the importance of Jacobsohn's essay by placing his work within the broader stream of American constitutional exceptionalism scholarship. When scholars were optimistic about democracy's prospects (Part II infra), structural arguments did not loom large in the constitutional imagination as democracy appeared to work tolerably well in polities that exhibited wide institutional variation. Consequently, normative debates crowded out questions of constitutional design. Scholars focused on courts, rights instruments, and constitutional values. Jacobsohn's essay focuses on constitutional values but strikes a discordant note by arguing that America's constitutional identity is, comparatively speaking, weak when measured against democratic values.

The era of democratic optimism has been replaced by one of democratic concern and pessimism (Schor 2020a). Consequently, scholarly attention has started to shift to the structural issues that permeate democratic politics (Part III infra). The issue is whether constitutional design matters. Jacobsohn was right to point out that the foundations of America's constitutional project might prove rickety were the nation ever to elect a demagogue president. The problem, though, is not that the American Constitution applies with a "lighter touch," as Jacobsohn argues, but that it applies with a heavy, almost Trumpian hand under the conditions of contemporary American democracy. The framers thought they had solved the problem of democratic, or republican, erosion by crafting a complex machinery of government. The paradox of the American constitutional project is that America's complex, eighteenth-century Constitution is facilitating and accelerating, rather than preventing, democratic erosion in the twenty-first century.

18.1 AMERICAN COMPARATIVE CONSTITUTIONAL SCHOLARSHIP DURING THE ERA OF DEMOCRATIC OPTIMISM

When constitutionalists were optimistic about democracy's prospects, they focused on judicial review (Schor 2008). Normative debates crowded out questions of institutional design as democracy was believed to be impregnable in long-standing, wealthy democracies. Americanists wrote about the counter-majoritarian difficulty whereas comparative constitutionalists wrote about the spread of judicial review.

The spread of judicial review after World War II was a remarkable phenomenon. Although the United States Constitution is no longer the pre-eminent global model, it has become almost unthinkable that a modern polity would lack a written constitution enforced by courts and formally entrenched against change. In a world replete with written constitutions, it is ironic that America's unwritten practice of judicial review is its most successful ideological export. Comparative constitutionalists who wrote about the United States during this era sharply disagreed over the extent of American constitutional exceptionalism with comparative "splitters" emphasizing differences and comparative "lumpers" focusing on similarities.

The scholarly consensus was that the differences mattered more than the similarities, but scholars disagreed on which differences mattered. In an important empirical study, Law and Versteeg (2012) conclude that the influence of the United States Constitution as a model is declining. They focus on the text of rights instruments and argue that the United States Constitution is an "increasingly unpopular model" (Law and Versteeg, 769). The Bill of Rights reflects its eighteenth-century origins whereas rights instruments around the globe have evolved. Contemporary global rights instruments typically protect positive socio-economic rights, do not protect gun rights, and have limitations clauses that provide elected officials with some leeway in enacting legislation.

Weinrib (2006), in an influential account, is skeptical that constitutional text explains American exceptionalism and focuses on constitutional politics. She argues that the United States played a critical role in the development of a post-World War II paradigm of rights protection but parted from global trends with the advent of originalism. *Brown v. Board of Education*[2] provided a model for how judges could undermine authoritarian enclaves. This model developed as a response to gross human rights abuses. It rests on the notion that the role of the judiciary is to adapt abstract constitutional principles to a "changing society within a changing world" (Weinrib 2006, 85).

The post-war paradigm took root in Europe and spread around the globe. Legal entrepreneurs rejected the idea common in Europe before the war that the political branches should interpret and enforce rights (Cruz 1987). Scholars believed that courts should displace the political branches since they are normatively better equipped to effectuate rights (Ferreres 2009). The rights instruments adopted after the Second World War are "universal" since constitutional designers and judges borrow liberally from other nations. Rights are not "absolute negations" on "state authority" as the different branches "operate co-operatively" (Weinrib 2006, 92). Courts rely on proportionality or balancing tests that are analogous to what American judges call intermediate scrutiny.[3]

Although the United States Supreme Court played a critical role in giving birth to the post-war paradigm, the ideological makeup of the Court has changed dramatically since *Brown v. Board of Education* was decided in 1954. Originalism is now the dominant ideology. Originalism differs markedly, Kim Scheppele (2013, 24) argues, from purposive interpretation which is the norm "in many other advanced

---

[2] 347 U.S. 483 (1954).
[3] Justice Breyer, for example, has analogized intermediate scrutiny to proportionality and argued that courts should prefer balancing tests over strict scrutiny (Breyer 2010).

democracies." Originalism rejects engagement with global constitutionalism and interprets the text by examining how constitutional language may have been understood when it was adopted. Purposive interpretation, on the other hand, is employed routinely by judges around the globe (Robertson 2010) and builds on insights developed by judges in the early American republic.[4] Purposive interpretation privileges the present over the past by seeking to determine the contemporary lessons that might be drawn from the circumstances under which constitutions were drafted.

The claims of splitters have not gone unchallenged. Academic lumpers, however, are a distinct minority when it comes to comparative studies of the United States. Stephen Gardbaum (2008), for example, concedes that the United States is exceptional when it comes to the content of rights, but argues it is not exceptional in how rights claims are analyzed. Constitutional rights jurisprudence around the globe, Gardbaum argues, is organized by a shared analytical structure. Courts employ a two-step analysis which examines "first whether a right has been infringed and second whether that infringement is justified" (Gardbaum 2008, 430). Judges around the globe, in short, employ similar methodological and intellectual tools in analyzing rights claims.

Versteeg and Zackin (2014) critique the American constitutional exceptionalism scholarship for failing to assess the role of state constitutions. They point out that state constitutions are "central to the American constitutional tradition" (Versteeg and Zackin 2014, 1644). The United States Constitution is considered exceptional because of its brevity, difficulty of amendments, and lack of positive socio-economic rights. State constitutions, on the other hand, are long and detailed, frequently amended and replaced, and contain positive socio-economic rights. Constitutional specificity combined with flexibility, moreover, is an important drafting strategy because it shifts power to ordinary citizens and away from courts. American state constitutionalism falls within the pattern of global constitutionalism where constitutions are detailed and frequently amended or replaced.

Gary Jacobsohn (2018) made a seminal contribution to the American constitutional exceptionalism literature in *A Lighter Touch: American Constitutional Principles in Comparative Perspective*. Although Jacobsohn's work fits within this post-war stream of scholarship as it focuses on constitutional values, it provocatively debunks the idea that the United States is the paradigmatic example of a democracy safeguarded by its constitution. Jacobsohn (2018, 14) argues that a "comparative national assessment of constitutional principles reveals a less decisive constitutive significance in the American case than is widely assumed." Contemporary constitutions embrace foundational commitments that limit democratic contestation (Müller 2012). The United States Constitution, on the other hand, does not preclude the American people from amending representative government out of

---

[4] In *McCulloch v. Maryland*, 17 U.S. 316 (1819), for example, Justice Marshall interpreted the necessary and proper clause by examining the purposes of the Constitution.

existence (Ackerman 1991, 3–33; Roznai 2017) or place effective limits on their power to undermine republican government (Tolson 2021). The Constitution, Jacobsohn concludes, applies with a lighter touch that is true of our peer democracies and he rightly worries what might happen if our institutions were to face a stress test.

18.2 AMERICAN CONSTITUTIONAL EXCEPTIONALISM DURING AN ERA OF DEMOCRATIC PESSIMISM

Following Donald Trump's election and the Brexit vote in the United Kingdom in 2016, scholars turned pessimistic about democracy's prospects. Although there was considerable evidence of democratic erosion before 2016 (Bermeo 2016), scholars understandably became concerned that democracy was under pressure in the two polities – the United Kingdom and the United States – that had played a critical role in spreading liberal constitutionalism around the globe and defending democracy during two world wars. A remarkable outpouring of monographs explored what the events of 2016 might portend for democracy's future (Ben Ghiat 2020; Dixon and Landau 2021; Ginsburg and Huq 2018; Haggard and Kaufman 2021; Howell and Moe 2020; Lepore 2018; Levitsky and Ziblatt 2018; Mettler and Lieberman 2020; Mounk 2018; Mudde and Kaltwasser 2017; Norris and Inglehart 2019; Przeworski 2019; Rosenfield 2018; Runciman 2018). These concerns jumped from the pages of scholarly monographs to the opinion pages when a mob broke into the United States Capitol on January 6, 2021, to prevent Congress from certifying the election of Joe Biden as President of the United States. Pundits, not surprisingly, opined on the demise of American exceptionalism.[5]

Given democracy's global travails, the role constitutions may play in stemming authoritarianism has become a critical research issue. Courts, rights, and constitutional values, which were the focus of scholarly attention during the era of democratic optimism, are likely to recede in importance as it is politics and the role constitutions play in shaping conflict that plays the starring role in democratic

---

[5] Abigail Abrams, "Inside the Capitol: a photographer's view of American exceptionalism under siege," *Time*, Jan. 7, 2021; Whitney Eulich, "Democracy on the brink? U.S. has familiar echo for Latin Americans," *Christian Science Monitor*, Jan. 19, 2021; Skelton George, "American exceptionalism is a myth. Our Constitution is the only thing keeping us from authoritarianism," *Los Angeles Times*, Jan. 11, 2021; Kaia Hubbard, "Running riot on American exceptionalism," *U.S. News & World Report*, Jan. 11, 2021; Charles Lane, "America is not exceptional after all," *Washington Post*, Jan. 18, 2021; John Patrick Leary, "America's obsession with peaceful transitions crashes into reality," *The New Republic*, Jan. 8, 2021; Siobhan O'Grady, "World stunned by subversion of U.S. democracy after pro-Trump throng breaches Capitol," *Washington Post*, Jan. 6, 2021; Ilhan Omar, "I never expected to see it here," *The Atlantic*, Jan. 21, 2021; Sergio Pecanha, "The end of American exceptionalism," *Washington Post*, Jan. 7, 2021; Ronald W. Preussen, "The Capitol riot exposes the myth and pathology of American exceptionalism," *The Conversation*, Jan. 7, 2021; Austin Sarat, "After attack on the Capitol, we need a new way to think about America," *The Hill*, Jan. 11, 2021; Ishaan Tharoor, "The end of the road for American exceptionalism," *Washington Post*, Jan. 7, 2021; NPR Weekend edition, "The Myth of American exceptionalism," *National Public Radio*, Jan. 10, 2021.

breakdown and erosion. On this issue, Publius and the framers of Germany's Basic Law had it right. *The Federalist* warns of the dangers of demagogues and the violence of political factions and argues that the structure of the proposed constitution would help impede republican breakdown. The framers of Germany's Basic Law were "seasoned politicians" who understood how Hitler came to power and sought to make dictatorship constitutionally impermissible by operationalizing the idea of a militant democracy (Kommers 1991, 853). The American and German constitutions, in short, were designed with an eye toward the lee shore.

The conceptual linkages between American and German constitutionalism have been obscured by scholars who emphasize that Germany's solution to the problem of democratic breakdown runs counter to contemporary American ideas of free speech (Issacharoff 2015) or Anglo-American ideas of liberty (Capoccia 2013). The scholarly focus on courts, rights, and values, moreover, provides an incomplete picture of how constitution makers may seek to prevent democratic breakdown as it ignores the role of structural provisions (Schor 2021). James Madison articulated the design issues clearly. In *Federalist 10*, he warns that the vice of popular governments is that they can break down if interest groups or factions turn violent. Constitution makers may ameliorate the problem by limiting liberty or by fashioning a "republican remedy for the diseases most incident to republican government" (Madison 1788). Germany and the United States illustrate these two divergent paths.

The framers of Germany's post-war order, unlike the framers of the American Constitution, had first-hand knowledge of how mass, representative democracy could break down (Golay 1958, 113–137). They took two lessons from Germany's democratic collapse. The first was that the power to amend the Constitution had to be limited. The "eternity clause" of the German basic law prevents political majorities from lawfully amending democracy out of existence (Kommers 1991, 45). The second was that "Germany's militant democracy obliges the state to actively oppose persons and groups who would use the rights and institutions of free government to subvert or destroy democracy" (Kommers 1991, 854). Militant democracies can take "illiberal measures" to prevent anti-democratic actors from using speech and elections to destroy it (Müller 2012, 1253). These measures "range from prohibitions on forms of speech," "bans on certain parties," "ideological acceptance of the bases of the democratic state," or the "exclusion of individuals from eligibility" (Issacharoff 2015, 36).

The framers of the American Constitution were seasoned politicians as well, but they, of course, had no experience or knowledge of how representative mass democracies might erode or collapse. The American Revolution was, by the standards of the late eighteenth century, a transformative, small d democratic social movement (Wood 1992), but the era of mass democracy was far off into the future. In *Federalist 10*, Madison warns that the "dangerous vice" of "popular governments" is their "propensity" to break down due to the "violence of faction[s]." Madison observed that the "most frivolous and fanciful distinctions" could elicit violence, but the chief cause of political polarization was the "various and unequal distribution of property." Madison believed the cure for this vice of self-government was to fashion institutions that would obstruct the emergence of factions built around economic issues (Rakove 2017, 54–95).

Timing matters. The federal Constitution was debated and written in the 1780s during a severe economic depression that many historians believe was the "worst economic climate suffered by the nation until the Great Depression of the 1930s" (Klarman 2016, 75). Contemporaneous state constitutions, on the other hand, were drafted during the heady days following the Declaration of Independence in 1776. They were largely small d democratic documents that weakened executives and strengthened legislatures (Wood 2018, 127–161). Ordinary citizens used their newfound power to enact debt relief legislation to deal with the economic dislocations occasioned by the Revolution. It was this so-called "excess" of democracy that played a critical role in the framing of the federal Constitution (Klarman 2016, 75–101). The antidote to an excess of democracy, or so the framers believed, was the federal Constitution, which was designed to make it difficult for majorities to govern. It is, as the historian Richard Hofstadter (1970, 42–70) concluded, "the constitution against parties."

The United States Constitution was undemocratic compared to contemporaneous eighteenth-century state constitutions (Fritz 2007) and is remarkably undemocratic when compared to those of its peer democracies that have continuously been in operation since 1950 (Dahl 2001, 164). The exceptional features of America's constitutional order include a

> political class that has the power to insulate itself from the electorate by gerrymandering and voter restrictions; staggered elections; strong bicameralism with two houses of equal strength; malapportionment in the Senate that privileges rural, small population states; the electoral college; a Supreme Court poorly constrained by checks and balances; a federal government that may lack the power to solve national problems (at least according to a majority of the Supreme Court given its current ideological makeup); and an extremely high bar to constitutional amendment. (Schor 2020b, 111)

These structural features have proven remarkably resilient. Germany introduced the idea of an eternity clause to prevent anti-democratic amendments. The American framers hit upon the idea of the functional equivalent of an eternity clause to protect the anti-democratic features of the constitutional order.[6] By combining a high bar to amendment with a governance structure tilted against political parties, structural reforms, no easy task in any democracy, become exceptionally difficult. These structural features are largely invisible, moreover, to Americans who understandably spend little energy discussing or contemplating how their immobile Constitution structures politics (Levinson 2006).

---

[6] The equal representation of each state in the Senate is formally protected against amendment. U.S. Const. Art. V.

A long-simmering debate over whether the American Constitution (and by extension any constitutional project) is, at bottom, about rights and values or structural provisions is coming to a boil.[7] When comparative scholars were optimistic about American democracy, for example, they argued about courts, rights, and values while discounting the importance of design and structure. The assumption that scholars should focus on rights rather than structure is being put to the test by the exogenous shocks – climate change, globalization, illegal migration, new information technologies, and a pandemic – now buffeting democracies around the globe. The Global Trends 2040 report, published by the National Intelligence Council, paints a dystopian picture of the future as "governments in every region are likely to face persistent strains and tensions because of a growing mismatch between what publics need and expect and what governments can and will deliver."[8] In facing these challenges, the United States will find it considerably more difficult to enact legislation to deal with these crises than its peer democracies. The results of this natural experiment will not be known for some time, but the early returns are not good as the United States elected a demagogue president in 2016 and may do so again in 2024.

Demagogues thrive on crisis and emergency. Their path to power is greased by lies and identity politics (Posner 2020). They promise to fix the nation's ills by destroying the institutions, the so-called "deep state," that "undermine" the interest of the "true" people (Mudde and Kaltwasser 2017). It is a thin view of democracy that privileges plebiscitary leaders over representative institutions (O'Donnell 1994).

The political market for demagogues turns on supply and demand factors (Schor 2020b). Insofar as the supply side is concerned, presidential regimes, which are exceptional among long-standing democracies, are, on balance, more susceptible than parliamentary regimes to the election of political outsiders (Carreras 2014). Presidentialism, unlike parliamentarism, divorces the job of chief executive from the job of managing a political party in the national legislature. Consequently, presidentialism facilitates the election of leaders with short timelines (since their relationship to a party is transactional and opportunistic) who are thin on experience but long on media exposure and well versed in propaganda techniques (Schor 2020b, 100–108).

All political–constitutional systems may generate demagogues or populist authoritarian leaders, though, under the right conditions. The real question is why citizens sometimes opt for leaders who promise to degrade democracy. Populist authoritarians thrive in an environment where the government cannot meet the demands of ordinary citizens (Foa 2021; Pildes 2021). The claim that only a strong leader can fix the nation's ills lies at the core of populism's appeal. The rhetoric employed by

---

[7] The debate began during the founding of the American republic as Federalists and Anti-Federalists argued over whether the plan of the convention needed a bill of rights or not (Maier 2011).
[8] Global Trends 2040, at 16, www.dni.gov/files/ODNI/documents/assessments/GlobalTrends_2040.pdf.

populists across space and time is remarkably similar. They purport to represent the true people and attack and undermine institutions and experts alike for failing to serve the people. Their day in the democratic sun is shining brightly, moreover, as new information technologies facilitate the spread of misinformation and divisive rhetoric (Rosenfield 2018).

There are two profound sets of issues that all polities must navigate: who gets what and who we are. The framers believed that overly democratic institutional arrangements facilitated the violence of factions. They designed a constitutional system intended to protect the interests of economic elites by making it exceptionally difficult for majorities and political parties to govern. The American Constitution, in this sense, has been remarkably successful. The United States has the highest Gini coefficient of any long-standing, wealthy democracy; positive, socio-economic rights have been effectuated in our peer democracies but remain deeply contested in the United States (Schor 2020b, 112–116).

Madison was wrong, however, to believe that economic issues are the primary source of polarization. That was likely true in a slaveholding republic, but economic issues have not been the primary cause of democratic erosion in wealthy, long-standing democracies (Norris and Inglehart 2019). Citizens in advanced democracies can and do compromise over economic issues but find it difficult to compromise over identity issues. Since the 1980s, Americans, who are uniquely disabled in advancing an economic program, have become more polarized over identity issues than citizens in our peer democracies (Boxell et al. 2021).

America's eighteenth-century institutional arrangements are having perverse consequences in the twenty-first century. Contemporary democracies are felled by demagogues who use the very tools of democracy – elections and speech – to undermine it. The limits placed by militant democracies on electoral politics raise serious questions of liberty but are aimed at the right danger. The American Constitution, on the other hand, does not limit electoral politics but seeks to blunt democratic erosion by preventing majorities from governing. Demagogues, unlike democratic majorities, have a protected place under the American Constitution. It is easier to rely on lies and misinformation to mobilize voters by means of divisive identity issues than it is to mobilize voters by legislating and providing government outputs. The Constitution, in short, has a Trumpian lean under the conditions of contemporary American politics.

Political scientists divide the world's democracies into two categories. In exceptional democracies, power is mediated by elections, civil society, and institutions. This is a thick version of democracy that, like any healthy ecosystem, is remarkably complex. No formal constitution adequately models its complexity (Llewellyn 1934). Flawed democracies, on the other hand, are unexceptional and were once thought to be located primarily in the global South. This is a thin version of democracy that posits that leaders are "entitled to govern as he or she sees fit" (O'Donnell 1994, 59) subject only to periodic elections that are constantly subject to "recalibration"

(Przeworski 2018). Plebiscitary democracy, or populism, is a "permanent shadow of modern representative democracy, and a constant peril" (Müller 2016, 10).

The Trump presidency ruthlessly exploited and exposed the flaws of American democracy. Flawed democracies share the following features: "loyalty to the leader supplants loyalty to institutions; clientelist policies are used to buy votes; electoral rules are manipulated to protect incumbents; and emergencies are normalized as a means of cementing power by exhausting voters and thereby weakening civil society" (Schor 2020b, 99–100). American pundits were right to point out that American democracy was no longer exceptional following the attempted *autogolpe* of January 6, 2021, but the root cause of our difficulties can be found in our exceptional constitution.

CONCLUSIONS

Constitutions have two faces: one points toward courts, rights, and values; the other toward politics and the role institutions play in structuring politics. When democratic times were good, comparative studies of the United States focused on courts, rights, and values. The assumption underpinning this literature was that design or structure did not matter much since polities with varying institutional arrangements appeared to operate tolerably well.

Jacobsohn made a seminal contribution to the American constitutional exceptionalism literature in *A Lighter Touch: American Constitutional Principles in Comparative Perspective*. He asked a critical question that other scholars had ignored by linking America's unusual constitutional arrangements to questions of her constitutional identity and the endurance of democracy. He provocatively and presciently argued that the American Constitution was exceptionally weak in values or principles that might be employed to fend off democratic erosion. Jacobsohn was right to point out that values matter when political actors threaten democracy.

When democratic times become troubled, however, issues of constitutional design loom large. There are two divergent paths constitution makers take toward the problem of democratic erosion. One is to enable democratic majorities to govern but limit their liberty to destroy democracy. This is the path taken by Germany's militant democracy. The other is to largely prevent majorities from governing while placing few if any limits on the liberty of elected officials and ordinary citizens alike to chip away at democracy. The latter is the path taken by the framers of the American Constitution.

The American version of militant democracy, designed for a slaveholding republic, is showing considerable strain. It may be that the attempt to preserve republican government for the long haul by obstructing majorities from governing while not limiting the freedom to erode institutions will protect neither democracy nor liberty. The promises of a demagogue that he alone can fix the nation's ills may prove alluring for a nation facing profound exogenous shocks and saddled with a government that makes it exceptionally difficult for majorities to govern. The problem, though, is not simply that the American Constitution applies with a lighter touch but that under the conditions of contemporary politics, it also applies with a heavy, almost Trumpian hand.

REFERENCES

Ackerman, Bruce. 1991. *We the People: Foundations.* Cambridge: Harvard University Press.
Ben Ghiat, Ruth. 2020. *Strongmen: Mussolini to the Present.* New York: W. W. Norton & Co.
Bermeo, Nancy. 2016. "On Democratic Backsliding." *Journal of Democracy.* 27: 5–19.
Boxell, Levi, Matthew Gentzkow, and Jesse M. Shapiro. 2021. "Cross-Country Trends in Affective Polarization," NBER Working Paper No. 26669 (August 2021).
Breyer, Stephen. 2010. *Making Our Democracy Work: A Judge's View.* New York: Alfred Knopf.
Capoccia, Giovanni. 2013. "Militant Democracy: The Institutional Bases of Democratic Self-Preservation." *The Annual Review of Law and Social Science.* 9: 207–226.
Carreras, Miguel. 2014. "Outsiders and Executive-Legislative Conflict in Latin America." *Latin American Politics and Society* 56: 70–92.
Ceaser, James W. 2012. "The Origins and Character of American Exceptionalism." *American Political Thought.* 1: 3–27.
Cruz Villalón, Pedro. 1987. *La formacion del sistema europeo de constitucionalidad (1918–1939).* Madrid: Centro de Estudios Constitucionales.
Dahl, Robert A. 2001. *How Democratic Is the American Constitution?* New Haven: Yale University Press.
Dixon, Rosalind and David Landau. 2021. *Abusive Constitutional Borrowing: Legal Globalization and the Subversion of Liberal Democracy.* New York: Oxford University Press.
Farber, Daniel. 2007. "The Supreme Court, the Law of Nations, and Citations of Foreign Law: The Lessons of History." *California Law Review.* 95: 1335–1336.
Ferreres Comella, Víctor. 2009. *Constitutional Courts and Democratic Values: A European Perspective.* New Haven: Yale University Press.
Foa, Roberto Stefan. 2021. "Why Strongmen Win in Weak States." *Journal of Democracy.* 32: 52–65.
Fritz, Christian G. 2007. *American Sovereigns: The People and America's Constitutional Traditions Before the Civil War.* New York: Cambridge University Press.
Gardbaum, Stephen. 2008. "The Myth and Reality of American Constitutional Exceptionalism." *Michigan Law Review.* 107: 391–466.
Golay, John Ford. 1958. *The Founding of the Federal Republic of Germany.* Chicago: University of Chicago Press.
Ginsburg, Tom and Aziz Huq. 2018. *How to Save a Constitutional Democracy.* Chicago: University of Chicago Press.
Graber, Mark. 2018. "Race and American Constitutional Exceptionalism." In *Comparative Constitutional Theory,* edited by Gary Jacobsohn and Miguel Schor, 456–475. Northampton, UK: Edward Elgar Publishing.
Haggard, Stephen and Robert Kaufman. 2021. *Backsliding.* Cambridge, UK: Cambridge University Press.
Hamilton, Alexander. 1788. *Federalist 1.* https://avalon.law.yale.edu/18th_century/fedo1.asp.
Hofstadter, Richard. 1970. *The Idea of a Party System: The Rise of Legitimate Opposition in the United States, 1780–1840.* Berkeley: University of California Press.

Howell, William G., and Terry M. Moe. 2020. *Presidents, Populism, and the Crisis of Democracy*. Chicago: University of Chicago Press.

Issacharoff, Samuel. 2015. *Fragile Democracies: Contested Power in the Era of Constitutional Courts*. New York: Cambridge University Press.

Jacobsohn, Gary. 2018. "A Lighter Touch: American Constitutional Principles in Comparative Perspective." In *The Cambridge Companion to the United States Constitution*, edited by Karren Orren and John W. Compton, 13–44. New York: Cambridge University Press.

Klarman, Michael J. 2016. *The Framers' Coup: The Making of the United States Constitution*. Boston: Harvard University Press.

Kommers, Donald P. 1991. "German Constitutionalism: A Prolegomenon." *Emory Law Journal*. 40: 837–873.

Law, David S. and Mila Versteeg. 2012. "The Declining Influence of the United States Constitution." *New York University Law Review*. 87: 762–858.

Lepore, Jill. 2018. *These Truths: A History of the United States*. New York: W. W. Norton & Co.

Levinson, Sanford. 2006. *Our Undemocratic Constitution: Where the Constitution Goes Wrong (And How We the People Can Correct It)*. New York: Oxford University Press.

Levitsky, Steven and Daniel Ziblatt. 2018. *How Democracies Die*. New York: Crown Books.

Llewellyn, Karl. 1934. "The Constitution as an Institution." *Columbia Law Review*. 34: 1–40.

Madison, James. 1788. *Federalist 10*. https://avalon.law.yale.edu/18th_century/fed01.asp.

Maier, Pauline. 2011. *Ratification: The People Debate the Constitution, 1787–88*. New York: Simon & Schuster.

Mettler, Suzanne and Robert C. Lieberman. 2020. *The Recurring Crises of American Democracy: Four Threats*. New York: St. Martin's Press.

Mounk, Yascha. 2018. *The People vs. Democracy: Why Our Freedom Is in Danger and How to Save It*. Boston: Harvard University Press.

Mudde, Cas and Cristobal Rovira Kaltwasser. 2017. *Populism: A Very Short Introduction*. New York: Oxford University Press.

Müller, Jan Werner. 2012. "Militant Democracy." In *The Oxford Handbook of Comparative Constitutional Law*, edited by Michel Rosenfeld and Andras Sajo, 1253–1269. New York: Oxford University Press.

Müller, Jan Werner. 2016. *What Is Populism?* Philadelphia: University of Pennsylvania Press.

Norris, Pippa and Ronald Inglehart. 2019. *Cultural Backlash: Trump, Brexit, and Authoritarian Populism*. New York: Cambridge University Press.

O'Donnell, Guillermo. 1994. "Delegative Democracy." *Journal of Democracy*. 5: 55–69.

Pildes, Rick. 2021. "Political Fragmentation in Democracies of the West." https://papers.ssrn.com/sol3/papers.cfm?abstract_id=3935012

Posner, Eric. 2020. *The Demagogue's Handbook: The Battle for American Democracy from the Founders to Trump*. New York: St. Martin's Press.

Przeworski, Adam. 2018. *Why Bother with Elections?* Boston: Polity Press.

Przeworski, Adam. 2019. *Crises of Democracy*. New York: Cambridge University Press.

Rakove, Jack N. 2017. *A Politician Thinking: The Creative Mind of James Madison*. Norman: University of Oklahoma Press.

Robertson, David. 2010. *The Judge as a Political Theorist*. Princeton: Princeton University Press.

Rosenfield, Sophia. 2018. *Democracy and Truth: A Short History*. Philadelphia: University of Pennsylvania Press.

Roznai, Yaniv. 2017. *Unconstitutional Constitutional Amendments: The Limits of Amendment Powers*. New York: Oxford University Press.

Runciman, David. 2018. *How Democracy Ends*. New York: Basic Books.

Scheppele, Kim Lane. 2013. "Jack Balkin Is an American." *Yale Journal of Law & the Humanities*. 25: 23–42.
Schor, Miguel. 2008. "Mapping Comparative Judicial Review." *Washington University Global Studies Law Review*. 7: 257–287.
Schor, Miguel. 2020a. "Constitutional Democracy and Scholarly Fashions." *Drake Law Review*. 68: 359–370.
Schor, Miguel. 2020b. "Trumpism and the Continuing Challenges to Three Political-Constitutionalist Orthodoxies." *Constitutional Studies* 7: 93–122.
Schor, Miguel. 2021. "Militant Democracy in America." *International Journal of Constitutional Law Blog*. www.iconnectblog.com/2021/02/militant-democracy-in-america/.
Tolson, Franita. 2021. "Countering the Real Countermajoritarian Difficulty." *California Law Review*. 109: 2381–2405.
Versteeg, Mila and Emily Zackin. 2014. "American Constitutional Exceptionalism Revisited." *University of Chicago Law Review*. 81: 1641–1707.
Weinrib, Lorraine E. 2006. "The Postwar Paradigm and American Exceptionalism." In *The Migration of Constitutional Ideas*, edited by Sujit Choudry, 84–111. New York: Cambridge University Press.
Wood, Gordon S. 1992. *The Radicalism of the American Revolution*. New York: Alfred A. Knopf.
Wood, Gordon S. 1998. *The Creation of the American Republic, 1776–87*. Chapel Hill: University of North Carolina Press.

PART IV

Emerging Trends

19

Constitution Making and Disharmonic Identity

Aslı Bâli and Hanna Lerner

INTRODUCTION

Gary Jacobsohn's *Constitutional Identity* is an elegant work of comparative political and constitutional theory that develops the concept of "constitutional identity" as central to understanding any constitutional order. Jacobsohn directs our attention to the dissonances internal to a constitutional text – as well as the ways that a constitution may come to be in tension with the political evolution of a society – as critical to defining and interpreting constitutional identity. By drawing our focus to the contested quality of any constitutional order, and the relationship between the intrinsic contestability of constitutions and their evolution, Jacobsohn provides a dynamic account of constitutionalism that enriches both constitutional theory and the study of comparative constitutionalism.

In this chapter, we explore the ways in which the concept of a disharmonic constitution provides a particularly compelling framework for comparative constitutional analysis. In our own work, we have explored constitution making in religiously divided societies in the Middle East and South Asia. In this context, we have theorized about the limitations of the liberal constitutional paradigm for understanding constitutional realities in societies where many of the presumptions of that model remain deeply contested. Jacobsohn's thesis in *Constitutional Identity* complements – and arguably converges with – the approach we have taken to studying constitutional design in polities beyond the West. Jacobsohn observes that disharmonies are endemic to all constitutional orders. While our focus has been on a subset of societies that are characterized by deep divisions, we believe that insights from these cases may have important applications for societies that exhibit a lesser degree of division but nonetheless have the disharmonies that Jacobsohn's theory underscores.

Our work on constitution making in religiously divided societies has focused on constitutional design strategies that enable and allow for disharmonies – including choices to include ambiguity and even contradiction within a constitutional text as well as to defer certain questions for incremental resolution through ordinary politics rather than textual entrenchment. In a sense, these features of our own argument build on and hone some of the concepts central to Jacobsohn's work when he highlights the utility and even centrality of dissonances in interpreting the "unfinished symphony" that is constitutional identity. Our comparative study also overlaps to some extent with Jacobsohn's in terms of case selection in examining these themes, allowing us to highlight the ways in which the drafting strategies we study are especially well suited to an approach to constitutionalism that is attentive to disharmonies.

To explore the complementary and convergent dimensions of Jacobsohn's study of the "three I's" –India, Ireland, and Israel – in *Constitutional Identity*, with our own work, we first reconstruct what we take to be the central elements of his argument. Next, we offer a brief review of our argument concerning the limitations of the liberal constitutional model for a comparative study of religiously divided societies. We then turn to short summaries of our examination of constitutional design in the Turkish and Israeli cases, both of which are discussed by Jacobsohn in *Constitutional Identity* (Jacobsohn 2010).[1] In both countries, the constitutional discussions at the foundational stage centered around intra-religious divisions, namely the rift between conservative and progressive ideologies concerning religion–state relations. In addressing these disagreements, both countries adopted constitutional solutions that deviated – albeit in different ways – from the familiar liberal model. By comparing our approach to Jacobsohn's, we highlight the ways in which the concept of "disharmonic constitutionalism" enhances our argument, emphasizing the significance of dissonance in ways that parallel our own focus on devices such as ambiguity, contradiction, and deferral as important elements of a constitutional design toolkit for religiously divided societies.

19.1 THE "DISHARMONIC" CONSTITUTION

Over the first thirty or so pages of Jacobsohn's seven-chapter study in *Constitutional Identity*, he unpacks his argument that "the dissonance within and around the constitution ... is key to understanding its identity" (Jacobsohn 2010, 15). For Jacobsohn, constitutional identity does not imply a unitary constitutive vision. Instead, it "consists of identifiable continuities of meaning within which dissonance and contradiction play out" (Jacobsohn 2010, 4). This "playing out," moreover, suggests that constitutional identity is something that is forged over time, in an evolutionary process in which meaning and content are neither fixed nor preordained, but rather open to reinterpretation through contestation. A nation's constitution incorporates more than the specific document, for Jacobsohn, and may over time "come to mean quite different things, even as the alternative possibilities retain identifiable

---

[1] Israel is one of Jacobsohn's three main cases in *Constitutional Identity*, while examination of a Turkish constitutional controversy serves as a framing device in the introduction and conclusion of the book.

characteristics enabling us to perceive fundamental continuities persisting through any given regime transformation" (Jacobsohn 2010, 4).

On Jacobsohn's account, then, dissonance is a built-in characteristic of all constitutional identity that sets the framework for the terms of contestation and debate through which identity politics – and attendant constitutional change – occur. The features of a constitution that are entrenched – the basic, regime-defining elements – attest to fundamental continuities although even these norms may be fundamentally contested and subject to revision. Textual barriers to such revision – such as unamendable provisions – are theoretically designed to obstruct ruptures with constitutional identity. Yet, as Jacobsohn notes, a constitutional text "is neither a discrete object of invention nor ... a heavily encrusted essence embedded in a society's culture." (Jacobsohn 2010, 7). The text is the expression of a shared historical context – often heavily influenced by earlier texts and experiences – neither invented nor immune to reinterpretation. Constitutional identity emerges dialogically, representing commitments that are "expressive of a nation's past ... and the determination of those within the society to transcend that past" (Jacobsohn 2010, 7).

Dissonance, here is not incoherence but rather the key to identity understood as an evolving process of self-definition, with its very contestability as the necessary condition for it to serve as a framework that sets the terms of debate in a democratic society. For this reason, constitutional change – even revolution – is more often the product of incremental developments that transform identity over time rather than sudden ruptures and moments of deconstitution and reconstitution. Jacobsohn concedes that a constitutional order may furnish those committed to its subversion with the lawful means to secure their objective, but it also poses substantive constraints. First and foremost, Jacobsohn follows Lon Fuller in defining the morality of law as requiring constraints on pervasive arbitrariness in the conduct of public affairs. From this it follows that constitutional change that alters the parameters of the debate in ways that are permissive of such arbitrariness does represent a form of deconstitution rather than evolution. But such acts of abrogation must be distinguished from the regular and necessary forms of contestation that often give rise to heated claims that one side is the true guardian of an authentic identity in need of protection. Jacobsohn observes that those who claim that the "personality of the constitution must remain unchanged" may oppose contestation in constitutionalism, because they view constitutional change as a threat to their own specific commitments to one side of a debate (Jacobsohn 2010, 18–19). In short, for Jacobsohn, the "we" of the "people" is fundamentally divided and the resulting ambivalences, tensions, inconsistencies, and ambiguities are not forms of dysfunction but rather reflections of the competing commitments present in the society.

Implicit in this conception of constitutional identity are a number of elements that we view as in tension with the prevailing liberal constitutional paradigm. The appreciation of the disharmonic elements of constitutional identity is at odds with a more univocal understanding of the "we the people" who act at a founding moment of rupture and perform an act of self-invention through the drafting of a constitution. Not only is Jacobsohn's understanding of identity more ambivalent, it is also more sticky, with identity understood as an incomplete, evolving and dialogic process that is historically situated. The idea that basic constitutional commitments remain contestable and cannot be resolved by reference to first principles alone further distinguishes Jacobsohn's work from a conventional, liberal account of constitutionalism. Indeed, implicit in *Constitutional Identity* is an acknowledgment, on our reading, that the liberal paradigm may not correspond to the reality of constitutional politics in any context, and may be especially inapposite for divided societies where "the people" do not agree on a single specific set of (liberal) values. In the next section, we turn to our own analysis of the limitations of what we define as the liberal paradigm in the context of religiously divided societies, before offering brief case studies to illustrate our argument from two such societies that Jacobsohn also examines.

19.2 THE LIBERAL CONSTITUTIONAL PARADIGM IN THE CONTEXT OF RELIGIOUS DIVISIONS AND ITS LIMITS

In very broad and general terms, we argue that the paradigm of liberal constitutionalism views constitutions as a written document, expected primarily to limit governmental power by crafting an institutional system that distributes powers between various branches of the government and provides a formal basis for the protection of fundamental rights (Elster, 1993). These protections are identified with *individuals* who are the basic components of the underlying society, while group rights are either secondary or excluded altogether. The commitment to individual rights in the liberal tradition is tied to a conception of secularism as the strict separation between religion and the public sphere (Sajo 2008, 625).

Since constitutional rules provide the legal framework for the political order, constitutions, according to the liberal worldview, are conceived as distinct from and superior to ordinary legislation (U.S. Constitution 1787, VI; Alexander 2010, 7–8; Raz 1998, 153–154). Their adoption has thus been described as "higher lawmaking," resting on greater democratic legitimacy than does "normal lawmaking," conducted by elected representatives (Ackerman 1992, 16). Given that the Western constitutional imagination is grounded in the American and French experiences, it perceives the moment of constitution making in revolutionary terms, as a moment of rupture (Ackerman 1992; Arendt 1965; Preuss 1995).

This paradigm of liberal constitutionalism dominates both legal scholarship, influenced as it is by the Anglo-American constitutional experience, and also the comparative politics literature of constitutional design (Bisarya 2013, 1). This edited volume is a testament to Jacobsohn's own contributions to this literature, as well as that of the many authors who have contributed chapters. There is, of course, much to learn from the constitutional design literature that develops institutional solutions based on the liberal constitutional paradigm (Choudhry ed. 2011; Horowitz 1985; Miller ed. 2010; Widner 2008). This paradigm may offer a good fit for projects of constitution writing or re-writing that take place in societies characterized by what John Rawls defined as "overlapping consensus" (Rawls 1996, 134–172) regarding the religious/secular vision of the state. Liberal constitutions may well be the best choice for societies that inhabit, in Charles Taylor's terms, "a secular age," where societies are characterized by the institutional separation between religion and state, a decline of belief and practice, and general skepticism toward "a naïve acknowledgment of the transcendent" (Taylor 2007).

However, a liberal constitutionalist approach may be far less apposite when constitutions are written in societies divided over the religious/secular definition of the state, in which disagreements concerning religious symbols, practices, or law are constitutive of core constitutional debates. Some religiously divided societies that do not begin from liberal commitments have developed constitutional solutions for conflict mitigation worth studying. In our work, we have studied these less well understood contexts to identify the variety of alternative institutional design strategies they adopt. Strikingly, we note that despite their variance from aspects of liberal constitutional design, these settings are grappling with aspects of constitutional identity that emphasize disharmonies at the time of constitution drafting and thus may offer lessons more broadly, given Jacobsohn's important insight that such disharmonies are endemic to all constitutional orders.

Recent experiences have underscored the degree to which constitution writing can be a high-stakes game (Cross 2016). In the presence of intense polarization between competing visions of the state, drafting a constitution risks undermining fragile forms of political stability and derailing fledgling efforts at democratization. This has been a troubling challenge where constitutional debates occur in a context of deep divisions over foundational values. In these cases, efforts at constitution drafting that have sought to entrench one set of commitments over another, rather than embracing a more disharmonic approach, have catalyzed renewed conflict instead of contributing to state building.

The question, then, is how to address the complex challenge of drafting a democratic constitution under conditions of disagreement regarding the role religion should play in the constitution and the state. As the next section demonstrates, drafting processes may tell us a great deal about why proposed constitutional solutions in the presence of religious divisions succeed or fail. Such processes offer a microcosm of the ways in which religiously divided societies address their internal polarization over the nature of the state and seek (sometimes without success) to produce convergence by adopting a constitutional identity capable of accommodating contestation and ambivalence. Importantly, when considered against the backdrop of Jacobsohn's concept of disharmonic constitutional identity, these strategies for addressing deep division may have pertinence to a wider range of cases as well, where there may be fewer ostensible divisions and yet important disharmonies persist.

19.3 DEBATING CONSTITUTIONAL RELIGIOUS IDENTITY IN ISRAEL AND TURKEY

The challenge in deeply religiously divided societies is how to grapple with constitution making in the absence of consensus on the shared norms or values underpinning the state. As the cases of Israel and of Turkey illustrate, constitutional arrangements formulated under conditions of deep divisions are neither a product of prior "thick" consensus (on the cultural, national, or religious identity of the state) nor is it grounded in a "thin" consensus around a shared liberal political culture. In both cases, the dissonance of constitutional identity is an especially prominent element of the debates around establishing a new framework for the formal constitutional order in the midst of contested interpretations of the existing text.

19.3.1 *Israel*

The debate on the state's religious identity has been central to Israeli constitutional politics since its foundation. Israel is one of only three countries in the world that refrained from adopting a formal constitution. But unlike the other two countries with no written constitutions – the United Kingdom and New Zealand – Israel also refrained from adopting a comprehensive Bill of Rights. Its list of thirteen basic laws includes only two that concern fundamental rights: the Basic Law on Human Dignity and Liberty and the Basic Law on Freedom of Occupation. Both were adopted in 1992, nearly four and a half decades after independence. One of the central reasons for the Israeli avoidance of enacting additional basic laws on human rights is Jewish religious parties' consistent rejection of constitutional recognition of the right of equality, particularly gender equality. Another reason for this avoidance is the consistent failure of large parts of the political system to embrace the protection of liberal rights for the entire population, including the non-Jewish minority of Palestinians, which comprise around 20 percent of the population.

Formally, two attempts have been made to draft a complete formal constitution in Israel. The first was between 1948 and 1950 immediately after independence. The second was between 2003 and 2006 when the Constitution, Law, and Justice Committee of the Israeli Knesset initiated *The Constitution in Broad Consent Project*. While by no means the only reason that Israel does not have a formal constitution, religious conflicts on both the inter-religious level (between the Jewish majority and the Palestinian minority) and the intra-religious level (within the Jewish population) continue to be one of the main reasons for the blockage in the long-lasting process of constitution making in Israel (Lerner 2011, 2013).

In the absence of a written constitution, religion–state relations in Israel evolved through ordinary legislation or through informal means during the early years of the state. These arrangements, known as "the religious status quo," stipulate the non-separation between religion and state in various areas of life, including a religious monopoly on marriage and divorce, limitations on public transportation on the Sabbath, public funding for autonomous religious schools, and exemptions from military service for Orthodox yeshiva students and religious women. The political leaders at the foundational stage of the state may have hoped that the incrementalist approach to constitution making they embrace would allow for liberal and secular reforms in the future. Nevertheless, seven decades after independence, the political system by and large refrained from advancing significant changes in the religious status quo.

In the past decade, the nature of the Israeli debate on its future constitution has changed with the enactment of two new basic laws: the Basic Law: Referendum (2014) and the Basic Law: Israel the Nation State of the Jewish People (2018). Both basic laws were initiated by right-wing political parties and their passing was accompanied by major political controversies. The enactment of the two basic laws marked a shift in the debate over Israel's disharmonic constitutional identity from religious to more ethnic/nationalist questions concerning the relationship between Israel's Jewish majority and the Palestinian minority.

Another important difference between the foundational debates on the Israeli constitution and the constitutional debates during the past two decades concerns the role and powers of the Supreme Court. In the 1990s, following a series of rulings concerning religion–state relations, and the Court's self-empowerment to review Knesset legislation, known as Israel's "constitutional revolution," the Orthodox and right-wing parties raised concerns about future judicial constitutional interpretation (Cohen 2020). The "counter revolution" culminated in 2023 with an attempted judicial overhaul, which included a proposal to limit the Supreme Court's authorities and to politically control the judicial appointment system, among other elements. In reaction, the liberal camp voiced growing demands for completing Israel's formal constitution making project. In a landmark decision published in January 2024, the Israeli Supreme Court ruled by a majority of twelve out of fifteen that the Court has the authority to perform judicial review on the content of Basic Laws. The Court also ruled (by a majority of eight to seven) that such intervention is required in the case of a recent amendment to Basic Law: The Judiciary, which revoked the standard of reasonableness.

The ongoing struggle over Israel's constitution, which seems far from over, represents an extreme version of a disharmonic constitution. It emphasizes, on the one hand, the inherent difficulty in entrenching formal and informal constitutional principles under conditions of deep disagreements over the state's identity. At the same time, it also highlights the stickiness of such disharmonies over time. Paradoxically, the ongoing conflict over Israel's constitutional identity has become a central part of the country's constitutional identity.

19.3.2 *Turkey*

Turkey has a long history of constitutionalism, dating from the first Ottoman Constitution of 1876 to the current constitution, written as part of a transition out of military rule in 1982 and radically amended several times, most recently in 2017.[2] All of these constitutions have been written in top-down, elite-led processes that entrench a repressive model of state–religion relations lacking popular support. Moreover, despite numerous high-profile ruptures in the country's constitutional order – including several military interventions and other non-conventional coups (and attempted coups) – the *de jure* configuration of republican state regulation of religion has proven fairly durable. Over time, the constitutional formula governing religion has been recalibrated in ways that reflect a shift of the pendulum from one end of the underlying societal polarization to the other, not through formal amendment or wholesale constitutional reform so much as by incremental shifts in the interpretation of a stable textual formula, which has survived numerous redrafting exercises. At present, Turkey is governed by a party widely understood as instantiating political Islam yet the constitutional orientation on matters of religion has been transformed by means of regulatory and legislative change, while the constitutional text defining the state as secular has remained static. Where many analysts see profound constitutional ruptures in the country's experience, particularly following the 2017 amendments, we find much continuity.

At the Republic's founding, Turkey opted for a tutelary constitution that sought to establish a pedagogical state which, over time, might forge consensus around constitutional secularism. Yet the reality of the dissonance between constitutional text and the underlying politics of religious contention played out across a century in a way that eventually neutralized the tutelary institutions. Despite efforts to shore up the entrenched constitutional formula through military and judicial interventions, the same textual formula and institutional design that once supported the top-down imposition of secularism is now used by the ruling party to advance an Islamist conception of Turkey's constitutional identity.

Secularism in Turkey consists not of separation of state and religion (or even state neutrality on questions of religion) but rather state control and regulation of religion in the interest of maintaining the autonomy of the political realm (Özbudun and Gençkaya 2009, 27–32). Under this definition aligned with the founding ideology of the Republic, known as "Kemalism," secularism is the basis for intrusive state policies governing many aspects of private religious expression and practice. The state monopolizes the domain of religious education, producing a state-sanctioned orthodoxy on Islam, excluding the beliefs and practices of heterodox Muslim communities like the Alevis. This definition of secularism was entrenched in the 1982 Constitution, which listed secularism as one of the unamendable characteristics of the Republic (Turkey 1982, art. 2(4)). In addition, the constitution protects freedom of religion while maintaining the Directorate of Religious Affairs – the state-controlled

---

[2] Turkey has had four different constitutions in the post-Ottoman period: the national liberation constitution of 1921, the first republican constitution of 1924, the post-military coup constitution of 1961 (revised in 1971 and 1973), and the post-military coup constitution of 1982. None of the three republican era constitutions were written by a broadly representative constituent assembly. Further, in the cases of the 1961 and 1982 constitutions, the drafters were selected by the military.

administrative apparatus for regulating Muslim religious institutions and affairs – and according special protection to the eight principal reform laws dating to the founding of the Republic that enshrined the Kemalist conception of secularism through public education, civil marriage, and language and dress reforms (Turkey 1982, art. 174).

Constitutional evolution on matters of state–religion relations has proceeded through reinterpretation of these arrangements. The 1990s witnessed the emergence of Islamist political parties in Turkey that performed well in national elections. Though several of these parties were shut down on the grounds of alleged anti-secular activities, by 2002 the emergence of the Justice and Development Party (known by its Turkish acronym, AKP for *Adalet ve Kalkınma*) led to the consolidation of the Islamist political camp within the center-right of the country's political spectrum. Since it first participated in national elections in 2002, the AKP has dominated the Turkish political scene, winning the plurality of votes in successive elections, and, as of this writing, still in power more than twenty years later.

The AKP's election platform promised to address the widespread demand to replace the 1982 Constitution through a broadly representative constitution-drafting process. Yet four electoral victories did not translate into successful constitutional revision until the party declared a state of emergency following a failed coup attempt and imposed its own version of constitutional transformation in 2017, continuing the pattern of top-down, unrepresentative constitutional revision. The main change introduced by these amendments was a transition to presidentialism, concentrating power in the executive and enabling the massive expansion of the Directorate of Religious Affairs. The textual definition of constitutional secularism remained untouched. Instead of amending the provisions on constitutional secularism, the AKP has used its parliamentary majority to alter regulatory and legislative frameworks in favor of its constituents' preferences for less intrusive secularism – permitting the wearing of headscarves on university campuses, in secondary schools and government offices (Toksabay and Villelabeitia 2010), as one example (Toksabay 2020).[3] The dissonance today between the lived reality of state–religion relations under AKP rule and the continued textual commitment to Kemalist secularism may, in the end, be resolved by a new constitutional text that reflects a real rupture. But it is also possible that the dissonance will remain a characteristic of the constitutional order, mediated by shifting constitutional interpretation that sometimes reflects preferences for greater state-sanctioned religiosity but also retains the possibility of providing interpretations more aligned with secularist commitments.

Turkey's divided inheritance on questions of state–religion relations and the meaning of secularism has produced efforts to quash disharmonies and resolve tensions

---

[3] Beyond the changes pertaining to the headscarf, the AKP also introduced restrictions on the sale of alcohol, vastly expanded the number of religious Imam-Hatip secondary schools, built towering monumental mosques in the country's republican public spaces and most recently converted the Hagia Sophia museum into a mosque.

definitively in favor of one constitutional interpretation by both Kemalist secularists and their Islamist antagonists. Each side's willingness to resort to anti-democratic readings of constitutional identity has introduced increasingly coercive dynamics in the dialogic process of contestation. Still, there is reason to hope that the discordant strands of the complicated inheritance of Ottoman and republican legacies may yet make way for more attenuated and accommodationist aspirations on each side.

19.4 INCREMENTALISM AND DISHARMONY IN CONSTITUTION MAKING

The brief discussion of the Israeli and Turkish cases reveals both the limitations of the liberal paradigm in addressing religious conflicts through constitution making and the relevance of Jacobsohn's insights concerning disharmonic constitutionalism. In both cases, would-be constitution drafters have been split over the question of the appropriate relations between religious law and the secular law of the state, or the relation between particular religious identities and the general identity of the state. Under such circumstances, liberal constitutional arrangements are not seen as a neutral solution to allow for further deliberation but rather as a victory of one side in the debate. This is particularly the case where religious divisions are intra-religious and concern the religious or secular character of the state.

Given the high degree of instability in the context of religiously divided societies, the presence of deep religious divisions in these cases requires different institutional, political, and judicial mechanisms for conflict resolution than the formulae prescribed in liberal models. Indeed, rather than relying on the prevalent techniques of institutional design choices from Western models, constitutions drafted in societies lacking cohesion around values or religious identity often develop conflict mitigation mechanisms which allow for an incrementalist and gradual resolution of the religious conflict through constitutional means. These include, in some cases, strategies such as deferral of clear decisions, the use of ambiguous language, the inclusion of conflicting provisions or principles in a written constitution, or the adoption of non-justiciable clauses. In other cases, constitutionalism itself is deferred either by not adopting a written constitution or by using ordinary legislative procedures to amend an existing text when broader repeal and revision prove unworkable. These strategies are under-emphasized in the liberal constitutional toolkit, which presumes greater underlying consensus around a set of foundational values, including on questions of religion–state relations. Yet Jacobsohn's insight that disharmonies are endemic to all constitutional orders suggests that a drafting toolkit premised on shared liberal values may be in need of expansion generally. As such, the study of strategies adopted for constitution drafting and constitutional interpretation in divided societies may provide tools for constitutional design that better reflect and accommodate disharmonic constitutional identity even in countries that face fewer ostensible deep divisions.

In both Israel and Turkey, we see that when drafters are faced with the complex political reality of religiously divided societies, the arrangements they design concerning the role of religion, or concerning the religious identity of the state, do not always represent a moment of "new beginning" in the long-lasting relations between religion and state. Given the deep disagreements over the religious/secular identity of the state that characterize religiously divided societies, drafters may refrain from formally defining a set of supreme constitutional principles which are intended to guide future generations, as in the Israeli case. The expectation that constitutions would establish clear legal limitations on governmental power often fails to be realized when political actors adopt more flexible constitutional arrangements which allow greater freedom for political decisions on divisive religious issues. And even where constitutional commitments are entrenched, as in the Turkish case, underlying disharmonies reflected elsewhere in the text may dictate wide latitude in the interpretation of those commitments.

Both Israel and Turkey involve the promulgation of constitutions in the absence of a clear consensus on the most divisive questions in the underlying society. The divergent strategies of the two cases – deferral in the first and constitutional entrenchment of secularism combined with a state-run religious directorate in the other – have both resulted in mechanisms that generally correspond to an incrementalist approach to constitution making (Bâli and Lerner 2016).

Incrementalist strategies such as deferral, ambiguity, and conflicting constitutional principles may, of course, have the effect of empowering particular institutions – notably apex courts that assert a predominant role in the interpretive exercises that produce constitutional evolution – and generating institutional conflict, particularly between the legislative and judicial branches in democratizing contexts.[4] Yet, in societies deeply divided over religious issues, an attempt to resolve state–religion relations by adopting an entrenched and clearly defined constitutional formula may run the greater risk of exacerbating polarization while limiting the institutional channels for conflict mitigation. Moving away from Western constitutional paradigms affords fresh perspective on the question of whether constitutionalism must operate as a form of higher lawmaking definitively set apart from the day-to-day politics of the underlying society (Ackerman 1991). For societies marked by deep and foundational divisions, a more incremental and evolutionary conception of constitutionalism may allow for gradual convergence around normative commitments and frequent renegotiation through informal reinterpretations in the course of ordinary politics. Jacobsohn's work on disharmonic constitutions reminds us that a constitutional framework capable of accommodating such frequent renegotiation may also be appealing and appropriate beyond the context of deeply divided societies.

---

[4] In contrast, the strategy of non-justiciability also has an impact on the distribution of power amongst the branches of government. Here, by disempowering the judiciary, specifically apex courts.

We recognize, at the same time, that the risks of incrementalism are significant. Perhaps foremost is the risk that by failing to resolve questions concerning the state's relationship to religion, divisions in the realm of ordinary politics may persist or deepen, setting in motion processes that exacerbate existing cleavages. For instance, deferral may set the stage for a conflict between the legislature and the judiciary over defining the state's role in regulating religion, as the recent political crisis in Israel has demonstrated (Lerner 2022). Or it may produce political strategies that promote communities' definition of themselves in increasingly insular ways that undermine the emergence of any common public sphere in which compromises can be negotiated (Barry 1975).[5] Incrementalism is also often a conservative strategy, one that may provide stability at the expense of the entrenchment of specific rights protections. Yet the risks associated with insisting upon restrictive constitutional concepts and the entrenchment of strong normative commitments in the presence of deep dissensus is the creation of permanent insiders and outsiders and channeling conflict away from the constitutional institutions toward extra-political violence.[6]

It is true, especially in post-colonial cases, that quite nearly everyone in a society undergoing transition cares about the Constitution, but they may care about it for very different reasons. For some, constitutions are imbued with the markers of sovereignty and a break with a past that has fallen into disgrace. For others, constitutions may be valued for the relationship between constitution making and political autonomy from external forces. Very often, symbolic provisions become the focal point for debate rather than the more substantive provisions, such as those allocating power between the branches. Still, even in a context of deep disagreements over these symbolic commitments, the parameters of debate are often relatively clear and reflect continuities with earlier debates. In this sense even the constitution drafting at independence may not, on our account, be an act of forging new identity, though certainly it is a moment in which novel political configurations of power are established. In the Turkish case, despite the formal rupture with an imperial past, the framing of constitutional secularism reprised debates about modernization and westernization that consumed Ottoman elites for much of the century preceding the founding of the Republic. Israel, too, adopted a formula on state–religion relations that reflected Ottoman antecedents even as the ideological commitments of the founding instantiated a profound rupture from earlier arrangements. In both cases, despite deep polarization over religion–state relations that if anything intensified after the constitutional founding, the initial formulae adopted have proven relatively durable. Here, too, our reading converges with Jacobsohn's.

---

[5] This has been the case to a large extent in Lebanon, producing one of the main critiques of the model of consociationalism.
[6] A notable example of the relationship between a top-down restrictive constitutional formula and the onset of extra-political violence is evident in the Egyptian case (Weaver and McCarthy 2013).

CONCLUSION

Much of the comparative constitutional literature reflects the view that liberal constitutionalism is normatively better than the alternatives. In contrast, we have argued in our work that strategies of incrementalism are devices that represent the best solution where the prerequisites of the liberal constitutional paradigm are not available. Indeed, we believe that incrementalist strategies may actually offer preferable design solutions for societies that are grappling with heightened dissensus, where the disharmonies of constitutional identity have become especially salient. In this sense, expanding the constitutional design toolkit to take note of drafting strategies adopted in religiously divided societies provides a particularly useful lens through which to think through and complement Jacobsohn's account of constitutional identity more generally. The sets of design solutions that we identify with incrementalism are well suited to enabling a dialogic process to unfold without producing the zero-sum dynamics of entrenching a univocal constitutional identity.

We argue that approaches to constitutionalism that depart from liberal expectations may well offer the first best institutional arrangements for polities where constitution-drafting exercises do not begin from a prior political consensus but rather are undertaken, sometimes as conflict mitigation strategies, in the presence of significant contestation over core normative commitments. For this reason, Jacobsohn's emphasis on the tensions internal to all constitutional identity is deeply resonant with our approach. Coming to shared norms or defining a shared conception of the collectivity constituting itself in the drafting process may be an aspirational ideal, but when the attempt to forge such shared commitments devolves into conflict or coercion, incrementalist strategies may well be better than available alternatives. Drawing on Jacobsohn's view that disharmonies are endemic to all constitutional identity, we believe these strategies may have important applications to a broader range of constitutional orders than countries described as "deeply divided."

REFERENCES

Ackerman, Bruce. 1991. *We the People: Foundations*. Cambridge: Harvard University Press.
Ackerman, Bruce. 1992. *The Future of Liberal Revolution*. New Haven: Yale University Press.
Alexander, Larry. 2010. "What Are Constitutions, and What Should (and Can) They Do." *Social Philosophy and Policy* 28: 1–24.
Arendt, Hanna. 1965. *On Revolution*. New York: Viking Press.
Bâli, Aslı and Hanna Lerner. 2016. "Constitutional Identity Without Constitutional Moments: Lessons from Religiously Divided Societies." *Cornell International Law Journal* 49 (2): 227–308.
Barry, Brian. 1975. "The Consociational Model and Its Danger." *The European Journal of Political Research* 3: 393.
Bisarya, Sumit. 2013. *Constitutional Building: A Global Review*. Stockholm: International IDEA.
Choudhry, Sujit ed. 2011. *Constitutional Design for Divided Societies: Integration or Accommodation?* Oxford: Oxford University Press.

Cohen, Amichai. 2020. *The High Court Wars: Constitutional Revolution and Counter Revolution*. Jerusalem: IDI.
Cross, Ester, 2016. "Contested Constitutions: A Microcosm of Post-Arab Spring Divisions." *Oxpol*, July 26, 2016. https://blog.politics.ox.ac.uk/making-arab-spring-constitutions/.
Elster, Jon. 1993. "Introduction." In *Constitutionalism and Democracy*, edited by Jon Elster and Rune Slagstad. Cambridge: Cambridge University Press.
Gençkaya, Ömer Faruk and Ergun Özbudun. 2009. *Democratization and the Politics of Constitution-making in Turkey*. Budapest: Central European University Press.
Horowitz, Donald. 1985. *Ethnic Groups in Conflict*. Berkeley: The University of California Press.
Jacobsohn, Gary J. 2010. *Constitutional identity*. Cambridge: Harvard University Press.
Lerner, Hanna. 2011. *Making Constitutions in Deeply Divided Societies*. Cambridge: Cambridge University Press.
Lerner, Hanna. 2013. "The Political Infeasibility of 'Thin Constitutions': Lessons from Israeli Constitutional Debates 2003–2006." *Journal of Transnational Law and Policy* 22: 85–121.
Lerner, Hanna. 2022. "Permissive and Unpermissive Constitution Making." *Law and Ethics of Human Rights* 16: 2.
Miller, Laurel E. ed. 2010. *Framing the State in Times of Transition: Case Studies in Constitution Making*. Washington: United States Institute of Peace.
Preuss, Ulrich K. 1995. *Constitutional Revolution: The Link between Constitutionalism and Progress*. Atlantic Highlands, NJ: Humanities Press.
Raz, Joseph. 1998. "On the Authority and Interpretation of Constitutions: Some Preliminaries." In *Constitutionalism: Philosophical Foundations*, edited by Larry Alexander, 152–154. Cambridge University Press.
Rawls, John. 1996. "Lecture IV: The Idea of an Overlapping Consensus." In *Political Liberalism*, 133–173. New York: Columbia University Press.
Sajo, Andras. 2008. "Preliminaries to a Concept of Constitutional Secularism." *International Journal of Constitutional Law* 6 (3–4): 605–629.
Taylor, Charles. 2007. *A Secular Age*. Cambridge: Belknap Press and Harvard University Press.
Toksabay, Ece. 2020. "Erdogan Declares Hagia Sophia a Mosque after Turkish Court Ruling." *Reuters*, July 10, 2020. www.reuters.com/article/us-turkey-museum-verdict-idUSKBN24B1UP.
Toksabay, Ece and Ibon Villelabeitia. 2010. "In Quiet Revolution, Turkey Eases Headscarf Ban." *Reuters*, October 17, 2010. www.reuters.com/article/us-turkey-headscarf-idUSTRE69GoDX20101017.
Weaver, Matthew and Tom McCarthy. 2013. "Egyptian Army Suspends Constitution and Removes President Morsi." *Guardian*, July 3, 2013. www.theguardian.com/world/middle-east-live/2013/jul/03/egypt-countdown-army-deadline-live.
Widner, Jennifer. 2008. "Constitution Writing in Post-Conflict Settings: An Overview." *William & Mary Law Review* 49: 1513–1541.

LEGISLATION

Turkey. 1982. *Constitution of the Republic of Turkey*.
U.S. 1787. *Constitution*.
Israel. 1984. Basic Law: The Judiciary.
Israel. 1992. Basic Law: Human Dignity and Liberty.
Israel. 1992. Basic Law: Freedom of Occupation.
Israel. 2014: Basic Law: Referendum.
Israel. 2018. Basic Law: Israel - the Nation State of the Jewish People.

20

Constitutional Identity and Unamendability

Oran Doyle[*]

INTRODUCTION

Constitutional theory has become a global enterprise, aspiring to general accounts of constitutional phenomena informed either by large-N statistical analysis or case studies drawn from an increasingly wide range of constitutional systems. Gary Jacobsohn's work on constitutional identity was an early exemplar of this work, testing and refining broad theoretical claims against deep analysis of constitutional developments in diverse constitutional systems. One aspect of Jacobsohn's rich and multi-textured theory is the claim that constitutional identity constrains amendment powers. In this chapter, I explore that claim through the lens of the two seminal Irish cases with which Jacobsohn engages: *State (Ryan) v Lennon*[1] and *Re Article 26 and the Information (Services outside the State for the Termination of Pregnancy) Bill 1994*.[2] These cases, while rejecting unamendability, illustrate Jacobsohn's central distinction between generic constitutional identity and particular constitutional identity.[3] Jacobsohn correctly claims that generic constitutional identity – conformity to the moral values of constitutionalism – constrains constitutional amendment, but the salience he assigns to a country's distinctive constitutional identity is problematic. I interpret Jacobsohn's particular constitutional identity not as a substantive constraint on amendment but rather an argumentative frame for debate about the legitimacy of amendments. This argumentative frame lacks a sound normative basis and encourages an excessive focus on the constitutional past, diminishing the potential of constitutional amendment as a site of democratic deliberation.

---

[*] I am grateful to all who commented at a TriCON workshop on 21 March 2023, and in particular to Li-Kung Chen, Daniel Gilligan, Chien-Chih Lin, Andrea Pin and Rachael Walsh for their detailed written comments. I am grateful to Po-Jen Chung for research assistance.
[1] [1935] IR 170.
[2] [1995] 1 IR 1, hereinafter the *Abortion Information* case.
[3] The Supreme Court has since endorsed the relevance of constitutional identity but not unamendability. *Costello v Government of Ireland* [2022] IESC 44 (Rainford 2023).

20.1 IDENTITY AND AMENDABILITY

Constitutions can be identified formally – that is, with reference to content-neutral considerations such as the fact that they are accepted as such by law-applying officials in a particular place at a particular time (Doyle 2018b) – or substantively. Jacobsohn's signal contribution to constitutional theory has been the analysis of what it means for a constitution to have a substantive identity. For Jacobsohn, constitutional identity is neither static nor unchanging:

> [A] constitution acquires an identity through experience … this identity exists neither as a discrete object of invention nor as a heavily encrusted essence embedded in a society's culture, requiring only to be discovered. Rather, identity emerges dialogically and represents a mix of political aspirations and commitments that are expressive of a nation's past, as well as the determination of those within the society who seek in some ways to transcend that past. It is changeable but resistant to its own destruction, and it may manifest itself differently in different settings. (Jacobsohn 2010, 7)

He argues for: 'a more fluid concept of identity, in which constitutional assertions of self-definition are just part of an ongoing process entailing adaptation and adjustment as circumstances dictate. It is not fluidity without boundaries, however, and textual commitments such as are embodied in preambles often set the topography upon which the mapping of constitutional identity occurs' (Jacobsohn 2010, 13). As intellectually stimulating as the discernment of substantive constitutional identity may be, its significance depends on its relevance to other important questions. Constitutional identity could play a doctrinal role across several legal systems, one example being a national law limit to the scope of the EU's competence (De Witte and Fromage 2021). A further example is the constraint of constitutional amendment powers with reference to constitutional identity. In Germany, the Constitutional Court has explained the textual limits on constitutional amendment as protecting a core constitutional identity (Heun 2011, 29). In Colombia, the Constitutional Court has held that constitutional amendments cannot amount to constitutional replacements (Bernal 2013). The question for constitutional theory, however, is whether the fact that several jurisdictions constrain amendment with reference to identity counts as support for the general claim that constitutional identity constrains amendment. At the level of empirical observation, many jurisdictions do not constrain constitutional amendment in this way: are they mistaken and, if so, what type of mistake are they making?

Jacobsohn argues that constitutional identity implies limits on the amendability of all constitutions (Jacobsohn 2006, 2010). He speaks of constitutional identity *constraining* amendment (Jacobsohn 2010, 18, 35, 78). The existence of constraints on the power of constitutional amendment in general – that is, not contingent on the doctrines or practices of a particular jurisdiction – can be advanced on either a conceptual or normative basis (Doyle 2017). Conceptual constraints are necessary features of the phenomenon being analysed; normative constraints require justification under a theory of political morality.[4] It is difficult, given the numerous examples of constitutional texts that grant apparently unconstrained amendment powers, to maintain a conceptual argument that constitutional amendment powers are necessarily constrained by constitutional identity. In any event, the better reading of Jacobsohn is that powers of constitutional amendment are *normatively* constrained to respect constitutional identity. In other words, irrespective of the breadth of amendment power that a constitution appears to grant, constitutional amenders *ought not* exercise that power inconsistently with their constitution's identity. This formulation does not determine the appropriate response by judges to amendments inconsistent with constitutional identity. I now turn to the Irish examples to illustrate Jacobsohn's claims in more detail.

20.2 IRELAND AND CONSTITUTIONAL UNAMENDABILITY

20.2.1 *The Constraint of Generic Identity*

In the aftermath of Ireland's war of independence, the Constitution of the Irish Free State 1922 was enacted by the Oireachtas in Dublin sitting as a constituent assembly and then enacted by the Westminster Parliament (Cahillane 2016). Article 50 of the 1922 Constitution allowed amendments by way of ordinary legislation for the first eight years; thereafter a referendum would be required. In 1929, the Oireachtas amended Article 50 to extend the period for amendment by ordinary legislation for a further eight years. The legislative power of amendment was then deployed to circumvent constitutional protections for human rights and the rule of law in the face of significant challenges to the authority of the state both from the Irish Republican Army, a paramilitary organisation which rejected the legitimacy of the Irish Free State on the grounds that it was not sufficiently independent from the United Kingdom, and from the Blueshirts, a conservative movement that bore mostly superficial similarities to fascism. In 1931, the Seventeenth Amendment introduced Article 2A, a draconian crime control provision. For instance, prescribed offences were to be tried not by judges but by military tribunals authorised to impose a greater penalty (including the death penalty) than that stipulated by law if the tribunal thought it was necessary or expedient.

In *State (Ryan) v Lennon*, the Supreme Court rejected a challenge to the constitutionality of Article 2A.[5] FitzGibbon J viewed Article 2A as an egregious departure from constitutional standards, but his strongly textualist approach meant

---

[4] I later consider the implication of moralised concepts that potentially draw together these two strands. But to advance the argument, it is clearer to keep the strands separate for now.
[5] [1935] IR 170.

this departure could not translate into a finding of unconstitutionality. The Constitution as originally enacted allowed amendment by the Oireachtas within the initial eight-year period and did not preclude the Oireachtas amending the Constitution to extend that eight-year period. The Seventeenth Amendment was validly made within that extended period because it did not infringe any explicit prohibition on amendment.

Kennedy CJ, however, vigorously dissented, identifying several grounds on which the amendment was unconstitutional. First, the constitution had – at least from the Irish perspective – been enacted by the Oireachtas sitting as a constituent assembly. The relevance of this was not the Schmittian distinction between constituent and constituted authority. Rather, members of the Oireachtas qua constituent assembly had not been required to take an oath of fidelity to the British monarch, in contrast to the later members of the Oireachtas qua legislature. The constituent assembly and the referendum-amendment process could therefore, in Kennedy CJ's view, more authentically express the will of the people than could the Oireachtas acting as legislature under the 1922 Constitution.[6] Second, since the Constitution Act stated that all power came from God to the people, any act would be unconstitutional if it could not be justified under authority derived from God. The actions and conduct authorised by Article 2A could not be reconciled with the Natural Law and were therefore null and void.[7] Third, the Constituent Assembly had expressed fundamental principles in a way that conveyed they were immutable and absolute subject only to specific qualifications. Given that Article 6 provided that personal liberty was inviolable, albeit that it could be deprived in accordance with law, the constitution could not be amended to permit indefinite detention without charge on the say-so of a soldier or police officer.[8] Fourth, Article 50 effectively created two powers of amendment: the time-limited power conferred on the Oireachtas and the indefinite power conferred on the people. The Oireachtas could not exercise the former power in such a way as to seize the latter power.[9]

Placed in its historic context – a fledgling state in 1930s Europe facing a significant threat from political violence seeking its overthrow; legal norms that emphasised the literal interpretation of statutes; several decades prior to any court in the world declaring a constitutional amendment unconstitutional (Roznai 2013) – the result in *Ryan* should not surprise. Moreover, while a setback for the value of constitutionalism in the short run, *Ryan* was shortly followed by the enactment of the new Constitution of Ireland (1937), which required referendum approval for all amendments after an initial unextendible three-year period. This requirement has underpinned rights protection and foreclosed possibilities for democratic backsliding

---

[6] [1935] IR 170, 210–211.
[7] [1935] IR 170, 204–205.
[8] [1935] IR 170, 208.
[9] [1935] IR 170, 213–219.

(Doyle 2018a, 198–203), thereby meeting a pre-*Ryan* objective of Prime Minister Éamon de Valera to identify which provisions of the 1922 Constitution should be regarded as fundamental and protected from change (Coffey 2012). While counterfactual examples are fraught, there is significant reason to doubt that a Supreme Court decision to strike down Article 2A would have strengthened protection of constitutionalism in Ireland over the medium to long term. Without losing sight of that historical context, however, *Ryan* provides a useful test for theories about constraints on the power of constitutional amendment.

In Jacobsohn's theory of constitutional identity, *State (Ryan) v Lennon* belongs in a category of cases where constitutional identity categorically prohibits amendment. In Jacobsohn's view, Article 2A was a 'constitutional monstrosity', the majority judgements allowing an 'amendment process functioning in total difference to itself and its own system of legality' (Jacobsohn 2010, 41, 44). This suggests that Article 2A infringed what Jacobsohn elsewhere characterises as the most important, *generic* constraint provided by constitutional identity (Jacobsohn 2010, 18). While each constitution has a specific and distinctive constitutional identity, there are also – following Lon Fuller's account of the morality of law (Fuller 1977) – certain criteria that determine the very existence of constitutional governance. In this light, the problem with Article 2A was its departure from the very characteristics of constitutional governance itself thereby depriving the Irish Free State Constitution of its identity qua constitution.

20.2.2 *The Constraint of Particular Constitutional Identity*

The 1937 constitution retained many of the provisions of the 1922 constitution but gave greater prominence to scholastic natural law theory as the basis for law and rights while also enhancing the people's role as the ultimate source of political power. On the one hand, Article 41 referred to the family as possessing 'inalienable and imprescriptible rights, antecedent and anterior to all positive law' while Article 43 stated that 'man, in virtue of his rational being, has the natural right, antecedent to positive law, to the private ownership of external goods'. On the other hand, Article 6 referred to all powers of government deriving, under God, from the people, whose right it was 'to designate the rules of the State and, in final appeal, to decide all questions of national policy, according to the requirements of the common good'. Whereas the unamendability question under the Irish Free State Constitution had focused on a diminution in generic constitutional identity, the question under the 1937 Constitution concerned whether its particular constitutional identity – that is, its endorsement of natural law as the basis for law and rights – circumscribed the range of constitutional amendments that the people could validly approve.

In 1983, the constitution was amended to give explicit recognition to the right to life of the unborn child, subsequently interpreted to preclude the distribution within the state of information relating to the provision of abortion services outside the state.[10] In 1992, an amendment was approved by referendum to qualify the right to life of the unborn as not limiting the freedom to obtain or make available information relating to services lawfully available in other states. The Houses of the Oireachtas then passed a Bill to allow for the provision of such information. The President exercised her power to refer the Bill to the Supreme Court for a decision as to its constitutionality. Counsel assigned to argue on behalf of the unborn advanced an argument developed in legal commentary since the constitutional amendment was passed: the Bill was unconstitutional because the constitutional amendment underpinning it was itself unconstitutional (O'Hanlon 1993). The constitutional provisions endorsing the antecedence of natural law and natural rights provided some support for this argument. Moreover, the courts had frequently elaborated on those provisions, with Walsh J in *McGee v Attorney General* perhaps going furthest when stating that the constitutional provisions indicated, 'justice is placed above the law and acknowledge[s] that natural rights, or human rights, are not created by law but that the Constitution confirms their existence and gives them protection'.[11] These provisions and dicta were the basis for the claim that the Constitution was subordinate to natural law, rendering invalid any amendments that infringed the natural law.

The Supreme Court must agree a collegial judgement, in practice delivered by the Chief Justice, within sixty days of the presidential reference, leaving little opportunity to develop sophisticated judicial reasoning. Even by that standard, however, the Court's judgement in *Re Article 26 and the Information (Services outside the State for the Termination of Pregnancy) Bill 1994*,[12] was deeply unsatisfactory (Doyle 2003). The Court cited constitutional provisions and court decisions that emphasised the state was subject to the Constitution but failed to grapple with the constitutional provisions and case law that suggested the Constitution itself was subject to natural law. As a result, the Court cursorily rejected the possibility of substantive limits on the amendment power, a position re-emphasised in subsequent cases.[13]

Jacobsohn criticises the Supreme Court judgement not on the basis that it should have declared the amendment unconstitutional, but rather that its reasoning was instructively deficient for failing 'to confront the fundamental dilemma concerning constituent power and constitutional identity' (Jacobsohn 2010, 48). In Jacobsohn's view, the referendum provision allowed the Court to rely simply on the constituent authority of the people rather than engage with more fundamental questions of what an amendment is or what a constitution is. As thin as the Court's reasoning

---

[10] *Attorney General (The Society for the Protection of Unborn Children Ireland Limited) v Open Door Counselling Limited* [1988] IR 593.
[11] [1974] IR 245, 310.
[12] [1995] 1 IR 1 (hereinafter the *Abortion Information Case*).
[13] *Riordan v An Taoiseach* (No2) [1999] 4 IR 343.

was, it is somewhat short-changed by Jacobsohn's criticism. The Court did not rely on the amendment provision in coming to its conclusion but rather on other provisions, most tellingly the statement in Article 6 that the people retain the right, in final appeal, to determine all questions of national policy. The judgement's deficiency lies more in its neglect of the natural law strands of constitutional text and jurisprudence, failing to attempt any reconciliation of that strand with the strand endorsing popular sovereignty and an unlimited amendment power. Irish scholars have attempted such reconciliations (Duncan 1995; Whelan 1995; Whyte 1997).

Plausible accounts of Ireland's particular constitutional identity could, in my view, have been constructed that *either* empowered judges to review whether constitutional amendments cohered with the constitution's substantive vision of democracy *or* empowered the people as authoritative interpreters of the natural law to which constitutional amendments must conform (Doyle 2003, 73–80). These more nuanced accounts might find favour with Jacobsohn, who rejects the claim that the validity of Irish constitutional amendments could be conditional on their strict adherence to natural law. Even a right with a natural endowment should be open to modification. And while there might be 'grounds for principled resistance to excision of a constitutionally prescribed right ... the claim on behalf of resistance would still have to be made upon a demonstration that the result of this more radical change [was] at least constitutionally incoherent' (Jacobsohn 2010, 49).

The *Abortion Information case* illustrates that particular constitutional identity constrains constitutional amendment in a very different way from generic constitutional identity. If constitutional identity 'emerges dialogically and represents a mix of political aspirations and commitments that are expressive of a nation's past, as well as the determination of those within the society who seek in some ways to transcend that past', then it will always be open to argument whether an amendment is precluded by constitutional identity. The indeterminacy here is not merely that associated with all contested concepts. Rather, the constraint of constitutional identity validates diametrically opposed directives: past political aspirations and commitments *but also* the determination to transcend those aspirations and commitments. In this analysis, the Supreme Court decision was flawed not for its outcome but for its failure to assess the legitimacy of the abortion information amendment as an identity-consistent transcension of past commitments.

Particular constitutional identity, as presented by Jacobsohn, does not constrain the power of constitutional amendment in the sense of foreclosing certain substantive changes. Rather, the constraint of particular identity lies in its imposition of a mode of argumentation. As an argumentative frame, this governs those who exercise the power of amendment, not just the judges who might review the lawfulness of particular amendments. I derive this point from Jacobsohn's suggestion that judicial power to strike down amendments – for breaches of both generic and particular identity – should be commensurate with amendment difficulty, with a stronger presumption against judicial review where onerous amendment requirements encourage or even guarantee moderation. But even in those situations, retaining a judicial power 'could serve to remind politicians and citizens that ... constitutional change is inherently bounded' (Jacobsohn 2010, 82–83).

20.3 THE NORMATIVE JUSTIFICATION FOR IDENTITY-BASED CONSTRAINTS ON AMENDMENT POWERS

Jacobsohn considers that the Supreme Court in *State (Ryan) v Lennon* should have struck down the constitutional amendment on the grounds that it failed to respect generic constitutional identity, that is, the Fullerian internal morality that a posited constitution must exhibit in order to be truly a constitution. While it is plausible that the value of constitutionalism constrains amendment powers (Dixon and Landau 2015), we could capture this insight without reference to identity, as illustrated by removing references to identity from the following statement: 'Whatever one might think of the identity of an authority that does not provide Magna Carta-like liberties, it is not an identity that is properly constitutional' (Jacobsohn 2010, 75).

The strike-throughs reflect a broadly legal-positivist approach that separates the concept of a constitution from its evaluation. Jacobsohn's Fullerian move, in contrast, works as follows: just as a positive legal system that failed to conform to the internal morality of law – through non-promulgation, retroactivity, etc. – would not truly be a legal system, so a constitutional amendment that offended the value of constitutionalism would deprive its constitution of its generic constitutional identity. Constitutions are not simply posited facts of human existence but rather instantiate at least an aspiration to constitutional values – Magna Carta-like liberties of due process, in Jacobsohn's terminology. An extreme failure to instantiate those values results not simply in a bad constitution but a defective constitution, a document that is constitutional in a peripheral sense but not in the focal sense.[14] This account integrates the moral value of constitutionalism – in the sense of negative, legal constraints on government to protect individual liberties (Barber 2015) – with a concept of constitutions. Jacobsohn's Fullerian move has sound jurisprudential underpinning but, in my view, risks a value-monist assessment of constraints on constitutional amendment, potentially blind to other constraints or seeking to maximise the instantiation of constitutionalism irrespective of the cost to other values, such as democracy (Doyle 2017). I shall return to this concern below but for now wish to focus on the differences between generic and particular constitutional identity.

Generic constitutional identity derives normative force from a moral theory of constitutionalism. Despite the semantic similarity, particular constitutional identity cannot derive normative force from the same source. A particular constitutional identity, unlike generic constitutional identity, can be malign. Even a constitution that adequately conforms to generic constitutional identity may have a particular

---

[14] This formulation is my adaptation of John Finnis's explanation of *lex iniusta not est lex* (Finnis 2011, 364).

identity that is malign in certain respects.[15] Is there an obligation to preserve a malign constitutional identity? Jacobsohn considers this challenge with reference to how the US Constitution, as originally enacted, envisaged the continuation of slavery. The reconstruction amendments abolished slavery and guaranteed equal protection of the laws. Jacobsohn (Jacobsohn 2010, 60) identifies two views on the relationship of the reconstruction amendments to constitutional identity: a radical transformation (Brandon 1998, 200–203); or the non-rupture of constitutional identity (Murphy 1987). Ultimately, Jacobsohn considers that whether or not the reconstruction amendments 'radically reconstituted the American polity or enabled it in time to make due on its inaugural promise', they represented the dialogical interaction of internal and external constitutional disharmonies (Jacobsohn 2010, 354). In other words, the US Constitution contained a sufficient aspiration towards justice at its adoption that even the radical change of abolishing slavery and guaranteeing equal protection of the laws could be understood as an evolution rather than a rejection of identity.

While Jacobsohn's account may be persuasive as a matter of US constitutional law and history, it raises two broader problems for the theoretical claim that particular constitutional identity constrains the power of constitutional amendment. First, it avoids rather than answers the challenge of malign constitutional identity. A possible answer to that challenge – not canvassed by Jacobsohn – is that the obligation is only pro tanto: particular constitutional identity should only be preserved to the extent that it is not malign. The difficulty with this answer is that it increases the imprecision of the constraint imposed by constitutional identity, exacerbating the second problem. In this regard, Jacobsohn's treatment of the US reconstruction amendments strengthens the concern that arose from the *Abortion Information* case. The dialogic account of identity – that 'mix of political aspirations and commitments that are expressive of a nation's past, as well as the determination of those within the society who seek in some ways to transcend that past' – does not circumscribe outcomes. Rather than prohibit certain amendments, particular constitutional identity dictates a mode of argumentation around amendment. Proposed amendments must be assessed for legitimacy in terms of whether they are straightforwardly consistent with particular constitutional identity, or a reconciliation of the constitution's disharmonic elements, or perhaps a justified response to a malign constitutional identity. This frame orients debate away from the merits of any proposed amendment to its relationship to constitutional identity.

If particular constitutional identity were tied to the political aspirations and commitments expressive of a nation's past, a broadly Burkean account could justify its

---

[15] In 2018, the Irish Constitution was amended to replace a near-absolute prohibition on abortion with a general competence for the Oireachtas to introduce abortion. This amendment did not affect the constitution's generic constitutional identity but – depending on one's perspective – the constitution's particular constitutional identity had a malign dimension either before or after the amendment.

constraint on constitutional amendment (Jacobsohn 2010, 69–104). Constitutions being 'artifacts of time and experience' implies that amendments are only legitimate if the old constitution survived without loss of identity. The basic core of constitutional identity should be protected against radical changes that would disrespect fundamental law as an 'idea of continuity'. It is doubtful, however, whether Burke's account of developing a UK-style constitution easily translates to the amendment of mastertext constitutions. His rejection of radical change would equally apply to the issue of constitutional replacement, which most doctrines and theories of unconstitutional constitutional amendments assume to be unconstrained. A closer fit as a justificatory theory, therefore, might be Dworkin's theory of integrity (Dworkin 1986), translated to require consistency of constitutional treatment across time. In that justificatory frame, constitutional replacement might overcome the demands of integrity.

Neither justification, I suggest, is open to Jacobsohn's theory of particular constitutional identity given the way he considers Burke's theory of constitutional identity incomplete because of its failure to allow for required innovation as a radical departure from constitutional continuity (Jacobsohn 2010, 98). For Jacobsohn, the past influences the developmental path of constitutional identity, but constitutional disharmony – aspirational content, dialogical articulation, and generic/local balancing – infuses constitutional identity with its dynamic quality, infusing an element of uncertainty regarding its future course. Consistent with this allowance for radical change, he explicitly rejects Dworkin's account for its 'acceptance of a central, unifying idea that confers unambiguous and lasting meaning to American constitutionalism' (Jacobsohn 2010, 4). In short, while constraint by a static concept of constitutional identity could be justified on conservative or consistency grounds, a fluid constitutional identity that allows radical change cannot be justified on those normative bases. Conceiving particular constitutional identity as an argumentative frame rather than substantive constraint softens potential normative objections at the cost of severance from any potential normative justification.

I wish to go a little further here, however, and suggest that there is a normative cost for jurisdictions that, through their contingent doctrinal decisions, limit the power of constitutional amendment with reference to identity. Joseph Raz argued that while the authority of new constitutions may derive from their authors – because of the particular esteem in which those authors were held by their contemporaries – old constitutions, if morally valid at all, must derive their authority from other sources (Raz 1998, 169). This argument is founded on the possibility that psychological facts can support normative conclusions. We might develop this insight in relation to constitutional identity and query whether constitutional values are best served by a requirement that amendment debates be conducted through the argumentative frame of constitutional identity. Constitutional amendment provides a site for democratic deliberation, helping to build societal consensus about desirable changes (Doyle and Walsh 2022). The scope of democratic deliberation is restricted by an argumentative frame of constitutional identity. As Jones observes, 'powerful connections to a collective founding, to a national identity ... can all combine to enhance the potential effects of constitutional idolatry, and stifle constitutional change' (Jones 2020, 163). Openness to change through democratic deliberation, in contrast, could reinforce respect for the particular constitution on which the realisation of generic constitutional values depends.

The Irish experience provides an illustration of this. The enactment of the 1937 Constitution was a deeply partisan affair reflecting the still bitter divide between the erstwhile opponents of the civil war that followed independence, with only 56 per cent of those voting in support. Over time, de Valera's civil war opponents came to accept his constitution. But as they did so, a cleavage between religious-conservative forces and secular-progressive forces became more salient, with the constitution a significant site of controversy (Sinnott 2002). With the resolution of that cleavage in favour of secular-progressive forces, partly through constitutional amendments on issues such as same-sex marriage and abortion in the 2010s, the Constitution no longer exists at a contested divide in Irish society. Amendment debates were conducted not with reference to constitutional identity but rather on the merits of the change on its own terms. Democratic engagement in constitutional amendment, untrammelled by an argumentative frame of constitutional identity, engendered a greater respect for the Constitution than it had ever garnered before. Unlike Jacobsohn's valorisation of the moderation encouraged by an onerous amendment rule, this democratic perspective valorises the constitutional respect encouraged by participation in amendment. There is value in an amendment process that allows us to start a new future rather than re-interpret our past.

CONCLUSION

Jacobsohn provides a rich and provocative account of constitutional identity that distils into theoretical form the instincts that lie behind many doctrines of constitutional unamendability. Generic constitutional identity constrains – at least pro tanto – powers of constitutional amendment. But it is difficult to articulate any equivalent moral theory that conveys normative force on particular constitutional identity. While Jacobsohn's dialogic account of particular constitutional identity avoids some of that concept's unpleasant implications, it simultaneously disconnects constitutional identity from the conservative or consistency-focused theories that could provide a justification. More broadly, Jacobsohn's work is testament to the value of deep and sustained engagement with the principles and culture of other constitutional systems. Notwithstanding the greater attention to comparative experience that Jacobsohn's work has been to the forefront in fostering, I suspect constitutional scholars share a tendency to project lessons learned from our own constitutional system onto the general constitutional world. If what we are familiar with works tolerably well, it is easy to derive from this success a normative position that unfavourably evaluates other constitutional approaches. In the spirit of diversifying those projections rather than making categorical claims, I have drawn attention to the Irish example as an illustration of the possible benefits of enabling rather than constraining constitutional amendment.

REFERENCES

Barber, Nick. 2015. 'Constitutionalism: Negative and Positive.' *Dublin University Law Journal* 38: 249.

Bernal, C. 2013. 'Unconstitutional Constitutional Amendments in the Case Study of Colombia: An Analysis of the Justification and Meaning of the Constitutional Replacement Doctrine.' *International Journal of Constitutional Law* 11 (2): 339–357.

Brandon, Mark E. 1998. *Free in the World*. 1st ed. Princeton: Princeton University Press.

Cahillane, Laura. 2016. *Drafting the Irish Free State Constitution*. Manchester: Manchester University Press.

Coffey, Donal. 2012. 'The Need for a New Constitution; Irish Constitutional Change 1932–1935.' *Irish Jurist* 48 (2): 275.

De Witte, Bruno, and Diane Fromage. 2021. 'National Constitutional Identity Ten Years on: State of Play and Future Perspectives.' *European Public Law* 27 (3): 411–426.

Dixon, R., and D. Landau. 2015. 'Transnational Constitutionalism and a Limited Doctrine of Unconstitutional Constitutional Amendment.' *International Journal of Constitutional Law* 13 (3): 606–638.

Doyle, Oran. 2003. 'Legal Validity: Reflections on the Irish Constitution.' *Dublin University Law Journal* 25: 56.

Doyle, Oran. 2017. 'Constraints on Constitutional Amendment Powers.' In *The Foundations and Traditions of Constitutional Amendment*, edited by Richard Albert, Xenophon Contiades, and Alkmene Fotiadou, 73–95. Oxford: Hart.

Doyle, Oran. 2018a. *The Constitution of Ireland: A Contextual Analysis*. Oxford: Hart Publishing.

Doyle, Oran. 2018b. 'The Silent Constitution of Territory.' *International Journal of Constitutional Law* 16 (3): 887–903.

Doyle, Oran, and Rachael Walsh. 2022. 'Constitutional Amendment and Public Will Formation: Deliberative Mini-Publics as a Tool for Consensus Democracy.' *International Journal of Constitutional Law* 20 (1): 398–427.

Duncan, William. 1995. 'Can Natural Law Be Used in Constitutional Interpretation?' *Doctrine and Life* 45: 125.

Dworkin, Ronald. 1986. *Law's Empire* (1st ed.). Cambridge, MA: Belknap Press of Harvard University Press.

Finnis, John. 2011. *Natural Law and Natural Rights* (2nd ed.). Clarendon Law Series. Oxford; New York: Oxford University Press.

Fuller, Lon L. 1977. *The Morality of Law* (Revised ed.). New Haven: Yale University Press.

Heun, Werner. 2011. *The Constitution of Germany: A Contextual Analysis*. Oxford; Portland: Hart Publishing.

Jacobsohn, Gary Jeffrey. 2006. 'An Unconstitutional Constitution? A Comparative Perspective.' *International Journal of Constitutional Law* 4 (3): 460–487.

Jacobsohn, Gary Jeffrey. 2010. *Constitutional Identity*. Cambridge: Harvard University Press.

Jones, Brian Christopher. 2020. *Constitutional Idolatry and Democracy: Challenging the Infatuation with Writtenness*. Cheltenham, UK; Northampton, MA, USA: Edward Elgar Publishing.

Murphy, Walter F. 1987. 'Slaughter-House, Civil Rights, and Limits on Constitutional Change.' *The American Journal of Jurisprudence* 32 (1): 1–31.
O'Hanlon, Rory. 1993. 'Natural Rights and the Irish Constitution.' *Irish Law Times* 11: 8.
Rainford, Seán. 2023. 'Costello v Ireland and an Irish Constitutional Identity.' *The Irish Judicial Studies Journal* 7 (1): 70.
Raz, Joesph. 1998. 'On the Authority and Interpretation of Constitutions.' In *Constitutionalism: Philosophical Foundations*, edited by Larry Alexander. Cambridge: Cambridge University Press.
Roznai, Yaniv. 2013. 'Unconstitutional Constitutional Amendments – The Migration and Success of a Constitutional Idea.' *American Journal of Comparative Law* 61 (3): 657–719.
Sinnott, Richard. 2002. 'Cleavages, Parties and Referendums: Relationships between Representative and Direct Democracy in the Republic of Ireland.' *European Journal of Policy Research* 41: 811.
Whelan, Anthony. 1995. 'Constitutional Amendments in Ireland: The Competing Claims of Democracy.' In *Justice and Legal Theory in Ireland*, edited by Gerard Quinn, Attracta Ingram, and Stephen Livingstone, 35–71. Durham: Oak Tree Press.
Whyte, Gerry. 1997. 'Natural Law and the Constitution.' *Doctrine and Life* 45: 481.

21

Illiberal Constitutionalism and the Abuse of Constitutional Identity

Gábor Halmai and Julian Scholtes

Gary Jacobsohn's work on constitutional identity impressively illustrates identity's conceptual salience to the study of constitutionalism. Jacobsohn shows how constitutions always stand in relation to and in interaction with the social order within which they are situated, and how constitutional identity is not limited to constitutional text but always also a result of precisely this interactive relationship (Jacobsohn 2010). The concept of constitutional identity, as Jacobsohn presents it in his work, can provide a key to understanding constitutional diversity – to how even in a world where constitutional discourse and the conceptual arsenal of constitutionalism have seemingly globalised, constitutionalism is primarily a socially contingent practice.

In a perfectly self-contained polity, only in the rarest moments would the idea of constitutional identity become an explicit, self-conscious normative concept asserted in defence of the constitution. Only where a constitution is facing existential threats that touch upon the essentials on which it rests, does constitutional identity become an argument to be asserted in defence of the constitution, rather than something that tacitly evolves within a polity's constitutional and social processes.[1] However, in Europe, constitutional orders have become increasingly self-aware and increasingly willing to seize the normative power of the notion of constitutional identity. The prime cause for this has been the increasing development of supranational constitutional claims on the part of, for instance, the European Union (EU) and the Council of Europe's European Convention on Human Rights (ECHR). As the ascent of supranational constitutional claims has started to irritate and unsettle the monopoly of state-based constitutionalism (Walker 2002), discourses on constitutional identity and its assertion, recognition and preservation alongside (and against) competing

---

[1] Consider, for instance, the Indian *Kesavananda* case, where constitutional identity was evoked to fend off a number of abusive constitutional amendments.

constitutional sites have started sprawling (Alejandro Saiz-Arnaiz and Alcoberro Llivina 2013; Claes 2016; Perju 2020)

Especially in the European context, constitutional identity has thus become a key concept in the negotiation of authority between national and supranational constitutions. This can be seen both in national constitutional case law as well as in the law of the EU and the ECHR. Many national constitutional courts set limits to the primacy of EU law around their constitutional identity. Most prominently, perhaps, the German Constitutional Court has asserted the possibility of conducting an 'identity review' of EU law for conformity with the principles enshrined by the eternity clause in Art. 79(3) of the German Constitution (Polzin 2016). Other examples can be found in the Italian Constitutional Court's *controlimiti* doctrine, which, though not explicitly mentioning constitutional identity, protects the 'fundamental principles' of the Italian Constitution against violation through EU law, but also in the case law of the constitutional courts of Spain, France, Poland, Belgium, and others (Calliess and van der Schyff 2019). On the side of the EU, Art. 4(2), commonly labelled the 'identity clause', demands that the Union respect Member States' 'national identities, inherent in their fundamental structures, political and constitutional'. In the ECHR, the recognition of constitutional identities is managed through the Court's 'margin of appreciation' doctrine that gives national legal orders room for manoeuvre where no sufficient European consensus on a question arising under the Convention has emerged (Dzehtsiarou 2015; Sajó and Giuliano 2019).

The assertion of constitutional identity in a context of constitutional pluralism raises questions about the cogency and value of constitutional identity as an argument that, in a situation where, if constitutional normativity were entirely self-contained, would perhaps not be asked. Under what circumstances is 'constitutional identity' a valid argument? Wherein lies the value of constitutional identity and why should different constitutional identities deserve recognition? Is constitutional identity valuable in and of itself, just by virtue of being labelled as such, or is it tied to certain 'constitutional' qualities?

In this chapter, we argue that constitutional identity should not be seen as an unconditional source of value – it only deserves recognition to the extent that it serves the ideals of constitutionalism. We argue in favour of thinking more explicitly about constitutional identity as a normative argument. Where constitutional identity is invoked as a normative argument, the expectation of constitutionalism is implied – claims from constitutional identity that stand at odds with the ideals of constitutionalism, in fact, invoke the former ironically and frivolously. Secondly, we will consider some examples where constitutional identity has been invoked to justify forms of 'illiberal' constitutionalism – especially in Poland and Hungary. These invocations of constitutional identity, we argue, should be considered abuses of the concept, as they do not live up to the normative expectations which they evoke.

21.1 CONSTITUTIONAL IDENTITY AND CONSTITUTIONALISM – A COMPLEX RELATIONSHIP

The complexity of the relationship between constitutional identity and constitutionalism should not be understated.[2] Constitutional identity can neither be fully collapsed into a specific normative theory of constitutionalism, nor can constitutionalism be entirely presented as a matter of a polity's given identity. It encompasses both an abstract idea of the constitution as well as its specific expression in constitutional practice. Bosko Tripkovic usefully distinguishes between the 'general' and 'particular' aspects of constitutional identity. Whereas the 'general' aspect 'derives its force from the fact of having an entrenched and written constitution containing the basic moral commitments of the community [and] is relatively independent of any of these commitments in particular', the 'particular' aspect of constitutional identity 'arises from the concrete constitutional spirit or tradition, and refers to the specific constitutional experience of the community in question' (Tripkovic 2017, 31).

Constitutional identity is shaped by the ways in which the principles of constitutionalism are translated and interpreted within a particular society. As a socially contingent political practice that organically develops over time rather than an abstract set of normative principles, constitutionalism is inseparable from a country's particularities and specificities that are a matter of constitutional identity. Normative ideals are important for the appraisal and critique of the exercise of political power. However, constitutions are usually contingent products of concrete clashes of interests and values that can at best hope to approximate a higher normative ideal. Constitutions have to be legitimate based on the standards of reasonableness that constitutionalism poses, but they also have to be based on an actual agreement (Rosenfeld 2010, 25).

However, on the other hand, to the extent that constitutionalism does not merely describe any given polity's constitutional practice but represents context-independent normative aspirations to a legitimate form of government, constitutional identity as a normative argument should necessarily be seen as constrained by those normative aspirations and requirements (Sartori 1962). Ultimately, constitutional identity cannot be severed from the idea of constitutionalism that it entails. Invoking constitutional identity to undercut the requirements of constitutionalism means to use the notion ironically, in a way that is self-legitimating and normatively hollow. Without the constraints of a prior conception of constitutionalism, constitutional identity collapses into a mere statement of fact. Any normative force of constitutional identity is dependent upon external criteria of legitimacy that identity itself is unable to provide. Without any form of normative filter, 'identity' becomes an argument for the veneration of the factual.

---

[2] This section (21.1) on a part in Chapter 5 of Julian Scholtes, *The Abuse of Constitutional Identity in the European Union* (OUP 2023). Reproduced by permission of Oxford University Press.

21.1.1 *Constitutionalism and Constitutional Identity*

How to define 'constitutionalism' itself is, of course, an integral part of the controversy. Any conclusive definition of what 'constitutionalism' is and requires is bound to attract contestation. However, at least in the European context, a relatively dense net of normative expectations that enable States to yield authority to one another in the context of legal integration (see Somek 2014, 200–201), from the values articulated in Art. 2 Treaty of the European Union (TEU) to the European Convention of Human Rights, give some shape to constitutionalism. With this in mind, some general contours of the idea of constitutionalism – at least as it is prevalent in the European context that will be discussed in the second half – can be outlined, and their relevance to normative invocations of constitutional identity highlighted.

Understood through the lens of constitutionalism, constitutions are not mere power maps, but they set out to deliberately organise and structure the exercise of public authority (Sadurski 2006, 9). Constitutions presume – and set out to organise – the relation of citizens to one another and to the state in a pluralistic society (Rosenfeld 2010, 21). This pluralism of modern societies requires a vantage point from which to negotiate these different perspectives. Accordingly, a constitution cannot be characterised by a view of legitimacy that aims at the actualisation of a single comprehensive worldview. Conceptions of 'strong popular sovereignty' that locate legitimacy in conformity with pre-legal political predispositions of the people fail to sufficiently account for how such dispositions could be credibly discerned (Vinx 2013).

In this sense, the central legitimating devices of liberal constitutionalism – such as the rule of law, democratic government, and respect for human rights – serve to certify that whatever is claimed as a polity's 'constitutional identity' can truly be attributed to that polity. Democratic government, based upon the rule of the majority, is the cornerstone of constitutionalism (Grimm 2010). At the core of (representative) democratic government lies not just that 'the people' are the reason and limit of government, but also that nobody personally *embodies* the power of the state. In the words of Claude Lefort, democracy '[represents] power in such a way as to show that power is an *empty place* and to have thereby maintained the gap between the symbolic ['sovereignty', etc.] and the real ['government', 'politics', etc.]' (Lefort 1988, 225). In order for democracy to be able to reproduce itself past its initial exercise, it has to be subject to conditions that enable the place of power to remain an 'empty place'. The 'limits' placed upon democracy through the rule of law and respect for basic rights are simultaneously 'enabling conditions' for continuous democratic government (Habermas and Rehg 2001). The rule of law aims not just to prevent the arbitrary exercise of power; it also provides the language for power to express itself legitimately (Krygier 2017). Respect for basic rights ensures that democratic government and collective self-determination do not turn into forms of social domination, but rather preserve the voice and stake of every citizen in the polity. Both the rule of law and basic rights, far from merely 'restraining' the democratic sphere of action, frame and constitute that sphere to begin with.

Of course, there are many varieties of institutional configuration and value orientation that can fit under these general parameters. It is not our aim to make an argument for the best configuration, or even the best starting point for constitutionalism. Which specific forms of legitimation and institutional structure are taken in practice for the realisation of these goals is something that our account can (and ought) not describe. The space for reasonable disagreement around these specific forms is, indeed, partially captured by the idea of constitutional identity. For instance, whether or not a constitutional system should be based on 'legal' or 'political' constitutionalism, for instance, is less a matter of the normative merits of one or the other than it is a matter of which is best suited to the local political and constitutional imaginary (Latham-Gambi 2020).

Nevertheless, to claim a constitutional identity means to move within this conceptual sphere of constitutionalism. When constitutional identity is invoked in a normative way, as an argument for authority, the meanings of this shared understanding of constitutionalism are implied alongside. Constitutional identity has value insofar as it gives expression to a prior concept of constitutionalism. To claim something as one's constitutional identity implies an act of collective self-determination that requires the basic conditions guaranteeing its legitimacy. As Hans Lindahl has impressively demonstrated, the conditions of constitutionalism and the 'ontology of collective selfhood' are deeply intertwined with one another (Lindahl 2008). He argues that 'questionability' is at the core of what he calls the 'ontology of collective selfhood': any act of identity formation and formulation on behalf of a polity can only be considered legitimate if it can be subsequently questioned. Assertions of constitutional identity, if these are to carry normative weight and elicit normative recognition, are not mere statements of fact, but the product of a political process governed by conditions of legitimacy. These conditions form part of the normative expectations that are implicit whenever one speaks of 'constitutional identity'.

21.2 'ILLIBERAL CONSTITUTIONALISM' AS AN ABUSE OF CONSTITUTIONAL IDENTITY

After the constitutional backsliding in Hungary since 2010 and in Poland between 2015 and 2023, a new identity politics has been promoted by both governments, and their court ideologists based on the concept of 'illiberal constitutionalism'. This part of the paper will argue that this invention abuses the idea of constitutionalism described in the previous part as the basis of constitutional identity, therefore it also abusively refers to constitutional identity.

21.2.1 Is There Such a Thing as 'Illiberal Constitutionalism'?

Prime Minister Viktor Orbán admitting that his governing party, Fidesz did not aim to produce a liberal constitution said the following about the new constitutional order, introduced by the 2011 Fundamental Law of Hungary:

> In Europe the trend is for every constitution to be liberal, this is not one. Liberal constitutions are based on the freedom of the individual and subdue welfare and the interest of the community to this goal. When we created the constitution, we posed questions to the people. The first question was the following: what would you like; should the constitution regulate the rights of the individual and create other rules in accordance with this principle or should it create a balance between the rights and duties of the individual. According to my recollection more than 80% of the people responded by saying that they wanted to live in a world, where freedom existed, but where welfare and the interest of the community could not be neglected and that these need to be balanced in the constitution. I received an order and mandate for this. For this reason, the Hungarian constitution is a constitution of balance, and not a side-leaning constitution, which is the fashion in Europe, as there are plenty of problems there. (Kossuth Radio 2013)

Orbán also refused the separation of powers, checks and balances as concepts alien to his illiberal constitutional system, arguing that 'checks and balances are a U.S. invention that, for some reason of intellectual mediocrity, Europe decided to adopt and use in European politics' (Simon 2014). Similarly, Tünde Handó, that time head of the National Judicial Office, a close ally of Orbán said, 'The rule of law over the State, like, for example, in the United States, is not the right way' (Népszava 2019).

The ideological foundation of Orbán's illiberal state can be found in the works of his two court ideologues, the sociologist and former liberal MP, Gyula Tellér and András Lánczi, a political scientist. It is easy to prove that Orbán in his infamous 2014 speech on 'illiberal democracy' (Orbán 2014) recited a study of Tellér published earlier in that year, which Orbán assigned as compulsory reading for all his ministers (Tellér 2014). Tellér claims that the 'system of regime-change' has failed because the liberal constitution did not commit the government to protect national interests, therefore the new 'national system' has to strengthen national sovereignty, and with it the freedom of degree of government activity. This, Tellér argues, is necessary against the moral command of the liberal rule of law regime, according to which 'everything is allowed, what does not harm others' liberty'.

Lánczi's anti-liberal ideas can be found in his book *Political Realism and Wisdom*, which was published in English in 2015, as well as in an article published in 2018, after Fidesz' third consecutive electoral victory. Lánczi's critique is an outright rejection of liberalism as a utopian ideology, which is – similar to Communism – incompatible with democracy.

Similarly to Orbán, the then Polish Prime Minister Beata Szydło (with Kaczyński, ruling from behind the scenes as he held no official post), has described the actions of the PiS (Prawo i Sprawiedliwość [Law and Justice]) government dismantling the independence of the Constitutional Tribunal and the ordinary courts as a blitz to install an illiberal state. Ryszard Legutko, the main ideologue and MEP of PiS, similarly to his Hungarian counterpart, Lánczi, also likens liberal democracy to Communism, both being fuelled by the ideas of modernisation and progress, arguing that liberalism – in its 'sterility' has little if anything to say about substantive, human moral questions, indeed liberalism is 'comparably simplistic and equally impoverishing as communist thought was' (Legutko 2016, 118). Another critique of liberalism expressed by Legutko is its inauthenticity, 'being more and more remote from reality' (Legutko 2016, 13). As Paul Blokker observes, Lánczi makes a similar point in his *Political Realism and Wisdom* that liberalism fails to engage with reality (Blokker 2019). According to Legutko, a further problem with liberalism is that it drives to egalitarianism, which renders 'all social hierarchies as immediately problematic because they were obviously, not natural' (Legutko 2016, 132). In his communitarian reading, human rights become 'arbitrary claims, ideologically motivated, made by various political groups in blatant disregard of the common good, generously distributed by the legislatures and the courts, often contrary to common sense and usually detrimental to public and personal morality' (Legutko 2016, 140).

21.2.2 *Illiberal Constitutionalism as Constitutional Identity*

Increasingly, this illiberal constitutionalism is being defended inside Europe as a matter of 'constitutional identity'. Both in Poland and in Hungary, the ways in which 'constitutional identity' is being asserted stand fundamentally at odds with the constitutionalism the latter notion evokes. Both should be considered abuses of constitutional identity as a normative concept.

21.2.2.1 Hungary

From the very beginning, the government of Viktor Orbán has justified non-compliance with the principles of liberal democratic constitutionalism enshrined also in Article 2 of the Treaty of the European Union (TEU) by referring to national sovereignty. In reaction to the EU's efforts to solve the refugee crisis, the government has advanced the argument that the country's 'Christian' constitutional identity, guaranteed in Article 4 (2) TEU, conflicted with the acceptance of Muslim refugees. The government's refusal to participate in the refugee relocation scheme is part of a broader move towards a hostile refugee policy that has seen asylum seekers interned for prolonged periods of time in so-called 'transit zones' in inhumane conditions, which was subsequently declared illegal under EU law (CJEU 2020).

Following a series of unsuccessful political efforts, such as a referendum and an attempted constitutional amendment, the politically captured Constitutional Court passed down a decision on the protection of constitutional identity in the Hungarian constitutional order. The Court held that 'the constitutional self-identity of Hungary is a fundamental value not created by the Fundamental Law – it is merely acknowledged by the Fundamental Law, consequently, constitutional identity cannot be waived by way of an international treaty' (Hungarian Constitutional Court 2016; see also Halmai 2018). Therefore, the Court argued, 'the protection of the constitutional identity shall remain the duty of the Constitutional Court as long as Hungary is a sovereign State' (Hungarian Constitutional Court 2016). Orbán took this judgment as a sign that the Court has the government's back in its resistance against refugee relocation, publicly stating that he 'threw [his] hat in the air' when he heard of the decision as it meant that 'the cabinet can't support a decision made in Brussels that violates Hungary's sovereignty' (Halmai 2018, 36). However, the idea that granting protection to a relatively small number of refugees would threaten the homogeneity of a 'Christian' society to such an extent that it would endanger that society's identity makes assumptions about constitutional identity that are hard to square with the basic requirements of constitutionalism in an open society. It transforms constitutional identity from a set of shared political commitments that frame and enable constitutionalism in the light of society's particularities into a set of claims that purport to substantially encompass and embody a society, thereby surrendering the pluralism of values and interests that constitutionalism sets out to reconcile to begin with.

This picture becomes clearer when one looks at two constitutional identity-related constitutional amendments that were subsequently passed: firstly, the Seventh Amendment to the FL (Fundamental Law) introduced the state's obligation to protect Christian culture, which – besides its potential to limit fundamental rights – strengthens the role of religion to constitutionally legitimise an ethnic concept of nationhood. In this concept, the 'nation' comprised by the FL is not just a community of ethnic Hungarians but is also a Christian community – meaning that those who do not associate themselves with Christianity, can feel themselves excluded from the nation as well. In this constitutional order, the state is not necessarily obliged to tolerate all religions, and the representatives of the Christian religion can feel themselves entitled to be intolerant towards the representatives of other religions.

The Ninth Amendment to the Hungarian Fundamental Law, introduced in November 2020 amidst the second wave of the COVID-19 pandemic, used this other crisis as a pretext to fix children's gender identity at birth so that later gender changes can never be reflected in the birth register. It blatantly rejects the self-determination rights of children as part of their human dignity. Article XVI of the Hungarian Constitution now states that: 'Hungary protects children's right to their identity in line with their birth sex, and their right to education according to our country's constitutional identity and system of values based on Christian culture'. In the explanatory note to the amendment, it is argued that the Fundamental Law 'unambiguously lays down the values that transpire through the legal system', and that amendments serve to clarify these values already established by the constitutional drafters (Rovo and Kovács 2020).

These amendments turn national and constitutional identity into a political and normative straitjacket with which the entire country is made to conform. What is asserted as 'constitutional identity' in Hungary turns identity from the frame of constitutionalism into a means of political closure. The closure of Hungarian society on the one hand – the marginalisation of opposing or diverging worldviews, the erosion of checks and balances, the fending off of refugees, and the subversion of and resistance to EU law are thus two sides of the same coin, both intent on ensuring the 'homogeneity' of Hungarian society (Scholtes 2023).

Furthermore, by denying the basic rights of refugees and refusing participation in the joint European solution of the refugee crisis,[3] Hungary asserts a constitutional identity that is inconsistent with the requirement of sincere cooperation of Article 4(3) TEU. It promotes national constitutional identity without accepting the constitutional discipline demanded by the European legal order (on constitutional tolerance, see Weiler 2003). The reference to national constitutional identity of Article 4(2) TEU is legitimate only if the Member State refuses to apply EU law in a situation where a fundamental national constitutional commitment is in play (Kumm and Comella 2005). This abuse of constitutional identity, aimed at not taking part in the joint European solution to the refugee crisis, is not merely an exercise of 'national constitutional parochialism' (see Kumm 2012, 492), but an attempt to abandon the common European liberal democratic constitutional whole.

21.2.2.2 Poland

In Poland, it was not refugee policy but the government's erosion of the rule of law and undermining of judicial independence that were raised as issues of constitutional identity (Chancellery of the Prime Minister 2018). As has been widely discussed, between 2015 and 2023, the Polish government was engaged in a systematic effort to establish political control over the Polish court system and undermine the rule of law (Pech and Scheppele 2017; Sadurski 2019). Among other 'reforms', it lowered the retirement age for judges of the Supreme Court in order to force early retirement of politically unfavourable judges. Furthermore, it established political control of the National Council of the Judiciary in order to exercise greater control over the appointment of new judges. Finally, a new 'Disciplinary Chamber', staffed entirely with government loyal judges, that can discipline and suspend judges for giving unfavourable judgments.

---

[3] In an article, Viktor Orbán warned the 'unionists' of the EU who call for a United States of Europe and mandatory quotas, if they refuse to accept the 'sovereigntists' desire for a Europe of free and sovereign nations who will not hear of quotas of any kind, the mainstream will follow precisely the course that Hungary has set forth to affirm its constitutional affirmation of Christian roots, its demographic policy, and its effort to unify the nation scattered across borders. See V. Orbán, 'Hungary and the Crisis of Europe: Unelected Elites versus People' *National Review*, 26 January 2017.

These reforms gradually became subject to great controversy within the EU, as the erosion of judicial independence endangers the legitimacy of judicial cooperation with Poland. The Court of Justice has consequently established rule of law standards and, among other things, declared the new disciplinary regime incompatible with EU law. (CJEU 2018a, 2018b, 2019, 2020, 2021a, 2021b) The 'constitutional identity' defence has since become a staple in the Polish government's rhetorical repertoire for fending off these reproaches. In a widely cited 'White Paper', it asserted that the organisation of courts was wholly a matter of constitutional identity in the European Union and as such, any political or judicial reproaches of its judicial reform would run afoul of the requisite respect for constitutional identity. Furthermore, the packed Constitutional Tribunal protected the government's unconstitutional actions by referring to national constitutional identity in a judgment declaring the CJEU's rule of law jurisprudence in violation of the Polish constitution (The Chancellery of the Prime Minister 2018). On 7 October 2021, the Constitutional Tribunal issued its judgment on the interpretation of the Polish Constitution, initiated by the Prime Minister in case K 3/21 concerning the place of EU law in the Polish legal order. According to the Tribunal's press release the judgment explicitly invokes constitutional identity, arguing that 'the [organisational structure of courts] belongs to the Polish constitutional identity', and further emphasising that the 'organisational structures of the judicial systems in EU Member States do not at all fall under the common constitutional identity of the Member States' (Polish Constitutional Tribunal 2021).

However, like its Hungarian counterpart, the Polish government and Constitutional Tribunal were merely abusing the idea of constitutional identity. Insofar as constitutional identity can only be expressed legally, the rule of law and the independence of judges are fundamental framing conditions for the expression of constitutional identity. They are safeguards for the authenticity of constitutional commitments. The institutional interplay established by the separation of powers, of which the guarantee of judicial independence is an integral part, creates the conditions that make it plausible and legitimate for an act to be attributed to 'the people' in the first place (Scholtes 2023, see also Lindahl 2008). Rather than an assertion of constitutional identity, the Polish government's attack on the rule of law marked a 'loss of constitutional identity' (Wyrzykowski 2019, 418).

Ultimately, the Polish government and captured judiciary similarly leveraged constitutional identity as a means of eroding constitutionalism and achieving 'political closure' by constitutionalising a fixed worldview. This also shows in the 'abortion judgment' passed down by the Constitutional Tribunal in late 2020. The abortion case decided in October 2020 by the packed Constitutional Tribunal, which finds that terminating pregnancies due to severe foetal abnormalities is unconstitutional, also has relevance to constitutional identity (Polish Constitutional Tribunal 2020).[4]

---

[4] In the absence of an English translation of the decision we relied on the generous help of Michal Ziolkowski in translating these passages.

While the majority reasoning does not use the constitutional identity argument, the separate votums of two unconstitutionally elected ('fake') judges do. Mariusz Muszyński, for instance, argues that the judgment 'protects the individual Polish specificity (legal tradition), systemic and cultural distinctiveness, shaped historically and expressed in normative form in the Constitution, that is protects the Polish constitutional identity' against the 'so-called imperialism of jurisprudence of international tribunals' (Muszyński in Polish Constitutional Tribunal 2020). Jaroslaw Wyrembak's separate votum contains a similar reference to the 'axiological foundations' and 'identity' of the Constitution, which prevent the Parliament from liberalising the abortion law after the judgement. Where exactly this 'constitutional identity' is to be found in the Polish constitutional text, however, is something that neither of the judges explain (Gliszczyńska-Grabias and Sadurski 2021).

CONCLUSION

The use of constitutional identity as a normative argument in boundary conflicts such as the one between the EU and its Member States warrants closer theoretical scrutiny. If our argument is correct, playing 'the constitutional identity card' always attempts to elicit a host of normative expectations about the constitutional order in question – above all, that whatever is claimed as 'constitutional identity' speaks, in some profound way, to the 'collective selfhood' of a polity that has enabled itself to live within a 'constitutionalist' order of political freedom. In other words, claiming 'constitutional identity' presupposes open constitutional procedures and a division of powers that would allow such a 'collective selfhood' to meaningfully emerge to begin with. Accordingly, the substance of what can be claimed as especially protected in the name of constitutional identity is not boundless. Where governments or courts evoke constitutional identity without living up to the normative connotations the latter elicits, the notion is being abused. This is, indeed, the case in Hungary and was in Poland until 2023. These abuses of constitutional identity do not merely undermine the authority of EU law by threatening to declare (or actually declaring) its non-applicability. Above all, they subvert the core promises that have been made in the name of constitutionalism in Europe by establishing closed societies where only some voices are heard and only some people are afforded dignity. The concept of constitutional identity needs to be reclaimed from those who abuse it.

REFERENCES

Alejandro, Saiz-Arnaiz and Carina Alcoberro Llivina, eds. 2013. *National Constitutional Identity and European Integration*. Cambridge: Intersentia.
Blokker, Paul. 2019. 'Populist Counter-Constitutionalism, Conservatism, and Legal Fundamentalism'. *European Constitutional Law Review* 15 (3), 519–543.
Calliess, Christian and van der Schyff, Gerhard. 2019. *Constitutional Identity in a Europe of Multilevel Constitutionalism*. Cambridge: Cambridge University Press.

Claes, Monica. 2016. 'The Validity and Primacy of EU Law and the "Cooperative Relationship" between National Constitutional Courts and the Court of Justice of the European Union.' *Maastricht Journal of European and Comparative Law* 23 (1): 151–170.
Constitutional Court of Hungary. 2016. Decision 22/2016 AB (30 November 2016).
Court of Justice of the European Union. 2018a. Case C-64/16 *Associação Sindical dos Juízes Portugueses* (27 February 2018) ECLI:EU:C:2018:117.
Court of Justice of the European Union. 2018b. Case C-216/18 PPU *LM* (25 July 2018) ECLI:EU:C:2018:586.
Court of Justice of the European Union. 2019. Case C-585/18 *A.K. and others v Sąd Najwyższy* (19 November 2019).
Court of Justice of the European Union. 2020. Case C-924/19 PPU Országos Idegenrendészeti Főigazgatóság Dél-alföldi Regionális Igazgatóság ECLI:EU:C:2020:367.
Court of Justice of the European Union. 2021a. Case C-824/18 *AB* (2 March 2021) ECLI:EU:C:2021:153.
Court of Justice of the European Union. 2021b. Case C-791/19 *Commission v Poland* (15 July 2021) ECLI:EU:C:2021:596.
Dzehtsiarou, Kanstantsin. 2015. *European Consensus and the Legitimacy of the European Court of Human Rights*. Cambridge: Cambridge University Press.
Gliszczyńska-Grabias, Aleksandra, and Wojciech Sadurski. 2021. 'The Judgment That Wasn't (But Which Nearly Brought Poland to a Standstill): 'Judgment' of the Polish Constitutional Tribunal of 22 October 2020, K1/20.' *European Constitutional Law Review* 17 (1): 130–153.
Grimm, Dieter. 2010. 'The Achievement of Constitutionalism and Its Prospects in a Changed World'. In *The Twilight of Constitutionalism*, edited by Martin Loughlin and Petra Dobner, 3–22. Oxford University Press. Accessed 5 October 2020. http://oxford.universitypressscholarship.com/view/10.1093/acprof:oso/9780199585007.001.0001/acprof-9780199585007-chapter-1.
Habermas, Jürgen, and William Rehg. 2001. 'Constitutional Democracy: A Paradoxical Union of Contradictory Principles?' *Political Theory* 29 (6): 766–781.
Halmai, Gábor. 2018. 'Abuse of Constitutional Identity. The Hungarian Constitutional Court on Interpretation of Article E) (2) of the Fundamental Law.' *Review of Central and East European Law* 43: 23–42.
Jacobsohn, Gary Jeffrey. 2010. *Constitutional Identity*. Cambridge: Harvard University Press.
Kossuth Radio. 2013. A Tavares jelentés egy baloldali akció [Interview with Viktor Orbán]. https://2010-2014.kormany.hu/hu/miniszterelnokseg/miniszterelnok/beszedek-publikaciok-interjuk/a-tavares-jelentes-egy-baloldali-akcio.
Krygier, Martin. 2017. 'Tempering Power'. In *Constitutionalism and the Rule of Law*, edited by Maurice Adams, Anne Meuwese, and Ernst Hirsch Ballin, 34–59. Cambridge: Cambridge University Press.
Kumm, M. 2012. 'Rethinking Constitutional Authority: On Structure and Limits of Constitutional Pluralism.' In *Constitutional Pluralism in the European Union and Beyond*, edited by M. Avbelj and J. Komárek, 51. Hart.
Kumm, M. and V. Ferreres Comella. 2005. 'The Primacy Clause of the Constitutional Treaty and the Future of Constitutional Conflict in the European Union' 3 ICON 473–492.
Lánczi, András. 2015. *Political Realism and Wisdom*. Palgrave.
Lánczi, András. 2018. 'The Renewed Social Contract–Hungary's Elections.' *Hungarian Review* 9 (3). www.hungarianreview.com/article/20180525_the_renewed_social_contract_hungary_s_elections_2018.
Latham-Gambi, Alexander. 2020. 'Political Constitutionalism and Legal Constitutionalism – An Imaginary Opposition?' *Oxford Journal of Legal Studies* 40 (4): 737–763.

Lefort, Claude. 1988. *Democracy and Political Theory*. Cambridge: Polity Press.
Legutko, Ryszard. 2016. *The Demon in Democracy: Totalitarian Temptations in Free Societies*. New York: Encounter Books.
Lindahl, Hans. 2008. 'Constituent Power and Reflexive Identity: Towards an Ontology of Collective Selfhood'. In *The Paradox of Constitutionalism*, edited by Neil Walker and Martin Loughlin. Oxford: Oxford University Press. www.oxfordscholarship.com/view/10.1093/acprof:oso/9780199552207.001.0001/acprof-9780199552207-chapter-2.
Népszava. 2019. Handó: Nem kell a bíróságoknak szembehelyezkedniük az állammal, https://nepszava.hu/3029940_hando-nem-kell-a-birosagoknak-szembehelyezkedniuk-az-allammal.
Orbán Viktor. 2014. Speech at Băile Tuŝnad (Tusnádfürdő) of 26 July 2014. *Budapest Beacon*. http://budapestbeacon.com/public-policy/full-text-of-viktor-orbans-speech-at-baile-tusnad-tusnadfurdo-of-26-july-2014/.
Pech, Laurent, and Kim Lane Scheppele. 2017. 'Illiberalism Within: Rule of Law Backsliding in the EU'. *Cambridge Yearbook of European Legal Studies* 19 (December): 3–47.
Perju, Vlad. 2020. 'Identity Federalism in Europe and the United States'. *Vanderbilt Journal of Transnational Law* 53 (1): 207–274.
Polish Constitutional Tribunal. 2020. Case K 1/20 (22 October 2020). https://ipo.trybunal.gov.pl/ipo/view/sprawa.xhtml?&pokaz=dokumenty&sygnatura=K%201/20.
Polish Constitutional Tribunal. 2021. Press Release after the Hearing: Case K 3/21 (7 October 2021). https://trybunal.gov.pl/en/news/press-releases/after-the-hearing/art/11664-ocena-zgodnosci-z-konstytucja-rp-wybranych-przepisow-traktatu-o-unii-europejskiej.
Polzin, Monika. 2016. 'Constitutional Identity, Unconstitutional Amendments And The Idea of Constituent Power: The Development of The Doctrine of Constitutional Identity in German Constitutional Law.' *International Journal of Constitutional Law* 14 (2), 411–438.
Rosenfeld, Michel. 2010. *The Identity of the Constitutional Subject: Selfhood, Citizenship, Culture, and Community*. Oxfordshire: Routledge.
Rovo, Attila and Kovács, Zoltán. 2020. 'Hungarian Constitutional Amendment to Crack down on Gender Issues, Narrow Definition of Public Funds'. Telex, 10 November 2020. https://telex.hu/english/2020/11/10/hungary-constitutional-amendment-gender-family-public-funds-special-legal-order.
Sadurski, Wojciech. 2006. 'European Constitutional Identity?' EUI Law Working Paper Series, no. 2006/33.
Sadurski, Wojciech. 2019. *Poland's Constitutional Breakdown*. Oxford: Oxford University Press.
Sajó, András and Sergio Giuliano. 2019. 'The Perils of Complacency: The European Human Rights Backlash'. In *The Challenge of Inter-Legality*, edited by Jan Klabbers and Gianluigi Palombella, 1st ed., 230–249. Cambridge: Cambridge University Press.
Sartori, Giovanni. 1962. 'Constitutionalism: A Preliminary Discussion'. *The American Political Science Review* 56 (4): 853–864.
Scholtes, Julian. 2023. *The Abuse of Constitutional Identity in the European Union*. Oxford: Oxford University Press.
Simon, Zoltán. 2014. 'Hungary Premier Orbán Sticks to Maverick Path as U.S. Ties Sour.' *Bloomberg*. www.bloomberg.com/news/articles/2014-12-15/hungary-premier-orban-sticks-to-maverick-path-as-u-s-ties-sour.
Somek, Alexander. 2014. *The Cosmopolitan Constitution*. Oxford: Oxford University Press.
The Chancellery of the Prime Minister. 2018. 'White Paper on the Reform of the Polish Judiciary'. www.premier.gov.pl/files/files/white_paper_en_full.pdf.
Tellér, Gyula. 2014. *Született-e Orbán-rendszer 2010 és 2014 között? [Was an Orbán system born between 2010 and 2014?]*. Nagyvilág.

Tripkovic, Bosko. 2017. *The Metaethics of Constitutional Adjudication*. Oxford: Oxford University Press.
Vinx, L. 2013. 'The Incoherence of Strong Popular Sovereignty.' *International Journal of Constitutional Law* 11: 101–124.
Walker, Neil. 2002. 'The Idea of Constitutional Pluralism'. *Modern Law Review* 65 (3): 317–59.
Weiler, J. H. H. 2003. 'In Defence of the Status Quo: Europe's Constitutional Sonderweg.' In *European Constitutionalism Beyond the State*, edited by J. H. H. Weiler and M. Wind, 7–20. Cambridge: Cambridge University Press.
Wyrzykowski, Miroslaw. 2019. 'Experiencing the Unimaginable: The Collapse of the Rule of Law in Poland.' *Hague Journal on the Rule of Law* 11: 417, 418.

22

Deconstructing Constitutional Identity in Light of the Turn to Populism

Michel Rosenfeld

INTRODUCTION

Gary Jacobsohn and I each published a book on constitutional identity the same year (Jacobsohn 2010, Rosenfeld 2010). Our approaches to the subject differ significantly, but, as I understand them, they are more complementary than divergent. Given that constitutional identity must transcend the mere fact of constitutional ordering or the actual content of a particular constitution, it emerges in the context of a dynamic process that must constantly weave together self-identity's two facets, namely sameness and selfhood. Indeed, as Paul Ricoeur has emphasized, the identity of the self is generated along two axes: sameness and selfhood (Ricoeur 1990). I am the same self that I was last week as my image in the mirror looks identical, but sameness does not account for how the fully grown adult that I am relates to the young adolescent I once was. In the latter case, it is the experience of selfhood that accounts for my identification with whom I once was, but with whom I am in most respects no longer identical. Analogously, constitutional identity belongs to a collective self that combines notions of sameness and selfhood, but there are several different conceptions of how the dynamic between the two may end up yielding a distinct constitutional identity. According to Jacobsohn, it is constitutional disharmony that drives the dynamic in question and the process involved is dialogical in nature. As he specifies,

> a constitution acquires an identity through experience ... [T]his identity exists neither as a discrete object of invention nor as a heavily encrusted essence embedded in a society's culture, requiring only to be discovered. Rather identity emerges dialogically and represents a mix of political aspirations and commitments that are expressive of a nation's past, as well as the determination of those within the society who seek ... to transcend that past. (Jacobsohn 2010, 7)

In essence, Jacobsohn's disharmony is caused by departures from the past manifested in the present or in a projected future and they relate to the content of the constitution or to its assumed social and political context. The disharmony at stake may be linked to great gaps or to more modest ones (Jacobsohn 2010, 23), and the dialogical process intended to foster unity through convergence toward a commonly shared constitutional identity.

Unlike Jacobsohn, my focus is above all dialectical, though it by no means minimizes the importance of dialogue. For me, constitutional identity is a meaning-endowing construct that aims to unify all those that are encompassed within a single constitutional order. Constitutional identity is distinguished from national identity – one can easily conceive of the French or German nation without reference to a constitution – but both are constructed and projected as what Benedict Anderson has labeled 'imagined communities' (Anderson 1991). Although both these identities may share elements in common, they must ultimately emerge as distinct. As I conceive it in its broadest terms, the place and function of constitutional identity are determined by the need for dialectical mediation of existing, evolving, and projected conflicts and tensions between poles of identity and poles of difference that divide those within the polity into self and other, and set the latter against those intended to remain beyond the bounds of the constitutional unit meant to be constructed or preserved. Conceiving of constitutional identity as belonging to an imagined community that must carve out a distinct self-image, I have argued that constitutional identity first emerges as a *lack* that must be overcome through a discursive process that relies on three principal interpretive tools: negation, metaphor, and metonymy (Rosenfeld 2010, 45–65). For example, in eighteenth-century France, the new constitutional project had to negate the *ancient regime*, but in order to project a positive image it had to reprocess material within the French heritage through metaphorical processes based on analogy and through metonymic processes based on displacements or relations of contiguity.

What is key, for present purposes, is that both Jacobsohn's dialogical approach and my dialectical one aim to allow for the greatest possible common unity and cohesion within the relevant constitutional unit. Populism, in contrast, is characterized by its commitment to subtract some long-established members of the constitutional unit within which it operates from its definition of "The People" (Müller 2016). More generally, constitutional identity as elaborated in pluralist settings committed to liberal constitutionalism emerges as a project of construction that aims at rallying all those concerned. As against that, present-day populist efforts to transform an existing liberal constitution into an illiberal one require altering the prevailing constitutional identity, but this seems for the most part to require deconstruction rather than construction in order to achieve exclusion of some of those who were theretofore an integral part of the extant imagined constitutional community. How constitutional identity deconstruction differs from construction is not self-evident as the latter includes the interpretive tools of negation and centrifugal metonymy alongside that of unifying metaphor. In what follows, I will first briefly describe how the same interpretive tools fare in projects of populist deconstruction as contrasted to projects of liberal constitutional construction. I will then focus on populist appropriation of the process of constitutional identity formation and finally explore whether the populist imagined constitutional community is ultimately consistent with or destructive of the core ideals of modern constitutionalism.

22.1 CONSTRUCTING AND DECONSTRUCTING CONSTITUTIONAL IDENTITY THROUGH NEGATION, METAPHOR, AND METONYMY

Revolutionary constitutions, as exemplified by the American and French late eighteenth-century ones, are often characterized as creations *ex nihilo* (Preuss 1994). The new constitution negates the overthrown monarchical order and starts anew in the name of the people. Whatever its content, a new liberal constitution – that is, one that limits the powers of government, provides for the rule of law, guarantees certain fundamental rights, and secures a basic level of democracy – must project a positive identity to foster the allegiance of those who are to be subjected to it. Moreover, in its journey leading to a new, distinct constitutional identity, the image-creating and meaning-endowing process must combine discarding certain existing tokens of common identity; drawing from, aggregating, and stringing along others; while recharacterizing yet others, and moving them from one context to another. Thus, the old regime must be negated but some of its attributes that have a strong hold on national identity, such as past national heroes who warded off foreign enemies, artists, and culturally marking literature, must be reintroduced either through linkage to revolutionary heroes and cultural artifacts or through recontextualization to hide or dissimulate unwelcome linkages to the deposed regime. In this process, negation, metaphor, and metonymy may contribute to the elaboration of a constitutional identity either by working separately to fashion distinct images or by working together to chisel the same distinct identity-inducing image. Regardless of particulars, what binds all these efforts together in all cases involving liberal constitutions is the search for an all-inclusive image or narrative.

In the case of populism, on the other hand, the same tools of interpretation, image making, and narrative construction are used, but this with the purpose of disaggregating previously projected unifying constructs so as to set a part as the whole and to turn the latter against those newly left out. Thus, for example, a populist project may negate previously accepted narratives of origins – say that two ethnic groups co-founded the nation and constitutional unit preceding the turn to populism – in order to reinvent or recast them so as to foment animosity between those that populism portrays as belonging and those it seeks to divest of any common constitutional identity – say that one of the two ethnic groups that goes all the way back to the founding is now recast as a bunch of hostile intruders lacking any true allegiance to their country or to its constitutional mission. In the latter case, negation does the work of erasing the previous image of ethnic cooperation at the outset; metaphor that of linking together all the historical and imagined highlights that cast the now favored ethnic group as the legitimate bearer of peoplehood; and metonymy that of decontextualizing and recontextualizing historical and imagined narratives to portray the now disfavored ethnic group as strangers or enemies worthy of exclusion from the benefits of peoplehood.

The difference between liberal constitutional identity construction and illiberal populism's identity deconstruction can be well illustrated by reference to the notion of "We the People" prominently at the head of the Preamble to the 1787 US Constitution. Taken by itself, "We the People" amounts to an empty signifier and therefore, from the standpoint of constitutional identity, as a lack open to a wide range of interpretations and paths to being filled in. Indeed, when contrasting "the people" to "the nation," peoplehood looms as much more undifferentiated than nationhood. Any nation must be an imagined community with a distinct identity. The French nation cannot thus be confused with the German or the American one. But who is "the people" in any of these three national settings? Were women part of the French or the American people at the time that both countries carried out revolutions that dislodged the sovereignty of the monarch to invest it in their respective peoples? The French and American peoples became sovereign, but in neither country were women given the vote or any official voice within the constitutional unit to which they had become subjected. Or were French and American women nevertheless part of their respective peoples as they belonged to the same territory, society, and national and political spheres as did the empowered men with whom they shared their lives?

The "We the People" that gave itself the US Constitution certainly did not include the black slaves or the women who were inhabitants in the newly independent country. Moreover, the mere constitutional legitimation of slavery (U.S. Constitution, Art. 1 Sec. 2)[1] disqualified the 1787 US Constitution from admission within the precincts of liberal constitutionalism. But after the stain of slavery was removed and women granted full citizenship, a retrospective bird's eye view of *who* the "We the People" has become over the past 150 years fits well within an inclusivist identitarian narrative. Indeed, today's US population is made up principally of the descendants of various waves of immigration spreading over centuries that have been incorporated – not without bumps and periodic regressions – into the citizenry in ways that at least partially emulate the metaphor of the "melting pot." The physiognomy of the present-day American people was certainly inconceivable when the 1787 Preamble was drafted, and the narrative of its growth and integration is fairly deemed inclusivist.

As against that, former US president Trump's nationalist-populist imagery and rhetoric was unabashedly exclusivist. Taken together, it peels off the attributes of

---

[1] Providing that non-free persons shall count as three-fifths of a free person for purposes of determining the number of representatives that each state is to be attributed within the US House of Representatives.

peoplehood from various groups who had gradually achieved greater integration into American peoplehood and nationhood. Trump started his presidential campaign by attacking immigrants from Mexico (Hee Lee 2015) in ways that demeaned the millions of US citizens of Mexican and other Latin American origin. One of his first presidential acts was the institution of a "Muslim ban" barring travel from several Muslim countries in the midst of inciting statements claiming that "Islam hates us" and suggesting that US Muslims could not be loyal Americans.[2] Although never explicitly embracing the mantle of white supremacy, Trump often associated with some of its proponents and used or repeated their rhetoric. Thus in 2017, in commenting on a march by fully armed Neo-Nazis in Charlottesville, Virginia, Trump insisted that there were some "fine people" among the rabidly anti-Semitic and racist marchers (Thrust and Haberman 2017). On future immigration, Trump indicated that he wished to close the door to those originating in Black Africa while welcoming those hailing from Norway (Davis, Kaplan, and Stolberg 2018). Finally, in the midst of the COVID-19 crisis which he handled very poorly, Trump turned to blaming China and to referring to the disease as "the Chinese virus" (Jakes, Rogers, and Swanson 2020). This resulted in an alarming rise in anti-Asian-American hate crimes (Hswen et al. 2021). As Trump lost his bid for re-election and did not actually undertake any constitutional transformations, the above examples are only suggestive of what a Trumpian populist constitutional identity would consist of. Finally, a Trumpian constitutional identity would go well beyond peeling off layers of American peoplehood. Trump has attacked the US press as "the enemies of the people" (Davis 2018) and Democrats, one of the two political parties with significant power in shaping the country's democratic destiny, as "un-American" and as liable to "destroy our country" if allowed to govern (Taylor 2018). Presumably, a Trumpian constitutional identity would have to negate the place of pride in freedom of the press traditionally inscribed in the American constitutional firmament – as attested by proud proclamations of American constitutional superiority over its British counterpart in the context of Prime Minister Margaret Thatcher's restrictions on her country's press during the Falklands war (Harris 1983). Also, although not in the Constitution itself, the American two-party political system is now well ingrained within the country's prevailing constitutional identity. A Trumpian constitutional revolution would therefore have to negate or recontextualize that latter identitarian mainstay in order to ban or disempower the "un-American" Democrats.[3]

---

[2] *See* EXEC. ORDER NO. 13769, 82 FR 8977 (2017).
[3] It should be noted that during the Cold War, the American Communist Party was frequently referred to as un-American. That characterization is, however, distinguishable to the extent that it was embedded in rhetoric that portrayed the US Communists as traitors in the service of the Soviet Union. Whereas a Trumpian may analogize communist or socialist policies with those of the Democrats insofar as predicting that they would all lead to economic and political bankruptcy, accusing the Democrats as traitors and mere agents of a hostile foreign power is quite unlikely to gain any traction.

22.2 POPULIST DECONSTRUCTIVE APPROPRIATION OF THE PROCESS OF CONSTITUTIONAL IDENTITY FORMATION

Before inquiring into an actual example of populist constitutional identity formation, that of Orbán's Hungary, a few preliminary observations are in order to better ground the distinction between construction aimed at unity, and deconstruction aimed at exclusion. That liberal constitutionalism aims at a unified constitutional identity does not entail that it succeeds or that, even if it does, the resulting imagined constitutional community is to be deemed equally fair to all involved or not subject to pressure for changes or adjustments. Thus, for example, Quebec did not acquiesce to the 1982 Canadian Constitution, has flirted with secession, and has wanted recognition within Canada as "a distinct society."[4] Nevertheless, efforts at Canadian constitutional unity and accommodation have been ongoing between Quebec and the remaining Canadian provinces as attested by the initially agreed upon but ultimately unsuccessful 1987 Lake Meech Accord.[5] Similarly, the 1978 Spanish Constitution was meant to be inclusive of Catalonia through the creation of "autonomous communities" and understood as such by the latter (Bofill 2019). And it is only in more recent times that tensions, calls for Catalonia's independence, and profound differences regarding Spanish constitutional identity have intensified – as evinced by the controversial Spanish Constitutional Court decision invalidating Catalonia's law providing for a referendum on the question of independence.[6] More generally, even in countries with no threats of secession, the prevailing constitutional identity is always subject to change and to interpretive disputes among those with a more pluralistically inclusive identity vision and those with a more restrictive one.[7]

Turning now to populism, first a distinction must be drawn between a case such as that of Trumpism in the US, with no direct constitutional purchase to date, and that of Orbán in Hungary where a new populist constitution actually became effective in 2012.[8] Movements, such as Trumpism may have an effect *within* an existing constitutional identity by reinforcing certain sides of existing splits – for example, expansive interpretations of executive powers and restrictive views regarding the right to abortion – but they do not of themselves transform an identitarian project oriented toward unity into one dominated by the will to exclude.

---

[4] Reference Re Secession of Quebec, 2 S.C.R. 217 (1998).
[5] Meech Lake Accord, Draft Constitutional Amendment (1987).
[6] See Law on the Referendum on Self-determination of Catalonia (Spanish Constitutional Court) Judgment 114/2017 (October 17, 2017).
[7] In the US, one area that clearly illustrates this is the one relating to the constitutional rights of the LGBTQ community. For a discussion of Justice Kennedy's inclusivist use of metaphoric analogy in this area, see Rosenfeld 2010, Ch.3.
[8] Magyarország Alaptörvénye [The Fundamental Law of Hungary], Alaptörvény (Jan. 1, 2012).

Regarding populism itself, two important points must be stressed at the outset. First, populism is not necessarily tied to constitutionalism; and second, although populism privileges exclusion it nonetheless cannot succeed without carving out inclusion. Relating to the first point, based on Sartori's distinction between substantive or *garantiste* constitutions and merely formal or "façade" ones (Sartori 1962; Sajo 2021), populism can certainly function without a substantive power-limiting constitution. This would happen under the authoritarian rule of a charismatic leader who is venerated with near-religious fervor by the sector of the population within the relevant polity that has been designated as *the* people while maintaining oppressive control over all those now cast as the regime's internal enemies. Concerning the second point, on the other hand, all constitutional identity formation must include both inclusion and exclusion. Indeed, any division between self and other can only become determinate on account of certain correlated inclusions and exclusions. What is crucially different between liberal constitutionalism and populism boils down to the following: the former seeks to manage the interplay between inclusions and exclusions so as to carve out the unity of the community of individuals and groups assembled into a constitutional unit; populism, in contrast, reconstitutes the unit in question by deploying an interplay of inclusions and exclusions meant to culminate in the expulsion from full membership of certain individuals and groups who had enjoyed the full benefits of peoplehood within the about to be replaced constitutional order. Moreover, upon such expulsion, those spared are poised to migrate from their former status as a part of the people to that of the whole people, thus becoming entitled to (exclusive) inclusion (as full-fledged members) within the nascent populist constitutional order.

Orbán's Hungary provides a propitious case study because his populist party and its parliamentary allies carried out a substantive constitutional transformation that procedurally and, on the surface at least, satisfied *garantiste* minimums. Many experts on the region have highly disputed that Orbán's constitution amounts to more than a façade (Sadurski 2019), but assessment of these criticisms is better postponed till Part III below. Hungary's populism is mainly ethnic-based, but Orbán has also embraced the Christian religion against what he has characterized as the evils of Western European liberalism (Brubaker 2017; Coakley 2021). Furthermore, Orbán has sided with the common Hungarian everyday citizen against the cosmopolitan elites whom he has personalized by demonizing George Soros, an American philanthropist who happens to be a Jewish Holocaust survivor of Hungarian origin (Foer 2019).

The identitarian particulars of Orbán's populist constitution are clearly framed by the Preamble to his 2012 Constitution. This new constitution, meant to replace the extant liberal one that prevailed in the country since its transition from communism,[9] was tellingly undertaken in the name of "the Hungarian Nation" instead of

---

[9] Ironically, the constitution in question was the 1949 Socialist one which became a liberal democratic one through radical use of the amendment process (Kovács and Tóth 2011).

"the People of Hungary."[10] Consistent with this, the Preamble's first proclamation states: "We are proud that our king Saint Stephen built the Hungarian State on solid ground and made our country a part of Christian Europe one thousand years ago."[11] To this, the Preamble adds that "We recognize the role of Christianity in preserving nationhood" and that "we honour the Holy Crown, which embodies the constitutional continuity of Hungary's statehood and the unity of the nation. We do not recognize the suspension of our historical constitution due to foreign occupations."[12] Pointedly, this embrace of Christianity as a constitutional foundation seems difficult to take at face value as, contrary to neighboring populist Poland where religious belief has a profound imprint, Hungary is one of the least religious countries in all of Europe.[13] Also, as one commentator put it, "Orbán's embrace of Christian nationalism is a relatively recent turn for a once-avowed atheist" (Tharoor 2015).

The constitutionally relevant identitarian consequences of the combined references to the Hungarian nation, Christianity, and the rejection of the periods of foreign occupation can be interpretively accounted for in terms of a transformation of Hungary's imagined community into a populist one. Starting with religion, all of negation, metaphor, and metonymy are enlisted to achieve an uprooting from liberal constitutionalism to launch a reorientation toward populism.

Grounding the new constitution in Christianity negates the non-religious Hungarian people's immediately preceding liberal secular constitutional tradition. Christianity, moreover, is used metaphorically to link together Saint Stephen, the first king of Hungary in 1000, the Ottoman – and hence anti-Christian – invasion and occupation of Hungarian territory starting in 1521 and ending in in 1699 (Bohlen 1991; Brubaker 2017), the Soviet imposed (atheist) communist era from 1949 till 1989, and the post-communist threat to Christianity posed by secular cosmopolitan elites, including those at the helm of the EU. Finally, Christianity is used metonymically in that it is not the religion itself, but its appeal as a principal token of cultural identity that unifies the narrative of ethnic Hungarians projected as a unified and continuous nation (though one in captivity during the Ottoman and Soviet periods) from 1000 till 2012, the year of the constitutional turn to populism. Continuing with emphasis on the Hungarian *Nation*, in addition to its crucial linkage to (cultural) Christianity, it serves to distinguish between the ethnic Hungarians who are *the* people of 2012 and other Hungarian citizens, such as the country's Jews and Roma who, pursuant to the new constitution's Preamble, are "The nationalities living with us [who] form part of the

---

[10] See European Commission for Democracy Through Law (Venice Commission) Opinion 720/2013.
[11] Magyarország Alaptörvénye [The Fundamental Law of Hungary], Alaptörvény, pmbl. (2011).
[12] Magyarország Alaptörvénye (2011).
[13] "Church attendance is pretty low in Hungary ... According to the latest study, 'Beliefs about God across Time and Countries' by Tom W. Smith (University of Chicago), only 9.6% of the population has a strong belief in God as opposed to 35% in the United States and 25.8% in Ireland. Hungary is closer to Great Britain, Sweden, and the Czech Republic as far as religious devotion is concerned. At the same time the percentage of atheists is relatively high: 23.1%" (Hungarian Spectrum 2012).

Hungarian political community and are constituent parts of the State."[14] Accordingly, non-ethnic Hungarians excluded from the Hungarian nation, but included in their country's political sphere and counted as citizens of the Hungarian state become akin to second-class citizens deprived of full membership within the Hungarian people. Finally, the reference to explicit (constitutional) negation of foreign occupations has both a positive and a negative connotation: positively, it strengthens the image of a strong, free, continuously united nation and people bound together by ethnicity, religion, culture, and tradition; negatively, it is invoked to justify militance against Muslim immigration – which Orbán ruthlessly evoked while systematically denying entry to Syrian refugees at his borders (Tharoor 2015) – and to use the image of Soviet oppression against all enemies internal and external who a populist may cast as posing threats to the indissoluble link that unites Hungarian nationhood and peoplehood.

Constitutional identity narratives tend to be overdetermined and hence the above account is certainly subject to further elaboration and nuancing. To illustrate this, suffice it to briefly expand on the seeming paradox, inscribed in the 2012 Preamble, of at once investing Christianity with an ethno-national cultural valence that separates the Hungarians as descendants of King Stephen and with a pan-European unifying bond that links Hungary to the rest of the continent. The paradox involved is highlighted by Orbán's rejection of Western European secular liberalism and its "ruthless capitalism and selfish individualism," in favor of a national populist illiberal ethnocentric democracy (Müller 2014). Does that not stand against emphasizing whatever links together virtually the whole of Europe as Christian along a metaphoric axis that incorporates Eastern Orthodox and Western Catholic and Protestant Christianity as well as the attenuated mainly cultural Christian heritage prevalent in certain highly secularized countries, such as France or the UK? Upon closer consideration, the juxtaposition of Hungarian and European Christianity does bind together several facets of Orbán's nationalist-populist project from an identitarian standpoint. Hungary, as part of Christian Europe, performs an important identitarian nexus given the Hapsburg military victory that resulted in the end of Ottoman occupation of Hungarian territory;[15] the Austro-Hungarian Empire that gave Hungary its most glorious golden age both because of its unification with one of Europe's greatest powers and civilizations and because it gave Hungary sovereignty over the greatest proportion of ethnic Hungarians – such as those who at present are citizens of other countries such as Romania, Serbia, or Slovakia – that it ever had under its jurisdiction (Barberá and Vladisavljevic 2020); and the EU that provides Hungary financial support that Orbán needs to maintain his popularity among "his" people (Ash 2019). These European-wide connections may appear to pull Hungary away from populism, but Orbán has used them

---

[14] Magyarország Alaptörvénye [The Fundamental Law of Hungary], Alaptörvény pmbl. (2011).
[15] The Ottomans ceded Hungarian territory to Austria pursuant to the Carlowitz Treaty (1699). www.britannica.com/event/Treaty-of-Carlowitz.

to bolster his populist project. Indeed, he has used the Ottoman invasion image to promote not only a Hungarian anti-Muslim front but also to counter the EU pro-immigration and asylum-accommodating policies. Reminiscing the glory days of the Austro-Hungarian empire abruptly dismembered by the 1920 Trianon Treaty, Orbán and (even more so) his extreme right parliamentary allies have suggested that ideally Hungary and its new constitution should unify not only Hungarian nationals within the country's present borders, but also ethnic Hungarians who are currently citizens of neighboring countries, such as Romania, Serbia, and Slovakia. The Trianon Treaty has been characterized as a national tragedy for Hungary (Sandford and Magyar 2020) and some Hungarian politicians have toyed with the idea of incorporating ethnic Hungarians living in bordering contemporary countries into a "greater Hungary" (Barberá and Vladisavljevic 2020). Finally, Hungary's projection as being at once pro- and anti-EU definitely appears to serve Orbán's populist objectives. As a populist anti-European, Orbán protects the Hungarian nation against transnational cosmopolitanism. At the same time, by remaining within the EU and avoiding any Brexit-like movement, Orbán secures EU money for *his* people and those powerful "friends" that bolster his illiberal populist rule.

Taken out of its overall context, Hungary's populist constitutional identity building project differs little from that of its typical liberal counterpart insofar as they both proceed through a series of demarcations involving an interplay between inclusions and exclusions. It is important to emphasize, however, that taken as a whole the Hungarian populist project is above all exclusionary. And this is true of even its most far-reaching aspiration (which for now is nothing but a distant dream for some) of including all the ethnic Hungarians living beyond its current borders within a reconstituted "greater Hungary." On the face of it, that aspiration seems overwhelmingly inclusionary, but its realization seems inconceivable without some prior wars to annex now foreign-held territory with large clusters of ethnic Hungarians and without disenfranchizing the non-ethnic Hungarian Serbs, Slovaks, or Romanians who would assume second-class citizenship status in a newly formed greater Hungary.[16]

22.3 POPULIST EXCLUSIONARY CONSTITUTIONAL IDENTITY AND THE CORE IDEALS OF MODERN CONSTITUTIONALISM

As already noted, many experts have concluded that populist rule in Hungary and Poland does not square with the essentials of modern liberal constitutionalism. In defending the legitimacy of his newly minted 2012 Constitution, Orbán insisted that rejection of the "liberal understanding of society" and its "emphasis on

---

[16] It should also be pointed out that a large proportion of ethnic Hungarians living in neighboring countries have little desire to give up their current country of citizenship in order to become part of a greater Hungary (Terenzani, Francelova and Minarechova 2020).

accountability and checks and balances,"[17] and relying instead on periodic elections (he was re-elected in 2014, 2018, and 2022), national pride, Christianity, and family values, did not go against European democracy or constitutional rule. Instead, they were the expression of a *Kulturkampf* between his vision and that of the Western European Left (Müller 2014). Be that as it may, Orbán's more recent conduct as prime minister – including his securing virtually absolute powers from his parliament during the COVID-19 pandemic[18] – belies any good faith claim that his populist rule conforms with the mainstays of modern constitutionalism. Similarly, Poland's law and justice populist rule under Kaczynski's command has also gone heavily against constitutional essentials, and done so without even changing their constitution as, unlike Orbán, they have not enjoyed having the requisite majorities for doing so (Sadurski 2019, 4). Actually, at this writing, both Hungary and Poland are in conflict with EU institutions based on the latter's claims that the two countries have violated their obligations to adhere to the rule of law (Pronczuk 2021).[19]

Actual developments in Hungary or Poland, however, are not determinative of the larger question of whether exclusionary identarian populist constitutional narratives are ultimately compatible with modern constitutionalism ideals. Indeed, many liberal constitutions fall short of ideals without thereby negating the plausibility of adherence to the latter. In view of this, two questions emerge as crucial: first, are all populist exclusionary narratives inherently contrary to modern constitutional ideals; and second, are clearly exclusionary identitarian elements within liberal constitutions always cogently distinguishable from their populist counterparts?

With respect to contemporary populism, a distinction must be drawn between left-wing and right-wing populism (Tushnet 2018). Left-wing populism may be class oriented and anti-elite, but it arguably raises no identitarian issues of its own. Indeed, one may contend that present-day liberal constitutionalism has facilitated the greatly increasing inequalities in wealth that have posed problems in many Western democracies and that left-wing populism might figure as an antidote for shifting powers from the richest 1 percent to more popular classes. At least in theory, such populism does not exclude anyone and accordingly, it will not be further addressed here. In contrast, right-wing populism, such as that in Hungary and Poland, excludes on the basis of ethnic, national, or religious identity. A constitutional identity that favors one among many such groups within the polity to the point of depriving those excluded from some of the key attributes of peoplehood is in obvious contradiction with modern constitutionalism's universalist aspirations within the relevant constitutional unit. Moreover, constitutional identity-based

---

[17] Viktor Orbán as cited in Müller 2014.
[18] *Magyar Közlöny* Act XII of 2020 on the containment of coronavirus (as in force on March 31, 2020) (Hung.). https://perma.cc/9LMR-YS3L.
[19] Ref. No. P 7/20, POL. CONST. TRIBUNAL (2021); Case C-204/21, EUROPEAN COMMISSION V REPUBLIC OF POLAND, 2021 E.C.R. 878; Case C-791/19, EUROPEAN COMMISSION V. REPUBLIC OF POLAND, 2021 E.C.R. 592.

exclusion seems potentially more pernicious than exclusion within the constitution itself or exclusionary judicial interpretations of constitutional provisions. And that is because identitarian markers that solidify the bonds of solidarity meant to sustain the imagined community coalescing into a distinct constitutional self seem particularly prone to becoming internalized in ways that suppress or dull the capacity or desire to engage in critical appraisal. An outright racist or religiously biased constitutional provision or judicial opinion appears certain to provoke objections in a country that purports to live according to the dictates of liberal constitutionalism. In contrast, just as the national imagined community may engender strong affective bonds of solidarity coupled with strong reprobation of those who take exception, so too the prevalent imagined constitutional community may consciously and subconsciously place its strong imprint on all that is constitutional while at the same time harboring hostility toward those who refuse to go along.

Turning now to the second question posed above, even fully admitting that right-wing populism's exclusionary identitarian mission is incompatible with liberal constitutionalism, how can that be consistently distinguished from outright exclusionary narratives that have been incorporated into the identity of seemingly indisputably liberal constitutions? For example, some constitutions in multi-ethnic countries prohibit the institution of ethnic-based political parties (Constitution of Bulgaria, Art. 11 Sec. 4). Similarly, some religiously pluralistic polities constitutionally enshrine an official state religion (Rosenfeld 2020). The multi-ethnic polity case with ethnic plurality inscribed in its national identity but negated in its constitutional identity may well ultimately evince an inclusionary rather than an exclusionary objective. Indeed, in a country where there are serious ethnic tensions, prohibiting ethnocentric political parties may lead quite plausibly to greater mutual accommodation and to reduced opportunities for ethnic conflict. The case of the official state religion may at times come closer to the line but is still much more likely to be consistent with inclusionary rather than exclusionary designs. In some cases, such as that of the UK, the official state status of the Church of England looms as mainly ceremonial, and it does not perceptively impact equal toleration of the other religions practiced within the country. In other cases, such as that of the official state Greek Orthodox Church in Greece, the latter does enjoy enough political clout to prevent strict equal toleration of minority religions within the polity (Rosenfeld 2020). Nevertheless, as freedom of religion is widely protected under the Greek Constitution (Constitution of Greek, Art. 13), the advantages of the state religion in Greece have no exclusionary effects comparable to those associated with the denial of peoplehood to segments of the population in right-wing populist constitutional polities.

CONCLUSION

In conclusion, leaving aside whether a thoroughly right-wing populist constitutionally grounded regime may sustain over time limitations on the powers of government or unflinching adherence to the rule of law, the preceding analysis clearly indicates that such a regime seems bound to fail to meet the minimum identitarian requirements of liberal constitutionalism. Such populist regimes require predominantly exclusionary constructs relating to constitutional identity, which seem bound to run squarely against the normative prerequisites of modern constitutionalism.

REFERENCES

Anderson, Benedict. 1991. *Imagined Communities: Reflections on the Origin and Spread of Nationalism*. London; New York: Verso.
Ash, Timothy Garton. 2019. "Europe Must Stop This Disgrace: Viktor Orbán Is Dismantling Democracy." *The Guardian*, June 20, 2019. www.theguardian.com/commentisfree/2019/jun/20/viktor-orban-democracy-hungary-eu-funding.
Barberá, Marcel Gascón and Vladisavljevic, Anja. 2020. "Orbán's 'Greater Hungary' Map Creates Waves in Neighborhood." *Balkan Insight*, May 7, 2020. https://balkaninsight.com/2020/05/07/orbans-greater-hungary-map-creates-waves-in-neighbourhood/.
Bofill, Hèctor López. 2019. "Hubris, Constitutionalism, and 'The Indissoluble Unity of the Spanish Nation': The Repression of Catalan Secessionist Referenda in Spanish Constitutional Law." *International Journal of Constitutional Law* 17: 943–969.
Bohlen, Celestine. 1991. "Glimpsing Hungary's Ottoman Past." *New York Times*, March 10, 1991. www.nytimes.com/1991/03/10/travel/glimpsing-hungary-s-ottoman-past.html.
Brubaker, Rogers. 2017. "Between Nationalism and Civilizationalism: The European Populist Moment in Comparative Perspective." *Ethnic and Racial Studies* 40 (8): 1191–1226.
Coakley, Amanda. 2021. "Hungary's Orbán Tries to Snatch Mantle of Christian Democracy." *Foreign Policy*, August 3, 2021. https://foreignpolicy.com/2021/08/03/hungary-orban-fidesz-christian-democracy-right/.
Davis, Julie Hirschfeld, Sheryl Gay Stolberg, and Thomas Kaplan. 2018. "Trump Alarms Lawmakers With Disparaging Words for Haiti and Africa." *New York Times*, January 11, 2018. www.nytimes.com/2018/01/11/us/politics/trump-shithole-countries.html.
Davis, William P. 2018. "'Enemy of the People': Trump Breaks Out This Phrase During Moments of Peak Criticism." *New York Times*, July 19, 2018. www.nytimes.com/2018/07/19/business/media/trump-media-enemy-of-the-people.html.
Foer, Franklin. 2019. "Viktor Orbán's War on Intellect." *The Atlantic*, June 2019. www.theatlantic.com/magazine/archive/2019/06/george-soros-viktor-orban-ceu/588070/.
Harris, Robert. 1983. *Gotcha!: The Media, the Government and the Falklands Crisis*. London: Faber & Faber.
Hswen, Yulin, et al. 2021. "Association of '#covid19' Versus '#chinesevirus' with Anti-Asian Sentiments on Twitter: March 9–23, 2020." *American Journal of Public Health* 111: 956–964.
Hungarian Spectrum. 2012. "Church and State in Hungary." April 21, 2012. https://hungarianspectrum.org/2012/04/21/church-and-state-in-hungary/.
Jacobsohn, Gary. 2010. *Constitutional Identity*. Cambridge: Harvard University Press.
Jakes, Lara, Katie Rogers, and Ana Swanson. 2020. "Trump Defends Using 'Chinese Virus' Label, Ignoring Growing Criticism." *New York Times*, March 18, 2020. www.nytimes.com/2020/03/18/us/politics/china-virus.html.
Kovács, Kriszta and Tóth, Gábor Attila. 2011. "Hungary's Constitutional Transformation." *European Constitutional Law Review* 7: 183–203.

Lee, Michele Ye Hee. 2015. "Donald Trump's False Comments Connecting Mexican Immigrants and Crime." *The Washington Post*, July 8, 2015. www.washingtonpost.com/news/fact-checker/wp/2015/07/08/donald-trumps-false-comments-connecting-mexican-immigrants-and-crime/.

Müller, Jan-Werner. 2014. "Moscow's Trojan Horse: In Europe's Ideological War, Hungary Picks Putinism," *Foreign Affairs*, August 6, 2014. www.foreignaffairs.com/central-europe/moscows-trojan-horse.

Müller, Jan-Werner. 2016. *What is Populism?* Philadelphia: University of Pennsylvania Press.

Preuss, Ulrich K. 1994. "Constitutional Power Making for the New Polity: Some Deliberations on the Relations between Constituent Power and the Constitution." In *Constitutionalism, Identity, Difference and Legitimacy: Theoretical Perspectives*, edited by Michel Rosenfeld, 143–164. Durham: Duke University Press.

Pronczuk, Monika. 2021. "Europe Tightens Purse Strings to Try to Pressure Poland and Hungary." *New York Times*, October 8, 2021. www.nytimes.com/2021/09/24/world/europe/hungary-poland-eu.html.

Ricoeur, Paul. 1990. *Soi-même comme un autre*. Paris: Seuil.

Rosenfeld, Michel. 2010. *The Identity of the Constitutional Subject: Selfhood, Citizenship, Culture and Community*. London: Routledge.

Rosenfeld, Michel. 2020. "Constitution and Secularism: A Western Account." In *Handbook on Constitutions and Religion*, edited by Susanna Mancini, 21–40. Cheltenham: Edward Elgar Publishing.

Sadurski, Wojciech. 2019. *Poland's Constitutional Breakdown*. Oxford: Oxford University Press.

Sajo, Andras. 2021. *Ruling by Cheating: Governance in Illiberal Democracy*. Cambridge: Cambridge University Press.

Sandford, Alasdair and Magyar, Ádám. 2020. "Trianon Trauma: Why Is the Peace Treaty Signed 100 Years Ago Seen as a National Tragedy for Hungary?" *Euronews*, June 4, 2020. www.euronews.com/2020/06/04/trianon-trauma-why-is-the-peace-treaty-signed-100-years-ago-seen-as-a-national-tragedy.

Sartori, Giovanni. 1962. "Constitutionalism: A Preliminary Discussion." *The American Political Science Review* 56: 853–864.

Taylor, Jessica. 2018. "Trump: Democrats 'Un-American,' 'Treasonous' during State of the Union." *NPR*, February 6, 2018. www.npr.org/2018/02/05/583447413/trump-democrats-un-american-treasonous-during-state-of-the-union.

Tharoor, Ishaan. 2015. "Hungary's Orbán Invokes Ottoman Invasion to Justify Keeping Refugees Out." *The Washington Post*, September 4, 2015. www.washingtonpost.com/news/worldviews/wp/2015/09/04/hungarys-orban-invokes-ottoman-invasion-to-justify-keeping-refugees-out/.

Thrust, Glen and Haberman, Maggie. 2017. "Trump Gives White Supremacists an Unequivocal Boost." *New York Times*, August 15, 2017. www.nytimes.com/2017/08/15/us/politics/trump-charlottesville-white-nationalists.html.

Terenzani, Michaela, Nina Hrabovska Francelova, and Radka Minarechova. 2020. "Slovak election to test Orbán's clout among ethnic Hungarians." *Reporting Democracy*, February 12, 2020. https://balkaninsight.com/2020/02/12/slovak-election-to-test-orbans-clout-among-ethnic-hungarians/.

Tushnet, Mark. 2018. "Comparing Right-Wing and Left-Wing Populism." In *Constitutional Democracy in Crisis?* edited by Mark A. Graber, Sanford Levinson, and Mark Tushnet, 639–650. Oxford: Oxford University Press.

23

Unconstitutional Constitutional Identities in The European Union

Pietro Faraguna

23.1 CONSTITUTIONAL IDENTITY: THE EUROPEAN SONDERWEG OF A UNIVERSAL CONCEPT

Terminological ambiguity and conceptual contestation raise serious challenges to any academic discussion around the notion of identity. Within this ambiguity, the expression 'constitutional identity' has been loaded with a rapidly changing emotional content: twenty years ago, it seemed to be a much more acceptable alternative if compared with the old concept of sovereignty. Nowadays, the scholarly debate seems to condemn the use, and particularly, the abuse of the concept (Halmai 2018; Kelemen and Pech 2018; Fabbrini and Sajó 2019; Tripkovic 2020; Scholtes 2021).

Constitutional identity is certainly a global concept,[1] as the debate hosted in this volume witnesses, but some specificities in the European constitutional experience are clearly emerging. Within the frame of the European public law debate, constitutional identity is far from a novel notion. On the contrary, the notion emerges from the basic scholarly foundations of contemporary constitutional law, starting from the seminal work of Carl Schmitt (Schmitt 1928). An entire chapter of *Verfassungslehre* is devoted to the exploration of the concept of constitutional identity though, where Schmitt claims that the power of constituted powers to amend the constitution only exists 'under the presupposition that the identity and continuity of the constitution as an entirety is preserved' (Schmitt 2008, 150).

However, recent developments around this concept suggest that there is a peculiar European *Sonderweg* in the way of approaching the concept. Among the many reasons that may illustrate this peculiarity, two of them seem particularly remarkable. First, Europe is a small continent with deep legal integration and wide differentiation of legal regimes. Second, EU law provides for an identity clause in Article 4(2) TEU, a unique example of a constitutionalization of the legal concept of identity in modern supranational constitutionalism.

---

[1] The universal character of the concept brightly emerges from the seminal works of Gary Jacobsohn and Michel Rosenfeld (Rosenfeld 2009; Jacobsohn 2010).

The two elements are intertwined: the EU has an identity clause, as the EU needs one. The EU needs one because the EU is a relatively small territory characterized by significant legal heterogeneity. As usual, constitutional law follows history, and history follows politics, while politics follows society. Therefore, an historical perspective may be an illuminating one in the analysis of the concept of constitutional identity from a European perspective. In this chapter, I will briefly explore what I consider a story of success (the legalization of the concept of constitutional identity in the EU) and conclude by investigating some current concerns and challenges arising from some new transformations of this key concept.

23.2 CONSTITUTIONAL IDENTITY IN THE EU: ITS POLITICAL ROOTS AND LEGAL TRANSFORMATION

The identity clause in EU law was first introduced in the Treaties of 1992. Ahead of the introduction of the clause with the Treaty of Maastricht, some constitutional courts of EU member states – particularly the Italian *Corte costituzionale* (Cartabia 1990; Faraguna 2015), and the German *Bundesverfassungsgericht* (Polzin 2016) – already engaged a judicial dialogue with the European Court of Justice (CJEU) around possible tools of protection of national constitutional peculiarities before 1992. However, it was only with the approval of the Treaty of Maastricht that the Treaties were complemented with an explicit clause providing for the principle of respect of member states' national identities. At the time of the Maastricht Treaty, the terms of the clause were rather vague and ambiguous. The introduction of the clause was considered a wise point of balance of colliding forces: on the one side, the centripetal force pushing in the direction of a stronger and deeper political integration; on the other side, a State-centered centrifugal reluctance to transfer too many state competences at the supranational level. Against this background, and to make a long story short, the political turn marked by the Treaty of Maastricht has been counterbalanced through the introduction of some legal tools with the aim of reassuring member states and their concerns about the impact of the new path of the European integration process on the integrity of their statehood. These legal tools include the protocol on subsidiarity, a significant number of opt-outs, the design of differentiated integration tools, and, finally the principle of respect of member states' national identities (on these developments see further Faraguna 2016).

For some decades, the value of the identity clause has mostly been considered only as a political statement: Among the reassuring tools in the process of balancing mentioned above, the identity clause was the less legally impacting tool within the package. The clause did not make any explicit reference to constitutional elements and textually referred to 'national identity', and – above all – it was kept outside the jurisdiction of the Court of Justice of the EU. Therefore, the clause was considered rather as an interpretative complement or as a political statement, than a proper constitutional provision. However, the political message of the identity clause was very clear and rather precious, particularly from the perspective of those countries in Central and Eastern Europe that, after decades of limitation of sovereignty due to the soviet influence, viewed the subjugation under new 'European' ties with understandable suspicion (Bartole 2020). The language of identity was considered far more acceptable compared with the language of sovereignty (Weiler 2002).

The legal impact of the identity clause in its Maastricht formulation has been rather limited. Between 1992 and 2009 (when the Treaty of Lisbon amended its formulation), the clause has never been used in any decision of the Court. However, implicit references to the identity clause are usually recognized in a group of decisions issued before the reformulation of the clause by the Treaty of Lisbon in 2009: among these cases, *Anita Groener*,[2] *Omega*,[3] *Grogan*,[4] *Re Azores*,[5] *Gibraltar*[6] are the most famous. In this stream of case law, the CJEU did not make explicit reference to the identity clause, but it implicitly referred to it.

The situation has changed, both in the Treaties and in the legal consequences, after the reformulation of the identity clause in the Treaty of Lisbon in 2009. The Treaty of Lisbon rephrased the identity clause and enhanced its legal and constitutional nature. In its current formulation, the clause makes explicit reference to the member states' 'fundamental structures, political and constitutional'. Moreover, the Treaty of Lisbon brought Art. 4(2) TEU under the jurisdiction of the CJEU. Nonetheless, the impact of this reformulation on the case law of the CJEU was rather light. In fact, even if it is true that after the adoption of the Lisbon Treaty, Art. 4(2) TEU made it finally and openly into the legal reasoning of the CJEU, the impact of the rephrasing of the clause on the CJEU case law should not be overestimated.

If we screen in detail the most important cases where the identity clause and identity-related arguments made it into the legal reasoning of the Court, we realize that the legalization of the identity clause did not have a revolutionary impact on CJEU case law. The CJEU adopted a cautious and self-restrained approach in the interpretation of the clause even after its constitutionalization: the clause made it into the legal reasoning of some decisions of the CJEU; however, the number of cases is limited and their constitutional tone is, in my opinion, rather poor.

On a different yet connected front, there are many more cases in which the identity clause was invoked by the referring courts and/or by national governments intervening in the hearings, but not picked up by the CJEU: *Torresi*[7] and

---

[2] Case C-379/87, Anita Groener and the Minister for Education and the City of Dublin Vocational Education Committee, 1989 E.C.R. 3967.
[3] Case C-36/02, Omega Spielhallen und Automatenaufstellungs-GmbH v. Oberbürgermeisterin der Bundesstadt Bonn, 2004 E.C.R. I-9641.
[4] Case C-159/90, Society for the Protection of Unborn Children Ireland Ltd. v. Stephen Grogan and Others, 1991 E.C.R. 4685.
[5] Case C-88/03, Portugal v. Commission, 2006 E.C.R. I-7145.
[6] Case C-145/04, Spain v. United Kingdom, 2006 E.C.R. I-7961.
[7] Joined cases c-58/13 and C-59/13, Angelo Alberto Torresi and Pierfrancesco Torresi v Consiglio dell'Ordine degli Avvocati di Macerata, EU:C:2014:2088.

M.A.S. e M.B.[8] (also known as Taricco II) are quintessential examples of this dynamic. Paradoxically, the 'constitutionalisation' of the identity clause provided for by the Treaty of Lisbon had a much higher impact on the case law of member states' supreme and constitutional courts.[9] The number of cases where member states' constitutional and supreme courts opposed some sort of constitutional reservations to the principle of primacy of EU law significantly increased after 2009.

This trend began after the reformulation of the identity clause by the Treaty of Lisbon in 2009 but has escalated in the last five years. In fact, some early signals emerged when the Czech Constitutional Court issued its famous *Landtova* judgment,[10] declaring a decision of the CJEU ultra vires. Then, the German *BVerfG* engaged in a rough judicial dialogue with the CJEU in the famous *OMT* saga,[11] submitting its first reference for preliminary ruling in 2014, and finally, in its 'final judgment' of the case in June 2016, decided not to declare any act of European institution ultra vires, after the CJEU issued its reassurances with its decision in 2015.[12] In the same year, the *BVerfG* issued an important decision on the European Arrest Warrant,[13] where identity-related arguments have been used to perform a peculiar 'national constitutional identity-oriented interpretation' of EU law. Some years later, the German *BVerfG* was involved in a new saga. In the so-called *Weiss* saga, the Constitutional Court of Germany – for the first time in the history of its European case law – declared an act of the European Central Bank (ECB), along with the *Weiss* decision of the CJEU[14] (upholding the validity of the mentioned act of the ECB) to be ultra vires.[15]

Some years earlier, in 2016, the Hungarian Constitutional Court issued a substantially EU law 'unfriendly' decision;[16] developing a fundamental rights review and an ultra vires review, the latter composed of a sovereignty review and an identity review, by explicitly making reference to the case law of the *BVerfG*. Then,

---

[8] Case C-42/17, M.A.S. and M.B., EU:C:2015:555.
[9] In this analysis, I will consider both groups of cases where constitutional identity emerges openly and cases where it emerges in disguise (under different tags as sovereignty control, ultra vires review, counter-limits and similar notions, etc.). In fact, the legal reasoning of many of these decisions does not rely on constitutional identity as a central argument to support its legal effects, but is rather based on the principle of conferral and the connected ultra vires review, "a rather clear-cut concept that limits actions emanating from the EU to its competences manifested in the Treaties" in this sense Spieker 2020, 264. However, the identity and ultra vires reviews are independent, but related concepts, in particular when a violation of the democratic principle is at stake. See BVerfG, BvR 2728/13, OMT I, para 27. See further Calliess 2019, 175.
[10] Czech Constitutional Court, Judgment of 31 January 2012, case no. Pl. ÚS 5/12, *Slovak Pensions XVII*. See comments by Komárek 2012; Kühn 2016.
[11] On the impact of the OMT saga on the national constitutional identity discourse, see Claes and Reestman 2015, 917.
[12] Case C-62/14, *Gauweiler and others*.
[13] *BVerfG*, Order of 15 December 2015, 2 BvR 2735/14.
[14] Case C-493/17, *Weiss and Others* [2018], ECLI:EU:C:2018:1000.
[15] *BVerfG*, BvR 859/15 – 2 BvR 1651/15 – 2 BvR 2006/15 – 2 BvR 980/16, 5 May 2020.
[16] Constitutional Court of Hungary, Decision 22/2016 (XII. 5.) AB.

the Danish Supreme Court ruled a CJEU decision as ultra vires.[17] The Italian Constitutional Court engaged in a vibrant judicial dialogue with the CJEU in the so-called *Taricco* saga.[18]

Among the recent cases challenging EU law authority in the member states, the 'Taricco saga' seems to provide the most topical example of the above-illustrated slightly paradoxical developments. In fact, the 'constitutionalisation of national identity' provided by the post-Lisbon Article 4(2) TEU formulation has impacted the understanding of constitutional identity by the member states' national courts much more than the CJEU's case law.

While the Constitutional court of Italy, in its reference for a preliminary ruling, expressly invoked the protection of 'constitutional identity', and explicitly referred to Article 4(2) TEU, the CJEU avoided referring to identity in its legal reasoning while grounding its accommodating decision on the territory of common constitutional traditions. It is extremely telling that the CJEU decision on *M.A.S. M.B.*[19] (also known as 'Taricco II') did not even mention the word 'identity' once.

23.3 CONSTITUTIONAL IDENTITY FROM ITS USE TO ITS ABUSE

In light of the briefly overviewed developments, the legal scholarship signalled the light impact of the constitutionalization of the identity clause, and signalled, in the best case, the lack of utility of the notion. While in the worst case, the legal scholarship denounced the dangers arising from constitutional identity, and specifically from its abuse. The abuse of the notion emerged in particular under two circumstances I only mentioned marginally in the previous list.

The first occasion was the infamous, above-mentioned decision of the already captured Hungarian Constitutional Court, where the Court assisted the Orbán Government in affirming, with a legally rather sophisticated decision, that the EU policy of assigning quotas in the relocation of migrants consisted in a violation of Hungarian constitutional identity.

The second occasion was the explicit invocation of constitutional identity by the Polish Government in defence of its heavily criticized judicial reform, illegitimately packing the Polish higher courts, later culminated in the decision by the Constitutional Tribunal of October 2021,[20] openly challenging the principle of primacy of EU law. In 2018, the government affirmed that differences in the

---

[17] Supreme Court of Denmark, Case no. 15/2014 *Dansk Industri*.
[18] Italian Constitutional Court, order 24/2017 (in the so-called *Taricco* saga).
[19] Case C-42/17, M.A.S. and M.B. [2017] (Paris 2017; Piccirilli 2018; Scaccia 2020).
[20] Polish Constitutional Tribunal, Case K 3/21. An official translation of the summary of the decision is available on the website of the Tribunal: https://trybunal.gov.pl/en/hearings/judgments/art/11662-ocena-zgodnosci-z-konstytucja-rp-wybranych-przepisow-traktatu-o-unii-europejskiej.

composition of the judiciary were a matter of constitutional identity. In the words of the White Paper on the Reform of the Polish Judiciary published in 2018, 'it is obvious that there are differences in legal systems within the EU, this follows from the separate constitutional identities of individual states, and this diversity is protected by the TEU' (Chancellery of the Prime Minister of Poland 2018). The White Paper expressly referred to the case law of the German Constitutional Court on identity, as well as the European Court of Justice's case law on Art. 4(2) TEU, in order to corroborate its argument.

Then, with a decision issued in October 2021, anticipated by some signals in July 2021,[21] the Polish Tribunal held that the first and the second subparagraphs of Article 1 TEU have allowed for a new stage of European integration, whereby the EU institutions act beyond the limits of competences enshrined in the Treaties and transferred by Poland in accordance with Article 90 of the Polish Constitution. In particular, the Tribunal challenged the second subparagraph of Article 1 in which the TEU is described as marking 'a new stage in the process of creating an ever closer union among the peoples of Europe'. According to the judgment, this new stage of integration, in which the CJEU's competencies go beyond those conferred on the EU, is incompatible with Articles 2 and 8 of the Polish Constitution according to which the Republic of Poland is a democratic state, and the constitution is its supreme law.

The Tribunal ruled then that Articles 2 and 19(1) TEU are incompatible with the Polish Constitution insofar as they allow lower national courts and the Polish Supreme Court to disapply the Constitution. Specifically, the Polish constitutional court referred to the well-known judicial saga concerning the procedure for the appointment of judges in Poland and the alleged violation of the rule of law. The Tribunal argued that by deriving a right to examine the organization and structure of a member state's judicial system from Article 19(1) TEU, the CJEU has essentially granted itself a new competence. According to the Tribunal, this competence may by no means be derived from Article 2 TEU which is a list of values of merely 'axiological significance' as opposed to setting clear rules.

23.4 ABUSIVE CONSTITUTIONAL BORROWING

On the one side, the temptation to explore the cases illustrated above by putting everything in the same basket is high. On the other side, there is the opposite risk of discerning between fair contestations of EU law authority coming from the 'good' Western courts from the malicious and rude contestations coming from

---

[21] In its decision in the case P 7/20 issued on 14 July 2021, the Polish Constitutional Tribunal ruled on the saga concerning the independence of the judiciary in Poland, affirming the incompatibility of EU Treaty Law with the Polish Constitution, as long as it caused application of measures concerning the organization of the judiciary in Poland.

Eastern Europe (Drinóczi and Bień-Kacała 2021). Against the two risks, uses and abuses[22] of constitutional identity should be identified by exploring details of the judgments and their institutional context.[23] Against this background, the decision of the Hungarian Constitutional Court, openly referring to the European case law of the *BVerfG*, is grounded on relatively intriguing and elegant legal reasoning. It argues that the EU policy of the relocation of migrants with compulsory quotas for Member state infringes on the fundamental rights of migrants, imposing on them a different destination from what they aimed at. The judgment, far from rude from a purely legal perspective, should nonetheless be located into a broader picture. The broader picture shows that the Constitutional Court cared more about having the ruling majority's back than about protecting the fundamental rights of migrants (Halmai 2018). However, the decision of the Hungarian Court abused the notion of constitutional identity through a legally refined – and therefore possibly particularly insidious – legal reasoning. Formally, the Court did not attack the core values of constitutionalism, but seemingly and only formally acted to protect those values.

On the contrary, the recent decision of the Polish Constitutional Court seems to be a bright example of abusive constitutional borrowing (this terminology draws from Dixon and Landau 2021).

In fact, it is true that the decision echoes some legal categories of the *BVerfG*, and it is true that Warsaw undermines the legal authority of the CJEU, as Karlsruhe did just a few months earlier. However, the Polish decision departs from the German case law significantly.

First, while the German *BVerfG* argued that a decision of the ECB, and the consequent judgment of the CJEU upholding that decision, had been adopted in violation of the European Treaties and were, therefore, ultra vires, the decision of the Polish Constitution Tribunal put in question the principle of primacy of EU law. While Karlsruhe affirms that the European Treaties should be respected and supports a strict interpretation of EU law, Warsaw openly challenges the foundational principle of primacy of EU law.

Second, the German Court put into question a contested monetary and its possible economic consequences and therefore addressed a policy that in a 'traditional' national constitutional democracy is usually open to political contestation. It might be considered a move of constitutional paternalism, the fact that a non-political actor, that is, a constitutional court, acts in protection of a space for political *manoeuvre* for political bodies who should be vested with the appropriate powers to exercise their political voice. However, this aspect is completely different to what happened

---

[22] Abusive constitutional borrowing is a growing phenomenon: for a recent overview see Dixon and Landau 2021.
[23] Antonia Baraggia and Giada Ragone, Symposium – Introduction: The Polish Constitutional Tribunal Decision on the Primacy of EU Law: Alea Iacta Est. Now What?, Int'l J. Const. L. Blog, Oct. 15, 2021, at: www.iconnectblog.com/2021/10/symposium–introduction–the-polish-constitutional-tribunal-decision-on-the-primacy-of-eu-law-alea-iacta-est-now-what/.

in Warsaw, where the contested legislation represents a violation of core principles characterizing a constitutional democracy.

Third, the German *BVerfG* has been accused of a sort of political alliance with political actors, aiming at protecting national interests. However, this connection has nothing to do with the action of a captured court, such as the Polish Constitutional Tribunal, which lacks any independence from political power.

Fourth, the Polish Court stresses the primacy of the entire constitution on EU law, as point 1b) of the operative part of the decision suggests, and not only of an essential core of the Polish Constitution (as commonly happens in many member states, including Germany).[24]

Fifth, the institutional background is remarkably different. The Polish Constitutional Tribunal itself is an unlawfully established court, and the decision was triggered by the Polish prime minister. The Constitutional Tribunal played a far from counter-majoritarian role, by supporting the hostile action of the Executive against the authority of the EU. On the contrary, the decision of the Polish Constitutional Tribunal resembles the decision of the Hungarian Constitutional Court in 2016. In both decisions, the actions of the constitutional Court were triggered by the government, which solicited a judgment from the captured Constitutional Tribunal to have its back in keeping its solipsistic little constitutional bubble intact, and it delivered.[25]

CONCLUSIONS

Moving from these epiphanies of identity arguments, the scholarly discourse around constitutional identity was subject to a new rapid emotional transformation. While in the last decade of the twentieth century constitutional identity seemed to be a more than acceptable safety clause to reassure member states' concerns in front of an important 'constitutional moment' of the European integration process, many scholars are now advocating the lack of utility, or the 'dangers' (Fabbrini and Sajó 2019) deriving from constitutional identity. Some scholars have demanded that member states engaging in constitutional identity talks should not take part in EU legal integration at all and leave the Union entirely.

My personal view is that abandoning the notion of constitutional identity because of its recent abuses is far from a wise option.[26] First of all: constitutional identity is

---

[24] Matteo Bonelli, Symposium – Part III – Let's Take a Deep Breath: On the EU (and Academic) Reaction to the Polish Constitutional Tribunal's Ruling, Int'l J. Const. L. Blog, 17, 2021, at: www.iconnectblog.com/2021/10/symposium–part-iii–lets-take-a-deep-breath-on-the-eu-and-academic-reaction-to-the-polish-constitutional-tribunals-ruling/.

[25] Julian Scholtes, Symposium – Part II – From Constitutional Pluralism to Constitutional Solipsism, Int'l J. Const. L. Blog, 16 October, 2021, at: www.iconnectblog.com/2021/10/symposium–part-ii–from-constitutional-pluralism-to-constitutional-solipsism/.

[26] In the same sense, see Scholtes (2021).

nowadays a matter of blackletter EU law – Art 4(2) TEU is part of the Treaties and it is also subject to the jurisdiction of the CJEU. A Treaty reform with the abrogation of Art. 4(2) is a completely unrealistic scenario, and therefore – as lawyers – we should acknowledge that constitutional identity exists as a legal notion. Second: advancing a sort of theoretical abjuration of identity because of the risks emerging from abuses is, in my opinion, counter-productive and more dangerous than the dangers this strategy aims to neutralize.

In my view, there is a much more effective and simple alternative, and this is acknowledging the legal success of the process of legalization and 'positivization' of constitutional identity in the EU and focusing on abuses and of the notion. To a certain extent, the same fact that the clause is increasingly subject to abusive manipulations is a clear symptom of its success. The same is true for many other key concepts of public law, such as democracy, freedom and liberalism: these are all indeterminate, and, as such, they are and have been prone to abusive misinterpretations.

The destructive potential of constitutional identity is not an essential character of the clause per se but is a possible consequence of its abuse. The challenge is, then, recognizing abuses and building legal remedies against them. As legal scholars, we might have some responsibilities on both fronts. As for the first front, the recognition of abuses of constitutional identity should rely on the massive literature on constitutional identity. The option advocated by some scholars of abandoning the discourse on constitutional identity just because the notion might be open to abuse sounds absurd to me.

First, we could say that constitutional identities shall be respected as far as they are constitutional and not unconstitutional constitutional identities. Keeping the play on words aside, respecting constitutional identities is a blackletter fundamental principle of the EU that shall be balanced with other fundamental principles of the EU. Among these, the fundamental principles mentioned in Article 2 TEU are certainly to be included as core principles identifying EU constitutional identity.[27] Article 2 and Article 4(2) TEU are on the same level: therefore, claiming that Article 4(2) TEU protects a national measure that violates Article 2 can be recognized as an abusive application of the identity clause.

If an identity is to be constitutional, it needs to refer to the specific principles of a given constitution of a specific member state, but also to the principles pertaining to having a constitution in general. This requires that, according to a normative conception of the concept of constitution, already originating from Article 16 of the French Declaration of Man and of the Citizen of 1789, where it stated that 'Any society in which the guarantee of rights is not assured, nor the separation of powers determined, has no Constitution'.

---

[27] For an account of constitutional identity as attached to unamendable provisions of any constitutional system, regardless of the legal label attached to those principles, see Roznai (2017).

In this sense, the rejection of unconstitutional constitutional identity claims would moreover lead to an affirmation of a European constitutional identity: this is a relatively overlooked topic that needs to be theoretically framed and strongly affirmed in the European legal scholarship.

Once discerned between uses and abuses of constitutional identity, the next challenge is to identify legal remedies to tackle abuses. Recent developments put legal categories in danger, but are also formidable occasions to test legal remedies in action. In fact, on the one hand, the 'political' mechanism provided for by Article 7 TEU proved inefficient, as it is easily paralyzed by the unanimity required for its activation. Therefore, the infringement procedure under Article 258 TEU is one of the most likely options to be activated, as happened in the reaction to the *Weiss* decision for Germany and to the decision issued in October 2021 by the Polish Constitutional Tribunal. However, the judicial follow-up was soon neutralized by a political accommodation in the *Weiss* case, while the infringement procedure against Poland is still pending.

On a different front, European actors decided to also follow alternative routes, mainly connected to mechanisms of financial pressure.[28] Among these mechanisms, the most innovative route consisting of the application of the new rule of law conditionality mechanism is another option. The CJEU upheld this option with its seminal twin decisions issued in February 2022.

REFERENCES

Bartole, Sergio. 2020. *The Internationalisation of Constitutional Law: A View from the Venice Commission*. London: Bloomsbury Publishing.

Calliess, Christian. 2019. "Constitutional Identity in Germany. One for Three or Three in One?" In *Constitutional Identity in a Europe of Multilevel Constitutionalism*, edited by Christian Calliess and Gerhard van der Schyff, 153. Cambridge: Cambridge University Press.

Cartabia, Marta. 1990. "The Italian Constitutional Court and the Relationship Between the Italian Legal System and the European Community." *Michigan Journal of International Law* 12 (1): 174–203.

The Chancellery of the Prime Minister of Poland, White Paper on the Reform of the Polish Judiciary, Warsaw, 7 March 2018, para. 177. Available at www.statewatch.org/media/documents/news/2018/mar/pl-judiciary-reform-chanceller-white-paper-3-18.pdf.

Claes, Monica and Jan-Herman Reestman. 2015. "The Protection of National Constitutional Identity and the Limits of European Integration at the Occasion of the Gauweiler Case." *German Law Journal* 16 (4): 917–970. https://doi.org/10.1017/S2071832200019957.

---

[28] Financial measures have already been adopted, with the order of the Vice-President of the Court of Justice to condemn Poland to pay a periodic penalty of €1 000 000 euros per day: Court of Justice of the European Union: PRESS RELEASE No 192/21, Luxembourg, 27 October 2021m Order of the Vice-President of the Court in Case C-204/21 R. Additionally, the Commission may suspend approving the Polish Recovery plan until the rule of law breaches have been fixed by Poland, with significant economic consequences for Polish citizens, civil society and businesses.

Dixon, Rosalind and David Landau. 2021. *Abusive Constitutional Borrowing: Legal Globalization and the Subversion of Liberal Democracy*. Oxford Comparative Constitutionalism. Oxford: Oxford University Press.

Drinóczi, Tímea and Agnieszka Bień-Kacała. 2021. *Illiberal Constitutionalism in Poland and Hungary: The Deterioration of Democracy, Misuse of Human Rights and Abuse of the Rule of Law*. London; New York: Routledge.

Fabbrini, Federico and András Sajó. 2019. "The Dangers of Constitutional Identity." *European Law Journal* 25 (4): 457–473.

Faraguna, Pietro. 2015. *Ai confini della Costituzione. Principi supremi e identità costituzionale*. Milano: FrancoAngeli.

Faraguna, Pietro. 2016. "Taking Constitutional Identities Away from the Courts." *Brooklyn Journal of International Law* 41 (2): 491–578.

Halmai, Gábor. 2018. "Abuse of Constitutional Identity. The Hungarian Constitutional Court on Interpretation of Article E) (2) of the Fundamental Law." *Review of Central and East European Law* 43 (1): 23–42.

Jacobsohn, Gary Jeffrey. 2010. *Constitutional Identity*. Cambridge: Harvard University Press.

Kelemen, R. Daniel and Laurent Pech. 2018. "Why Autocrats Love Constitutional Identity and Constitutional Pluralism." Reconnect Working Paper 2. *RECONNECT – Reconciling Europe with Its Citizens through Democracy and Rule of Law*.

Komárek, Jan. 2012. "Czech Constitutional Court Playing with Matches: The Czech Constitutional Court Declares a Judgment of the Court of Justice of the EU Ultra Vires; Judgment of 31 January 2012, Pl. ÚS 5/12, Slovak Pensions XVII." *European Constitutional Law Review* 8 (2): 323–337.

Kühn, Zdenek. 2016. "Ultra Vires Review and the Demise of Constitutional Pluralism: The Czecho-Slovak Pension Saga, and the Dangers of State Courts' Defiance of EU Law." *Maastricht Journal of European and Comparative Law* 23 (1): 185–194.

Paris, Davide. 2017. "Carrot and Stick. The Italian Constitutional Court's Preliminary Reference in the Case Taricco." *QIL QDI* (blog). March 31, 2017. www.qil-qdi.org/carrot-stick-italian-constitutional-courts-preliminary-reference-case-taricco/.

Piccirilli, Giovanni. 2018. "The 'Taricco Saga': The Italian Constitutional Court Continues Its European Journey: Italian Constitutional Court, Order of 23 November 2016 No. 24/2017; Judgment of 10 April 2018 No. 115/2018 ECJ 8 September 2015, Case C-105/14, Ivo Taricco and Others; 5 December 2017, Case C-42/17, M.A.S. and M.B." *European Constitutional Law Review* 14 (4): 1–20.

Polzin, Monika. 2016. "Constitutional Identity, Unconstitutional Amendments and the Idea of Constituent Power: The Development of the Doctrine of Constitutional Identity in German Constitutional Law." *International Journal of Constitutional Law* 14 (2): 411–438.

Rosenfeld, Michel. 2009. *The Identity of the Constitutional Subject: Selfhood, Citizenship, Culture, and Community*. London; New York: Routledge.

Roznai, Yaniv. 2017. *Unconstitutional Constitutional Amendments: The Limits of Amendment Powers*. Oxford Constitutional Theory. Oxford; New York: Oxford University Press.

Scaccia, Gino. 2020. "The Lesson Learned from the Taricco Saga: Judicial Nationalism and the Constitutional Review of E.U. Law." *American University International Law Review* 35 (4).

Schmitt, Carl. 1928. *Verfassungslehre*. Berlin: Duncker & Humblot GmbH.

Schmitt, Carl. 2008. *Constitutional Theory. Tradotto da Seitzer*. Durham, NC: Duke University Press.

Scholtes, Julian. 2021. "Abusing Constitutional Identity." *German Law Journal* 22 (4): 534–556. https://doi.org/10.1017/glj.2021.21.

Spieker, Luke Dimitrios. 2020. "Framing and Managing Constitutional Identity Conflicts: How to Stabilize the *Modus Vivendi* between the Court of Justice and National Constitutional Courts." *Common Market Law Review* 57 (2): 361–398.

Tripkovic, Bosko. 2020. "Constructing the Constitutional Self: Meaning, Value, and Abuse of Constitutional Identity." *Union University Law Review* (Forthcoming). https://papers.ssrn.com/abstract=3744008.

Weiler, J. H. H. 2002. "A Constitution for Europe? Some Hard Choices." *JCMS: Journal of Common Market Studies* 40 (4): 563–580.

24

What Counts as Constitutional Identity?

Mila Versteeg[*]

INTRODUCTION

Do nations' constitutions and constitutional law have a distinct identity? (Rosenfeld 2007, 756).[1] One of Gary Jacobsohn's major contributions to the literature has been to argue that they do. Where do we find such identity? Jacobsohn notes that constitutional texts themselves often appear to be signaling an identity (Jacobsohn 2010, 348–349).[2] Judicial decisions can further develop and crystallize it, such as when courts resist laws that undermine their notion of constitutional identity (Fletcher 1994, 223; Sajó 2019, 3269). More generally, some see constitutional identity as broader than the text and its interpretations, but as also encompassing the important popular values. For example, Jacobsohn argues that a "constitution acquires an identity through experience," which means that it "emerges *dialogically* and represents a mix of political aspirations and commitments that are expressive of a nation's past, as well as the determination of those within the society who seek in some ways to transcend that past" (Jacobsohn 2010, 7).

In part because of its complexity, the concept of constitutional identity is especially difficult to quantify. In addition to the fact that there is simply no consensus on the concept, understanding a nation's constitutional identity entails more than reading the constitutional text; it requires careful observation of the nation's constitutional conventions and the "disharmonies" that arise in constitutional interpretation and practice (Jacobsohn 2010, 15).

And yet, in this era, many social phenomena are measured. Among other things, we have data measuring the rule of law (Ginsburg and Versteeg 2017, 100), human rights performance (Merry 2011, 52), democracy (Coppedge 2011, 247), the costs of doing business (World Bank 2020), and many other aspects of socio-legal life.

---

[*] I thank Apinop Atipiboonsin for excellent research assistance. I thank Yaniv Roznai and Ran Hirschl for helpful comments and suggestions.
[1] "'Constitutional identity' is an essentially contested concept as there is no agreement over what it means or refers to."
[2] "To establish the identity of a constitution, it obviously makes sense to scrutinize carefully the text itself."

A recent wave of research studies constitutions and constitutional law empirically (Elkins et al. 2009; Chilton 2020). So it is no surprise that the editors of this volume dedicated to the work of Gary Jacobsohn asked me to reflect on whether we can measure constitutional identity.

I argue that there is a potential role for large-N empirical work in improving our understanding of constitutional identity. Even if we cannot simply count and measure all aspects of constitutional identity, empirical analysis can help us better understand the concept.

In what follows, I first reflect on whether and how large-N empirical studies can aid understanding of constitutional identity. I identify two broad approaches. The first is to study statements of identity in constitutional texts. Such statements can appear anywhere in the document, but especially promising parts are preambles and amendment provisions making certain parts harder to amend or unamendable. A second approach is to explore popular values and how they relate to the constitution. For instance, one might explore whether popular values relate to the values articulated in the constitution. Relatedly, one might use surveys to explore whether and how people believe that their values are represented in the constitution.

Next, I present original data from nationally representative surveys conducted in five countries that capture whether people believe they are represented by the constitution. (This is a small companion piece to a larger paper where we look at drivers for different kinds of constitutional support (Crabtree and Versteeg n.d.).) The five studied countries represent different constitutional settings, and, presumably, they have different constitutional identities. The main finding from this exercise is a common pattern in those who feel represented. Respondents who are older, male, higher educated, and have high income feel more represented than younger, female, lower-educated, and low-income respondents. In essence, groups that are relatively well off in society feel better represented by the constitution. While it does not directly tell us what the constitution's identity is, these data do tell us something about the nature of the relationship between the constitution and those governed by it. Most notably, this finding is consistent with accounts of constitutions as reflecting elite interests (Beard 1913; Hirschl 2004; Parenti 2011).

24.1 EMPIRICAL APPROACHES TO UNDERSTANDING CONSTITUTIONAL IDENTITY

Can empirical analysis aid understanding of constitutional identity? Before I take up this question, I should note some caveats and clarifications. First, the approaches identified below are guided by what is feasible with existing data. Second, these approaches are by no means the only ones; it is likely that creative empiricists can come up with other ways to explore constitutional identity. Third, empirical approaches, as I use the term here, are meant to capture research designs that use large-N data, including large-N cross-national analyses and surveys. (Case studies, of course, are also empirical in nature; but I exclude them here.)

24.1.1 Constitutional Text

How might one go about measuring constitutional identity? An obvious starting point is to simply look at what the constitution says about its own identity. Many, if not most, constitutions make important statements about the nation's highest values and its history. Such statements can be seen as part of the more symbolic or expressive function of constitutional texts. For example, Beau Breslin has argued that a primary function of constitutions is to "imagine and then help to realize a shared collective existence" (Breslin 2009, 5).

In his seminal work on constitutional identity, Gary Jacobsohn appears to see constitutional text as a starting point for understanding a constitution's identity. He observes that in order "[t]o establish the identity of a constitution, it obviously makes sense to scrutinize carefully the text itself" as "[t]his provides us with a documentary transcript of how a particular group of framers provided for the governance of their polity, and it often includes their aspirations for its subsequent development" (Jacobsohn 2010, 348–349). At the same time, Jacobsohn observes that what we can learn from the text is limited, as "there can be important dissonances between the identity expressed in the constitution and actual constitutional politics of the country" (Jacobsohn 2010, 348–349).

If we were to try to find constitutional identity in the text of the constitution, where would we look? Perhaps an obvious place to start is the preamble. One of the primary goals of the preamble is to articulate the nation's highest values, narrate its history, and express aspirations for the future. Jeff King describes preambles as "mission statements" (King 2013, 73). In a similar vein, Wim Voermans and co-authors argue that preambles seek to "strengthen citizenship" (Voermans 2017, 93).

Many preambles make important statements of the nation's highest values, its history, and its hopes and aspirations for the future. For example, the Constitution of Ireland is pronounced in "the Name of the Most Holy Trinity, from Whom is all authority and to Whom, as our final end, all actions both of men and States must be referred" and "humbly" acknowledges "our obligations to our Divine Lord, Jesus Christ, [w]ho sustained our fathers through centuries of trial" and "gratefully" remembers "their heroic and unremitting struggle to regain the rightful independence of our Nation" (Constitution of Ireland 1937). As a different example, the Constitution of Ecuador recognizes "our age-old roots, wrought by women and men from various peoples," celebrates "nature, the Pacha Mama (Mother Earth), of which we are a part and which is vital to our existence," invokes "the name of God and recognizing our diverse forms of religion and spirituality," calls upon "the wisdom of all the cultures that enrich us as a society," and decides to build a "new form of public coexistence, in diversity and in harmony with nature, to achieve the good way of living, the sumak kawsay" in a "society that respects, in all its dimensions, the dignity of individuals and community groups" (Constitution of the Republic of Ecuador 2008). According to my own coding of all of the world's written constitutions since 1946, about 25 percent of all constitutions today contain preambles that make statements indicating their values and identities in this way (Law 2016; Versteeg 2014, 1140–1142).

But these kinds of expressions are not confined to preambles. Constitutions can also contain specific provisions that appear to reflect history and identity. For example, the constitution of Sweden protects the "right of the Sami population to practise reindeer husbandry is regulated in law."[3] While the constitution of Bhutan requires the state "to promote those conditions that will enable the pursuit of Gross National Happiness" (Constitution of the Kingdom of Bhutan 2008, Art. 9.1). The Constitution of Bolivia notes that the "State adopts and promotes the following as ethical, moral principles of the plural society: ama qhilla, ama llulla, ama suwa (do not be lazy, do not be a liar or a thief), suma qamaña (live well), ñandereko (live harmoniously), teko kavi (good life), ivi maraei (land without evil) and qhapaj ñan (noble path or life)" (Political Constitution of the State of Bolivia 2009, Art. 8.1). Gunter Frankenberg observes that these types of statements are, in fact, quite common, though to my knowledge, nobody has tried to code such "oddities" (as Frankenberg calls them) (Law and Versteeg 2011; Frankenberg 2018).

It is also noteworthy that constitutions commonly describe the nation's flag, the anthem, the motto, and other national symbols. According to data from the Comparative Constitutions Project, some 69 percent of constitutions in force mention their flag in the constitution (Constitution of the Dominican Republic 2015, Art, 30–35).

Another textual representation of identity can be found in amendment procedures. Some constitutions make some of their parts unamendable, or harder to amend than others. When this is the case, constitution-makers signal that the values protected by these unamendable (or hard-to-amend) provisions are especially important. Indeed, some of the first theories of constitutional identity, tracing back to Carl Schmitt, were about such eternity clauses, which could only be replaced by a constituent assembly representing the people as a whole (Sajó 2019, 3262). Jacobsohn likewise considers such provisions important to understanding constitutional identity (Jacobsohn 2011, 129). Unamendability provisions, he observes, are "designed to preserve a pre-existing identity by obstructing the removal of those attributes without which the object in question would become something very different" (Jacobsohn 2010, 129). He further observes that "[w]hen those who frame a constitution act to prevent future actors from changing certain elements of their handiwork, they are in effect establishing an insurance policy in favor of a present identity against an imagined future identity that is deemed unacceptable" (Jacobsohn 2010, 129). Yaniv Roznai has likewise linked unamendability to constitutional identity (Roznai 2017, 148).

---

[3] Regeringsformen [RF][Constitution], Art. 17 (Swed.).

Data on heightened amendment thresholds and eternity clauses is readily available from the Comparative Constitution's project as well as other data collection efforts (Hein 2018), and several scholars have analyzed these provisions (Roznai 2017).[4] But of course, constitutional texts alone do not fully capture whether parts of the constitution are unamendable. In many settings, it is courts that deem parts of the constitution unamendable, as with the "basic structure" doctrine in India (to name just one of many examples) (Krishnaswamy 2011). Coding unamendability and tiered amendment structures beyond the text of the constitution alone is more difficult, but most likely possible. A team of researchers could collect this information and quantify it. To my knowledge, this data has not yet been systematically collected. With it, one could explore the drivers of unamendability, and whether the values that are insulated from easy change correlate with widely held popular values.

More generally, the advantage of quantifying statements of identity in constitutional texts is that it allows us to compare countries systematically. It also allows us to employ statistical methods to explore the correlates of textual aspects of identity. For example, are statements of identity correlated with democracy, constitutional compliance, or rule of law? The answer to these questions might be of interest to those doing theoretical work on constitutional identity.

24.1.2 *The Relationship between Constitutional Texts and Popular Values*

Many have conceptualized constitutional identity as going beyond the constitution and its interpreters. Michel Rosenfeld, for example, emphasizes the connection between constitutional identity and the values of the constitution's subjects, or "we the people." That is, he distinguishes between the "national identity" of the nation's different people(s) and the identity of the constitution (Rosenfeld 2009, 18). He sees the relationship as a paradox: on the one hand, the constitution is to constrain majorities, and forces them "to renounce" part of their "pre-constitutional self" by agreeing to "certain levels of self-constraint" (Rosenfeld 2007, 762); on the other hand, "a constitution should not veer too far off a constituent group's identities, for that would impair its viability and undermine its implementation" (Rosenfeld 2007). Rosenfeld, then, conjectures that, at least to some extent, constitutional identity is linked to the identity of its subjects.[5] As an empirical matter, this means that we should expect to see at least some degree of congruence between the values enumerated in the constitution and those held by the (majority of the) people (Rosenfeld 2009, 113).

---

[4] *But see* Van Der Schyff 2020, 309.
[5] Many have sought to explore the relationship between national identity and constitutional identity. See, e.g., Ackerman 1991, 36 ("the narrative we tell ourselves about our CONSTITUTION'S roots is a deeply significant act of collective self-definition; its continual re-telling plays a critical role in the ongoing construction of national identity").

When building popular values into our concept of identity, several questions emerge that lend themselves to empirical exploration. The first is whether and to what extent the constitution matches the values held by the people whom the constitution is supposed to represent. This is an empirical question: we can explore whether and to what extent the constitution reflects the values held by popular majorities in different countries.

In prior work, I have made an initial attempt at doing just that (Versteeg 2014, 1137–1138). Specifically, I looked at twelve values that many countries enumerate in the constitution and contrasted those values with popular opinion data on the same values. The constitutional values I considered were: (1) the protection of family life; (2) the right to rest/ leisure; (3) the right to work; (4) the protection of the environment; (5) the protection of marriage; (6) the right to petition; (7) the right to assembly; (8) the right to strike; (9) the protection of equality regardless of sexual orientation; (10) the prohibition on abortion (through protection of the unborn); (11) gender equality in labor relations; and (12) the protection of motherhood. I compared these twelve constitutional features with data from World Values Survey, which measures public opinion on a range of issues in over ninety countries, covering 88 percent of the world population.[6] For example, I matched the constitution's protection of the family with what percentage of the population agrees with the statement "Do you think that a child needs a home with both a father and a mother to grow up happily?" Likewise, I matched the right to rest/leisure with the percentage of people who said that "leisure time" is "very important" or "rather important" in their life.

The main impression from this exercise was that there is low congruence between specific constitutional choices and prevailing popular opinion in a country. For instance, there was no statistically significant relationship between popular opinion on homosexuality and constitutional protection of gay rights; on popular opinion regarding abortion and constitutional protection of the unborn; or between popular values relating to the environment and constitutional protection of the environment.

Of course, it is not clear what the optimal level of congruence between popular values and constitutional values is. As Rosenfeld has pointed out, we want constitutions to both be somewhat disconnected from popular values – as majoritarian impulses sometimes must be restrained – and reflective of constitutional values. Yet, the exercise reveals that, if anything, constitutions are more about constraining majoritarian values, than seeking to reflect them. Thus, the exercise shows that constitutional identity is not simply a reflection of deeply held popular values. For a concept as complex as constitutional identity, knowing what it is *not* can be helpful in establishing its contours.

When building popular values into our concept of identity, another question that emerges is whether people actually feel represented by the constitution. That is, do

---

[6] See Inglehart 2008 describing the infrastructure of the World Values Survey.

people feel a sense of belonging within a constitutional polity? Michel Rosenfeld has argued that one of the roles of constitutions is to create such a sense of belonging and to create a "common identity" among different groups "rooted in a shared constitutional text" and constitutional discourse surrounding the text (Rosenfeld 2009). If the constitution is successful at doing so, one might think that people will feel that they are represented by the constitution.

This is something that we can explore empirically by asking people. Doing so does not necessarily provide an empirical account of what the constitution's identity is, but it allows us to explore which group of people feel that the constitution represents them. And by exploring the demographic characteristics of those who feel represented by the constitution, we may in turn be able to infer something about its identity. In the remainder of this contribution, I seek to do so by drawing on new survey data from five countries.

24.2 CONSTITUTIONAL REPRESENTATION: AN INITIAL EMPIRICAL EXPLORATION

To explore whether and to what extent people feel represented by the Constitution, I simply asked them. Specifically, I asked people the following question: "On a scale from 1 to 10, how much do you feel represented by the constitution?"[7]

Participants were recruited to take the survey online by a leading survey firm in each of these countries. The U.S. survey was conducted in October 2020 and had 4,068 respondents; the surveys in Japan, China, South Korea, and Taiwan were conducted in May 2020, and had 4,045, 2,580, 1,985, and 1,363 respondents, respectively. In total, over 14,000 people were surveyed.

I selected these countries in part because, along with my collaborators on related projects, I had an opportunity to conduct population surveys there. But they also represent a diverse set of countries. The U.S. is notorious for its old constitution which is particularly important in its democratic political culture.[8] It is well known that Japan's Constitution is imposed, and therefore unlikely to be very reflective of popular values.[9] And the Chinese Constitution operates in an authoritarian context.[10] If my findings on who feels represented were similar across these systems, then it is possible that they would generalize more widely.

---

[7] For Japan, there were 100 values; for other countries, there were 10. For Japan, we recoded the responses so that they were discrete numbers between 1 and 10.

[8] See Levinson 1979 discussing the implications of the constitution as part of the American civil religion.

[9] Compare Shōichi 1997, 98–109 (stating that the end of Japanese constitutional ideas happened when the government accepted the draft constitution without much debate) with Law 2013 (arguing against the idea that the Japanese Constitution was simply imposed by the occupation authorities).

[10] See Zhang 2012 (providing an account of the establishment and developments of the constitution of China within an authoritarian context).

24.2.1 Which Constitution Is the Most Representative?

I begin by exploring cross-country differences in the extent people feel represented by the constitution. A cursory analysis of the data reveals that people in the U.S. claim to have the highest levels of constitutional representation (or more precisely, the highest average scores on the question of whether people feel represented by the constitution), followed by China, Japan, Korea, and Taiwan.

Let me first discuss the United States. Figure 24.1 shows a histogram that depicts the portion of respondents that selected each of the different scores on the 10-point scale. The median American respondent gives 8 out of 10 to the question of whether they feel represented by the Constitution. The average response is 7.6, and 88 percent rate the extent to which the constitution represents them at 5 or higher.

The United States is followed by China, where respondents' perceived level of constitutional representation is actually remarkably similar to that of the United States. As Figure 24.2 reports, the median Chinese respondent's level of representation is 8 out of 10. The average is slightly lower than the United States: 7.3 out of 10, while 82 percent of Chinese rate the extent to which the constitution represents them as 5 or higher.

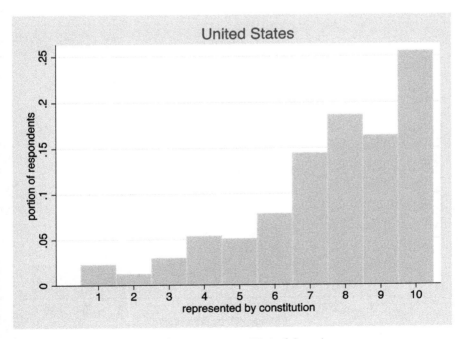

FIGURE 24.1 Represented by the constitution (United States)

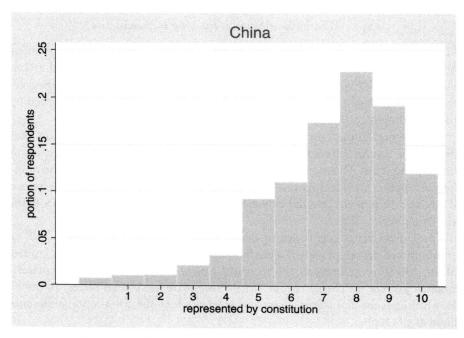

FIGURE 24.2 Represented by the constitution (China)

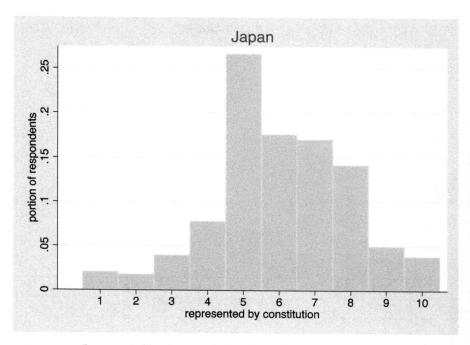

FIGURE 24.3 Represented by the constitution (Japan)

What Counts as Constitutional Identity? 321

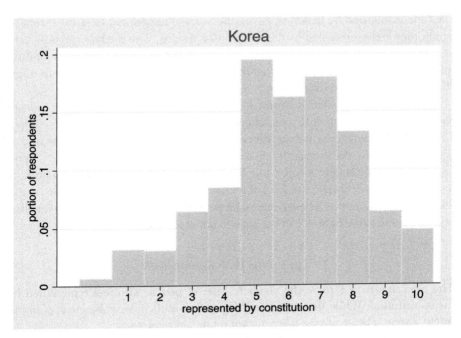

FIGURE 24.4 Represented by the constitution (Korea)

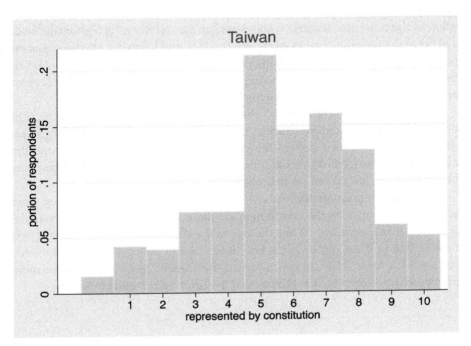

FIGURE 24.5 Represented by the constitution (Taiwan)

China is followed by Japan. In Japan, the average respondent rates the extent to which they feel represented by the constitution as 6.04. The median response is 6, and 58 percent of Japanese respondents gave a score of 5 or higher. This finding might be surprising, considering that the Japanese Constitution is notorious as an "imposed" constitution (Shōichi 1997, 68–97) (Figure 24.3).

Perceived representation is lowest in Korea and Taiwan. In Korea, the average respondent rates the extent to which they feel represented by the constitution as 5.9. The median response is 6 and 59 percent of Korean respondents gave a score of 5 or higher. In Taiwan, the average respondent rates the extent to which they feel represented by the constitution as 5.8, while the median response is also 6. In Taiwan, 54 percent of respondents rate the level of representation as 5 or higher. Notable here is that even in the countries where perceived representation levels are lowest, the median response is still at the right side of the scale (6 out of 10) (Figures 24.4 and 24.5).

24.2.2 Who Feels Represented?

The next step is to explore the characteristics of people who feel represented by the constitution. While the answer to the question is of course subjective, doing so might give us a sense of who the constitution in fact represents.

To do so, it is useful to break down the representation scores by basic demographic characteristics. Some demographic variables are available for all five countries: (1) age, (2) gender, (3) education level, and (4) income. I code these as binary values, whereby the value one denotes (1) above-median age, (2) male, (3) higher educated, and (4) in the upper-income brackets. For the U.S. and Japan, we also have data on political ideology (for the U.S., whether the respondent is Republican, Democrat, or Independent; for Japan, whether the respondents consider themselves right-of-center on a 10-point left-right scale) and for the U.S., we also have data on race.

Figures 24.6 to 24.10 break down the average representation scores for each of these groups in each country. The dots represent the means for the different groups, while the vertical lines represent the 95 percent confidence intervals around the means. When the confidence intervals for groups do not overlap, the differences between the groups' means are statistically significant.[11]

Overall, the impression from the analysis is that, across these five countries, those who feel represented by the constitution are those who are older, wealthier, male, and more highly educated. While the size of the effect differs across countries, it is notable that in these very different constitutional and political contexts, the basic pattern is the same. Thus, in general terms, the exercise reveals that it is the more privileged in society, or elites, that say that the constitution represents them.

---

[11] Note, however, that even when the confidence intervals do overlap, the differences between the groups' means might still be statistically significant. See Cornell Statistical Consulting Unit 2008.

What Counts as Constitutional Identity? 323

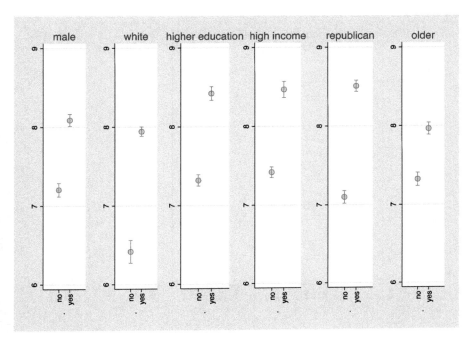

FIGURE 24.6 Who feels represented? (United States)

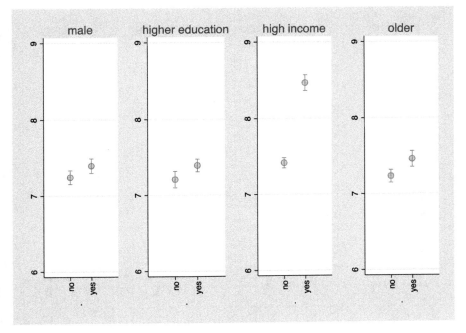

FIGURE 24.7 Who feels represented? (China)

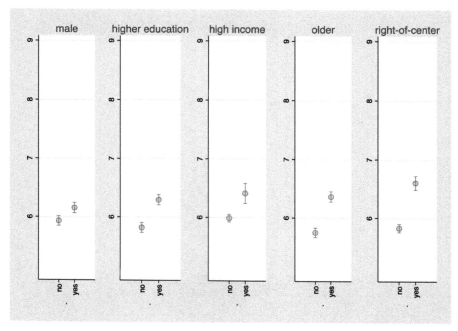

FIGURE 24.8 Who feels represented? (Japan)

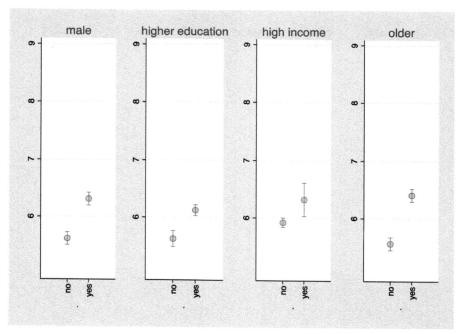

FIGURE 24.9 Who feels represented? (Korea)

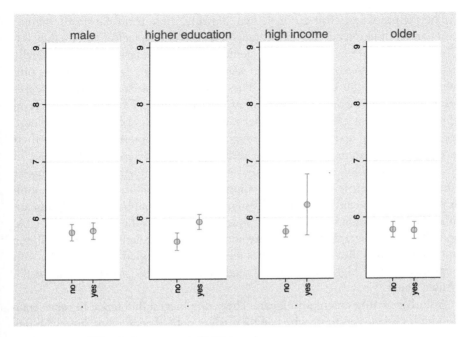

FIGURE 24.10 Who feels represented? (Taiwan)

Take the United States. Figure 24.6 depicts representation scores for those who are male, white, obtained higher education (a four-year college degree and/or graduate degree), have high income (over USD120,000), are Republican, and have an above-median age (over 43) and compares those to the scores of those who are not-male, not-white, did not obtain higher education, do not have high income, are not Republican, and have a below-median age. The figure reveals that each of these factors represents a statistically significant divide in representation scores. The average male has a constitutional representation score of 8.1, while the average female rates the extent to which they feel represented by the constitution at 7.1. The average white person rates their level of representation at 7.9, while the average non-white person has a representation score of 6.4. The average person *with* higher education rates their level of representation at 8.4, while the average person without higher education has a representation score of 7.3. The average person with a high income has a representation score of 8.5; those with lower incomes have an average of 7.4. The average Republican rates their level of representation at 8.5; the average non-Republican at 7.1. And the average person with above-median age in the sample rates their level of representation at 8; younger respondents have a representation score of 7.3. If we add these various factors together, we find that for the average middle-aged white Republican male with high education and high income, the representation score is 8.6.

The picture is less clear cut in China. Notably, there is no statistically significant gender difference in the extent to which respondents feel represented by the Chinese Constitution. Yet the other demographic characteristics are statistically significant predictors of representation scores, even though their effect is less pronounced than in the United States. The difference between high-income earners and non-high-income earners is most substantial: the former rate their level of representation at 7.8; while the latter rate it at 7.3. Older people also feel more represented; those above-median age (age 39 in our Chinese sample) rate their level of representation at 7.5; younger respondents have a representation score of 7.2. Higher education also seems to make a (small) difference: those with higher education rate their level of representation at 7.4; those without higher education at 7.2 (this difference is not statistically significant in the graphs, but it is significant in a simple regression in which the representation score is the dependent variable and all four demographic variables are added at the right-hand side). Overall, the impression is that also in China, elites feel more represented (older people, with high income and high education), though the difference is smaller than in the United States.

A similar picture emerges in Japan. There, the biggest difference in representation scores is between those who rate themselves right-of-center and those who rate themselves on the left or in the middle (on a 10-point scale). The average representation score for those on the right is 6.8 compared to 5.8 for those on the left or in the middle. Those with higher income also feel more represented; those with high income have a representation score of 6.4, compared to 6.0 for those with lower-income levels. Likewise, those with higher levels of education have a representation score of 6.3; while those without higher education have a score of 5.8. Age is also a factor: those above-median age (the median respondent in our Japan sample was 47) have a representation score of 6.4; younger respondents have a representation score of 5.9. Finally, men feel slightly more represented than women: male respondents have a representation score of 6.2; female respondents score 5.9 on average. While most of these differences are smaller than in the U.S., they are statistically significant.

The same impression again emerges in South Korea. Male respondents have an average representation score of 6.3; women of 5.6. Higher-educated respondents have a representation score of 6.1; those with higher education rate their level of representation as 5.6 on average. Likewise, those with high-income rate their level of representation at 6.3; those in lower-income brackets rate it as 5.9. And age is again a factor; those with above-median age (the median age in our Korean sample is 40 years) score 6.4; younger respondents rate their level of representation at 5.6.

Taiwan is arguably mostly an outlier (though we should also note that our sample in Taiwan is substantially smaller than in the other countries). In Taiwan, there is no statistically significant difference between male and female respondents, between high-income earners and lower-income earners, or between older and younger respondents. The only statistically significant variable is higher education; the average respondent with higher education rates representation at 5.9; the average respondent without higher education rates it at 5.3.

CONCLUSION

Large-N work on constitutional identity is surely no substitute for in-depth case studies. But even if limited, cross-national empirical analyses can provide certain insights. In this brief chapter, I presented some new data based on surveys in five countries that asked whether people feel represented by the constitution. Those who have theorized identity have conjectured that constitutions can help create a common identity. My main finding here is that those who are better off in society feel more represented by the constitution. This might be because the constitution actually reflects their values. But it might also be because the system works well for elites, and that as a result, they approve of it more. Exploring these pathways behind perceived constitutional representation is an avenue for future research. My objective here is more limited, which is to show that empirical approaches can provide insights that are useful to better understanding constitutional identity. That is, even if constitutional identity is not something we can easily count or measure, large-N analyses can nonetheless contribute to understanding its nature.

REFERENCES

Ackerman, Bruce. 1991. *We the People, Volume I: Foundations*. Cambridge: Harvard University Press.
Beard, Charles A. 1913. *An Economic Interpretation of the Constitution of the United States*. Stuttgart: Macmillan.
Breslin, Beau. 2009. *From Words to Worlds: Exploring Constitutional Functionality*. Baltimore: Johns Hopkins University Press.
Chilton, Adam and Mila Versteeg. 2020. *How Constitutional Rights Matter*. Oxford: Oxford University Press.
Coppedge, Michael et al. 2011. "Conceptualizing and Measuring Democracy: A New Approach." *Perspectives on Politics* 9 (2): 247 (2011).
Cornell Statistical Consulting Unit. 2008. "StatNews #73: Overlapping Confidence Intervals and Statistical Significance." Last updated September 2020. https://cscu.cornell.edu/wp-content/uploads/73_ci.pdf.
Crabtree, Charles and Mila Versteeg. n.d. *Constitutional Legitimacy*.
Elkins, Zachary et al. 2009. *The Endurance of National Constitutions*. Cambridge: Cambridge University Press.
Fletcher, George P. 1994. "Constitutional Identity." In *Constitutionalism, Identity, Difference, and Legitimacy*, edited by Michel Rosenfeld, 223–232. Durham: Duke University Press.
Frankenberg, Gunter. 2018. *Comparative Constitutional Studies: Between Magic and Deceit*. Cheltenham: Edward Elgar Publishing.

Ginsburg, Tom and Mila Versteeg. 2017. "Measuring the Rule of Law: A Comparison of Indicators." *Law & Society Inquiry* 42 (1): 100–137.
Hein, Michael. 2018. "The Constitutional Entrenchment Clauses Dataset." University of Göttingen. http://data.michaelhein.de.
Hirschl, Ran. 2004. *Towards Juristocracy*. Cambridge: Harvard University Press.
Inglehart, Ronald. 2008. "Foreword." In *Values Change the World*. World Values Survey.
Jacobsohn, Gary J. 2010. *Constitutional Identity*. Cambridge: Harvard University Press.
Jacobsohn, Gary J. 2011. "The Formation of Constitutional Identities." In *Comparative Constitutional Law*, edited by Tom Ginsburg and Rosalind Dixon, 129–142. Cheltenham: Edward Elgar Publishing.
King, Jeff. 2013. "Constitutions as Mission-Statement." In *The Social and Political Foundations of Constitutions*, edited by Denis Galligan and Mila Versteeg, 73–102. Cambridge: Cambridge University Press.
Krishnaswamy, Sudhir. 2011. *Democracy and Constitutionalism in India: A Study of the Basic Structure Doctrine*. Oxford: Oxford University Press.
Law, David S. 2013. "The Myth of the Imposed Constitution." In *The Social and Political Foundations of Constitutions*, edited by Denis Galligan and Mila Versteeg, 239–264. Cambridge: Cambridge University Press.
Law, David S. 2016. "Constitutional Archetypes." *Texas Law Review* 95 (2): 153–243.
Law, David S. and Mila Versteeg. 2011. "The Evolution and Ideology of Global Constitutionalism." *California Law Review* 99 (5): 1163–1257.
Levinson, Sanford. 1979. "'The Constitution' in American Civil Religion." *Supreme Court Review* 1979: 123–151.
Merry, Sally Engle. 2011. "Measuring the World: Indicators, Human Rights, and Global Governance: With CA Comment by John M. Conley." *Current Anthropology* 52: 83–95.
Parenti, Michael. 2011. *Democracy for the Few*. New York: St. Martin's Press.
Rosenfeld, Michel. 2007. "Constitutional Identity." In *The Oxford Handbook of Comparative Constitutional Law*, edited by Michel Rosenfeld and András Sajó, 756–776. Oxford: Oxford University Press.
Rosenfeld, Michel. 2009. *The Identity of the Constitutional Subject: Selfhood, Citizenship, Culture, and Community*. London: Routledge.
Roznai, Yaniv. 2017. *Unconstitutional Constitutional Amendments: The Limits of Amendment Powers*. Oxford: Oxford University Press.
Sajó, András. 2019. "On Constitutional Identity and Loyalties of the Constitutional Judge." *Cardozo Law Review* 40: 3253–3276.
Shōichi, Koseki. 1997. *The Birth of Japan's Postwar Constitution*, edited by Ray A. Moore. London: Routledge.
Van Der Schyff, Gerhard. 2020. "Member States of the European Union, Constitutions, and Identity: A Comparative Perspective." In *Constitutional Identity in a Europe of Multilevel Constitutionalism*, edited by Christian Calliess and Gerhard Van Der Schyff, 305–347. Cambridge: Cambridge University Press.
Versteeg, Mila. 2014. "Unpopular Constitutionalism." *Indiana Law Journal* 89: 1133–1190.
Voermans, Wim, Maarten Stremler and Paul Cliteur. 2017. *Constitutional Preambles: A Comparative Analysis*. Cheltenham: Edward Elgar Publishing.
World Bank Group. 2020. "Doing Business 2020." https://documents1.worldbank.org/curated/en/688761571934946384/pdf/Doing-Business-2020-Comparing-Business-Regulation-in-190-Economies.pdf.
Zhang, Qianfan. 2012. *The Constitution of China: A Contextual Analysis*. London: Bloomsbury Publishing.

LEGISLATION

Constitution of Ireland 1937.
Constitution of the Kingdom of Bhutan 2008.
Constitution of the Republic of Ecuador 2008.
Political Constitution of the State of Bolivia 2009.
Constitution of the Dominican Republic 2015.

25

Contrariness and Contradiction in Constitutional Law

Zachary Elkins and Tom Ginsburg

A foolish consistency is the hobgoblin of little minds, adored by little statesmen and philosophers and divines.

Ralph Waldo Emerson, *Self Reliance*

INTRODUCTION

In the 1990s (and perhaps to this day) the door to the computer lab in the Berkeley Political Science Department posted two very clear, if contradictory, rules:

1a. Absolutely no food or drink in the computer lab;
1b. If you do bring in food or drink, be very careful.

The rules' inconsistency would, at once, amuse and relieve undercaffeinated and undernourished graduate students. Perhaps surprisingly though, one finds similar examples of tension in law, such as the following pair of provisions:[1]

2a. Property rights are protected;
2b. The government should redistribute property equitably.

It seems that in recent years, many libraries have relaxed their rules and come to adopt something similar to the Berkeley policy, just as many constitutions in the developing world have versions of the second. One wonders, then, what other sort of logical and interpretive conflicts arise in constitutions? That, indeed, is our modest goal here: a survey of paradoxes, contradictions, and contrasts that are woven into constitutional texts.

The occasion for this inquiry is our reconsideration of a set of ideas beautifully articulated by our colleague Gary Jacobsohn with respect to the disharmonic elements of constitutional law. As Jacobsohn has shown, these disharmonic elements tell us much about the societies governed by these texts. Jacobsohn famously pulls most of his insights from three countries that all begin with the letter "I" and were influenced

---

[1] A stylized but, evidently, not fictional example (keep reading).

strongly by the UK legal tradition.[2] Our comparative advantage – to the extent that we have one – is in expanding the sample geographically, culturally, and temporally. Part of our interest is ecological; that is, in documenting the habitat of ideas – disharmonic ideas, in this case. Elkins calls this kind of exercise *conceptual ecology*. Another part is in exporting the Jacobsohnian view to other cases to see how well it travels. And a third is to take the Jacobsohnian idea of disharmony and use it as a point of departure toward a taxonomy of the kinds of disharmony on display in constitutions.

25.1 THE FUTILITY OF CONSISTENCY

It would be naive to expect consistency in constitutional documents since we see it so rarely in any set of plans. One might hope that, at least, a single individual – Solon, to take the paradigmatic example – could produce a cohesive constitution (Lanni and Vermeule 2012). Emerson's "hobgoblin" passage in our epigraph suggests that even this is impossible. One day Solon might want to protect the life and dignity of workers; the next day to protect the environment; and the next, to grow the economy and maximize economic production. These three objectives are often in tension with one another, but what leader wouldn't want all three? We are constantly beset by conflicting imperatives (Bendix 1978); it is the reason that human beings agonize over decisions. Elster (1987) identifies this as the problem of "multiple selves." Such indecision might lead one to leave decision-making to others and is one reason that societies tussle over the meaning of their founding documents.[3]

The example above suggests that one may hold competing objectives at even the same moment. Of course, as conditions change, the probability of multiple selves increases. The dipsomaniac swears off drink the morning after a bender, only to reach for a glass come happy hour. Conditions and, therefore, timing matter. Many constitutional provisions make sense given their context but less so later. Take Japan's well-known "peace clause" (Article 9) following World War II, which has come under pressure since the Cold War began. Another example is the ban on quartering soldiers, embodied in the Third Amendment to the U.S. Constitution. This made sense in 1787 but has never been adjudicated and now seems irrelevant, at least domestically. These examples indicate, simply, that preferences and conditions change. Why should we expect consistency in human behavior – much less a dynamic human creation authored across generations – when the ground underneath us is moving? Indeed, much of the tension in Jacobsohn's *Constitutional Identity* arises from shifts in societal conditions and preferences over time. Constitutions may struggle with changing conditions, but of course, their *raison d'être* is built on such. Constitutions

---

[2] We will call this set the "I-threes," and thus pay homage to the wonderful harmony of the trio of Jamaican voices of the same name, which stands in stark contrast to the disharmonic constitution.
[3] We note that this focus on the individual parallels a fascinating discussion in Jacobsohn 2010 about the connection between individual identity and constitutional identity.

are meant to solve exactly these concerns of "dynamic inconsistency" (see Amick, Chapman, and Elkins 2020). If we want to commit our future selves to a sober life, we will throw away the bottle of bourbon upon waking up and commit, constitutionally, to ginger ale – regardless (or because!) of how inviting the cocktail appears.

Since consistency is evidently impossible within a single organism, we might stop here in our proof. Any expansion beyond single individuals will only increase the dissonance, one would think. But since nearly all constitutions are the product of collaboration, we might plod on – if only for descriptive accuracy. After all, it could be that multiple voices are symphonic and, somehow, jointly consistent. The document drafted in Philadelphia in the summer of 1787 suggests otherwise. There, fifty-five men who shared the same religion, language, and cultural heritage put together a document for their small agricultural society. The document satisfied merely two-thirds of their co-delegates in Philadelphia and, upon returning to their states, a bare majority of their constituents in some places.[4] As we all know, the U.S. Constitution has had its share of disharmony, often explained by its cousin, compromise.[5]

But these days, one expects a constitution to capture the hopes and dreams of enormous societies inhabited by both city slickers and country folk, those of different means, those speaking different languages, those practicing different religions, those with ancestral claims to the land as well as new arrivals from different parts of the globe – all of whom inhabit separate municipalities and jurisdictions within the national boundary. Oh, and let's remember the expectations for public involvement these days. As Donald Horowitz (2021) points out, the drumbeat for ever-more public participation is deafening. The number of voices has exploded. Diverse groups and individuals will bring very different visions of the purpose, text, and process of constitution making. Coherence be damned.

All this to say that the idea of a constitutional identity – some sort of coherent core – amounts to exactly what Jacobsohn has said it is: a set of ideas woven, dialogically, from conflict and disharmony. Disharmony is everywhere, and inseparable from identity. But what kinds of disharmony do we see in these documents? Jacobsohn's examples pique our interest – and there must be all sorts of disharmony once we open up historical constitutions.

25.2 KINDS OF DISHARMONY

Our title invokes the duality of contraries versus contradictories, which is one important aspect of inconsistency identified in classical (Aristotelian) logic. We will review

---

[4] We are thinking about the U.S. Constitution's narrow victories in Massachusetts and New York, among other statehouses.

[5] Compromise may well be necessary, but it does come at the expense of coherence. We often think of Donald Horowitz's expectation that a "designed" constitution implies coherence (Horowitz 2000). In his recent thoughtful book (Horowitz 2021), he outlines a process of consensus (deliberation, not horse-trading or even voting), which may well be a recipe for such coherence.

these classic distinctions here, and go (slightly) beyond the state of the art circa 200 BC. In addition to Aristotle's framework, we elaborate on a further type of tension/inconsistency, which helps to exhaust the various forms in existence.

The formalism of these arguments may be jarring for some, but perhaps only fitting in a Festschrift for Gary Jacobsohn, whose writing plunges us into political philosophy often enough, though perhaps not formal logic. It seems to us that if one is to make arguments about inconsistency, formal logic is unavoidable. And, though formal logic can have a master-of-the-obvious quality, there is something to be said for "explicit" knowledge, as against the "tacit" variety. For it is often the case that ideas are obvious only after they have been articulated clearly.[6] Still, in our experience, formal logic is best served when one is well rested and open to logical puzzles, lest the experience be both unenlightening and unpleasant.

25.2.1 *Aristotelian Notions of Inconsistency*

The critical Aristotelian distinction that motivates us is that some ideas negate one another (**contradictories**), while others are in more indirect tension (**contraries**). Specifically, contraries refer to two statements that cannot both be true, but that can both be false (see, e.g., Bonevac 1998). So,

3a. citizens can leave the country freely;
3b. citizens cannot leave the country freely.

are **contradictories**. Stating that citizens can leave denies one that says they cannot. However, a pair of **contraries** might be:

4a. sovereignty resides with the people;
4b. sovereignty resides with the monarchy.

4a would seem to rule out 4b. But really, both could be false, as one could imagine a third source of sovereignty (an elite group, a religious cleric, etc.), though both cannot be true if one believes sovereignty is unitary. Handing the ultimate power to two separate entities is, thus, contrarian. A third category, **subcontraries**, is the reverse of contrariness – that is, two statements that both may be true, but cannot both be false. This typically occurs when each proposition makes a particular, rather than a universal, statement. An example might be,

5a. some property is eligible to be confiscated;
5b. some property is not eligible to be confiscated.

Both statements can be true (one can imagine some property that is explicitly off limits to confiscation and other property that is explicitly confiscable). But if one of

---

[6] As one example, consider Gary Herstein's 2009 treatment of the right to privacy.

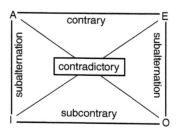

FIGURE 25.1 The Aristotelian square of opposition
Note: **A** propositions, or *universal affirmatives*, take the form: All S are P.; **E** propositions, or *universal negations*, take the form: No S are P; **I** propositions, or *particular affirmatives*, take the form: Some S are P; **O** propositions, or *particular negations*, take the form: Some S are not P. (Graphic and note reprinted from Fieser and Dowden 2011).

these is false (say, false that some property is off limits (5b) – that is, that all property is confiscable), it cannot be false that some property is confiscable, since we just said that it was *all* confiscable. Doubly false here thus would create two contradictory statements. If your head is *not* spinning at this point, you must have slept well last night, or you are wired for logic. The inference is that contradictories and contraries in a constitution would both be incoherent; subcontraries would not (Figure 25.1). It may be useful to classify elements of constitutions as one or the other type. But hold on, there is a fourth category of subtle tension, which is even more prevalent and more interesting.

In the interest of getting our foot in the door, we have waited to overwhelm the reader with notation, but at this point, some accounting makes sense. The "Aristotelian Square" (Figure 25.1), summarizes the kinds of conflict one might expect from any pair of four basic declarative statements: universal affirmatives (A), universal negations (E), particular affirmatives (I), and particular negations (O). (See the note in the figure for elaborations of these forms.) We've already discussed three kinds of Aristotelian "oppositional" logic that arise from the juxtaposition of these statements. A fourth is that of **subalternation**. Two statements relate in this way if one expresses a universal predicate and the other (the **subaltern**) suggests a partial condition of the same predicate. "All people are free" (A) is thus **superaltern** to the statement "some people are free" (I). The superaltern clearly implies the subaltern but not the reverse.

As we shall see, the redundant expression of the subaltern seems to cast doubt on the superaltern, though not logically oppose it. Why say that *some* people are free if you've already told us that *all* people are free? These sorts of relationships are, as we shall see, plentiful in constitutional law, in which one finds seemingly blanket freedoms expressed in one section, only to be accentuated by positive carve-outs in another section. If the Equal Rights Amendment (ERA), which provided for equality irrespective of sex, had become the Twenty-seventh Amendment to the U.S.

Constitution, it would have been subaltern to the Fourteenth Amendment, which had provided general equality.[7] These days, constitutional drafters commonly single out certain groups for *equal* treatment, as paradoxical as that sounds. Indeed, it is something of a dilemma for constitutional drafters as to which groups, exactly, to select for equal treatment. Gender, sex, race, religion, and age, are common candidates. But what about sexual orientation or language – surely you will leave some demographic markers out by going down this road of inclusion. And by including some, but not others, what are you doing except suggesting those groups that are excluded are not entitled to equal treatment? Subalterns, then, may not necessarily be inconsistent with their superaltern, but an inconsistency is implied. They emphasize one variant of the universal position, perhaps for a particular condition that would otherwise be neglected. But by so doing, that calls into question the blanket condition. Call this, for lack of an existing term, the emphasis-that-weakens-the-rule, the flip side of the well-known exception-that-proves-the-rule idea (about which more below).

Subalternate clauses have potentially far-reaching effects. Consider, for example, the case of enumerated versus unenumerated rights. What ought we to do if a constitution expresses a set of general rights with respect to, say, dignity, liberty, and equality, but follows it up with an enumerated set of particulars? Does the enumeration of these particular rights call into question any rights that would follow from a more general theory of the constitution? The U.S. founders hastened to add the Ninth Amendment, to clarify that "The enumeration in the Constitution, of certain rights, shall not be construed to deny or disparage others retained by the people." However, that amendment has not stopped those who would deny, say, the right to privacy as a fundamental right in the United States.

Importantly, partial propositions can read as contradictory when they reverse the sign of the predicate. We can read this off of Figure 25.1 easily enough if we travel from a universal affirmative (A) to a particular negation (O) (see Figure 25.1). So, "all people are free" is contradicted by "some people are not free." As we shall see, the U.S. founders' approach to female, Black, and Indigenous peoples seems to have traded in this sort of contradiction. We'll see that contradictions can sometimes be rendered coherent, in the sense of exceptions proving the rule. So, a "no parking," universal negation (E) statement combined with a "except on Sundays" particular affirmative (I) seems to be a contradiction but we know, of course, that suggesting a conditional affirmation can provide a sense of credibility to the universal negation. A blanket "no parking" sign is just not credible, at least to aggressive parkers.

---

[7] Alas, the ERA was not to be the Twenty-seventh Amendment, though it may well become the Twenty-eighth. One of us is institutionally committed to pointing out that it was a University of Texas undergraduate who is responsible for (finally, 200 years since its proposal) enacting the Twenty-seventh amendment (see Elkins 2022).

Finally, classical logic can take us only so far. "Modern" logic helps as it appreciates the possibility of fiction (and, therefore, facts) in identifying a null set.[8] Central here is the concept of "empirical import," which introduces the notion that the truth of the statement depends upon the idea that the subject actually exists. The implication is that some contraries are actually contradictories and that some contradictories are actually contraries (see our discussion of slavery below). That is, it may be theoretically (and rhetorically) possible that two statements can both be false, but facts in the world suggest that one or the other must be true (and vice versa). Given the famously theoretical nature of some constitutional texts, it may be that modern logic will prove relevant. We shall see.

If these logical categories are confusing, it is possible that some more, less stylized, examples from constitutional text will elucidate these various forms.

25.3 ILLUSTRATIONS

Do drafters write constitutional clauses that exhibit these kinds of logical inconsistency? What do they look like and how do they work? Or *do* they work?

25.3.1 *Contradiction and the Peculiar Institution*

Imagine a constitution that provides for individual freedom but also permits bondage and slavery.[9] The U.S. Constitution (or, in abolitionist William Lloyd Garrison's words, a "covenant with death") may well do this. As we know, the text forbids the end of the slave trade until 1808 (Article 1, Section 9, Paragraph 1), over-represents voters in slave states by three-fifths (Article 1, Section 2, Paragraph 3), under-counts individuals in slave states by two-fifths for tax purposes (Article 1, Section 9, Paragraph 4), returns fugitive slaves to their owners (Article IV, Section 2, Paragraph 3), and prohibits any amendment of the slave importation and taxing clauses until 1808 (Article V). The message is clear: some people are not free.[10]

The contradiction is evident when we read through the freedoms detailed in the First Amendment, as well as the extensive criminal procedural and detainment rights of Amendments Four through Eight and, of course, the natural rights implied by the Ninth Amendment. Not to mention the right against unjustified restraint in the habeas corpus clause in Article 1, Section 9, Paragraph 2.

Each of these provisions implies blanket freedom for those in the United States governed by the document. In Aristotelian terms, this amounts to an A–O relationship. A, "People are free from restraint" and O, "Some people are not free from

---

[8] By "modern," philosophers mean roughly the last two hundred years.
[9] We refer readers to Graber 2006 for indispensable background reading here.
[10] Another view is that of Oakes 2021, who suggests that the constitution empowered anti-slavery ideas more forcefully than most see it.

restraint." This is a clear contradiction, as corroborated by the Aristotelian square in Figure 25.1. The only logical resolution to this contradiction is one in which an entire category of people is denied citizenship, which is, of course, the odious assumption that the founders made. In logical terms, this is an example of "empirical import," in which the facts and context that define the subject (in this case, citizenship) matter. It is worth emphasizing that an abolitionist minority of citizens at the time were not at all on board with such a designation, lest we chalk up such thinking to a pre-enlightened consensus.

Of course, post-civil war amendments altered facts on the ground again and rendered some of the statements in the constitution more coherent. Specifically, the Fourteenth Amendment made clear that all those born in the country were citizens, a simple and inclusive rule. Nevertheless, the United States continues to struggle with its original sin, and what Graber (2006) calls the "Problem of Constitutional Evil."

25.3.2 Further Contradiction: Property Rights and Land Redistribution

Another seemingly explicit contradiction arises with those constitutions with both strong property rights clauses and a comprehensive plan to redistribute property. Of course, every right, including property, has its limits, with eminent domain and state takings being one of them. An aggressive agrarian reform program, however, would seem to be antithetical to strong property rights.

One example concerns the property clauses contained in Section 25 of South Africa's 1996 Constitution. That document embodied a grand bargain between the National Party and the African National Congress (ANC), which had long been committed to redistributive social and economic policies. The compromise included protection for individual property rights and a market-based economy; and for the ANC, formal commitments to broad and inclusive development. The property clauses embodied these somewhat competing goals. Section 25 (1) made clear that property rights, in general, were protected: "No one may be deprived of property except in terms of law of general application, and no law may permit arbitrary deprivation of property." Section 25(3) of the constitution provided that compensation for the expropriation of property was to be,

> just and equitable, reflecting an equitable balance between the public interest and the interests of those affected, having regard to all relevant circumstances, including the current use of the property; the history of the acquisition and use of the property; the market value of the property; the extent of direct state investment and subsidy in the acquisition and beneficial capital improvement of the property; and the purpose of the expropriation. [Section 25(3)]

At the same time, Section 25(5) and 26(2) provided that the state must "take reasonable legislative and other measures, within its available resources'" both to "foster conditions which enable citizens to gain access to land on an equitable basis" and "achieve the progressive realisation of" the right of access to housing. Section 26(3) further provided that "[n]o one may be evicted from their home, or have their home demolished, without an order of court made after considering all the relevant circumstances [and that] [n]o legislation may permit arbitrary evictions." And Section 25(7) required restitution or compensation for those dispossessed of lands after the passage of the Native Lands Act of 1913.[11] The 1996 Constitution thus effectively created a system in which property rights were protected, land reform was encouraged, and property holders could not evict tenants freely.

Logically, South Africa reflects the tension in the pair of statements (2a and 2b) with which we opened the essay and some of the tension of the statements in (5a and 5b), which we described as subcontraries. South Africa seems to suggest that (1) property rights matter; (2) property will be treated in accordance with law (generally); but (3) property must be redistributed to correct wrongs. One could view this as a set of compromises that led to a coherent bargain between parties engaged in negotiation (Dixon and Ginsburg 2011). But it is also possible to read the clauses as signaling quite incompatible things to different audiences: Property rights are secure, but redistribution of property is required. The same document speaks out of both sides of its mouth in two different registers: The result is disharmony.

Argentina is not much different. Article 17 begins with two statements reminiscent of Statements 2a and 2b:

6a. "Property is inviolable;"
6b. "…except by virtue of a judgment supported by law."

Regarding confiscation, one may view this as a universal negation (E) combined with a particular affirmative (I). That is, following the Aristotelian square, a contradictory. One imagines a claimant in the court of law arguing, "what part of 'inviolable' don't you understand?"

Then there is Zimbabwe:

Article 289. Principles guiding policy on agricultural land
In order to redress the unjust and unfair pattern of land ownership that was brought about by colonialism, and to bring about land reform and the equitable access by all Zimbabweans to the country's natural resources, policies regarding agricultural land must be guided by the following principles –

a. land is a finite natural resource that forms part of Zimbabweans' common heritage;
b. subject to section 72, every Zimbabwean citizen has a right to acquire, hold, occupy, use, transfer, hypothecate, lease or dispose of agricultural land regardless of his or her race or colour;

---

[11] "A person or community dispossessed of property after 19 June 1913 as a result of past racially discriminatory laws or practices is entitled, to the extent provided by an Act of Parliament, either to restitution of that property or to equitable redress."

Constitutional Law: Contrariness and Contradiction

c. the allocation and distribution of agricultural land must be fair and equitable, having regard to gender balance and diverse community interests;
d. the land tenure system must promote increased productivity and investment by Zimbabweans in agricultural land;
e. the use of agricultural land should promote food security, good health and nutrition and generate employment, while protecting and conserving the environment for future generations;
f. no person may be deprived arbitrarily of their right to use and occupy agricultural land.

This section seems to incorporate contradictory impulses of private property subject to many competing imperatives. It seems to imagine that there will be rights to own land, secure from arbitrary deprivation (clause f) while at the same time requiring land reform. It demands redistribution and increased productivity at the same time (clauses c and d), along with insurance that land use promotes other goals (clause e). This kind of constitutional language provides something for everyone, but the competing imperatives may actually increase the discretion of the government, which can always point to one of the goals it is advancing. Logically, a demand for both X and not-X is contradictory, meaning that nothing is legal, but in practice, everything is likely to be on the table.

25.3.3 Subalternation, Contrariness, and Contradiction: Non-discrimination and Discrimination

Constitutions are filled with universal affirmations, combined with both particular affirmations and particular negations, which can result in subalternation and contradiction, respectively.

25.3.3.1 Group Rights versus Individual Rights

Most organizations these days are doing whatever they can to be more diverse and inclusive. Part of avoiding the mistakes of the past is to avoid discrimination along demographic lines, both explicit and implicit. But of course it is exactly this proscription against favoring one group over another that thwarts efforts that would advantage minorities. One way to think about this is as a tension between individual and group rights. Individuals should be treated equally, but some groups will be advantaged.

Canada is a good example. Consider Article 15 of the 1982 document:

1. **Equality before and under law and equal protection and benefit of law.** Every individual is equal before and under the law and has the right to the equal protection and equal benefit of the law without discrimination and, in particular, without discrimination based on race, national or ethnic origin, colour, religion, sex, age or mental or physical disability.

2. **Affirmative action programs.** Subsection (1) does not preclude any law, program or activity that has as its object the amelioration of conditions of disadvantaged individuals or groups including those that are disadvantaged because of race, national or ethnic origin, colour, religion, sex, age or mental or physical disability.

One view of these clauses is a of a *universal negation* (no discrimination based on race, etc.) with a *particular affirmative* (discrimination for some based on race, etc.). These are contradictories in Aristotelian logic and not easily reconcilable, as has been obvious to anyone watching high courts, as well as admissions and hiring committees over the years. The resolutions tend to be messy and politically contested.

25.3.3.2 Identity Regimes and Equality

Consider a related source of tension: constitutions that privilege certain identities (presumably of the majority this time) while, again, providing for non-discrimination. Elkins and Sides have called these kinds of state privileges "identity regimes"; examples include provisions for official language, official religion, official political party, and descent-based citizenship (see, e.g., Elkins 2019). This kind of enhanced membership in the state is quite prevalent in constitutions.

For example, consider Article 2 of the Iraqi constitution, which actually includes two areas of tension, though we'll focus on the tension regarding identity regimes first: Article 2.

1. Islam is the official religion of the State and is a foundation source of legislation.
    a. No law may be enacted that contradicts the established provisions of Islam.
    b. No law may be enacted that contradicts the principles of democracy.
    c. No law may be enacted that contradicts the rights and basic freedoms stipulated in this Constitution.
2. This Constitution guarantees the Islamic identity of the majority of the Iraqi people and guarantees the full religious rights to freedom of religious belief and practice of all individuals such as Christians, Yazidis, and Mandean Sabeans.

We'll start with the tension between the first clause (official religion) of Article 2 and the second (non-discrimination) clause. What these identity regimes do, in effect, is to declare that one group (a religious group) is more central than are others. Put differently, some groups enjoy a more central position in the state than others. Imagine if we were to rewrite it as a universal affirmative and a particular affirmative. As in,

7a. Some residents are full 2(1);
7b. All residents are full members of the nation (Article 2(2)).

The statements are simplified, but reflect the spirit of "guarantees full rights and freedom" as against the preferential treatment of "official religion" and "foundational source of law." The pair of statements is a classic A/I combination, in which the second is subaltern to the first. We've seen this before, in the case of equality rights and the ERA above (recall, "everyone will be treated equally" and "women will be treated equally"). We understand this as an emphasis-that-questions-the-rule effect, which seems to follow from subaltern relationships: Singling some groups out as full members casts doubt on the universal that all groups have membership.

There are other ways to think about these identity regimes that do not involve subalternation in membership. Consider this more practical formulation with respect to official language:

8a. Some conversations (say, private meetings) can be conducted in your language;
8b. Some conversations (say, public meetings) cannot be conducted in your language.

These particular negations and particular affirmatives are subcontraries and, perhaps, easily reconcilable. They can both be true; they cannot both be false. It may not be an ideal situation (public meetings and school instruction may be very important to have in your own language). But it's not contradictory.

Of course, if one is to think of what these language clauses indicate about membership, then we have the same subaltern situation that we describe above in the Iraqi case.

25.3.4 Errors

Finally, lest one think that disharmony is deeply intractable, there are contradictions introduced by outright errors in constitutional texts. An early draft of the Brazilian Constitution of 1988 protected the right to life, even during cases of fatal illness. It is up to a reader to determine what they meant: prohibiting euthanasia? Ensuring maximum care for the elderly? Or simply an error? The rush to produce a final constitutional text sometimes leads to what are called "Scrivener's errors" which were unintended but make the text nonsensical, including missing article numbers and cross-references. Nicaragua's Constitution of 1950 seems to contain a mathematical error, providing for a target ratio of one-third minority members of the Senate that is not even achieved in the original allocation of one-quarter:

> In the Chamber of Deputies twenty-eight Representatives shall belong to the majority party and fourteen to the minority; in the Senate twelve Senators shall belong to the majority and four to the minority. With respect to the Senate, the law may change the ratio of the minority in order that this shall always be, as nearly as possible, one third of the total membership.

Minor errors, of course, are easy to fix. Scrivener's errors can be repaired through judicial interpretation. For more consequential matters, the legislature may have to amend the constitutional text accordingly. But whether it could actually do so might depend on the political consequences and the difficulty of mustering the proper majority. We thus have the possibility of lingering disharmonies as a matter of course.

CONCLUSION: DEALING WITH DISHARMONY

Even constitutions with these logical inconsistencies can "work" at some level, which recalls our quote from Emerson. Perhaps we need not be hung up on such inconsistencies. Like everything else in life, we can find a way to adapt and muddle through.

But what does "muddling through" look like with respect to constitutions? Well, of course, we should note that there exist gradations of disharmony, ranging from slight atonalities to very severe logical contradictions that simply cannot be harmonized, but must rather be overcome. But the difficulty of overcoming or resolving disharmony is a distinct dimension from the degree of disharmony. Putting the two dimensions together, we can identify four combinations.

Self Tuning. In this quadrant, we place disharmonies that are minor and easy to overcome. Imagine an orchestra in which the pre-concert tuning of instruments has not worked completely. As the concert starts, the lead violinist hears that one string is out of tune. Deftly grabbing her tuning peg, she can adjust the string during a lull in her part. The disharmony was slight, and even if audible to a listener, was easily resolved. Our category of "errors" fits easily into this category.

Cooperative Tuning. In this quadrant, we place those disharmonies that are relatively minor, but difficult to overcome. Like a pianist who discovers onstage that her piano is out of tune, there is little choice but to tolerate the disharmony for the duration of the concert and to fix the tuning before the next one. One might think of the clause in the Seventh Amendment to the U. S. Constitution, which requires a civil jury trial in any case in which more than twenty dollars is in dispute. With inflation, this proved impractical and the solution required legislation to limit the availability of federal courts for low-stakes cases. But the original text remains in place, as it cannot be easily removed.

The Conductor as Harmonizer. Next, we consider disharmonies that are more substantial but can be resolved through creative coordination. Imagine an orchestra reading a musical score in which both the brass and strings are playing loudly. This might be a substantial irritant to the listener. But if there is a conductor of the orchestra, she can rather easily signal to the players that they should behave differently, reducing the volume to be more harmonious. We think of courts as playing this conducting role when dealing with disharmony. In the case of the South African property clauses, the Constitutional Court has produced a long line of decisions interpreting and harmonizing apparently incompatible provisions. This has led to a workable regime, and something of a balance between redistribution and protection of property. Sometimes this has involved the Court looking to constitutional principles or goals, so as to help prioritize one rule over another. In other cases, the Court has used the jurisprudential technique of proportionality to harmonize competing rights claims. This technique involves balancing competing interests in a way that seeks to minimize constraints on rights.

Irreconcilable Disharmony. While such techniques work well in the realm of rights, where doctrines of proportionality and balancing are available, they are not always sufficient. Our fourth box includes substantial disharmonies that are also difficult to resolve. To our ears, the musical version might be Beethoven's symphony "Wellington's Victory," a notoriously bombastic composition that makes us want to run from the room. Others might put free jazz in the category. One person's disharmony might be beautiful in the eyes of another, but from the point of view of the listener, the disharmony cannot be resolved.

Consider the contradiction in the U.S. Constitution between freedom and slavery. The disharmony of the constitutional scheme invited political mobilization to confront what appeared to be irreconcilable contradictions. For abolitionists, slave-holders' interests could not be accommodated if the promise of American liberty was to be preserved; slave-holders saw in the other side a threat to their wealth that could not be accommodated. Ultimately, institutions did not protect the South; they had to lose a war. And even then, the legacies of the "peculiar institution" provide a great source of disharmony in American politics today.

Some disharmonies may take centuries to resolve if they ever do.

REFERENCES

Amick, Joe, Terrence Chapman, and Zachary Elkins. 2020. "On Constitutionalizing a Balanced Budget." *The Journal of Politics* 82 (3): 1078–1096.

Bendix, Reinhard. 1978. *Kings or People: Power and the Mandate to Rule*. Oakland: University of California Press.

Bonevac, Daniel. 1998. *Simple Logic*. Oxford: Oxford University Press.

Dixon, Rosalind and Tom Ginsburg. 2011. "The South African Constitutional Court and Socio-economic Rights as Insurance Swaps'." *Constitutional Court Review* 4 (1): 1–29.

Elkins, Zachary. 2019. "On the Paradox of State Religion and Religious Freedom." In *Oxford Research Encyclopedia of Politics*, edited by William R. Thompson. Oxford: Oxford University Press. https://oxfordre.com/politics/display/10.1093/acrefore/9780190228637.001.0001/acrefore-9780190228637-e-846?rskey=6hQL2J&result=1.

Elkins, Zachary. 2022. "Underestimated but Undeterred: The 27th Amendment and the Power of Tenacious Citizenship." *Political Science and Politics* 56 (1): 158–163.

Elster, Jon. 1987. *The Multiple Self*. Cambridge: Cambridge University Press.

Emerson, Ralph Waldo. 1983. "Self-Reliance (1841)." In *Ralph Waldo Emerson: Essays and Lectures*, edited by Joel Porte, 259–282. New York: Library of America.

Fieser, James and Bradley Dowden. 2011. "Aristotle: Logic." In *Internet Encyclopedia of Philosophy*. https://iep.utm.edu/aristotle-logic/#H5

Graber, Mark A. 2006. *Dred Scott and the Problem of Constitutional Evil*. Cambridge: Cambridge University Press.

Herstein, Gary. 2009. "What Formal Logic Can Do." *Science* 2.0. www.science20.com/inquiry_inquiry/what_formal_logic_can_do.

Horowitz, Donald L. 2000. "Constitutional Design: An Oxymoron?" *American Society for Political Legal Philosophy* 42: 253–284.

Horowitz, Donald L. 2021. *Constitutional Processes and Democratic Commitment*. New Haven: Yale University Press.

Jacobsohn, Gary J. 2010. *Constitutional Identity*. Cambridge: Harvard University Press.

Lanni, Adriaan and Adrian Vermeule. 2012. "Constitutional Design in the Ancient World." *Stanford Law Review* 64 (4): 907–949.

Oakes, James. 2021. *The Crooked Path to Abolition*. Arizona: Norton.

26

Conclusion

The Past, Present, and Future of Constitutional Identity

Christina Bambrick and Connor M. Ewing

INTRODUCTION

Taken together, the contributions to this volume illustrate the value of understanding constitutional identity not as entirely fixed, but as an emergent phenomenon. In scholarship and politics alike, constitutional identity is "an essentially contested concept" (Rosenfeld 2012, 756). Contributing to this pivotal insight, Gary Jacobsohn develops an understanding of constitutional identity in terms of disharmony throughout his corpus, and particularly in his 2010 book. In his own take on the concept, Michel Rosenfeld emphasizes a similar fluidity, describing constitutional identity as "determined by the need for dialectical mediation" of conflicts "between identity and difference ... that shape the dealings between self and other" (Rosenfeld 2012). Despite their differences, these accounts of constitutional identity, and others that have since built upon them, share the virtue of clarifying constitutional politics without diminishing its complexity. In particular, understanding identity in terms of disharmony and dialogue, or dialectical mediation, admits a crucial sensitivity to the vast range of forces driving constitutional politics. For example, Jacobsohn's dialogic take foregrounds such drivers of constitutional politics as competing commitments or interpretations of the constitutional project, incongruity between the constitutional text and lived experience, and variance between the values particular to a place and more universal principles associated with constitutionalism. On the one hand, constitutional identity must include some persisting or essential elements, an aspect that Michel Troper highlights in the arguments of French constitutional actors against the increasing power of EU institutions (Troper 2010). On the other hand, understanding the content of constitutional identity as abiding in conflict, uncertainty, and indeterminacy enables us to see constitutional politics ultimately as a product of continual exchange and unfolding.

In this concluding chapter, we focus on two central contributions that a dynamic understanding of constitutional identity makes to the study of constitutional politics. First, we discuss the relationship between constitutional identity and constitutional development, a connection of not only substantive but also methodological significance. Here we emphasize the ways in which the concept of constitutional identity engenders a mode of analysis that is both historically sensitive and attuned to the dynamics of political development. In doing so, we identify how constitutional identity differs from and can ultimately enrich the now-dominant understanding of political development within the literature.

Second, we describe lessons that the concept of constitutional identity offers both scholars and practitioners, particularly in light of current challenges to the foundations and practice of constitutional governance. From the rise of populism and challenges to the rule of law to democratic backsliding and intensifying constitutional rot, constitutionalism today confronts a potent set of obstacles (Bermeo 2016; Coppedge 2017; Eatwell and Goodwin 2018; Waldner and Lust 2018; Norris and Inglehart 2019; Revelli 2019; Balkin 2020). Although clearly concerning, these developments bring into focus issues that are in certain ways perennial in constitutional orders, such as how to treat difference and indeterminacy in constitutional politics. Indeed, constitutional government is born of the need to establish governing principles and rules amid differences that do not lend themselves to quick or easy resolution.

Some degree of harmonization and unity may be the point of a constitution. However, disharmony and diversity will persist as long as different people, with different projects and interests, are party to the constitutional enterprise. Likewise, the landscape of constitutionalism cannot but be shaped by shifting politics. To understand constitutional identity in terms of this disharmony and difference is thus to take constitutional politics on its own terms, as dynamic and largely contingent on how actors negotiate their position in and interpretation of the constitution's commitments. Such understandings offer students of (and, potentially, actors within) constitutional politics concepts to make sense of and act in their moment. However, it also proposes a basic humility as to any one person's ability to define constitutional identity amid this characteristic dynamism. Ultimately, this dynamism and indeterminacy creates space for agency. It allows actors to keep hope that they may improve their constitutional state of affairs, that authoritarian and antidemocratic voices hold neither a monopoly nor the last word on constitutional identity.

A certain dynamism underlies constitutional identity in the additional sense that scholars find space to build upon prior work by Jacobsohn, Rosenfeld, Troper, and others when they confront new challenges in constitutional politics, and perhaps even new conceptions of constitutionalism as a result. Taken together, the contributions to this volume point up a range of research agendas that scholars may fruitfully pursue, equipped with the tools that scholars of constitutional identity both forged and inspired. In the fourth section, we briefly address three of these. In doing so, we hope to connect constitutional identity's past and present to its possible futures, elucidating some possible research programs for future inquiry. Our comments in this regard are intended to be less prescriptive than interpretive. Indeed, the scholarly futures we discuss emerge as much from the political world in which constitutional governance must now proceed as from the progress that scholars have made toward understanding the aspirations of that enterprise.

26.1 CONSTITUTIONAL IDENTITY IN AND THROUGH TIME

The elaboration of constitutional identity as a central concern of constitutional theory both marked and catalyzed a renewed sensitivity to political history and political development in constitutional studies. The conceptual architecture of constitutional identity makes this orientation especially clear. Its theoretical foundations and key analytical mechanisms – disharmony, dialogue, dialectical processes, contestation – all reflect the centrality of temporal extension and diachronic analysis to understanding the identity of a constitutional order. Even in more static accounts of constitutional identity, such as those that emphasize legal principles discoverable by judicial actors (e.g., Troper 2010), judicial *interpretation* is portrayed as an iterated process embedded in the tumult of constitutional politics. Illustrating the dynamic interplay at the heart of constitutional identity, Jacobsohn writes, "The development of constitutional identity may thus be conceptualized as a maturation process involving ongoing interactions among multiple actors operating within the parameters of text and history" (Jacobsohn 2016, 122). While constitutional past and present are indissolubly linked, their relationship is mediated by the conflict, interaction, and uncertainty characteristic of constitutional disharmony and the dialectical processes by which identity is negotiated.

While the identity of a particular constitutional order is rooted in and informed by factors that can be apprehended in the moment, its constitutional identity is disclosed in and through time. In turn, this approach centers the dynamics of political development that have been elaborated both within and beyond the literature on constitutional identity. Studies of constitutional identity are thus variously distinguished by a sensitivity to historical contingency and a recognition of the significance of timing, sequencing, and path dependence. These analytical commitments are both cause and consequence of the remarkable breadth of disciplines and methodologies that have taken up various questions connected to constitutional identity. The scholarly development of constitutional identity has been a distinctly interdisciplinary and multi-method enterprise. Enriched by perspectives from political science and law and engaged both qualitatively and quantitatively, the rich variety of case studies, insights, and applications evident in the scholarship on constitutional identity stems from the underlying topic's irreducible complexity.

As illustrated by numerous contributions to this volume, constitutional identity's contingency and dynamism call for an analytical approach that matches the object of inquiry. But even as leading works have been distinguished by a commitment to historical and developmental analysis, the literature on constitutional identity has been enriched by empirical research on the content, character, and performance of constitutional regimes (Elkins et al. 2009; Ginsburg and Versteeg 2017). In this vein, Versteeg's contribution to this volume probes the empirical dimensions of constitutional identity, further underscoring the continued value of the porous disciplinary and methodological borders that have characterized research on constitutional identity to this point.

For all of the continuities between constitutional identity and political development scholarship, constitutional identity is premised on an understanding of political development that sets it apart from much scholarship concerned with political change. The prevailing definition of political development within that literature, formulated by Orren and Skowronek, centers on "durable shifts in governing authority" (2004, 123). On this understanding, political ideas and ideologies are relevant to political analysis to the extent that they are embedded in or transmitted by political institutions and political orders (Orren and Skowronek 2004, 14, 82–83). As a result, these ideas and ideologies are subsumed by institutions, becoming incidental to, rather than the focus of, developmental analysis.

Constitutional identity suggests a rather different conception of political development, one that simultaneously centers political ideas while also expanding the focus beyond discrete, formal shifts in authority. While the processes that elucidate constitutional identity – be they dialogical or dialectical – frequently stop short of producing shifts in political authority, they nonetheless structure and reconfigure the political terrain on which such shifts ultimately occur (or are prevented from occurring). As Rosenfeld's chapter in this volume illustrates, political developments – whether the creation of revolutionary constitutions in the eighteenth century or the emergence of populist constitutions in the twenty-first – crucially depend on the (de)construction of constitutional identity through negation, metaphor, and metonymy. At the same time, this understanding of the relationship between constitutional identity and political development also reveals that the ideals codified in a constitutional text and tradition supply normative parameters for political and constitutional development, "establish[ing] broad limits for the legitimacy of constitutional change" (Jacobsohn 2011, 411; cf. Greenstone 1993). These limits, in turn, give rise to the distinction, probed in this volume by Gardbaum, between constitutional evolution and constitutional revolution (see also Thomas 2011).

To focus only on formal shifts in authority would not only miss important precursors that contribute to and shape subsequent shifts; doing so would also risk impoverished descriptive and explanatory accounts of those developments. By centering the values, aspirations, and ideals embodied in a constitutional system, constitutional identity fosters a subtler understanding of political development, one oriented as much by the *normative commitments of constitutionalism* as the particular disharmonies and tensions operative within a constitutional order.

26.2 EMBRACING DIFFERENCE AND AGENCY IN CONSTITUTIONAL IDENTITY

We now turn from the ways that identity may inform work on constitutional development to other lessons about wrestling with difference and embracing agency that constitutional actors and scholars may glean from this concept. For one thing, the dynamism and contests at the center of different accounts of constitutional identity implicitly call for toleration of difference and diversity. The appreciation for disharmony in Jacobsohn's account, for example, presupposes that different articulations of the constitutional project exist and cautions against discounting accounts that may differ from one's own. Moreover, we find similar lessons in the discursive process involved in carving out constitutional identity that Rosenfeld recounts. When constitutional actors negotiate identity, they "shape the dealings between self and other" and so confront the urgent question of who is represented in that constitutional "self" versus other, who and what is counted as part of that identity versus difference (Rosenfeld 2012, 761). In their characteristic indeterminacy, these understandings of constitutional identity invite a powerful agency for those in the present to contribute to the shape of constitutional identity into the future. As constitutional identity is not entirely fixed but unfolds over time, constitutional actors are not relegated to the role of passive observer or powerless heir of a predetermined conception of identity. On the contrary, the disharmony and contestation that these scholars find in identity preserves some ability to argue for and give voice to certain conceptions of the constitution over others.

In understanding constitutional identity in terms of disharmony or the line between self and other, the fact of difference in the constitutional order necessarily comes to the fore – different interpretations and experiences of the constitutional project all come into focus as not merely incidental but part of the story. In Jacobsohn's telling, the disharmony resulting from such difference is not something that can be avoided but rather is par for the course in constitutional politics. Disharmony may be basically innocuous or even fruitful for the polity, as Bui Bgoc Son argues in his essay on Confucian influences on constitutional identity in Asia. On the other hand, disharmony may be symptomatic of the principal questions and challenges facing a polity, as Bâli and Lerner argue in the context of divided societies. The point is that disharmony and difference persist, even in identity. These are not things that can or should always be overcome, try as we might to pursue a "compelling unity" (Jacobsohn 2010, 84–135). Understanding disharmony and difference as part of the constitutional deal challenges us to be comfortable with diversity even as we wrestle with it. We can expect that competing understandings of the constitutional project will always exist. This may be a difficult pill to swallow when some understandings actually undermine crucial aspects of the constitutional project as we conceive it (Troper 2010), or even basic principles of constitutionalism (Jacobsohn 2012; Rosenfeld 2012, 761). However, even detrimental interpretations can and do become part of the constitutional story and, on this basis, are ignored at our peril.

At the same time, foregrounding disharmony or highlighting the line between self and other begins to engender a conception of constitutional identity that may challenge detrimental interpretations. Indeed, Jacobsohn's and Rosenfeld's takes on the concept lay an intellectual foundation crucial to resisting formulations of constitutional identity that aim to homogenize. In different ways, each of these accounts encompasses diverse perspectives, such that they unsettle alternative conceptions that would reduce identity simply to one ascriptive category, for example, or that absolutize a single element of the constitution at the cost of others. Chapters in this volume by Michel Rosenfeld, and Gabor Halmai and Julian Scholtes point to such tendencies in the cases of Hungary and Poland (see also Jacobsohn and Roznai 2020, Chapter 3), as does Victor Ferreres Comella in addressing certain downsides of constituent power. The Indian BJP's (Bharatiya Janata Party) Hindu nationalism and treatment of Muslims and other minorities as lesser citizens of the constitutional order provide further examples illustrating the value of understanding identity in terms of disharmony rather than, say, a more simple homogeneity or a single attribute (Jacobsohn 2010, 194–195). By foregrounding disharmony and difference as unavoidable, these understandings of constitutional identity have the capacity to resist authoritarian impulses that attempt to circumscribe the constitutional project to serve some parts of the population over others or to weigh disproportionately some constitutional commitments at the cost of others.[1]

Disharmony, contestation, and the sheer fact of evolving politics thus give rise to a kind of indeterminacy, an ability to chart the course of constitutional identity into the future. As George Thomas puts it in his essay, "Thinking in terms of constitutional disharmony we can better understand constitutional actors as constructing constitutional meaning rather than drawing out latent meaning" (Thomas 2024, 205). Identity may be bounded by certain ideas and practical realities. But much about identity consists in the dialogues and discourses emerging out of political developments, some anticipated, but many coming as jolts that no one expects. It is for this reason that constitutional identity cannot be fully discerned from judicial decisions alone, but emerges from a wide range of constitutional actors and even non-elite voices.

In this way, both practitioners and scholars have much to gain from appreciating such features as disharmony and contestation that admit of something yet undecided in identity; however, indeterminacy is not the whole of the story. Indeed, a study of constitutional identity depends on some prior, persistent identity. Heinz Klug and Justin Dyer both gesture toward this possibility in arguing that we might identify among various interpretations of constitutional identity certain "founding values" or "central animating aspirations," respectively. And even when constitutional actors

---

[1] See also Jacobsohn and Roznai's discussion of formal equality in Part III and substantive equality in Part IV of the Indian Constitution (Jacobsohn and Roznai 2020).

or scholars debate or disagree, they acknowledge there is some*thing* about which they are ultimately disagreeing – perhaps the role of religion in Israel, the proper meaning of secularism in Turkey, the demands of equality in India.

Constitutional identity proceeds in part on the basis of such continuities, even if these are often "continuities of conflict" (MacIntyre 1981, 206; cited in Jacobsohn 2010, 99) as different actors debate the meaning of certain concepts in the constitutional history and ongoing project. Even when complex and disputed, these continuities comprise bounds to constitutional identity – bounds as to what a particular constitutional order may support, and even bounds to what more general understandings of constitutionalism could mean. It is through this boundedness that one may argue that certain understandings are better rooted in constitutional history or aspirations than others. Hence, even while disharmony and contestation admit a diversity of inputs, there may still be better and worse accounts of a given constitution's identity, from both a normative and a descriptive perspective. In considering constitutional identity alongside Jacobsohn's early work on aspiration, the possibility and stakes of getting it wrong, so to speak, come into sharp relief (Jacobsohn 1986, 1993). Perhaps paradoxically, it is in the combination of indeterminacy and boundedness that those in the present may claim some agency to shape constitutional identity into the future. Put differently, it is within the bounds of identity that constitutional actors find some*thing* to work toward and, by extension, a renewed sense of agency in the choice of how to proceed.

26.3 THE FUTURE OF CONSTITUTIONAL IDENTITY

As the contributions to this volume attest, constitutional identity continues to motivate reflection on dimensions of constitutional politics that are both timely and enduring. This, in turn, reflects a central insight of the scholarship in this area: Constitutional identity is forged at the intersection of principle and contingency, in the interaction of constitutionalism's core commitments and the ever-changing particularities of politics. For this reason, the future of constitutional identity will, as a matter of course, be shaped by the challenges constitutional polities confront. It is fitting, then, to conclude by looking toward that future. In this section, we identify three promising areas for future scholarly reflection and briefly sketch the first steps of a research agenda oriented toward carrying forward the enterprise limned in these pages.

We begin with perhaps the most pressing concern facing those who see value in the concept of constitutional identity and its continued use, namely the weaponization of constitutional identity, what in his Preface to this volume Jacobsohn calls "abusive appropriations of the concept." Such invocations of constitutional identity – most prominent in Hungary's response to EU refugee relocation efforts though also discernible in debates over judicial power in Israel and identity politics in the United States – have led some to argue that its manifest dangers outweigh its potential benefits. Confronting this objection requires serious reflection on the distinction between good and bad, legitimate and illegitimate uses of the concept. These distinctions, in turn, presume some non-arbitrary sense of what an abuse looks like or entails. While multiple contributions to this volume take up this task in different ways (e.g., Faraguna, Halmai and Scholtes, and Mérieau), much remains to be done at the level of both conceptualization and application.

In the first place, such abuses are, perhaps ironically, an indication of the triumph of constitutional identity. Were it not seen as a meaningful claim with some justificatory power or political significance, it would not be invoked as it has been. Its deployment is thus a sign of its potential import and effect. Constitutional identity is an essentially contested concept, an assessment with which contributors to this volume are in broad agreement (see especially the chapters by Rosenfeld, Bhatia, and Doyle). Troubling invocations of constitutional identity would seem to exploit this characteristic, finding refuge in the welter of political contestation and using it as a shield against allegations of abuse. If the concept is contested, what grounds are there for condemning particular uses?

Those who see principled limits to constitutional identity's use would do well to recall that designating constitutional identity an essentially contested concept is not to concede that the concept is infinitely malleable, nor that abuses cannot be identified (Waldron 2002, 148–153). At least as the term was initially elaborated by Gallie (1956, 1964), an essentially contested concept has several constitutive criteria, ranging from an appraisive character to competition among competing usages that lead to greater conceptual coherence. To the extent that alleged abuses of constitutional identity involve conflicts between different conceptions of constitutional identity, evaluation in terms of Gallie's criteria may enable principled distinctions between those uses deemed by many to be pernicious and those widely seen as acceptable. Such an approach has proven valuable in the case of human dignity, another contested concept at the center of global constitutional politics (Rodriguez 2015). Examining the parameters of constitutional identity's essentially contested nature may supply the grounds for assessing claims made in its name, providing leverage for normative judgments about instances that are in tension – if not inconsistent – with central commitments of constitutionalism.

As Jacobsohn observed in discussions attending the development of this volume, responding to abusive appropriations of constitutional identity not only presents fraught substantive questions about conceptualization and application; it also confronts scholars with difficult prudential questions about how and when to respond to the weaponization of identity claims. While we abjure any intention to dictate how scholars or citizens should engage such questions, we nonetheless see great wisdom in Jacobsohn's admonition: to proceed considerately and deliberatively, mindful of the pitfalls that attend scholarly intervention in pitched political battles. We can think of few better models of this approach than those offered in this volume.

A second promising area of future inquiry concerns variability or development in the relationship at the heart of constitutional identity. Central to the concept of constitutional identity is a distinction that can be understood in terms of values and principles. While the former are local practices and commitments, the latter are the commitments entailed by (perhaps implicit in) constitutionalism (Jacobsohn 2012, 777). As Troper puts it, "one could easily argue that a constitutional identity derives not only from features unique to the country's constitution, but also of [sic] a combination of features common to several constitutions, and essential to each" (2010, 196). These common and essential features – the principles that define conceptions of constitutionalism as such – "need to be reconciled with the particularistic commitments of local traditions and practices; the substance of a nation's constitutional identity will to a large extent reflect how the essentials of constitutionalism combine and interact with the attributes of a constitution that are expressive of unique histories and circumstances" (Jacobsohn 2016, 115).

The tension between values and principles becomes especially apparent when they diverge. Given the relationship between the two, this is principally a consequence of local commitments increasingly coming into tension with what are widely believed to be the constitutive or essential commitments of constitutionalism (Hirschl 2014). At the same time, though, the principles of constitutionalism are themselves a function of historical development. Contemporary conceptions of the range of rights protections that constitutions should include are the result of waves of constitution making since the first modern constitutions in the late eighteenth century. So too with the institutions oriented toward the protection of those rights. In turn, these changes in constitutional practice have given rise to new challenges and tensions within the enterprise of constitutionalism (see, e.g., Hirschl 2004; Loughlin 2022). Because many of the forces that shape the political demands that feed into constitution making are not limited to single countries, shifts in constitutional understandings can take on a systemic quality. In this way, constitutional identity is importantly shaped by the context of constitutionalism, itself a political variable subject to contestation and change. As a consequence, the future of constitutional identity will be importantly structured by the future of constitutionalism. Accordingly, the contemporary challenges confronting constitutionalism as such – ranging from democratic backsliding and yawning economic inequality to constitutional rot and corrosive partisanship – should remain at the center of scholarship on constitutional identity. Furthermore, the evolving, emergent nature of constitutionalism calls for continued attention to the character of constitutional self-government as a global phenomenon.

Finally, there is a matter of particular professional interest, namely, the methodological dimension of scholarship oriented toward understanding and applying constitutional identity. As several contributions in this volume attest, constitutional disharmony has been and remains a vitally important component of inquiry related to constitutional identity. At the same time, fundamental questions remain about the meaning, range, and contours of constitutional disharmonies. As one contributor asked during the development of this volume, what distinguishes constitutional disharmonies from issues that simply rile constitutional politics? Future research should take up this question directly, probing the possibility and value of further conceptual refinement of constitutional disharmony. Pursuing answers to this question will involve further elaboration of the fundamental nature of constitutional identity. In particular, efforts to formalize or typologize disharmony deductively should lead us to examine what limitations (if any) are imposed on such efforts by the indeterminacy inherent in constitutional identity. To the extent that a deductive approach reduces (or assumes away) epistemic uncertainty, a fault line may emerge between such approaches and those rooted in individual case studies. But one need not choose one approach to the exclusion of the other. In this respect, the "conceptual ecology" approach outlined in Elkins and Ginsburg's chapter represents a promising mode of inquiry and analysis. As has been the case for so much research in the area of constitutional identity, continued dialogue between methodological orientations can advance the collective enterprise while also resisting a lapse into methodological homogeneity or analytical parochialism.

CONCLUSION

The sheer diversity of voices comprising this volume is a fitting tribute to the complexity of constitutional identity, in which resolution and definition are achieved through disharmony and dialectic. Despite indeterminacy and conflict, though, constitutional identity is neither amorphous nor without content. We can expect disharmony (Jacobsohn 2010) and must be comfortable with diversity (Rosenfeld 2010), but need not accept any manner of politics under the constitution or any meaning that happens to be attributed to a constitution (Troper 2010). A constitution cannot mean just anything at all, but rather is bound at least somewhat by text, history, aspirations, and, in Jacobsohn's words, continuities of conflict. Moreover, and perhaps more salient in light of contemporary challenges, it seems that any discussion of constitutional reform or change must begin with an idea of what it is that requires reform in the first place. In other words, it is only with reference to some constitutional identity that we may choose how to proceed into the future, both as practitioners and scholars.

Likewise, any discussion of reform should acknowledge the norms toward which one intends to work, perhaps certain general principles of constitutionalism, for example. Even as articulations of constitutionalism are bounded by past and present realities, the concept itself is an emergent phenomenon whose development bears the marks of political, social, and economic change. Indeed, it is out of particular instantiations, from actual constitutional contexts, that the idea of constitutionalism is made meaningful and accrues any practical significance. As new challenges and questions arise in the fora of constitutional politics, so too may our conceptions of constitutionalism shift to accommodate hitherto unimagined possibilities. In this way, a kind of bidirectionality ensues, with certain general principles of constitutionalism serving as a lodestar for particular constitutions, and particular constitutional contexts giving light to new possibilities and challenges through which the practical requirements of constitutional commitments are understood.

The concept of constitutional identity, elaborated over a rich and generative body of work by such scholars as Jacobsohn, Rosenfeld, and Troper, holds the potential to clarify all of this and more. In foregrounding disharmony and difference, the various accounts of constitutional identity make space for aspiration and the hope that constitutional promises may be realized ever more if not ever perfectly. Equally present is a call for humility. Humility of constitutional scholars to study politics as it presents itself, even while informed by certain norms of their own. And humility of constitutional actors to accept difference, even while embracing persistent indeterminacy as an opportunity to secure the constitution's ends.

REFERENCES

Balkin, Jack. 2020. *The Cycles of Constitutional Time*. New York: Oxford University Press.
Bermeo, Nancy. 2016. "On Democratic Backsliding." *Journal of Democracy* 27 (1): 5–19.
Coppedge, Michael. 2017. "Eroding Regimes: What, Where, and When?" *V-Dem Working Paper Series* 57.
Eatwell, Roger and Matthew Goodwin. 2018. *National Populism: The Revolt against Liberal Democracy*. London: Pelican Books.
Elkins, Zachary, Thomas Ginsburg, and James Melton. 2009. *The Endurance of National Constitutions*. New York: Cambridge University Press.
Gallie, Walter Bryce. 1956. "Essentially Contested Concepts." *Proceedings of the Aristotelian Society* 56: 167–198.
Gallie, Walter Bryce. 1964. *Philosophy and the Historical Understanding*. New York: Schocken Books.
Ginsburg, Tom and Mila Versteeg. 2017. "Measuring the Rule of Law: A Comparison of Indicators." *Law & Social Inquiry* 42: 100–137.
Greenstone, J. David. 1993. *The Lincoln Persuasion: Remaking American Liberalism*. Princeton: Princeton University Press.
Hirschl, Ran. 2004. *Towards Juristocracy: The Origins and Consequences of the New Constitutionalism*. Cambridge: Harvard University Press.
Hirschl, Ran. 2014. *Comparative Matters*. New York: Oxford University Press.
Jacobsohn, Gary. 1986. *The Supreme Court and the Decline of Constitutional Aspiration*. Totowa, NJ: Rowman and Littlefield.
Jacobsohn, Gary. 1993. *Apple of Gold: Constitutionalism in Israel and the United States*. Princeton: Princeton University Press.
Jacobsohn, Gary. 2010. *Constitutional Identity*. Cambridge: Harvard University Press.
Jacobsohn, Gary. 2011. "Rights and American Constitutional Identity." *Polity* 43 (4): 409–431.
Jacobsohn, Gary. 2012. "Constitutional Values and Principles." In *The Oxford Handbook of Comparative Constitutional Law*, edited by Michel Rosenfeld and András Sajó, 777–792. New York: Oxford University Press.

Jacobsohn, Gary. 2016. "Constitutional Identity." In *The Oxford Handbook of the Indian Constitution*, edited by Sujit Choudhry, Madhav Khosla, and Pratap Bhanu Mehta, 110–126. New York: Oxford University Press.

Jacobsohn, Gary and Yaniv Roznai. 2020. *Constitutional Revolution*. New Haven: Yale University Press.

Loughlin, Martin. 2022. *Against Constitutionalism*. Cambridge: Harvard University Press.

MacIntyre, Alaisdair. 1981. *After Virtue: A Study in Moral Theory*. South Bend: University of Notre Dame Press.

Norris, Pippa and Ronald Inglehart. 2019. *Cultural Backlash: Trump, Brexit and Authoritarian Populism*. New York: Cambridge University Press.

Orren, Karen and Stephen Skowronek. 2004. *The Search for American Political Development*. New York: Oxford University Press.

Revelli, Marco. 2019. *The New Populism: Democracy Stares into the Abyss*, trans. David Broder. New York: Verso.

Rodriguez, Philippe-André. 2015. "Human Dignity as an Essentially Contested Concept." *Cambridge Review of International Affairs* 28 (4): 743–756.

Rosenfeld, Michel. 2010. *The Identity of the Constitutional Subject: Selfhood, Citizenship, Culture, and Community*. New York: Routledge.

Rosenfeld, Michel. 2012. "Constitutional Identity." In *The Oxford Handbook of Comparative Constitutional Law*, edited by Michel Rosenfeld and András Sajó, 756–776. New York: Oxford University Press.

Thomas, George. 2011. "What is Political Development? A Constitutional Perspective." *Review of Politics* 73 (2): 275–294.

Thomas, George. 2024. "The Constitution at War with Itself: Race, Citizenship, and the Forging of American Constitutional Identity." In *Deciphering the Genome of Constitutionalism: The Foundations and Future of Constitutional Identity*, edited by Ran Hirschl and Yaniv Roznai, 205. Cambridge and New York: Cambridge University Press.

Troper, Michel. 2010. "Behind the Constitution? The Principle of Constitutional Identity in France." In *Constitutional Topography: Values and Constitutions*, edited by András Sajó and Renata Uitz, 187–203. The Hague: Eleven International Publishing.

Waldner, David and Ellen Lust. 2018. "Unwelcome Change: Coming to Terms with Democratic Backsliding." *Annual Review of Political Science* 21: 93–113.

Waldron, Jeremy. 2002. "Is the Rule of Law an Essentially Contested Concept (In Florida)?" *Law and Philosophy* 21 (2): 137–164.

Index

Adams, John, 36, 206, 209
Africa, 14, 61, 93, 138–140, 142, 144–148, 290, 337–338
   African National Union, 142
   sub-Saharan, 93, 139–140, 144–146 333, 338
amendments to existing constitutions, 3, 16–17, 38, 40, 45, 58, 68, 70–74, 89, 102, 110, 114, 116–117, 153, 159, 164, 214, 222, 235, 252, 259–270, 278–279, 292, 313, 315–316, 335–336, 342
   First Amendment, 50–51, 336
   Fourteenth Amendment, 198, 214, 218, 223–224, 335, 337
   unconstitutional constitutional amendments, 1, 92, 94, 268
America. *See* United States
Anderson, Benedict, 287
Angola, 142
Argentina, 338
atheist, 293
authoritarianism, 94, 125, 129, 233. *See also* autocracy; constitutional dictatorship
   authoritarian proclivities, xviii
authority, constituent vs. constituted 26, 29–31, 66, 262, 264
autocracy, 130, 173

Bangladesh, 1, 14, 125–135
Bantustan, 146
Barak, Aharon, 65, 190
Belgium, 39–40, 273
Bhutan, 315
Biden, Joe, 181, 189, 233
Bill of Rights, 173, 236
Bolivia, 315
Botswana, 142
Brazil, 1
Britain, 90, 158, 195, 219, 293. *See also* parliamentary supremacy

British colonies, 48, 146
British constitutional practice, 28

Canada, 5, 291, 339
   Quebec, 291
capitalism, 93, 294
China, 13, 101–104, 107–111, 156, 158, 290, 318–320, 322, 323, 326
Christians, xix, 9, 52–54, 223, 233, 278–280, 292–294
   nationalism, 52
citizenship, 1, 7, 15, 31–32, 127, 205–210, 212–214, 222, 289, 295, 314, 337, 340
   Black, 15, 205, 208, 210
civil rights, 48, 129, 189, 194
colonialism, 140, 147, 338. *See also* constitution, post-colonial; post-colonialism
communalism, 127–128
communists, 102, 109–110, 278, 290, 293
community, xvii–xviii, 4, 48, 70–71, 92, 106, 121, 128, 139, 142, 147, 150, 183, 204, 274, 277, 279, 287–289, 291–294, 297, 315, 338–339
   imagined communities, 5, 286–287
   a sense of, 4
Confucian, 13, 101–111, 349
consensus, 45–49, 52, 67, 80, 106, 116, 164, 183, 231, 249–250, 252, 254–255, 257, 268, 273, 312, 332, 337
consociational regime, 223
constituent power, 12–13, 23–31, 58, 63–69, 71–74, 92, 95, 160, 264, 350. *See also* constitution making; *pouvoir constituant*
   and God, 52, 73–74, 90–91, 155, 186, 219, 262–263, 293, 314
   natural vs. legal, 35, 64–65, 67, 73–74, 77, 80, 91, 160, 172, 199–200, 202, 209–211, 213, 226, 236, 263–265, 278, 336, 338
constitution, xviii, 5, 12, 14–16, 26, 34–37, 39–41, 46, 48, 52–53, 57, 64–65, 67, 70, 78–85, 90, 93, 102, 104–105, 107–109, 113–120, 125–134,

357

constitution (cont.)
        141–146, 150–161, 163–173, 180–185, 187–188, 190, 193–196, 199–201, 204–214, 216–218, 220–226, 229–239, 245–246, 248, 250, 253–254, 261–262, 264, 267, 269, 273, 279, 281–282, 289, 291–292, 295, 297, 305–308, 314–316, 318–322, 326, 331–332, 335–338, 340–343, 350
    contradictions, subalternation, and contrariness, 18, 153, 330, 336–337, 339
    democratic, 105, 249
    effects of, xviii, 40, 145, 269
    and equality, 2, 6, 10, 15, 18, 35–36, 38, 51, 67, 95, 105, 115, 126, 135, 163–165, 182, 187, 196, 200–202, 204–206, 208, 210–214, 217, 219–220, 222, 224, 227, 250, 317, 334–335, 341, 350–351
    errors, 341
    and existential threats, 114, 138–139, 147–148
    federal, 235
    and forms of power, 115
    as harmonization, 196, 346
    historic, xix
    imposed, 14, 150, 156–157, 159
    independence, 7–8, 48, 60, 78–85, 126, 128, 130–131, 133, 141–143, 163–164, 167, 169, 185, 194–195, 211, 250–251, 256, 261, 269, 278, 280–281, 291, 305, 307, 314
    and internal morality, 266
    and language, 3, 50, 57, 105, 108, 126–127, 131–132, 163, 170, 173, 180, 188, 193, 212, 217, 232, 253–254, 275, 302, 332, 335, 339–341
    militant vs. acquiescent, 30, 82, 84, 183
    political, 4, 189
    post-colonial, 14, 139
    prescriptive, 3, 101, 104, 108–109, 111, 347
    representative, 4, 28, 39, 48, 58, 63, 65, 67, 69–70, 77, 117–118, 128, 172, 207, 220, 248, 279, 289
    sham, 23, 29
    socialist, 102
    as supreme law, 68, 70, 305
constitution making, 24, 27, 29, 64, 68, 71, 76, 81–82, 86, 126, 131, 133, 148, 150–151, 154, 245, 250, 254, 332, 353
    external interference, 157
    incrementalism, 16, 245, 247, 252, 255–257
    remaking, 93, 214
constitutional aspiration, 15, 199–202
constitutional aspirationalism, 15, 199, 202
constitutional authorship. *See* constituent power
constitutional condition, xviii, 35, 138
constitutional democracy, 219, 226, 306.
    See also democracy
    paradox of, 28
constitutional development, 8, 15, 79, 108–109, 184, 205, 224, 346, 348–349

constitutional dictatorship, 234. *See also* authoritarianism; emergency, state of; military regime
constitutional disharmony, xviii, 11, 15, 18, 45–47, 85, 102, 147, 150–151, 204–205, 268, 286, 347, 350, 353
constitutional dis-identity, 12, 44, 47, 49
constitutional diversity, 147, 272
constitutional evil, 337
constitutional evolution, 170, 255, 348
constitutional exceptionalism, 15, 229, 233
constitutional exclusion, 114
constitutional faith, 13, 123
constitutional hierarchies, 4
constitutional identity, xvii–xix, 1–18, 23–24, 27–28, 30–32, 34–35, 40–42, 44–47, 49–53, 56–61, 76, 80–82, 85–86, 90–94, 101, 103–111, 113–115, 119–120, 122, 125, 127, 130, 134–135, 138–139, 147–148, 150–151, 154, 161, 163–166, 170, 172–173, 183, 185, 190, 201–202, 204–205, 208–209, 211–213, 216–218, 220–227, 229–230, 238, 245–247, 249–252, 254, 257, 259–260, 263–269, 272–276, 278–282, 286–292, 295–298, 300–301, 303–304, 306–309, 312–317, 327, 331–332, 345–355
    abusing, 17, 281
    of the colonizer, 49
    creation of, 5, 24, 26–28, 48, 109, 161, 256, 291, 348
    dual, 13, 113–114
    extra-, 151
    future of, 18, 345, 351
    large-N analysis, 17–18, 259, 313, 327
    militant, 16, 113, 119, 122–123, 234, 238
    national, 280–281
    and particularism vs. universalism, 150–151
    unconstitutional, 17, 300
constitutional mis-identity, 12, 44, 47, 49
constitutional moments, 70, 74, 109
constitutional norms, 11, 69, 103, 122, 273
    meta-, 114
constitutional order, xvii–xviii, 1, 5, 8, 10–11, 14, 16, 18, 26, 30, 53, 61, 68, 72, 91, 108–109, 115, 138–140, 142, 145–147, 183, 187, 194, 199, 201, 205, 208–209, 212, 214, 217, 225, 235, 245, 247, 250, 252–253, 277, 279, 282, 287, 292, 347–351
    American, 16, 194, 208–209, 214, 235
    and constitutional commitment, 102–104, 217, 220–221, 224–225, 227, 280
    global, 352
    pan-European, 1
constitutional pluralism, 168, 273
constitutional politics, 1, 10, 15–17, 67, 74, 138, 160, 165–166, 199, 216–227, 231, 248, 250, 314, 345–347, 349, 351, 354

constitutional provision, 6, 37–38, 46, 65, 107, 220, 264, 297, 331
constitutional recognition, 126, 139, 141–142, 147, 250
constitutional reform, 4, 152–153, 156–158, 252, 354
constitutional regime, 57, 222, 226
constitutional religious identity, 250
constitutional retrogression, 1, 7, 16
  democratic backsliding, xviii, 1, 7, 16, 262, 346, 353
constitutional revolution, 6, 14, 27, 56, 58–61, 108–109, 190, 217, 224, 290, 348
  The New Deal, 58
  nonrevolutionary, 60
constitutional rights, 38, 53, 95, 169, 291
constitutional silence, 182
constitutional theocracy, 10
constitutional theory, contemporary, 1
constitutional unamendability, 13, 16, 269
constitutionalism, xix, 2, 7, 10–12, 14, 16–18, 30, 32, 46, 54, 58, 89, 91–94, 103, 109–110, 127, 139–140, 148, 151, 155, 161, 164, 166, 174, 182, 184, 190, 206, 212, 214, 216, 218, 232–234, 245–248, 251, 254–255, 257, 259, 262, 266, 268, 272–282, 287, 289, 291–293, 295–298, 300, 306, 345–346, 348–349, 351–354
  American, 12, 14, 177, 222
  generic, 57
  globalised vs. social contingent practice, 274
  illiberal, 1, 7
  "large-C," 11, 45
  liberal, xix, 110, 292, 297
  modern, 17, 288, 296, 298
  "small-c," 3, 11
  transformative, 165
constitutionalist regime, 57, 222, 226
Corsica, 24–25
COVID-19 pandemic, impact of, 279
Croatia, 39
Czech Republic, 1, 9, 293, 303
  Landtova judgment, 303

democracy, xviii, 6–7, 13, 35–36, 38, 41, 64, 66, 71–72, 93, 95, 107, 109, 113–115, 119–120, 122, 125–126, 128–130, 133, 139, 147, 154, 163, 173, 193, 222, 226, 229–230, 232–238, 265–266, 275, 277–278, 288, 294, 296, 307–308, 312, 316, 340.
  See also constitutional democracy, paradox of; constitutional diversity; republic
  democratic process-normativism, 54
  democratization, 141–142, 249
  dormant, 26, 122, 161
  ethnic, 10
  flawed, 114, 265
  militant, 16, 113, 119, 122–123, 234, 238
  paradoxes of, 24
  secular, 113
Denmark, 304
Derrida, Jacques, 30
dialogue and dialogical process, 9, 28, 32, 44, 50, 287, 301, 303–304, 345, 347, 354
dialectics, 13, 49–50, 110, 287, 345, 347–348, 354
dictatorship, 60, 92, 118, 129, 234
despotism, 141, 220
disaggregation of unifying constructs, 17, 288
Dominican Republic, 315
Douglass, Frederick, 15, 182–183, 186–187, 194–196, 200–202, 208, 210–213
Dworkin, Ronald, 11, 189, 268

Ecuador, Republic of, 314–315
Egypt, 10
elite interests, 17, 25–27, 106, 111, 130, 187, 252, 296, 313, 333, 350
emergency, state of, 13, 114–115, 118–119, 122, 158, 253
entrepreneurship, 93
equality, definitions of, 35
Ethiopia, 93
Europe, xviii–xix, 1, 7, 9, 17, 40, 70, 90, 94, 231, 262, 272, 277–278, 280, 282, 293–294, 300, 305–306. *See also* constitutional order, pan-European
  Central Europe, 1, 7, 9, 302
  Council of Europe's European Convention on Human Rights (ECHR), 272
  Eastern Europe, 302
European Court of Human Rights (ECtHR), 1
European Union, xix, 8, 17, 39, 90, 93, 272, 274, 278, 281, 300, 309
  Court of Justice of the EU, 1, 301
  Treaty of Lisbon, 6, 9, 302–303
  Treaty of Maastricht, 6, 301
  Treaty on European Union, 6

Federalist Papers, 69
Fletcher, George, 3, 91, 312
France, 1, 4, 7, 13, 39, 60, 66, 68, 70, 113–117, 119–122, 151, 273, 287, 294
  French colonies, 115, 117–118, 120–121, 141
freedom of speech, 65, 170
Freeman, Elizabeth, 206
Fuller, Lon, 247, 263

Gebeye, Berihun Adugna, 93, 148
gender equality, 104. *See also* LGBTQ rights
  gender quota, 35–36, 38–40
gender identity, 279
Geneva, 24, 26

Germany, 12, 36–41, 60–61, 234–235, 238, 260, 303, 307, 309
　Basic Laws in Germany, 234
　Federal Constitutional Court of Germany, 1
Ghana, 143–144
Giddens, Anthony, 77
Global South, 95
Greece, 39, 297

Habermas, Jurgen, 30, 90, 275
Hamilton, Alexander, 64, 69–70, 229
Hannah-Jones, Nicole, 181–182, 185, 188, 201–202
hegemonic preservation thesis, 218, 221
Hindu, 126, 131, 350
Hirschl, Ran, 1, 10, 27, 89, 91, 95, 113, 216, 218, 221, 313, 353
homosexuality. *See* LGBTQ rights
Honig, Bonnie, 24, 30–31
human rights, 92–93, 95, 102, 122, 128, 130, 139, 147, 150, 152–153, 184, 231, 250, 261, 264, 275, 278, 312
Hungary, 1, 8–9, 17, 58, 185, 273, 276, 278–280, 282, 286, 291–296, 303, 350–351. *See also* Christians; communists; gender identity; populism; refugees; religion
　anti-cosmopolitanism in Hungary, 292–293
　Fundamental Law of Hungary (2011), 277
　"greater Hungary," 295
　homogeneity of society, 279
　King Stephen, 294
hybrid regime (integrated democracy and autocracy), 130

identity, xvii–xix, 1–18, 23–24, 27–28, 30–32, 34–35, 40–41, 44–53, 56–61, 71–72, 76–86, 90–94, 101, 104–109, 111, 113–115, 120, 122–123, 125–135, 138, 147, 150–151, 154, 160–161, 163–167, 170, 172–174, 179–180, 182–183, 185–186, 188, 190, 202, 204–205, 209, 213, 217–220, 222–223, 225–227, 236–237, 245–247, 249–251, 254–257, 259–260, 263, 265–269, 272–274, 276, 278–282, 286–291, 293–294, 296–297, 300–308, 312–318, 327, 331–332, 340–341, 345–355. *See also* constitutional identity
　ambivalent, 125, 248
　Aristotelian notion of, 57, 227, 332–334, 336–338, 340
　diachronic, 57, 151, 347
　entrepreneurship 93
　fluid, 2, 11–12, 44, 125, 165, 260, 268
　legal, 60–61
　national vs. constitutional, 4–5, 57, 59, 61, 125, 316
　politics, xvii, xix, 11, 131, 135, 236, 247, 276, 351

　regimes, 340
　state's, 114
　synchronic, 57
immigration, 2, 7, 227, 289–290, 294–295
impartial justice, 53
India, xvii–xviii, 1, 10, 14, 16, 35, 44, 60, 90–91, 126, 131, 163–165, 167–168, 170–171, 173–174, 183, 222, 246, 316, 351
　constitution of India, 91, 184
　Supreme Court of India, 166
Indigenous populations, 5
　institutions, 146
　legal traditions, 141
individual rights, 109, 248
individualism, 102, 294
Indonesia, 10, 78, 82–84
integrationist/assimilative approach, 126
integrity, theory of, 268
international law, 67–68, 226
international relations, 13, 76–77, 81, 86
Iraqi, 340–341
Ireland, 1, 16, 29, 35, 39, 58, 246, 259, 261, 264–265, 293, 302, 314
　abortion debates in Ireland, 264
　Constitution of Ireland (1937), 262
　Constitution of the Irish Free State (1922), 261, 263
Israel, xvii–xviii, 1, 10, 16, 35, 58, 60, 89, 113, 185, 190, 216, 223, 246, 250–251, 255–256, 351. *See also* constitution making, incrementalism; Jewish; Jews; Palestinians; religion
　attempts to complete a formal constitution, 190
　Basic Laws in Israel, 251
　constitutional revolution in Israel, 251
　counter revolution in Israel, 251
Italy, 1, 7, 39, 304

Jacobsohn, Gary Jeffrey, 2–6, 9–12, 23–24, 27–32, 34–35, 41–42, 44–45, 47, 53, 56–59, 61, 71–72, 76, 79, 82, 85–86, 89, 91–92, 101, 104, 107–111, 113, 125–126, 134, 138–139, 146–147, 150, 161, 164–167, 170, 173, 179, 183–184, 186, 194, 198–201, 204–206, 211, 213–214, 216–217, 220, 222, 229–230, 232, 238, 245–249, 254–257, 259–260, 263–269, 272, 286–287, 300, 312–315, 330–333, 345–355
Japan, 1, 14, 150–161, 318–322, 324, 326, 331
Jefferson, Thomas, 182, 213, 216, 219
Jewish, 1, 54, 113, 122, 185–186, 190, 220, 250–251, 292
Jews, 185, 190, 293

Katz, Rudolf, 41
Kennedy, Justice, 5, 291

Kenya, 141, 165
King, Martin Luther, 15, 193, 200–201, 220, 227

Lesotho, 142
Lewellyn, Karl, 237
LGBTQ rights, 10. *See also* gender equality
liberal tradition, 201, 248. *See also* individual rights
liberalism, 201, 218, 277–278, 292, 294, 308
liberty, 15, 27, 51, 109, 193–195, 198, 202, 204, 207–208, 210–211, 213, 224, 237–238, 262, 277, 335, 343
  Anglo-American ideas of liberty, 234
Lincoln, Abraham, 15, 31, 57–58, 182–184, 193–202, 210–213, 216–217, 219–221, 225, 227
Luxembourg, 39, 309

Madison, James, xvii, 64, 70, 179, 181–182, 204–206, 208, 234–235, 237
majoritarianism, xix, 217, 221, 230, 317
Malaysia, 10, 46, 48–49
Malta, 39
Mamdani, Mahmood, 140–141, 147–148
marginalized groups, xvii, 146. *See also* Indigenous populations
Marti, J.L., 9
Marxism-Leninism, 102
Middle East, 245
militarism, 152–154
  vs. pacifism, 153–154
military regime, 135. *See also* constitutional dictatorship
monarchy, 115, 117, 152, 333
Montesquieu, 66
Mozambique, 142–144
Muslims, 8, 14, 48–49, 118, 121, 126, 129, 131–134, 253, 278, 290, 294–295. *See also* Shari'a law
Islamo-secularism, 135
mysticism in constitution, 314

national identity, 5, 7, 9, 57, 59, 61, 80, 114, 125, 127, 129, 269, 286–288, 297, 301, 316
  composite, 202
nationalism, xix, 14, 83, 106, 125–127, 129, 131–135, 185, 293, 350
  'Christian nation', xix, 52, 293
  collective 132
  multi-national society, 131
  multiple, 125
nationality, 67, 119, 131, 202
natural rights tradition, 196, 199, 264, 336
Netherland, 7, 188
Nietzsche, Friedrich, 73
Nigeria, 93

Obama, Barak, 179

Pakistan, 10, 126, 129, 131
Palestinians, 121, 250–251. *See also* Israel
parliamentarism vs. presidentialism, 236
parliamentary supremacy, 28
"people, the," 12, 23, 25, 29, 67, 248, 289
peoplehood, 7, 25, 93, 289–290, 292, 294, 296–297
pluralism, 17, 30, 81, 95, 120, 133, 141, 168, 181, 275, 279, 307. *See also* constitutional pluralism
Poland, 1, 17, 24, 39, 273, 276, 278, 280, 282, 293, 295–296, 305, 309, 350
  abortion debates in Poland, 281
  undermining of judicial independence, 282
political authority, 12, 28, 139, 144, 146, 348.
  See also parliamentary supremacy
political morality, 64–66, 69, 261
polity, xvii, 1–6, 9–11, 15–18, 30–31, 59, 65, 91, 106–107, 109–110, 114, 142, 151–152, 155, 173, 186, 189–190, 199, 205–206, 208, 210, 216, 230, 267, 272, 274–276, 282, 286–287, 292, 296–297, 314, 318, 349
populism, 1, 16–17, 134, 236, 238, 286, 288–289, 291–294, 296–297, 346
Portugal, 39, 78, 302
positive law, 63, 65, 67–69, 263
post-colonialism, 83, 141
pouvoir constituant, 63, 70–71, 73. *See also* constitution making; constituent power
preambles of Constitutions, 82, 102, 115, 120, 126, 314
property rights, 337–338

queers. *See* LGBTQ rights

racism, 194, 201. *See also* colonialism; segregation
  critical race theory (anti-racist theory), 201
Rawls, John, 65, 249
referendum, 28, 67, 70, 80, 159, 261–262, 264, 278, 291
refugees, 52, 278–280, 294
Reid, Thomas, xvii
religion, 1, 10, 18, 46, 48, 50–53, 57, 80, 91, 113–115, 117, 120, 125, 128–129, 131, 133–135, 152, 173, 188, 226, 246, 248–256, 279, 286, 292–293, 297, 314, 318, 332, 335, 339–341, 351. *See also* constitutional religious identity
  state religion, 10, 125, 133–135, 297
republic, 25–26, 108, 115, 193, 198, 202, 209, 213, 219, 232, 236–238, 252, 256
republicanism, 201
  unrepublicanism, 121
revolution, 1, 5, 56, 58–59, 61, 89, 108–109, 125, 151, 154–155, 160–161, 194, 199, 201, 209–210, 247, 251. *See also* constitutional revolution
  American Revolution, 36, 59, 185, 234
  French Revolution, 63, 115

Ricoeur, Paul, 286
Romania, 294
Roosevelt, Kermit, 184
Rosenfeld, Michel, 2–6, 17, 24, 26–27, 49, 56, 91, 125, 150–151, 274–275, 286–287, 291, 297, 300, 312, 316–318, 345, 348–350, 352, 354–355
Rousseau, Jean-Jacques, 12, 23–28, 30–32, 66, 91. *See also* constituent power
sovereignty (according to Rousseau), 12
Roznai, Yaniv, 1, 6, 11, 23, 28–30, 56, 58–59, 61, 65, 71–72, 89, 91, 109, 114, 200, 216–217, 220, 222–223, 229, 233, 262, 308, 315–316, 350

Schmitt, Carl, 24, 73, 92, 300, 315
Second World War. *See* World War II
secularism, 14, 113, 119, 121–122, 125–129, 131, 133–135, 163–165, 174, 218, 226, 248, 252–253, 255–256, 351
nonsectarian, 53
secular humanism, 52
security, 13, 76–81, 83–86, 339
ontological security, 13, 76–77, 81, 85–86
segregation, 140, 188. *See also* colonialism; racism
Senegal, 141
Shari'a law, 1
Sieyès, Emmanuel-Joseph, 24, 63–64, 67
Singapore, 13, 101, 106–111
slavery, 15, 181–185, 187–188, 190, 195–198, 201, 204–208, 211–213, 216, 218–221, 224–225, 227, 267, 289, 336, 343
antislavery, 15, 205–206, 208, 210–214, 217–218, 220–221, 224–226
proslavery, 204–206, 211–212, 225–226
Slovenia, 39
social justice, 126, 130
social order, xviii–xix, 30, 47, 91, 110, 138, 272
socialism, 14, 110, 125–130, 134. *See also* constitution, socialist
South Africa, 60, 144–145, 338
African National Congress, 142, 337
South Asia, 245
South Korea, 13, 101, 104–111, 318, 326
sovereignty, 9, 12, 14, 26–27, 29–30, 40, 67, 73–74, 91, 95, 120, 132, 153–155, 161, 171–172, 183, 196, 256, 265, 275, 277–279, 289, 294, 300, 302–303, 333
divine vs. popular, 155
Spain, 5, 39, 60, 273, 302
Catalonia, 291
Sri Lanka, 10
state authority, 141, 231
Sweden, 293, 315

Taiwan, 1, 108, 318–319, 321, 322, 325–326
Tanzania, 141, 146
terrorism, 119
Thailand, 10, 113
Timor-Leste, 13, 76, 78, 80, 82–85
Toniatti, Roberto, 1
traditional authority, 14, 139–140, 143–145, 147–148
neotraditionalism, 145
tribal chieftaincies, 141
Troper, Michel, 3, 345–347, 349, 353–355
Trump, Donald, 181, 233, 238, 289–290
Tunis, 58
Turkey, 1, 16, 59, 147, 183, 250–253, 255, 351
1982 Constitution, 252
constitutional transformation (2017), 1, 5, 12, 253, 292
Kemalism, 252
Ottoman Constitution (1876), 251

Uganda, 142, 146
unconstitutional acts, 281
United Kingdom. *See* Britain
United Nations, 79
United States, xvii–xix, 5, 15, 45–46, 50, 52, 64, 68, 70, 151–152, 157–158, 179–180, 182–184, 187–190, 193, 202, 204, 207, 209–210, 216–222, 224–227, 229–238, 277, 280, 293, 319, 323, 325–326, 335–337, 351. *See also* civil rights; constitutional exceptionalism; constitutional order, American; constitutionalism, American; slavery
the 1619 Project, 15, 179, 181–183, 185–187, 189–190, 201, 204
African-Americans, 181
American Constitution, 64, 68, 185, 188, 204, 206–208, 214, 220, 222, 225–226, 248, 289, 331–332
American constitutionalism, 12, 14, 177, 222
American Revolution, 36, 59, 185, 234
Black Americans, 15, 208
Brown v. Board of Education, 188, 231
Civil War, 15, 204–205, 214
Declaration of Independence (1776), 31, 64, 181, 184, 193–195, 199–202, 204, 206, 211, 216–220, 224, 235
Missouri Crisis, 205–206, 208
and its protection of demagogues, 16

values, 2–6, 9–10, 12–14, 16–17, 30, 44–46, 50, 52, 69, 73, 83, 92, 94, 101–111, 114, 139, 145, 147–148, 180, 183, 218, 221–223, 225–226, 229–230, 232–234, 236, 238, 248–250, 254, 259, 266, 268, 274–275, 279, 305–306, 313–318, 322, 327, 345, 348, 350, 353

enduring, 11
family, 296
liberal constitutionalist, 53
popular, 312–313, 316–317
twelve values typical to constitutions, 317
value-normativism, 54

Weinrib, Lorraine E., 231
Wilentz, Sean, 182, 205
World War II, 1, 12, 14, 151–152, 160, 187, 230–231, 331

Zimbabwe, 142, 338
Zionism, 185

Milton Keynes UK
Ingram Content Group UK Ltd.
UKHW021008050824
446411UK00007B/25